A HAND-BOOK OF MOTTOES.

A

HAND-BOOK OF MOTTOES

THE NOBILITY, GENTRY, CITIES,

PUBLIC COMPANIES, &c.

*TRANSLATED AND ILLUSTRATED WITH NOTES
AND QUOTATIONS*

BY

C. N. ELVIN, M.A.

DETROIT
Gale Research Company • Book Tower
1971

This is a facsimile reprint of the
1860 edition published in London
by Boil and Daldy.

INTRODUCTION.

A MOTTO is a word or sentence usually inscribed on a scroll, either beneath the coat-of-arms, or above the crest. Of these mottoes some families bear two, one below their arms, and one above their crest; sometimes two are placed in either of these positions.

They in some respects resemble those ancient invocations of God, appeals to patriotism, or descriptions of the character of those who employed them, which are met with both in sacred and profane history; while in other points they almost entirely differ from them. The resemblance lies chiefly in the meaning, whether religious or patriotic, of the words and sentences employed. "I am that I am," is a sentence descriptive of the Divine Essence; "Who is like unto thee among the gods, O Jehovah?" the well-known words from which the Maccabees derived their name, embraces at once invocation and praise; "Jove the Preserver and Victory," the watchword of the Greeks at Cunaxa, literally resembled the chivalrous cri-de-guerre; while the inscription on the temple of Isis at Sais, "I am all that hath been, that is, and that shall be, and no mortal hath lifted my veil," is not unlike those enigmatical expressions of which heralds at a later period were so fond.

But if the mottoes of Modern Europe have some affinity to those of ancient times, yet the points in which they differ from them are of far greater importance; the resemblances proceed from the common laws of human nature; the differences from the peculiar feudal organisation of the races who overthrow the Roman empire. In the first place, then, heraldic mottoes differ from the ancient religious or patriotic cries, or sentiments, from the fact that they are always written. It is true we do find in Jewish History that the motto of the Maccabees was inscribed upon their standard, as well as S.P.Q.R. upon that of the Roman republic; and Capaneus is represented as bearing, at the siege of Thebes, a shield with the inscription, "I will burn the city;" but these were only exceptions, while, as a general rule, the cries or invocations of the Jews, Greeks, and Romans, were merely expressions elicited by the exigencies of the case, and for-gotten or relinquished as soon as the particular emergency was gone by.

Again, mottoes in the modern sense of the word belong not only to armies, or to whole nations, but also to families and individuals: the pride of the Jew lay, not in his immediate ancestors, but in his clearly traced descent from one of the sons of Jacob; the Greek was contented if he could prove that he was of pure free blood, of such a family of such a tribe; the Roman showed the images of his ancestors; and the sepulchral tablets which enumerated the conquests, offices, and virtues of each of those ancestors, served him instead of arms and motto; but not one of these nations had in war any personal or family cries, nor did they bear on their shields or helmets any inscriptions having a special reference to themselves.

Motto then, in its modern and definite sense, is "a written word or phrase assumed by an individual, and usually retained by his descendants." It admits of being divided into several classes, which I shall now proceed to enumerate. At a glance it will be seen that a very large proportion, especially of the earliest mottoes, like the inscriptions and war-cries of the Jews and Greeks, had a religious as well as a warlike tendency; in fact, that they were either supplications to God for aid in battle, or simple phrases containing encouragement to followers.

But there is another mode of classifying these "inscriptiones," which will, I think, be found convenient; namely into,—

First—Mottoes which have no reference whatever to the coat-of-arms, crest, or name; some being of a

religious character ; some loyal and patriotic ; others
again enigmatical, of which last the origin, unless preserved by tradition, written or otherwise, must necessarily
be doubtful.

Secondly — Mottoes which have a direct reference to
the bearings.

Thirdly — Mottoes which have a punning reference
to the name.

Fourthly — Mottoes which have a reference both to
the name and the bearing.

Mottoes, especially the more ancient ones, were
generally either in Latin or French, the two languages
employed by the Normans and by the clergy ; we, however, occasionally find them written in Greek, Italian,
Spanish, German, Scottish, Welsh, Cornish, and Irish,
and I have met with two or three in Hebrew ; while
many English, French, and Italian mottoes retain the
antique phraseology and spelling.

With respect to the relative antiquity of mottoes, it
may be said that, in all probability, such of them as bear
a punning reference to the family name of those who use
them, are of later date than the war-cries ; inasmuch as
family or surnames did not come into use until the beginning of the twelfth century, and that those which
refer to the bearings are of still more recent date, since
it was not till some time after the introduction of surnames
that the hereditary use of coat-armour was adopted.

However, these sentences or Mottoes became very
fashionable in the time of Edward III., who made use of
different ones adapted to various occasions and circumstances. Before his time they seem to have been less
commonly used ; and, perhaps, the earliest instance of one
on a seal is that afforded by the seal of Sir Johan de
Byron, which is affixed to a deed dated 21° Edw. I., the
motto " Crede Beronti " surrounding the arms.

In conclusion, I would observe that no mottoes are
necessarily hereditary, as may be seen even in the case of
that attached to the arms of England, which has been
altered more than once ; any individual, while he pre-
serves his family arms and crest, is at liberty to adopt

any motto he pleases ; yet still the pride of ancestry will induce most men of old descent to adhere to that phrase or sentiment which proves to all around them, that in their veins runs the blood of those who, long years ago, were renowned and rewarded for wisdom, or for skill, or patriotism, or for deeds of chivalry and daring.

Examples of the Four Classes of Mottoes.

Class I. Mottoes which do not refer either to name or bearing are so numerous, in fact, so greatly outnumber all the rest put together, that it would be useless and wearisome to multiply examples of them. It may be sufficient to give the following : "Che sara sara," Russell. "Je pense à qui pense plus," Cleland. "Alla ta hara," Mildmay. "In Deo fides, lux in tenebris," Hare. "Usque fac et non parcas," Peter. "Cause caused it," Elphin-stone.

Class II. Mottoes which have a direct reference to the bearings, e. g. "Game to the bone," crest, A game-cock. "Hinc garba nostra," crest, A hand holding a sickle, and there are three wheat-sheaves in the arms. "Percussa resurgo," crest, A football. "Illumino," crest, The sun rising. "True as the dial to the sun," crest, A sundial. "Repullulat," crest, An old trunk of a tree rebudding. "Ut reficiar," crest, A decrescent· "Deus pascit corvos," there is a raven in the arms. "Virtus mille scuta," there are four shields in the arms and a shield forms part of the crest. "Forward, kind heart," crest, A winged heart. "Juvat dum lacerat," crest, A plough. "Spes ultra," crest, a terrestrial globe. "Virtue my castle," crest, A castle. "A cuspide corona," the crest is a lance and crown.

Class III. Mottoes which have a punning reference to the name ; as, "Toujours gai," for Gay. Τῷ Θεῷ δόξα, Doxat. "Pro rege dimico," Dymocke. "Ut amnis vita labitur," Brooke. "Bene factum," Weldon. "Esto miles fidelis," Miles. "Pares cum paribus," Pares. "Fabula sed vera," Story. "Regis donum gratum bonum," Kingdon. "Mea dos virtus," Meadows. "Του αριστευειν ἑνεκα," Henniker. "Cheris l' espoir," Cherry. "Mon trésor," Montresor. "Vespertilionis," Batson. "Pure foy, ma joye," Purefoy. "Toujours jeune," Young. "Vows shall be respected," Vows. "Pauper non in spe," Poore. "Non sino sed dono," Seddon. "Speed well," Speed. "Trop hardi," Hardie. "Cave," Cave. "Pagit Deo," Pagit. "Ros cœli," Roskell. "Vive la joye," Joye. "Graves disce mores," Graves. "En grace affie," Grace. "Virtus semper viridis," Green. "Per se valens," Perseval.

Class IV. Mottoes which have a reference both to the name and the bearing. "Accendit cantu," Cockburn, crest, a cock. "Benedictus qui tollit crucem," Bennet, crest, A hand holding up a cross. "Hoc in loco Deus rupes," Hockin, crest, On a rock a seagull. "Ut palma justus," Palmes, crest, A hand holding a palm. "Holme semper viret," Holme, crest, A holme, or holly tree. "Nemo me impune lacessit," Nettles, in the arms are three nettle-leaves. "Quercus robur, salus patriæ," Oakes, crest, An oak-tree. "Turris mihi Deus," Towers, crest, A tower. "Latet anguis in herba," Anguish, crest, A snake in the grass. "At spes non fracta," Hope, crest, A fractured globe. "Deus major columna," Major, there are three columns in the arms. "Mon Dieu est ma roche," Roche, crest, On a rock an osprey holding in her claw a roach. "Cassis tutissima virtus," Helme, a helm is borne in the arms, and also as part of the crest. "Sicut oliva virens lætor in æde Dei," Olivier, in the arms is an olive-tree.

ABBREVIATIONS.

D., duke; m., marquis; e., earl; v., viscount; b., lord, or baron; bt., baronet; kt., knight; comp., company; co., county; c., city; t., town; sig., seal; O., Order of knighthood.

HERALDIC ABBREVIATIONS.

Or., gold; ar., argent; gu., gules; az., azure: sa., sable; vt., vert; erm., ermine; ppr. proper; chev., chevron; pass., passant; ramp., rampant; betw., between.

Those mottoes, to which no name is attached, have been collected from carriages, seals, hatchments, &c., whose owners I could not discover.

Words, or parts of words, printed as the following examples, are intended to point out the play upon the name; as,—
Cave! *Deus videt.* Beware! God sees. CAVE.
Fabula sed vera. A *story*, but a true one. STORY.
Mos le*gem regit.* Custom rules the law. MOSLEY, bt.
Pie*tatis causa.* In the cause of *Piety.* PYE.

MOTTOES.

A

A bonis ad meliora. From good things to better. GOODWRIGHT.

A clean heart and cheerful spirit. PORTMAN, b.

> " His mind was a thanksgiving to the Power
> That made him ; it was blessedness and love ! "—WORDSWORTH.

A cœur vaillant rien impossible. To a valiant heart nothing is impossible. HARTCUP.

A cruce salus. Salvation from the cross. BURGH. BOURKE. DE BURGHO. DOWNES, b. JEFFERSON, co. York. MAYO, e.

> A cross is borne in the arms of each of these families.
> " The Cross !
> There, and there only (though the deist rave,
> And atheist, if earth bear so base a slave),
> There, and there only, is the power to save."—COWPER.

A cuspide corona. By a spear a crown. BRODERICK. CHAPMAN. MIDLETON, v.

> A lance and crown is the crest of Broderick and Midleton, that of Chapman is an arm embowed in armour, in the hand a broken tilting-spear, encircled with a chaplet or victor's crown.
> " My sword, my spear, my shaggy shield,
> These make me lord of all below ;
> And he who fears the lance to wield
> Beneath my shaggy shield must bow.
> His lands, his vineyards must resign,
> For all that cowards have is mine."

A Deo et patre. From God and my father. THOMAS.

A Deo et rege. From God and the king. CHESTERFIELD, e. FAWKES. HAMPTON. HARRINGTON, e. LEWIS. SCUDMORE. bt. STANHOPE, e. STRACHY, bt.

A Deo in Deo. From God in God. TROYTE.

A Deo lumen. Light from God. KERR. OGLE. *Crest*—The sun.

> " Thou, O Sun !
> Soul of surrounding worlds ! in whom best seen
> Shines out thy Maker ! "—THOMSON.

A Deo lux nostra. Our light is from God. HOLLOWAY.

" *God, Light Himself*, dwells awfully retir'd
From mortal eye, or angel's purer ken ;
Whose single smile has, from the first of time,
Fill'd, overflowing, all those lamps of heaven,
That beam for ever thro' the boundless sky."—THOMSON.

A Deo victoria. Victory from God. GRAHAM. GRÆME.

A falcon towering in his pride of place. COWIE.

Crest— A falcon rising from the stump of a tree.

A Fenwyke ! A Fenwyke !! A Fenwyke !!! FENWICK.

A fin. To the end. AIRLIE, e. OGILVIE.

A fine. From the end. GRIFFITH, of Gloucester.

A foye. To faith. TEMPEST, Sir Richard.

A fyno duw a fydd. What God willeth will be. HUGHES.
MATTHEW. WALSHAM, bt.

A gair Duw yn uchaf. The word of God above all. MORRIS.

A Gadibus usque auroram. From West to East. SOUTH SEA COMP.

" Omnibus in terris quæ sunt a Gadibus usque
Auroram."—JUV. *Sat.*

A Home ! A Home ! A Home ! HOME, e.

"Beneath the crest of old Dunbar,
And Hepburn's mingled banners come
Down the steep mountain glittering far,
And shouting still 'A Home ! A Home !'"—SCOTT.

A jamais. For ever. JAMES, of Dublin, bt.

A l'amy fidele pour jamais. Faithful for ever to my friend.
SEYMOUR.

A la bonne heure. In good time. BONNOR.

A la constancia militar premio. Reward of military fortitude.
O. of St. Herminigilde.

A la vérité. In truth. BREMER.

" The only amaranthine flower on earth
Is Virtue ; the only lasting treasure, Truth."—COWPER.

A la volonté de Dieu. At the will of God. STRICKLAND, bt.

"I delight to do thy will, O my God." Ps. xl. 8.

A ma puissance. According to my power. STAMFORD, e. GREY.

A ma vie. For my life. O. of the Ear of Corn and Ermine.

A more floresco. I (MOORE) flourish according to my custom.
MOORE.

A Nilo victoria. Victory from the Nile. GOULD.

A posse ad esse. From possibility to being. CARTER.

A rege et victoria. From the king and by conquest. BARRY.
LIGONIER. THATCHELL.

A regibus amicis. From friendly kings. RUCK. KEENE.

'Α ΣΟΤ ΧΕΙΡ ΚΤΡΙΕ ΔΕΔΟΞΑΣΤΑΙ ΕΝ ΙΣΧΤΙ. Thy right hand,
O Lord, hath been glorified in strength. EMERSON-
TENNANT.

A tenir promesse vient de noblesse. To keep promise comes from
nobleness. NEVILL, Lord Abergavenny, temp. Hen. VIII.

A te pro te. From thee, for thee. SAVAGE. MORTON.

A toujours loyale. For ever loyal. FENWICK, of Longframlington.

A tout pourvoir. To provide for every thing. OLIPHANT, CO. Perth.

A vino duw derwd. When God willeth He will come. EDWARDS, bt. LLOYD.

A virtute orta. Sprung from courage. STEWART.

A vous entier. For you entirely. JOHN, Duke of BEDFORD, son of Hen. IV.

A wight man *never wants a weapon.* WIGHTMAN.
The word "wight" is used by old authors in the sense of quick or active.

Ab alto speres alteri quod feceris. Expect from Heaven what you have done to another. WYNDHAM.

Ab aquila. From the eagle. GILLY, co. Suffolk.
"Invited from the cliff, to whose dark brow
He clings, the steep-ascending eagle soars,
With upward pinions."—THOMSON.

Ab uno ad omnes. From one to all. PERTH and MELFORT, e.

Abest timor. Fear is absent. EWART. KER, of Sutherland Hall.

Abscissa virescit. By pruning it grows green. BISSET.
Crest—A branch sprouting from the stump of a tree.

Absit ut glorier nisi in cruce. May I glory in nothing but the cross. CLARKE, of Ardington.

Absque dedecore. Without stain. NAPIER, of Falside.

Absque Deo nihil. Nothing without God. PETERS, of Newcastle.

Absque labore nihil. Nothing without labour. STEELE, bt.

Absque metu. Without fear. DALMAHOY, of Ravelridge.

Absque virtute nihil. Nothing without virtue. ROGERS-HARRISON.

Abstinete, sustinete. Forbear, bear. SHIRLEY.

Abstulit qui dedit. He who gave hath taken away. HOWARD. JERNINGHAM.

Accendit cantu. He animates by crowing. COCKBURN, bt.
Crest—A cock crowing.
"Non præstantior alter
Ære ciere viros, Martemque accendere cantu."—VIRG. Æn. lib. vi. 164.

Accipe daque fidem. Receive and give faith. CRICKETT.

Accipe quantum vis. Take as much as you wish. BROWN.

Accipiter prædam sequitur, nos gloriam. The hawk seeks prey, we (seek) glory. HAWKER. STROTHER, Shooter's Hill, Kent.
Both these families bear a hawk for crest.
"Adurgens (accipiter velut
Molles columbas, aut leporem citus
Venator in campis nivalis
Æmoniæ)."—HOR. Car. i. 37, 17.

Acquirit qui tuetur. He obtains who defends. MORTIMER, of Auchenbody.

Acre. CAMERON, bt.
This word is borne on the chief of honourable augmentation granted for

services at Acre. The motto over the crest is " Arriverette," commemorative of the gallantry of Col. Cameron at the pass of the River
Gave, at Arriverette near Bayonne, in 1813. Under the arms is the
word "Maya," on account of the renown gained by him at that pass,
also in 1813.

Ad æthera virtus. Virtue to heaven. HEMMING.

" Ardens evexit ad æthera virtus."— VIRG. *Æn.* vi. 130.

Ad alta. To high things. CAIRNIE.

Ad amussim. By the plumb-line. CUNYNGHAM, bt.

Crest — A hand holding a plumb-rule.

Ad ardua tendit. He attempts difficult things. M‘OLUM.

" Who, not content that former worth stand fast,
Looks forward, persevering to the last,
From well to better, daily self-surpast."— WORDSWORTH.

Ad arma paratus. Prepared for arms. JOHNSTONE, of Corehead.

" Valour was harnessed, like a chief of old,
Armed at all points, and prompt for knightly gest ;
Fierce he stepped forward and flung down his gage,
As if of mortal kind to dare the best."— SCOTT.

Ad astra. To the stars. MOORSON. BIGSBY.

Ad astra per ardua. To the stars through difficulties. DRUM-
MOND, of Midhope. *Crest* —Three stars placed in chevron.

Ad astra sequor. I follow to the stars. TOTTENHAM, co. Wexford.

Ad astra virtus. Virtue rises to the stars. SALTMARSHE, co.
York.

Ad cœlos volans. Flying to the heavens. CLAVERING, co.
Northumberland. CAYTON.

" Virtus, recludens immeritis mori
Cœlum, negatâ tentat iter viâ."— HOR. *Car.* iii. 2, 21.

Ad cœlum tendit. He directs his course towards heaven. BOOKER.

Ad diem tendo. I journey towards the dayspring. STEIN.
STEVENS.

Crest — An eagle's head between two wings expanded.

Ad escam et usum. For food and use. GRADEN.

Crest — An otter devouring a fish, and in the arms there are three with
a chevron between.

Ad finem fidelis. Faithful to the end. COLVILLE. GILROY.
HOWSON. KERSLAKE, Banner Hall, co. Norfolk. PETO, bt.
WEDDERBURN. WHITEHEAD.

Ad finem spero. I hope to the last. OGILVIE.

Ad fœdera cresco. I grow for treaties. OLIVER.

Crest — An arm holding an olive-branch.

Ad gloriam per spinas. To glory through *thorns, i.e.* difficulties.
THORN, of Paddington.

This motto, which is a pun on the name, alludes to the death of an
ancestor of this family, Sir Nicholas de Thorn, who fell fighting the
Welsh, along with Sir Wm. Latimer, on St. Leonard's Day, Nov. 6,
1282 — when Llewelyn's brother rebelled against Edward I. The
motto used by John Thorn, Abbot of Reading, brother of the ancestor

of the present representative, W. Thorn, M.D., of Paddington, was, "Sæpe creat pulchras aspera spina rosas," translated by Ashmole, "The beauteous rose oft springs from prickly thorns." This motto was taken by him from the windows of Berr Court near Pangbourne. Allusion to the name was also made in the device "Ex spinis uvas colligimus," "We gather grapes from thorns," which was placed by the corporation of Bristol over the picture (still preserved) of Nicholas Thorn, nephew of the abbot, and father of Sir Robert Thorn, discoverer of Newfoundland. This Nicholas was a great benefactor to Bristol, and, with his brother, founded the grammar-school there.

Ad littora tendit. It makes for the shore. QUATHERINE. JAMIESON. *Crest* — A ship in full sail.

Ad littora tendo. I make for the shore. WATSON.

Crest — A ship under sail.

> " *Where* lies the land to which yon ship must go?
> Festively she puts forth in trim array,
> As vigorous as a lark at break of day :
> Is she for tropic suns or polar snow?
> What boots the inquiry?— Neither friend or foe
> She cares for ; let her travel where she may,
> She finds familiar names, a beaten way
> Ever before her, and a wind to blow.
> Yet still I ask, what haven is her mark."— WORDSWORTH.

Ad metam. To the mark. BOWER. COMBREY. COMRIE. COMREY. COMRY.

Crest of Bower — A dexter and sinister arm shooting an arrow from a bow.

Ad morem villæ de Poole. According to the custom of the town of Poole. TOWN OF POOLE.

Ad mortem fidelis. Faithful till death. CANDLER, of Acomb.

Ad rem. To the point. WRIGHT.

Ad summa virtus. Courage to the last. BRUCE, of Wester-Kinloch.

Ad te, Domine. To thee, O Lord. NEWMAN.

Ad virtus astra. Virtue to the stars. CRANE.

Adde calcar. Apply the spur. SPURRIER.

Evidently intended as a play upon the name.

Addecet honeste vivere. It much becomes us to live honourably. ADDISON.

Addit frena feris. He puts bridles on wild beasts. MILNER, bt.

Arms — Per pale or, and sa. a chev. betw. three horses' bits counterchanged.

" Addit
Fræna feris, manibusque omnes effundit habenas."— VIRG. Æn. v. 817.

Addicunt aves. Birds ratify it. LUTEFOOT, of Scotland.

Addunt robur. They give strength. HAMILTON, of Westport.

Addunt robur stirpi. They add strength to the stock. HAMILTON.

Ades y franes i frain pan dychre. The crow is the guardian of others when she is croaking. *Crest* — A crow.

Adest prudenti animus. Courage belongs to the prudent. HAMILTON, of Mount Hamilton.

Adhæreo. I adhere. BURRELL.

Crest — A hand holding a bunch of burdock:

Adhæreo virtuti.   I cling to virtue.   KENNEDY, bt.
   " Virtutis veræ custos, rigidusque satelles."— HOR. *Ep.* lib. i. 1, 17.
Adjuvante Deo.   God my helper.   PHILLIPS.   MALINS.
Adjuvante Deo in hostes.   God aiding against enemies.   DON-
   OVAN.   O'DONOVAN.
Adjuvante Deo, quid timeo ?   God helping me, what do I fear ?
   BRIDGMAN.
Adorn the truth.   WADDEL.
Advance.   BRAND.   FERRIER.   SPIERS, of Eldershe.
Advance with courage.   MARJORIBANKS, bt.
Adversa virtute repello.   I repel adversity by virtue.   DENISON.
   DENNISTOUN, of that Ilk.   LONDESBOROUGH, b.   MEDHURST.
Ægis fortissima virtus.   Virtue is the strongest shield.   ASPINALL.
Ægre de tramite recto.   Scarcely from the right path.   HORS-
   BURGH.   TAIT.
Æquabiliter et diligenter.   By consistency and diligence.   MIT-
   FORD.   MOORE.   REDESDALE, b.
Æqualiter et diligenter.   Calmly and diligently.   MOORE.
Æquam servare mentem.   To preserve an equal mind.   GREEN,
   bt.   HOYLE, of Denton Hall.   MATHEW.   RAYMOND.   RIVERS, b.
   TREACHER.   MOON, bt.
      These words are from the lines of Horace. lib. ii. Od. 3, in which he
      recommends equanimity under all circumstances : —
            " Æquam memento rebus in arduis
               Servare mentem, non secus in bonis."
Æquanimiter.   With equanimity.   HARBORO.   SHUTTLEWORTH,
   bt.   SUFFIELD, b.
Æquat munia comparis. (Hor. *Car.* ii. 5. 2.)   She fully dis-
   charges the duties of a partner.   O. of Saint Catherine.
      This Order was instituted by the Czar, Peter the Great, on the 25th of
      November. O. S., 1714, in honour of the Empress Catherine the First,
      whose prudence delivered him from the Turks on the banks of the
      river Pruth, in 1711. The other motto of the Order, "For love and our
      native land" is inscribed in Russian on the ribbon, and in French on
      the left of the Stomacher.
Æquitas actionem regulam.   Equity (makes) action the rule.
   MONTAGUE.
Æquitas actionum regula.   Equity is the rule of actions.
   BRADBURY.
Æquo adeste animo.   Be present with mind unchangeable.
   COPE, bt.
Æquo animo.   With equanimity.   PENNANT.   REPTON.
            "——— The virtuous man,
      Who keeps his temper'd mind serene and pure,
      And every passion aptly harmonized,
      Amid a jarring world with vice inflamed."—THOMSON.
Æquo pede propera.   Hasten with steady pace.   EAST, bt.
            Crest — A horse passant.
Afrad pôb afraid ; equivalent to *Qui non vigilat vastat.*   He

who does not watch lays waste. VAUGHAN, of Burlton Hall.

Age officium tuum. Act your office. ABBOTT, of Darlington, formerly of Suffolk and East Dereham, Norfolk.

This motto has been handed down as allusive to the office of superior of Warden Abbey, held by an ancestor of this family, to which also the pears in the arms refer.

Agendo gnaviter. By acting prudently. LEEKE, co. Salop. ROWE. WHITWORTH.

Agere pro aliis. To act for others. ASHTON.

Agincourt. LENTHALL, of Oxon. WALLER, bt. WODEHOUSE, b. WALKER, bt.

An ancestor of each of these families is said to have been at that famous battle.

Agitatione purgatur. It is purified by agitation. RUSSELL, bt.

Crest — A fountain.

Agite pro viribus. Act according to your strength. CAMPBELL.

Agnoscar eventu. I shall be known by the results. ROSS, of Auchlossen.

Agnus Dei mihi salus. The Lamb of God is my salvation. LAMMIN.

Intended as a play upon the name.

Aides Dieu ! Help, O God ! AUBERT. MILL, bt. MILLS.

"Help us, O Lord our God."—2 *Chron.* xiv. 11.

Aἰὲν ἀριστεύειν. Always to excel. BELGRAVE. MANNINGHAM· NEVE.

Aime le meilleur. Love the best. SINCLAIR, bt.

Aime ton frère. Love thy brother. FRERE. FREER.

"He who loveth God, loveth his brother also."—1 *John,* iv. 21.

Aimez loyaulté. Love loyalty. BOLTON, b. COWAN, bt. PAULET, bt. WINCHESTER, m.

Aim high. MINN.

Crest — A dexter and sinister arm shooting an arrow upwards from a bow.
"Such as our motive is, our aim must be."— COWPER.

Ainsi et peut estre meilleur. Thus and perhaps better. ROLLESTON, co. Stafford.

Ainsi il est. Thus it is. BELLINGHAM, bt.

Albuera. LUMLEY.

Sir W. Lumley, G.C.R., commanded the cavalry at Albuera.

Alba de Tormes. HAMILTON, of Woodbrook, bt.

This town, which is situated in the kingdom of Leon, was, in spite of the weakness of its defences, most gallantly defended by Sir John Hamilton with only fifteen hundred men, against 15,000 under Marshal Soult. Hence the motto, which is inscribed on the chief of augmentation.

ΑΛΗΘΕΙΑΝ ΚΑΙ ΕΛΕΥΘΕΡΙΑΝ. Truth and freedom. WAKEFIELD.

Ales volat propriis. The bird flies to its kind. TUFTON, bt.

Alert. CRASDALE.

Algiers. Exmouth, v. Pellew.

Edward Pellew entered the naval service of his country at an early age, and by his gallantry was raised to the Peerage as Baron Exmouth in 1814. His Lordship was advanced to a Viscounty in 1816, for bombarding and destroying the fleet and arsenal of Algiers.

Alienus ambitioni. Averse to ambition. Hawkins.

Alis aspicit astra. On wing he looks towards the stars. Carnegie, of Craigie.

The arms contain an eagle displ., and the crest is a star.

Alis et animo. With speed and courage. Munro.

Alis nutrior. I am fed by my wings. Simpson, of Udock.

Crest—A Falcon volant.

All for religion. Langton.

All is in God. Clovyle. Colvile. Colvell, co. Essex.

All my hope is in God. Frazer. Undey. Udney, of that Ilk.

All's well. Mudge.

All worship be to God only. (Matt. iv. 10.) Fishmongers' Comp. London.

Alla corona fidissimo. To the crown most faithful. Leche, of Carden.

This motto has reference to the origin of the arms, which is thus recorded in an old pedigree : " One of this ancient family living in Barkshire, near Windsor, in the time of Edward III. entertained and feasted three kings in his house ; viz. the king of England, the king of France, and the king of Scots ; which last two kings were at that time prisoners to king Edward. The king of England, to requite his good entertainment and other favours, gave him three crowns, on his chief indented gules, the field ermine ; which coat is borne by the name and family, dispersed into many other counties."

Alla ta Hara. God my help. Mildmay, bt.

Alleluiah. Tuite, bt.

Allons, Dieu ayde. Let us go on, God assists us. Blakely.

Al'merito militar. To military merit. O. of St. Ferdinand.

Alnus semper floreat. May the *Alder* always flourish. Aldersey.

Alta pete. Aim at high things. Glen, of Bar. Fletcher.

Alte fert aquila. The eagle bears on high. Monteagle, b.

Alte volat. He flies high. Dawson.

Alte volo. I fly aloft. Heywood, bt.

"The wintry blast of death
Kills not the buds of virtue; no, they spread
Beneath the heavenly beam of brighter suns,
Thro' endless ages, into higher powers."—Thomson.

Altera merces. Another reward. M'Lean, of Ardgour. Maclaine.

Crest—An axe in pale, before a laurel and cypress branch in saltire. The motto refers to the glory which is gained by death even when victory is not won.

Altera securitas. Another security. Henry VIII.

Alteri, si tibi. To another, if to thyself. Harvey, co. Norfolk. Saville-Onley.

"Deum amemus supra omnia, proximum vero juxta nos ipeos ; id est, ut alteri faciamus quod nobis velimus fieri."—Grotius *de Veritate.*

Alterum non lædere. Not to injure another. Keir.

Altiora in votis. Higher things are the object of my wishes.
Des Vœux, bt.
> A play on the name which means wishes or prayers.

Altiora pete. Seek higher things. Gordon, of Tichmurie.
Altiora peto. I seek higher things. Oliphant, of Newton, co.
Perth.
> "Seek things above."—*Col.* iii. 1.

Altiora spero. I hope higher things. Torr.
Altius ibunt qui ad summa nituntur. They will rise highest
who strive for the highest place. Forbes, bt. Fordyce.
Altius tendo. I aim higher. Kinlock.
Always. Stevens.
Always faithful. M'Kenzie, co. Inverness.
Always for liberty. Mawbey.
> " The love of liberty with life is given,
> And life itself the inferior gift of heaven."—Dryden.

Always helping. Gravine, of Edinburgh.
Always the same. Freebairn.
Ama Deum et serva mandata. Love God and keep his com-
mandments. Synnot.
> This motto evidently refers to the name (Sin-not), Synnot.

Ama gregem. Love the flock. Shepperd.
Amantes ardua dumos. The thorns which love the hills.
Thornhill.
> This motto and the crest, a thorn-tree, are intended as a rebus on the
> name ; the words are from Virg. *Georg.* iii. 315.

Amantibus justitiam, pietatem, fidem. To the lovers of justice,
piety, and faith. O. of St. Anne, of Sleswick.
Amat victoria curam. Victory and care are close friends. (lit.
Victory loves care). Clark, bt. Clerk, of Penicuik, co.
Edinburgh, bt. Clerk, of Norwich.
> This motto of Clerke refers as does "Free for a blast," (which see) to
> the adventure which secured their lands : and teaches that caution
> is necessary to ensure victory.

Ambition sans envie. Ambition without envy. Walch.
Amica veritas. Truth is dear. Nesbett.
Amice. Lovingly. Russel. Watts.
> "Nil ego contulerim jucundo sanus amico."—Hor. *Sat.* i. 5. 44.

Amicis prodesse, nemini nocere. To do good to my friends, to
injure nobody. Lowton.
Amicitia sine fraude. Friendship without deceit. Allen.
> " Thou art the same through change of times,
> Through frozen zones and burning climes ;
> From the equator to the pole,
> The same kind angel through the whole."

Amicitiæ virtutisque fœdus. The league of friendship and
virtue. Grand O. of Wurtemburg. Hippisley, bt. Nelson,
of Beeston, co. Norfolk.

B

Amicitiam trahit amor. Love draws on friendship. WIRE-DRAWERS' COMP.

Amico fidus ad aras. Faithful to my friend as far as conscience permits, or even to death, lit. even to the altar. RUTHER-FORD, of Fairningtoun.

> This fragment of a verse refers to the story of Orestes and Pylades, each of whom endeavoured to die instead of his friend when threatened with death at the altar of the Tauric Diana.

Amicos semper amat. He always loves his friends. CULLEY.

> In allusion to the Talbot in the crest.

Amicta vitibus ulmo. An elm covered with vine. ELMSALL.

> A play upon the name and crest, which is an *Elm(s)all* covered with vine.

Amicus amico. A friend to a friend. BELLINGHAM.

Amicus certus. A sure friend. PEAT, of Sevenoaks. PEIT.

Amicus vitæ solatium. A friend is the solace of life. BURTON.

> " Social friends,
> Attun'd to happy unison of soul ;
> To whose exalting eye a fairer world,
> Of which the vulgar never had a glimpse,
> Displays its charms."—THOMSON.

Amitié. Friendship. PITT.

Amo. I love. BUCCLEUGH, d. HOOPS. MAC KINDLAY. SCOTT.

> " Birds and beasts,
> And the mute fish that glances in the stream,
> And harmless reptile coiling in the sun,
> And gorgeous insect hovering in the air,
> The fowl domestic, and the household dog—
> In his capacious mind he loved them all ;
> Their right acknowledging he felt for all."—WORDSWORTH.

Amo, inspicio. I love him, I gaze upon him. SCOT.

> *Crest* — An eagle regarding the sun.

Amo pacem. I love peace. TOWLE.

Amo ut invenio. I love as I find. PERROT, bt.

Amor Dei et proximi summa beatitudo. The love of God and our neighbour is the highest happiness. DOBBS.

> " By swift degrees the love of nature works,
> And warms the bosom, till at last sublim'd
> To rapture and enthusiastic heat,
> We feel the present Deity, and taste
> The joy of God to see a happy world !"—THOMSON.

Amor et pax. Love and peace. IRELAND.

Amor et obedientia. Love and obedience. PAINTERS' COMP.

Amor patitur moras. Love endures delay. LUMISDEN, of that Ilk.

Amor proximi. The love of our neighbour. O. of NEIGHBOURLY LOVE.

> " Verus amor tum Dei tum proximi ; quo fit ut præceptis ipsius pareamus, non serviliter pœnæ formidine, sed ut ipsi placeamus, ipsumque habeamus pro sua bonitate patrem ac remuneratorem."
> —GROTIUS *de Veritate.*

Amor sine timore. Love without fear. READE.

Amorque et obedientia. Both love and obedience. PAINTERS' COMP.

Amore patriæ. By patriotism. SCOTT.
> "Our one best omen is our country's cause."—POPE'S *Homer.*

Amore sitis uniti. Be ye united in love. TIN-PLATE WORKERS' and WIRE-WORKERS' COMP.

Amore vici. I have conquered by love. M'KENZIE, bt.

Amore vinci. To be conquered by love. M'KENZIE.

Amour de la bonté. Love of goodness. COWELL.
> "Come, ye generous minds, in whose wide thought
> Of all his works, creative Bounty burns
> With warmest beam, and on your open front
> And liberal eye, sits, from his dark retreat
> Inviting modest want."—THOMSON.

Amour avec loyaulté. Love with loyalty. PARR, of Kendal, co. of Westmoreland. Of this family was Katherine, Queen of Henry VIII.

Anchor fast. GROAT.

Anchor, fast anchor. GRAY, b. GRAY, of Durham.
> *Crest* — An anchor.

Anchora salutis. The anchor of safety. O'LOGHLEN, bt.
> *Crest* — An anchor.

Anchora sit virtus. Let virtue be my anchor. FORD, of Essex.

Anchora spei Cereticæ est in te, Domine. The anchor of Cardigan's hope is in Thee, O Lord. T. of Cardigan.

Anguis *in herba.* A snake in the grass. ANGUISH, co. Norfolk.
> *Crest* — A snake in grass.
> "Frigidus, ô pueri? fugite hinc, latet anguis in herba."—VIRG. *Ec.* iii. 93.

An I may. DE LYLE. LYLE. MONTGOMERY.

Anima in amicis una. One feeling among friends. POWELL.

Animis et fato. By courageous acts and good fortune. THRIEPLAND, bt.

Animo et fide. By courage and faith. BURROUGHES, of Burlingham and Long Stratton, co. Norfolk. CORNOCK, co. Wexford. GUILDFORD, e. NORTH. PHILLIPS. TURNER.

Animo et prudentiâ. By courage and prudence. HOWETT. JOWETT. LYON. MELLOR.

Animo, non astutia. By courage, not by craft. GORDON, d. GORDON, bt. GORDON, co. Down. PEDLAR, of Hoo Mavey.

Animose certavit. He hath striven courageously. PRYME, of Cambridge.
> Alexander de la Pryme, the first of this family of whom anything is known, was of Flemish origin and followed Philip of Alsace from Ypres to the second Crusade, where he distinguished himself so much that he obtained a patent of gentility and a grant of arms with the foregoing motto. Charles de la Pryme, with about 800 other Protestant families, came to England about 1628-29 or 30, during the persecution of the Protestants at the siege of Rochelle.

Animum fortuna sequitur. Fortune follows courage. BEDFORD, co. Warwick. CRAIK, of Arbigland.

Animum ipse parabo. I myself will provide courage. NIBBERT.
" Qui donat et aufert ;
Det vitam, det opes ; æquum mî animum ipse parabo."—HOR. *Ep.* i. 18, 111.

Animum prudentia firmat. Prudence strengthens courage.
BRISBANE, of Scotland.

Animum rege. Rule thy mind. DAY. KEITH, bt. MOORE, of
Grimeshill. REEVES.
" Animum rege ; qui, nisi paret,
Imperat : hunc frænis, hunc tu compesce catenâ."—HOR. *Ep.* i. 2, 62.

Animus est nobilitas. The soul is the nobility. COBHAM.

Animus et fata. Courage and fortune. THRIEPLAND.

Animus non deficit æquus. Equanimity is not wanting. BUR-
RELL. WILLOUGHBY DE ERESBY, b.
"Quid petis, hic est ;
Est Ulubris, animus si te non deficit æquus."—HOR. *Ep.* i. 11, 30.

Animus, non res. Mind, not circumstance. HUTH.

Animus tamen idem. Yet our mind is unchanged. CUFFE, bt.
WHEELER.

Animus valet. Courage availeth. BOSWORTH.

Annoso robore quercus. An oak in aged strength. AIKENHEAD.
Crest — An oak-tree.
"Velut, annoso validam cum robore quercum
Alpini Boreæ, nunc hinc, nunc flatibus illinc
Eruere inter se certant ; it stridor, et altè
Consternunt terram concusso stipite frondes :
Ipsa hæret scopulis ; et, quantum vertice ad auras
Æthereas, tantum radice in Tartara tendit."—VIRG. *Æn.* iv. 441.

"King of the Forest ! well hast thou the name :
Majestically stern, sublimely great !
Laughing to scorn the wind, the flood, the flame ;
And e'en when withering, proudly desolate."

Ante ferit quam flamma micet. He strikes (it) before the fire
sparkles out. O. of the GOLDEN FLEECE.
The collar of the Order of the Golden Fleece is composed of double steels
interwoven with flint stones emitting sparks of fire. To these, which
were the ancient arms of Burgundy, the above motto alludes. The
motto engraven on the badge of this order is "Pretium non vile
laborum" (no mean reward for toils) ; while on the mantle "Je l'ay
empris" (I have won it) is several times repeated in letters of gold.

Ante et post cole Deum. Before and after worship God, *i.e.*
before and after (you *go to bed*) sunset. GOTOBED.

Ante omnia erit. It will be before all things. DUNCH.

Ante omnia sylvæ. The *woods* (or *forests*) before all things.
FORRESTER. FORSTER. WOODS.
"Pallas, quas condidit arces,
Ipsa, colat ; nobis placeant ante omnia sylvæ."—VIRG. *Æn.* ii. 61.

Antiqui mores. Ancient manners. MORRICE.

Antiquum assero decus. I claim ancient honour. ARROT.

Antiquum obtinens (sc. *honorem.*) Possessing our ancient honour.
BAGOT, b. BEAUMONT. COTGREAVE, of Netherleigh. SHA-
KERLY, bt.

An tu tonitru ? Wilt thou with thy thunder? Cox, of Charton.
This motto is borne over the crest, which is a demi-horse argent charged on the shoulder with a thunderbolt ppr. And under the arms is the motto, Chescun son devoir. Each man his duty.

Aperto vivere voto. To live without a wish concealed. AYLES-FORD, e. FINCH. CHAMIER. WRIGHT.

Apparet quod latebat. What lay hidden appears. EDGAR.
Crest—An oak-branch sprouting out leaves.

Appetitus rationi pareat. Cic. *de Off.* I. 39. 10. Let your desires obey your reason. CUSTANCE, of Weston, co. Norfolk.

Appropinquat dies. The day is at hand. JOHNSTONE, of Clathrie.

Aquila non captat muscas. The eagle catcheth not flies.
BEDINGFIELD, bt. BEDINGFIELD, of Ditchingham, co. Norfolk. BULLER, of Cornwall. CHINN, of Gloucester. DRAKE. GRAVES, b. GREAVES, of Mayfield. GOTHARD, of Newcastle. ILLIDGE. STEEL, bt. TRANT. WEDDEBURN. WESTON. WRIGHT.
This motto is evidently altered from the Greek proverb, Ἀιτὸς οὐ θηρεῦσι τὰς μυίας, An eagle will not follow after flies. An eagle forms part of the armorial bearings of these families.

Aquila petit solem. The eagle seeks the sun. KENDALL.

Aquilæ vitem pocula vitam. Let me avoid the cup—the sustenance of the eagle. BOTELER.
I imagine this motto has reference to an opinion, anciently entertained, that the eagle was sustained chiefly by drink, and therefore the cup is called the sustenance, or life, of the eagle.

Arr dduw y Gyd. All depend on God. PHILLIPS.

Arbor vitæ Christus, fructus per fidem gustamus. Christ is the tree of life, the fruit whereof we taste through faith. FRUIT-ERERS' COMP.

Arctæos numine fines. (I reached) the limits of the north by (the help of) God. ROSS.
This motto was borne by Sir John Ross, C.B., distinguished for his discoveries in the Arctic regions.

Arcui meo non confido. (Ps. xliv. 6.) I trust not to my bow. WILKES. Borne by the celebrated John Wilkes.
Crest —A cross-bow.

Arcus, artes, astra. The bow, arts, and stars. BIRNEY, of Salin. BURMEY.

Archoille. The woody hill. M'GREGOR, bt.

Ardenter amo. I love fervently. SCOT, of Harwood.

Ardenter prosequor alis. Eagerly do I pursue in my winged course. GRAEME.

Ardens. Fervent. PEAT, of Sevenoakes.

Ardet virtus, non urit. Valour inflames, but consumes not.
FYERS. FYRES.

Ardua petit ardea. The *heron* seeks high places. HERON, bt.
There are three herons in the arms, and the crest is a heron.

Ardua vinco. I overcome difficulties. STRATTON, of Montrose.

Ardua tendo. I rise on high. MALCOLM, bt.
  Crest—A pyramid entwined with laurel.

Arma pacis fulcra. Arms are the supporters of peace. AR-
TILLERY COMP.

Arma parata fero. I carry arms in readiness. CAMPBELL.
MACGUFFE.

Arma tuentur pacem. Arms maintain peace. FOWKE, bt.

Armat et ornat. For defence and ornament. BROWN, of Gorgy-
mill.
  Alluding to the flower and the thorns of the rose which forms the
  crest.

Armed with integrity. WADDILOVE.

Armet nos ultio regum. Let vengeance for princes arm us.
  PORTAL.
  When Blanche of Bourbon, queen of Castile, and sister-in-law of Henry
  V. of France, had been poisoned by her husband, Pedro the Cruel,
  400 knights, under the command of Bertrand du Guesclin, volunteered
  to go into Spain in order to avenge her death. Among these knights,
  Raymond de Portal held a distinguished place, and the foregoing motto
  was assigned him, in 1336, by the French king.

Armis et animis. By arms and courage. CARNAGIE. CARNEGIE.
GILFILLAN.

Armis et diligentia. By arms and diligence. BASKIN, of
Scotland.

Armis et fide. By arms and fidelity. CAMPBELL, of Auchawilling.

Armis et industria. By arms and industry. COCHRAN, of Bal-
barchan. *Crest*—A spear and garb in saltire.

Armis potentius æquum. Justice is more powerful than arms.
FALCONER of Newton, Scotland.

Arolla. MACDONALD, of Dalchosnie, co. Perth.
  This word is inscribed on the banner which forms part of the crest
  granted to Col. John Macdonald, C.B, in commemoration of the good
  service rendered by him at that place.

Arriverette. CAMERON, of Fassiefern, bt.
  For particulars of this motto see " Acre."

Arte conservatus. Preserved by skill. CHRISTOPHER.

Arte et animo. By skill and courage. FERGUSON.

Arte et Marte. By skill and valour. MIDDLETON. HUNTER.

Arte non impetu. By skill not force. HUNTER.

Arte non vi. By skill not force. JORDAN.

Arte vel Marte. By art or force. DEANS. DUNDAS.

Artes honorabit. He will do honour to the arts. HANGER.
  "From art how various are the blessings sent,
    Wealth, splendour, honour, liberty, content."— GOLDSMITH.

Artibus et armis. By arts and arms. ELTON, bt.

Artibus haud armis. By arts, not arms. GARDNER.

Artis vel Martis. By skill or valour. EASTOFT. EURE.
  Crest—A pen and sword in saltire.

Arts and trades united. FANMAKERS' COMP.

Ascendo. I rise. CATTY.

Ascendam. I shall rise. KENNAWAY, bt.

As God wills, so be it. BLACKSMITHS' COMP., London.

> The modern motto of this Company is, "*By* hammer and hand all arts do stand."

Asgre lan diogel ei phercen. A good conscience is the best shield. HERBERT of Llanarth Court. JONES. VAUGHAN.

> "What stronger breastplate than a heart untainted?
> Thrice is he arm'd that hath his quarrel just;
> And he but naked, though lock'd up in steel,
> Whose conscience with injustice is corrupted."—SHAKSPEARE.

As the hart the water brooks. (Ps. xlii. 1.) HUNTLEY.

Assher dure, see "*Assez dure,*" which I believe to be the correct motto.

Aspera ad virtutem est via. The road to virtue is rough. EDWARDES, of Gileston.

Aspera me juvant. Difficulties delight me. Low.

Aspera virtus. Virtue is difficult. SINCLAIR. bt.

Aspice et imitare. Look and imitate. BROOKS.

Aspira. Aspire thou. FELD.

Aspire, persevere, and indulge not. ADAM.

Aspiro. I aspire. BOLTON. CURRY. M'FEIL. RAMSAY, bt.

Assez dure. Sufficiently hard. IPONMONGERS' COMP.

Assiduitate. By assiduity. JOHNSTON of Anstruther. SKEEN.

Assiduitate non desidiâ. By assiduity, not by sloth. LOCH, of Drylaw and Rachan.

> "Vitanda est improba Siren
> Desidia."—HOR. *Ep.* ii. 3. 14.

Astra castra, numen, lumen munimen. The stars are my camp, the Deity is my light and guard. BELCARRES, e. LINDSAY, bt. LINDSEY.

> "Nor sun nor moon they need, nor day nor night;
> God is their temple, and the Lamb their light."—HEBER'S *Palestine.*

Astra et castra. The stars (or heaven) and the camp. LITTLER.

Atalanta. HARDINGE, bt.

> In the crest of augmentation granted to this family, are a Dutch and French flag in saltire, on the former of which the name "Atalanta," on the latter, "Piedmontaise," is inscribed. These words commemorate the gallantry of Capt. G. Nicholas Hardinge, who when in command of H M.S. Fiorenzo, took the Dutch frigate Atalanta, and afterwards fell in action with the French frigate Piedmontaise, which he also captured.

At all times God me defend. LYELL.

At servata fides perfectus amorque ditabunt. But faith kept, and perfect love will enrich. YOUNGE, co. Stafford.

At spes infracta. Yet my hope is unbroken. CONYNGHAM, bt. DICK. HOOD. HOPE, bt.

At spes non fracta. But *hope* is not broken. HOPE. HOPE-TOWN, e. KENNARD.

> The crest of Hope and Hopetown is a globe fractured at the top under a rainbow.

At spes solamen. Yet *hope* is my solace. HOPE, of Balcomy.

Attamen tranquillus. Tranquil notwithstanding. MAITLAND.

Attendez. Wait. BOYES, of Scotland.

Attendez vouz. Wait patiently. BOYS. BOYES.

Au bon droit. With good right. DALLING, bt. EGREMONT, e. WINDHAM.

Au plaisir fort de Dieu. At the all-powerful disposal of God. MOUNT EDGECUMBE, e.

Auctor pretiosa fecit. The Giver made them valuable. BARLEE.

Auctor pretiosa facit. The Giver makes them valuable. BUCKINGHAMSHIRE, e. HOBART. LUBBOCK, bt. RAYMOND.

Audacem juvant fata. The fates assist the bold. SOMERVILLE.

Audaces fortuna juvat. Fortune favours the bold. BARRON. BLOXHAM. BURROUGHES. CARPENTER. CHAMBERLAINE. DAVENPORT, of Bramall. KING, bt. HAYES. COSBY, of Stradbally. TURNBULL. MORGAN. STEWART. COSTELLO, of Ireland.

Audaces juvat. She (*i.e.* Fortune) favours the bold. CLEVELAND, co. Devon. CAMPBELL. GOODGE. GOOGE.

Audaces juvo. I assist the bold. CAMPBELL, of Jure and Achteny. M'CAUSLAND. BUCHANAN-HAMILTON.

Audacia. Boldness. GRANT, of Auchrraine.

Audacia et industria. Boldness and diligence. BUCHANAN.

Audacia et virtute adepta. Gained by daring and valour. PATON.

Audaci favet fortuna. Fortune favours the bold. TURNBULL.

Audaciter. Boldly. EWEN, of Craigton.

Audacter et aperte. Boldly and openly. CAMPBELL, bt.

Audacter et sincere. Boldly and sincerely. CLIVE. POWES, e.

Audacter et strenue. Boldly and earnestly. BLYTH. POLLOCK, bt.

Audax. Bold. ERTH.

Audax ero. I will be bold. BOLDERO.

A pun upon the name.

Audax et promptus. Bold and ready. DOUGLAS, bt.

Audax omnia perpeti. Daring (Hardi) to endure all things. HARDING.

Aude et prevalebis. Dare, and thou shalt prevail. FREND.

Audentes fortuna juvat. Virg. *Æn.* x. 284. Fortune favours the bold. MACKINNON. MOWBRAY. TURING, bt.

Audentior ibo. I will go more daringly. OLIVEIRA.

" Audentior ibo
In casus omnes."—VIRG. Æn. ix. 291.

Audeo. I dare. ROSE, of Houghton Conquest, co. Beds.

"I dare do all that may become a man."—SHAKSPEARE.

Audi alteram partem. Hear the other party. PEMBERTON.

Audio sed taceo. I hear, but say nothing. TROLLOP, of Durham.

Audito et gradito. Listen, and walk on. CRUIKSHANKS, of London.

Audi, vide, sile. Hear, see, be silent. TILLARD.

> " Ay, free off han' your story tell,
> When wi' a bosom cronie ;
> But still keep something to yoursel
> Ye scarcely tell to onie.
> Conceal yourself as weel 's ye can
> Frae critical dissection ;
> But keek thro' ev'ry other man
> Wi' sharpened sly inspection."—BURNS.

Au fait. In fact. SHAW.

Augeo. I increase. TRENT.

Augeor dum progredior. I increase as I proceed. DURHAM.
Crest—An increscent.

Auriga virtutum prudentia. Prudence is the directress of the virtues. MAWBEY, of Surrey.

Ausim et confido. I am brave and confident. ARESKINE. ERSKINE, of Kirkbuddo.

Auspice Christo. Under the guidance of Christ. DAVIE, bt. LAWLEY, bt. WENLOCK, b.

Auspice Deo. Under God's direction. SPEID.

Auspice Deo extuli mari. God being my leader, I brought him out of the sea. PHILLIPS-MARSHALL. PHILLIPS.

> *Crest*—Upon a mount vert, in front of a Newfoundland dog, sejant, reguardant ppr. an Escutcheon ar. thereon, in base, waves of the sea, and floating therein a naked man, the sinister arm elevated also ppr. The crest and motto are borne in consequence of the life of William Phillips, Esq., of Cavendish Square, having been saved from drowning in Portsmouth harbour by a strange dog ; this canine preserver was received into the family and passed the remainder of his days in ease and comfort.
> John William Phillips-Marshall, now deceased, was one of the Admirals of our Royal Navy ; he was a natural son of William Phillips, Esq., of Cavendish Sq. (whose life was saved as stated above). His brother (Phillips) a clergyman, Vicar of Eling. Hants, also bore the same crest and motto.

Auspice Numine. Under Divine direction. WELSH.

Auspice summo Numine. Under direction of Almighty God. IRVINE.

Auspice Teucro. Under the auspices of Teucer. TUCKER.
"Nil desperandum Teucro duce. et auspice Teucro."—HOR. *Od.* i. 7, 27.

Auspicio regis, senatus Angliæ. Under the auspices of the sovereign and senate of England. EAST INDIA COMP.

Auspicium melioris ævi. A pledge of better times. ST. ALBANS, d.

Aut manum aut ferrum. Either the hand or the sword. WAYLAND.

Aut mors aut vita decora. Either death or honourable life. GORDON, of Carnousie. SHAW.

Aut mors aut vita Deus. God is either death or life. GORDON, of Edinglassie.

Aut nunquam tentes aut perfice. Either never attempt or accomplish. BENNET. CRESWELL. CROUCH. DAY. DORSET, d. HUSTLER. SACKVILE.

Aut pax aut bellum. Either peace or war. DONALDSON, of Kinnardie. GUNN. HALL. HEATON. MORRIS. TWEEDIE.

Aut suavitate aut vi. Either by gentleness or by force. HOPKINS, bt.

Aut tace aut face. Either be silent or act. SCOTT, of Comeston.

Aut vi aut suavitate. Either by force or mildness. GRIFFITH.

Aut viam inveniam aut faciam. I will either find a road or make one. COCKBURN, bt. WIGHTWICK, of Bloxwich.

Aut vincam aut peribo. I will either conquer or perish. CHUDLEY.

Aut vincere aut mori. Victory or death. POWER.

Aut vita libera, aut mors gloriosa. Either a life of freedom, or a death of glory. SAVERY.

Autre n'auray. I will have none other. O. of the GOLDEN FLEECE.

Auxiliante resurgo. When he helps I rise again. GRAHAM, of Merickle.

Auxilio ab alto. By aid from on high. MARTIN.

Auxilio Dei. By the help of God. ERISBY. MOREHEAD. MUIRHEAD, of Bredisholm.

Auxilio divino. By divine aid. DRAKE, bt.

    This motto refers to the crest of the great circumnavigator's family, which is a ship drawn round a globe with a cable-rope, by a hand out of the clouds, all ppr.

Auxilium. Aid. MACHIN. PRICKETT.

Auxilium ab alto. Aid from above. CLONBROCK, b. DILLON, bt. KILLETT. NORMAND. ORDELL. KING. MARTIN, bt. ROSCOMMON, e.

Auxilium meum ab alto. My help is from above. BLAKENEY.

Auxilium meum a Domino. My help is from the Lord. COLLYER. LLOYD. PRICE, bt. MOSTYN, b.

    "My help cometh from the Lord."— *Ps.* cxxi. 2.

Avance ! Advance ! COLLYR, of Norwich. LONG. PORTMAN, e.

Avancez ! Advance ! CHALMERS, of Culto. CHAMBERS, of Scotland. CHURTON. HILL, bt.

    "That day 'gainst charge of sword and lance,
    As their own ocean rocks hold stance,
      The British host had stood;
    But when their leader said 'Advance !'
      They were that ocean's flood."—SCOTT's *Waterloo.*

Avant ! Forward ! STEWART, bt. STUART, bt.

Avauncez et archez bien. Advance and shoot well. SWINNERTON.

    An ancestor of this family having rallied the Christian archers in an engagement with the Turks, one of whom he slew with his own hand, took these words for his motto.

Ave Maria plena gratia. Hail, Mary, full of grace. (Luke, i. 28.) CUSACK.

Avec ce qui je tienne je suis. With what I hold I am. BRADSHAW.

Avi numerantur avorum. A long train of ancestry is enumerated. Grantley, b. Norton. Hitch. Perton. Pryce. Rede. Turberville.

This claim to long descent is taken from Virg. *Geo.* iv. 209.
"Genus immortale manet, multosque per annos
Stat Fortuna domûs, et avi numerantur avorum."

Avise la fin. Consider the end. Ailsa, m. Kennedy.

Avis la fin. Consider the end. Keydon.

Avita et aucta. (Honours) Inherited and acquired. O. of the Iron Crown.

These words may either refer to the good qualities which persons admitted into this Order were supposed to have received from their ancestors and to have themselves cultivated, or to the new honours which their admission added to their former ones. The Order itself was instituted by the Emperor Francis I., to commemorate the re-union of his Italian provinces under his sceptre, and the Iron Crown of the ancient kings of Lombardy was chosen as its appropriate badge. This crown, which is said to contain one of the nails of the true cross, was till recently preserved at Monza, ten miles from Milan, and with it the Emperors of Germany, from Charles the Great downwards, have been crowned.

Avitæ gloriæ memor. Mindful of ancestral glory. Acton.

No doubt this motto may be rendered as a rebus on the name, thus—
Act on mindful of your ancestral glory.

Avito evehor honore. I am exalted or influenced by ancestral honour. Holmes. Burnes.

Avito jure. By ancestral right. Wheeler.

Avito non sine honore. Not without ancestral honour. Leppington.

Avito viret honore. He flourishes through the honour of his ancestors. Bute, m. Stuart de Decies, b. Stewart de Rothsay, b. Mackenzie. Wharncliffe, b. Turner.

"Fortes creantur fortibus et bonis."— Hor. *Car.* iv. 4. 29.

Avitos notit honores. He knows his ancestral honours. Gusthart.

Avorum honori. For the honour of our ancestors. Barne.

Await the day. Mayne, of Teffont-Ewyas, co. Wilts.

Ay, forward. Brand, of Baberton.

Ayez prudence. Have prudence. Biss, of Durham.

Aymez loyaulté. Love loyalty. Bolton, b. Cowan. Paulett. Stratton. Winchester, m.

John Paulett, marquis of Winchester, garrisoned his house during the Civil Wars in the reign of Charles I., and held it against the Parliament forces nearly two years. The Marquis, in honour of the principles which actuated him, called his house "Aymez Loyaulté," and caused these words to be written with a diamond upon every glass-window, as if he would thus have a perpetual monument of his loyalty to his Prince. These words have ever since been used by his descendants for their motto.

Azincourt. Billam. Waller, bt. Lenthall, of Oxon.

Sir Rowland Lenthall was master of the robes to Henry IV. and attended Henry V. to France, where he had a command at the battle of Agincourt.

B

Βαλανους Δενδρον Βαλλει.   The tree drops acorns.   BALLY.
A direct allusion to the name.

ΒΑΛΙΖΕ ΤΗΝ ΕΥΘΕΙΑΝ.   Walk the straight way.   BALLI.

Barn ar agin.   Wrongly judged.   FLEMING.

Barn yn uchaf.   Buck uppermost.   BUCK.

Baroach.   NICHOLSON.

> The name of a fortress in the East Indies, borne as one of their mottoes by a branch of the Nicholson family to commemorate the services of Gen. Nicholson at the siege of the place.

Barbaria.   O. of BURGUNDIAN CROSS.

Barrosa.   GOUGH, v.

> At the battle of Barrosa, Viscount Gough, then Sir Hugh Gough, commanded the 87th Reg.; he also has for motto, "China," in commemoration of the attack on Canton, at which he had the command of the British troops, and for his services received a baronetcy. His third motto is "Goojerat," at the time of which battle he was commander-in-chief of the forces in India.

Basis virtutum constantia.   Constancy is the foundation of all virtue.   DEVEREUX.   HEREFORD, v.

Be as God will.   BRACEBRIDGE, of Atherstone.

𝔅𝔢 𝔞𝔰 𝔊𝔬𝔡 𝔴𝔦𝔩𝔩.   BRACEBRIDGE, co. Warwick.

Be bolde, be wyse.   GOLLOP, of Strode.

Be ever mindful.   CAMPBELL, of Moy.

Be faithful.   AGNEW.   VANS.

Be fast.   MEXBOROUGH, e.   SAVILE, of Rufford.

Be firm.   COATES, of Glasgow.   FERIE.   FERRIE.

Be hardie.   EDMONSTON.   EDMONSTOUN.

Be hardy.   EDMONSTON, of Newton, Scotland.

Be in the van.   BEVAN.

> *Intended as a play upon the name.*

Be it fast.   FOTHERINGHAM, of Lawhill and Powrie, N.B.

Be just, and fear not.   ASHBY.   ATKINS.   COLEMAN.   HEWITT. LILFORD, v.   PAYNE.   PEACOCK.   STRANGE.   WARREN.

> "Be just and fear not:
> Let all the ends thou aim'st at be thy country's,
> Thy God's, and truth's."—SHAKSPEARE.

Be mindful.   CAWDOR, e.   CAMPBELL, bt.   CALDER.   CLYDE. HOOKER.

Be mindful to unite.   BRODIE, of Lethen.

Be not wanting.   BAZILIE.

Be ready.   LAWRENCE, bt.

Be right and persist.   YOUNG, co. Bucks, bt.

Be steadfast.   CARNOCK.   CARVICK.   CLARBRICK.

Be sure.   PASLEY, of Craig.

Be traist.   Be faithful.   INNES, bt.   INNES, of that Ilk.   ROXBURGHE, b.   SHIELS.

Be treist. Be faithful. INNES, of Innes.

Be true. M'GUARIE.

> " His hope is treacherous only whose love dies
> With beauty, which is varying every hour;
> But, in chaste hearts influenced by the power
> Of outward change, there blooms a deathless flower,
> That breathes on earth the air of paradise."— WORDSWORTH.

Be trwgh and delygent. LUCY, of co. Warwick.

Be watchful. DAROCH. DARSCH.

Be wise as a serpent, harmless as a dove. (Matt. x. 16.) LEWIS.
There are serpents in the arms.

Bear and forbear. BEAR. BERNARD. BIRCHAM, of Reepham,
co. Norfolk. LANGFORD, b. MORELAND, bt. ROWLEY, of
Lawton.

> This motto in the case of the families of Bear and Bernard has an evident
> allusion to the name and crest, which is a bear's head, but was assumed
> by the family of Bircham under the following circumstances:—
> An ancestor of this family purchased a brewery at Reepham, in 1756, and
> shortly after settling there was invited to dine with the Rector, the
> Rev. St. John Priest, when Mr. Bircham asked him to suggest a motto
> for his adoption. A friend at the table submitted that it would be
> well to decide at once upon *"Beer for ever:"* to which Mr. Priest re-
> joined, "If our friend Bircham would do well to adopt your suggestion,
> I am decidedly of opinion that he would do far better to let it be
> *'Bear and Forbear,'"* and it was determined that this latter should be
> the motto, which has continued to be used by his family.

Beare *and forbeare.* BEARE.

Bear up. FULFORD, of Fulford.

Beati pacifici. Blessed are the peace-makers. (Matt. v. 9.)
JAMES. STEWART.

Beati misericordes, quoniam ipsis misericordia tribuetur. Blessed
are the merciful; for unto them mercy shall be granted
(Matt. v. 7). SCOT'S COMP.

Beati qui durant. Blessed are (the Durants) they who endure.
DURANT.

Bedhoh fyr ha heb drok. Let us be wise without guile; or, as
it is expressed in scriptural phrase, "Be ye wise as serpents,
and harmless as doves." CARTHEW, of East Dereham.

Bella! horrida bella! Wars! Horrid wars! LISLE, bt.
LYSAGHT.

> "Hark to that roar, whose swift and deaf'ning peals
> In countless echoes through the mountains ring.
> Startling pale Midnight on her starry throne!
> Now swells the intermingling din; the jar
> Frequent and frightful of the bursting bomb;
> The falling beam, the shriek, the groan, the shout,
> The ceaseless clangour, and the rush of men
> Inebriate with rage:— loud, and more loud,
> The discord grows; till pale Death shuts the scene,
> And o'er the conqueror and the conquered draws
> His cold and bloody shroud."— SHELLEY.

Bellement et hardiment. Handsomely and hardily. BUCK.

Bellicæ virtutis præmium. The reward of military valour.
O. of St. LOUIS and THE LEGION OF HONOUR.

Bello ac pace paratus. In war and peace prepared. BRACKEN-RIDGE, co. Somerset.

Bello palmam fero. I bear the palm in war. BELL.

Benedicite fontes Dominum. Oh, ye wells, bless ye the Lord. From the "Song of the Three Children." WELLS.

Benedic fontes, Domine. Bless (the) *wells*, O Lord! This motto was borne by JOHN WELLS, last Abbot of Croyland.

Benedictus qui tollit crucem. Blessed is he who bears the cross. BENNET. WOOLDRIDGE.

A play upon the name of Bennet, and the crest is a hand holding a cross.

Bene factum. Well done. WELDON.

Benefacere et lætari. To do well and be glad. GALLO, DUC DE.

Beneficio bene erit. He will succeed by kindness. RAISBECK.

Beneficiorum memor. Mindful of benefits. NICHOLSON. KELHAM.

Bene merentibus. To the well-deserving. O. of the LION OF LEMBOURG, and ST. CHARLES OF WURTEMBERG.

Bene paratum dulce. That which is rightly acquired is sweet. OGILVY, of Inchaven.

Bene præparatum pectus. A heart well prepared. JEX-BLAKE.

"Sperat infestis, metuit secundis
Alteram sortem bene præparatum
Pectus."— HOR. Car. ii. 10, 12.

Bene qui pacifice. He lives well who lives peacefully. ALLAR-DYCE, of that Ilk.

Bene qui sedulo. He lives well who lives industriously. ARKLEY.

Bene tenax. Rightly tenacious. BENNET.

Benigno Numine. By benign Providence. BENTLY. CHATHAM, e. DAVIES. COPELAND. GRENVILLE. HICKS. MEIGH. PITT. SMITH, of Dorchester.

"Benigno numine Jupiter
Defendit, et curæ sagaces
Expediunt per acuta belli."— HOR. Car. iv. 4, 74.

Betrayed, not conquered. HOWDEN, b.

Beware in time. LUMSDEN. LUMSDAINE. WHITE.

Bibl. The Bible. MORRIS.

"Is there no guide to show the path?
The Bible! He alone who hath
The Bible need not stray:
Yet he who hath, and will not give
That light of life to all who live,
Himself shall lose the way."— MONTGOMERY.

Bien est qui bien fait. Well is he that does well. WELLS.

Bien faire et ne rien dire. To do good and to say nothing. Sometimes, "*Bien faire, et ne rien craindre.*" To do good, and to fear nothing. DU RIEN, or DURIEN.

Bien sûr. Well sure. DE TUCH.

Bi'se mac na slaurie. Be thou the son of the crook. M'LAURIN.

Rebus on the name, and in the arms is a crook.

Bis vivit qui bene. He lives twice who lives well. BECHER, bt.

Blow, hunter, thy horn. FORRESTER, of Corstorphine, Scotland.
  Crest — A hunting horn.

Blow shrill. MERCIER, of Northumberland.
  Crest — A demi-huntsman winding a horn.

Bon fin. A good end. GRAHAM, of Fintry.

Bon accord. Good fellowship. TOWN OF ABERDEEN.

Bon temps viendra. The good time will come. GAGE.

Bold. SPENCE.

Bona benemerenti benedictio. A good benediction to the well-deserving. BRADSHAW.

Bona fide sine fraude. In good faith without fraud. SINGLETON.

Bonis omnia bona. All things are good to the good. ORR, of Barrowfield.

  "———— hæc perinde sunt, ut illius animus qui ea possidet ;
  Qui uti scit, ei bona ; illa, qui non utitur rectè, mala."—TER. *Heaut.* i. 2. 21.

Bonne espérance et droit en avant. Forward, good hope and right ! NUGENT.

Bonne et belle assez. Good and handsome enough. BELLASYSE.

Bono vince malum. Overcome evil with good. GERRARD. FINCH. KETTLE.

  " Be not overcome of evil, but overcome evil with good."—*Rom.* xii. 21.

Boulogne et Cadiz. HEYGATE, bt.

  Two of the ancestors of this family, father and son, served with distinction ; the first as Provost-marshal in the expedition to St. Quentin and Boulogne ; the last in that under the Earl of Essex to Cadiz, 1596.

Bound to obey and serve. JANE SEYMOUR, 3rd wife of Hen. VIII.

Boutez en avant. Push forward. BARRY, co. Chester. BARRYMORE, e. FOWLE, co. Wilts.

  From this motto is derived the name of Buttevaux, co. Cork, which is the second title of the Earls of Barrymore ; now extinct.

Boyne. KIDDER. CROSBY.

Britannia victrix. Britannia victorious. NORTHESK, e.

Bryreroderyri. Haste, herald of Snowdon ; or, High are the eagles at Snowdon. WYNN-WILLIAMS.

Buagh. Victory. TERNAN.

Butleirach abú. Butlers defying. BUTLER. This is the Hiberno-English war-cry of the family.

Bwch yn ychaf. Precedency to the he-goat.

By command of our superiors. WATERMAN'S COMP. London.

By degrees. BREY.

By faith we are saved. (Gal. ii. 20.) CATHCART, bt.

By faith I obtain. TURNERS' COMP. London.

By hammer and hand all arts do stand. BLACKSMITHS' COMP.

  " Swing in your strokes in order, let foot and hand keep time,
  Your blows make music, sweeter far than any steeple's chime ;
  But while ye swing your sledges sing ; and let the burden be,
  ' The anchor is the anvil king, and royal craftsmen we.' "
                                        Blackwood's Magazine.

By industry we prosper. GAVIN, of Lanton.
By the providence of God. ATKYNS. MAC SWEEN.
By these we shine, and it is fortified. MAC CONACK.
By truth and diligence. LUCY.
By the sword. ATKINS, of Fountainville, co. Cork.
By valour. HERN, or HERON, of that Ilk.
By wounding I cure. STIRLING, of Calden.
    Crest — A hand holding a lancet.
Bydand. Remaining. GORDON, d. GORDON, bt. GORDON.
Bydand to the last. GORDON, of Farsbank.
Byddwch gyfiawn ac nag ofnwch. Be righteous, and fear not.
    LEWIS, of Gilfach.
Byde. GORDON, of Cockclarochie.
Byde be. GORDON, of Ardmellie.
Byde together. GORDON, of Auchendown.

C

Cabool. BURNES, of Montrose and Ladbroke Square, London.
    This word is inscribed on the Mural Crown of the Crest of Augmentation (out of a mural crown per pale vert and gu. a demi-eagle disp. or, transfixed by a javelin ppr.) granted to James Burnes, D.C.L., F.R.S., Knight of the Guelphic Order, and the other descendants of his paternal grandfather, in commemoration of the devotion to their country shown by his brothers, Sir Alexander and Charles, who fell at Cabool, Nov. 2. 1841.
    The motto beneath the shield, "*Ob patriam vulnera passi*" (Virg. Æn. vi. 660) "Having sustained wounds for our country"— was granted with the same Crest, and refers to the same event, as well as to this family having "welcomed ruin" for the Stuarts in 1715, as duly recorded by the poet Burns, the cousin-german of Sir Alexander's grandfather. It would also apply to the fate of the gallant Lieut. George Holmes Burnes, the eldest son of the above James, who (as recorded on the monumental tablet erected to his memory by his brother-officers at Montrose), after a long and painful captivity, the consequence of his heroic efforts to save a helpless child from the fury of the mutineers, was savagely murdered at Lucknow, 19th Nov. 1857.

Cada uno es hijo de sus obras. Scarce one is the son of his works. BOSS.
    A Spanish proverb, equivalent to "Raised by his own exertions."

Cadarn ar cyfrwys. Strong and subtle. WILLIAMS.
    This motto refers to strength, typified by the crest, an eagle; and to subtlety, intimated by the foxes in the arms.

Cadenti porrigo dextram. I extend my right hand to the falling. PEARSE. KING, co. Somerset.

Caen, Cressie, Calais. RADCLIFFE, of Fox-Denton and Ordshall.
    Sir John Radcliffe of Ordshall served, during the wars of Edward III., at the sieges of Caen and Calais, and at the battle of Cressy. In remembrance of these services his descendants bear the motto as above.

Cæteris major qui melior. He is greater than others who is better. RADCLIFFE.

Cælestia canimus. We sing of heavenly things. SYNGE.

Cælestes pandite portæ. Open, ye celestial gates. GIBSON.

Cæsar aut nullus. Cæsar or none. WALL.

Caffraria. WILLSHIRE, bt.

For an account of this motto see "Khelát."

Calco sub pedibus. I trample it under my feet. ALCOCK.

This motto alludes to the crest, which is a cock trampling on a globe, and expresses contempt.

Calli*de et honeste.* Wisely and honourably. CALLEY, of Burderop.

Calm. M'ADAM, of Ballochmorrie.

Campi fero præmia belli. I bear the prizes of a fair field, or the rewards of the battle-field. CAMPBELL, of Skerrington.

Crest — A hand holding a garland.

Canada. PREVOST, bt. SMITH.

The first baronet, Lieutenant-General Sir George Prevost, was Governor-General in North America.

Candide. Candidly. STEWART, of Binny.

Candide comme la fleur. Fair as the flower. FENTON.

Crest — A fleur-de-lis.

Candide et caute. Candidly and cautiously. ELLIOT. GRIEVE.

Candide et constanter. Fairly and firmly. IRWINE. WARNER.

Candide et secure. Candidly and safely. GRAHAM. LYNE-DOCH, b.

Candide, sed caute. Candidly, but cautiously. SINCLAIR, bt.

Candide me fides. You will trust me favourably. HILL.

Candide, sincere. With candour and sincerity. GRIEVE.

Candider et constanter. Candidly and constantly. COVENTRY, e.

Candidiora pectora. Purer hearts ; *i.e.* whiter hearts. WHYTT.

Candor dat viribus alas. Truth gives wings to strength. HOGARTH. ROCHFORT.

Candore. By candour. ROBE.

Capta majora. Seek greater things. GEDDES, or GEDDEIS.

Caput inter nubila condit. (Virg. *Æn.* x. 767.) It hides its head among the clouds. TOWN OF GATESHEAD.

Car pawb, nod dy elyn. Love everybody, even thy enemy.

Caradoc. Caradoc. HOWDEN, b.

This motto is over the crest, which represents Caradoc, the Caractacus of the Romans.

Cari Deo nihilo carent. Those dear to God want nothing. WEEKES.

Caritas fructum habet. Charity bears fruit. BURNELL.

". . . Lasting Charity's more ample sway,
Nor bound by time, nor subject to decay,
In happy triumph shall for ever live,
And endless good diffuse, and endless praise receive."— PRIOR.

Carn na cuimhne. The rock of remembrance. FARQUHARSON.
Carpe diem. (Hor. *Od.* i. 11.) Seize the present opportunity.
    CLARKE. BERNS. PAYNTER. LANGFORD. WEBSTER.
Cassis tutissima virtus. Virtue is the safest helmet. ARMOUR.
    CHARRINGTON. CHOLMONDELEY, m. DELAMERE, b. HELME.
> Helmets form part of the armorial bearings of all these families ; and
> the motto is also a rebus upon the names of Armour and Helme.

Castra et nemus Strivilense. The castle and wood of Stirling.
    STIRLING.
Cattaro. HOSTE, bt.
> For account of this motto see "*Lissa.*"

Catus semper viret. The cautious man always flourishes. CATON.
> As a play on the name, "Caton always flourishes."

Cause caused it. ELPHINSTONE, b.
Caute et sedulo. Cautiously and carefully. ATKINS. BROWN,
    of Bonnington. HAMLYN.
Caute nec timide. Cautiously, not fearfully. FEARON, of Hun-
    stanton.
Caute non astute. Cautiously, not craftily. Ross, of Kindies.
Caute sed impavidè. Cautiously, but fearlessly.
Cautus sed strenue. Cautiously, but strenuously. HAMLYN.
Cautus a futuro. Cautious as to the future. BOWEN.
Cautus metuit foveam lupus. The cautious wolf fears the
    snare. CATON, of Binbrook. The name previously to 1599
    was spelled Catton.
Cave ! Beware ! CAVE.
> ". . . . Dico tibi,
> Ne temere facias, neque tu haud dicas tibi non prædictum : cave."
>   TER. *And.* 1, 2, 34.

Cave! adsum. Beware! I am present. ASHMORE. JARDINE, bt.
    JARDIN.
Cave ! *Deus videt.* Beware ! God sees. CAVE.
Cave Leam. Beware the lioness, or Lea. LEA.
Cave lupum. Beware the wolf. HUBBARD.
> *Crest* — A wolf passant.

Cave, paratus. Prepared, be cautious. JOHNSTON.
Cavendo. By taking care. CROWFOOT, of Beccles.
Cavendo tutus. Safe by being cautious. CAVENDISH, on which
    this motto is a play. BURLINGTON, e. DEVONSHIRE, d.
    CRUICKSHANK. HARDWICK. WATERPARK, b. WARING.
> " The wise are ever on their guard,
> For unforeseen, they say, is unprepared."—DRYDEN.

Cedamus amori. Let us yield to love. BLUNDEN, bt.
> "Omnia vincit amor : et nos cedamus amori."—VIRG. *Ecl.* x. 69.

Cedant arma. Let arms yield. BEST.
Cedant arma togæ. Let arms yield to the gown. READ, bt.
    READE, of Ipswich.
> This is a portion of a line quoted by Cicero (*Off.* 1. xxii.), in which he
> prefers civic to military deeds and honours : the remaining words are
> "concedat laurea laudi."

Ceidw, Owain *a gafodd.* Let Owen hold what he held. BULKELEY-OWEN, of Tedmore Hall, Shrewsbury.

Celer atque fidelis. Active and faithful. DUINE.

Celer et audax. Quick and bold. JACKSON.

Celer et vigilans. Quick and watchful. DOUCE.

Celeritas. Quickness. BECQUET.

Celeritas et veritas. Promptitude and truth. ROLLS.

Celeritate. With quickness. LANE, co. Hereford.

Celeriter. Quickly. LANE.

Celeriter et jucunde. Quickly and pleasantly. ROGERS.

Certa cruce salus. Sure salvation through the cross. GARRITTE. KINNAIRD, b.

Certamine parata. Acquired by strife. CAIRNCROSS.

Certamine summo. In the battle's height. BRISBANE, bt. M'ONOGHUY.

Certavi et vici. I have fought and conquered. O'FLANAGHAN.

Certior in cœlo domus. A surer home in heaven. ADAMS.

Certum pete finem. (Hor. *Ep.* i. ii. 56.) Aim at a sure end. CORSE. CROSSE. BUNDY. HOWARD. EVANS. BISSLAND. THOMPSON, bt. WICKLOW, e.

Cervus lacessitus leo. A stag when pressed becomes a lion.

Cervus non servus. A stag not enslaved. GODDARD, of Swindon. and Preston. THOROLD, bt.

A stag forms part of the armorial ensigns of these families.

C'est la seule vertu qui donne la noblesse. Virtue alone confers nobility. GREAME, co. York.

Ceteris major qui melior. Who is better is greater than the rest. RADCLIFFE.

Chacun sa part. Each his share. GWILT.

Chacun le sien. Every man his own. BOURKE.

Chase. GEARY, bt.

Cherche et tu trouveras. Seek and thou shalt find. SAWYER.

Crest—On a mount vert, a hound on scent or, spotted liver colour.

Cherche qui n'a. Let him seek who has not. MARGARY.

Chéris l'espoir. Cherish hope. CHERRY.

A play upon the name.

Che sarà sarà. What will be will be. BEDFORD, d. RUSSELL, bt.

Ches moy. At home. HONYWOOD.

Chescun son devoir. Every one his duty. COX.

Chi la fa l'aspetti. As a man does, so let him expect to be done by. MAZZINGHI, of London, originally from Germany.

China. GOUGH, v. For an account of this motto see " Barrosa."

Chi semini vertu racoglia fama. Who sows virtue gathers fame. COORE, of Scruton Hall.

Chounda. LITTLER.

Sir J. Littler, G.C.B., commanded the British forces at this place.

Christiana militia. Christian warfare. O. of CHRIST of Portugal.

Christi crux est mea lux. The cross of Christ is my light. NORTHCOTE, bt.

Christi pennatus sidera morte peto. Furnished with wings, (*feathers*, in allusion to the name) by the death of Christ I seek the stars. FETHERSTON.

Christo duce. With Christ for leader. RICHARD I.

Christo duce feliciter. Happily, under the guidance of Christ. BINNING.

Christus mihi lucrum. Christ is my gain. STEWART.

> " To look at Him who form'd us and redeemed."—COWPER.

Christus mihi vita. Christ my life. BIGG.

Christus pelicano. Christ is like the pelican. LECHMERE, bt.

> In allusion to the pelican shedding its blood for its offspring. The crest is a pelican vulning itself.

Christus pelicanus et agnus. Christ my pelican and my lamb. GODFREY.

> There are pelicans in the arms, and the crest is a holy lamb.

Christus providebit. Christ will provide. THOMSON.

Christus sit regula vitæ. Let Christ be the rule of life. SAMWELL, of Upton Hall.

Cia'll agos neart. Reason and power, or, Power used with judgment. O'CONNELL, of Derrynane Abbey, co. Kerry.

Cio che Dio vuole, io voglio. What God wills, I will. DORMER, b.

Cito fideliterque. Quickly and faithfully. GUTCH.

Cito, non temere. Quickly, not rashly. NORTHCOTE.

Civil and religious liberty. WOOD, of Singleton Lodge.

Clamabunt omnes te, liber, esse meum. All will cry, O book, that thou art mine. DESBRISAY.

Clamamus, Abba, Pater. (Rom. viii. 15.) Whereby we cry, Abba, Father. ABBOTT.

> This motto is on the stained glass in the Archbishop Abbot's Hospital, Guildford ; also on the great seat of the hospital.

Clareo foveoque. I am bright (*i.e. Clare*), and I cherish. CLARE.

> *Crest* — A sun.

Clarescam. I shall become bright. HEBBERT.

> *Crest* — A crescent.

Clarior e flammis. Brighter from the flame. GRAY.

> *Crest* — A phœnix.
>
> " As when
> The bird of wonder dies, the maiden phœnix,
> Her ashes new create another heir,
> As great in admiration as herself."—SHAKSPEARE.

Clarior e tenebris. The brighter from previous obscurity. BRIGHT. GRAY. LIGHTBODY. MILTOWN, e. PURVES. PURVIS.

Clarior ex obscuro. Brighter from obscurity. SANDERSON.

Clarior hinc honos. Hence the brighter honour. BUCHANAN.
MAC CAUSLAND.

Clariora sequor. I follow brighter things. BUCHANAN, of Ardock.

Clariores e tenebris. Men are brighter from previous obscurity.
PULESTON, bt. POLDEN. LEESON.

Claris dextra factis. (Virg. *Æn.* vii. 474.) A right hand employed in glorious deeds. BURGH. BYAM.

Clarum reddit industria. Industry renders illustrious. MILNE.

Clementia et animis. By clemency and courage. PANMURE, b.
MAULE.

> " The quality of mercy is not strained ;
> It droppeth as the gentle rain from heaven
> Upon the place beneath : it is twice blessed ;
> It blesseth him that gives, and him that takes."—SHAKSPEARE.

Clementia tecta rigore. Clemency concealed under (apparent)
rigour. MAULE.

Cœlestem spero coronam. I hope for a heavenly crown. BLAKE-
HUMFREY.

Cœlestes pandite portæ. Open, ye heavenly gates. GIBSON.

Cœlestia canimus. We sing (of) heavenly things. HUTCHINSON.
SYNGE, bt.

Cœlestia sequor. I follow heavenly things. M'DONALD. MONRO.

Cœlis exploratis. For the heavens explored. HERSCHEL, bt.

> This motto was granted to Sir W. Herschel for his great astronomical
> discoveries, and in the arms are a telescope, and the symbol of the
> planet Uranus, which he discovered.

Cœlitus datum. Given by God. BORTHWICK. FINLASON.
FINLAY. FINLAYSON.

Cœlitus mihi vires. My strength from heaven. RANELAGH, v.

Cœlitus vires. Strength from heaven. MALLET.

Cœlum non animum. You may change your climate, but not
your disposition. COMYN. STRACHEY, bt. RHODES, of
Bellair. WALDEGRAVE, e.

> " Si ratio et prudentia curas,
> Non locus effusi latè maris arbiter, aufert ;
> *Cœlum,* non animum, mutant, qui trans mare currunt."—HOR. *Ep.* lib. i. 12.

And is thus translated by Francis :—

> "They who through the venturous ocean range,
> Not their own passions but the climate change."

Cœlum, non solum. Heaven, not earth. HAYMAN, of South
Abbey. STEVENSON, of Newcastle-on-Tyne.

> " Hic tibi certa domus ; certi, ne absiste, penates."—VIRG. *Æn.* viii. 39.
> This motto was assumed by Hamo de Créve-Cœur, Lord of Chatham,
> and ancestor of the families of Hayman and Heyman, who at the same
> time altered his paternal coat.
> Having gone to the Holy Land, he lost all his three sons at the battle of
> Ascalon, and on his return, instead of his original arms, which were
> " or, three chevronels gules," took argent instead of or, in token of
> humiliation ; a single chevron instead of three chevronels, to show
> his solitary state ; and three martlets (birds of passage) to denote that
> his three sons had passed away to heaven, which, and not earth, was
> now their abode.

Cœlum quod quærimus ultra. Heaven, which we seek beyond. GODMAN.

Cœlum versus. Heavenward. DICKSON.

Cœptis aspirate meis. Be favourable to my undertakings. DAVIES.

Cœur fidèle. A faithful *heart.* HART.

Cnock Elachan. COLQUHOUN, bt.
> This was the war-cry of the clan Colquhoun.

Cogadh na sithe. Peace or war. MCCRUMMEN.

Cogit amor. Love compels. JOASS.

Cogito. I reflect. WEEMS.

Cognoies toy meme. Know thyself. BRADDYL.
> This saying is attributed to Thales of Miletus, one of the seven wise
> men of Greece.
> " Know then thyself, presume not God to scan :
> The proper study of mankind is man."—POPE.

Cognosce teipsum et disce pati. Know thyself, and learn to suffer. RAWLINGS, co. Cornwall.

Cole credeque Deum. Worship and believe God. HODILOW.

Colens *Deum et regem.* Honouring God and the King. COLLINS.

Collocet in cœlis nos omnes vis Michaelis. May Michael's strength place us all in heaven. LINLITHGOW, Scotland.

Coloony. GORT, v.
> This motto commemorates the gallant conduct of Charles, second
> Viscount Gort, in opposing at Coloony the invading French forces
> under Humbert, 5 Sep. 1798.

Color fidesque perennis. Its colour and our faith are imperishable. IRVINE.
> In allusion to the holly leaves in the arms and crest.

Come, ye blessed; when I was harbourless ye lodged me. This was the original motto of the INNHOLDERS' COMP. London.

Cominus et eminus. In close or distant combat. O. of the PORCUPINE, France.

Comitate quam viribus. By mildness rather than force. HALL.

Comiter sed fortiter. Courteously but firmly. SHEFFIELD, bt.

Comme je fus. As I was. MORE, co. Lancaster. WARD, e.

Comme je trouve. As I find. BUTLER, bt. KILKENNY, e. ORMONDE, m. GALMOYE, v. CAREY. BOWDEN.

Commit thy work to God. (Prov. xvi. 3.) CAITHNESS, e. SINCLAIR.

Commodum non damnum. A convenience not an injury. BACKIE. BAIKIE, of Tankerness.
> Crest —A flame of fire ; and there are three flames of fire in the arms, to
> which this motto alludes.

Communitates Burgi de Dorchestriâ. The CORPORATION OF THE TOWN OF DORCHESTER.

Compositum jus fasque animi. A mind which respects alike the *laws* of mutual justice and of God. ELLENBOROUGH, e. LAW. LAWS. NIGHTINGALE.

Conabimur. We will try. BIRT. GWYNNE.

Conamine augeor. By effort I am advanced. LESLY, of Colpnay.
Conanti dabitur. It will be given to him who strives. CONANT.
PIGOTT.
Con can an. Wisdom without reproach. CONCANON.
A very good play upon the name.
Concipe spes certas. Conceive sure hopes. SEALY.
Concordans. Agreeing. O. of CONCORD, Brandenburgh.
Concordant nomine facta. Our deeds agree with our name.
GRACE, bt.
Concordia et industria. By concord and industry. DENT.
Concordia et sedulitate. By union and diligence. GOLDSMID, bt.
Concordia, integritate, industria. By concord, integrity, and
industry. Baron de ROTHSCHILD. ROTHSCHILD.
Concordiâ parvæ res crescunt. Small things increase by con-
cord. MERCHANT TAYLORS' COMP.
Concordia præsto. With one consent we are ready. FORBES,
of Ballogie.
Concordia res crescunt. Things increase by union. BROM-
HEAD, bt.
Concordia res parvæ crescunt. Small things increase by concord.
THE STATES-GENERAL.
This motto refers to the crest, which is a sheaf of arrows.
"Concordia res parvæ crescunt, discordia maximæ dilabuntur."—
SALL. *Bell. Jug.*
Concordia vincit. Unanimity conquers. COCHRAN, of Aberdeen.
Concussus surgo. Though shaken, I rise. GARRIOCK. GARROW.
COUNT-JARNAC.
Conduct is fate. DE BEAUVOIR, bt.
Confide. Be confident. GEN. SIR R. GARDINER, G.C.B.
Confide in Deo. Trust in God. RUGELEY.
Confidence in God. COLEMAN.
Confide rectè agens. Doing rightly be confident. BROADHEAD.
GLANVILLE. FELLOWS. LONG. NEWDEGATE. NEWDIGATE.
Confido. I trust. BELL. BOYD, bt. BOYD, of Merton Hall.
BOYD, of Middleton Park. LE BON. MILLS. PETERS.
WINTER.
Confido conquiesco. I trust and am contented. DYSART, e.
HODGETTS. MAROY. TOLLEMACHE. TURNER.
Confido in Deo. (Ps. cxli. 8.) I trust in God. BACKHOUSE.
Confido in Domino. I trust in the Lord. PETERKIN.
Confido in probitate. I trust in my probity. CADELL.
Confido non confundar. I trust and shall not be confounded.
TYNDALE, of Hayling.
Confisus viribus. Confident in my own powers. WATSON.
Conjuncta virtuti fortuna. Good fortune is allied to bravery.
M'BETH.
Conjunctio firmat. Union gives strength. MIDDLETON.

Conquer or die. CROSTHWAITE.

Conquiesco. I am contented. METCALFE, bt.

Consequitur quodcunque petit. He hits whatever he aims at.
HEADFORT, m. DRUMMOND. TAYLOR, of Pennington.

> The crest of the Marquis of Headfort is a naked arm embowed, holding
> an arrow ppr. ; that of Taylor is a like arm in armour, the hand in a
> gauntlet, grasping a javelin all ppr., and Drummond's crest is a
> pheon, or.

Conserva me, Domine. Preserve me, O Lord. TAYLER.

Conservabo ad mortem. I will preserve it till death. JENNINGS.

> This motto refers to the crest, which is a dragon pass., vair, wings or,
> dexter claw resting on a shield az. charged with a golden fleece.

Consilii taciturnitas nutrix. Silence is the nurse of counsel.
JESSON, of Oakwood.

Consilio ac virtute. By prudence and valour. LEWIN.

Consilio et animis. By wisdom and courage. GIBSON. LAU-
DERDALE, e. MAITLAND, bt. RAMADGE.

Consilio et animo. By skill and spirit. MAITLAND.

Consilio et armis. By wisdom and arms. STEPHENS.

Consilio et prudentia. By wisdom and prudence. CLANCARTY, e.
LE-POER TRENCH.

Consilio non impetu. By counsel, not by force. AGNEW, bt.
AGNEW, of Barnbarroch, Dalreagle, and Lochryan.

Constans contraria spernit. The resolute man despises difficulties. EDGEWORTH.

Constans et fidelis. Constant and faithful. ARNETT.

Constans et fidelitate. Constant and with fidelity. O. of ST.
HUBERT.

Constans et prudens. Constant and prudent. CAMPBELL, of
Skerrington.

Constans fidei. Steady to my faith. COGAN. COGGAN. COL-
BORNE, b. RIDLEY, bt.

Constant. GRAY.

Constant and faithful. MACQUEEN.

Constant and true. ROSE, of Kilravock. Ross, of Belfast.

> This motto was anciently written "Constaunt and Trew." The motto
> over the crest of Rose is "Audeo."

Constant en tout. Constant in everything. STANDISH, of Duxburg.

Constante et firme. Constant and firm. OSBALDESTON.

Constanter. With constancy. DUKES. HORE of Pole Hore,
Harperstown, &c.

Constanter in ardua. With constancy against difficulties.
HARLAND.

Constanter et prudentia. Firmly and prudently. CAMPBELL,
of Sombey. CESSNOCK, of Treesbank and Fairfield.

Constantia. By constancy. GOODALL.

Constantia et diligentia. By perseverance and diligence. SPENCE.

Constantia et fidelitate. By constancy and fidelity. CLARKE, of Rossmore, bt.

Constantia et fortitudine. By constancy and fortitude. HERBERT.

Constantia et labore. By resolution and exertion. KIRBY.

Constantia et virtute. By constancy and virtue. AMHERST, e.

Constantia in ardua. Perseverance against difficulty. HARLAND, co. York.

Constantia, virtus. Constancy and valour. FITZ-WILLIAM.

Constare in sententia. To continue in my opinion. WILLIAMSON.

Constaunt an' trew. ROSE, of Worighton.

Consulto et audaciter. With prudence and daring. PLUMMER.

Contentement passe richesse. Contentment is preferable to riches. BOWYER, bt.

Contranando incrementum. Prosperity by swimming against the stream. T. of PEEBLES.

Copia ex industria. Plenty from industry. COMYN.

There are three garbs in the arms.

Copiosè et opportunè. Plentifully and opportunely. BUNTING.

Cor et manus concordant. My heart and my hand are in concord. FARREL.

Cor immobile. A steadfast heart. HUSSEY, co. Dublin. HYETT.

Cor nobyle, cor immobyle. A heart noble, a mind determined. HUSSEY. HUNT, of co. Somerset. VIVIAN, b.

Cor unum, via una. One heart, one way. CECIL. EXETER, m. MOUNTSANDFORD, b. SANDFORD. WILLS.

Cor vulneratum. A wounded heart. MACK.

Crest—A heart gu. thrust through with an arrow in bend sinister ar.

Corda serata fero. I bear a *locked heart.* LOCKHART.

Sir Simon Locard being one of those appointed to attend Earl Douglas to the Holy Land with the heart of Robert Bruce, had charge of one of the keys of the box which enclosed the heart. In memory of this he changed his name to Lockhart, added a heart within a padlock to his arms, and assumed the above motto.

Corda serata pando. I lay open *locked hearts.* LOCKHART, bt.

Corde et manu. With heart and hand. STEUART, of Auchlunkart. STEWART, of Carnousie. GOFFDON. WATLING.

A heart and hand form part of the armorial bearings of these families.

Corde fixam. Fixed in my heart. GODFREY.

Corde manuque. With heart and hand. GORDON, of Invergordon.

Crest—Out of a heart a hand holding a dagger ppr.

Cordi dat robora virtus. Virtue gives strength to the heart. PORCH, of Edgarley.

" When within
They shrink at sense of secret sin,
A feather daunts the brave."—SCOTT.

Cornu exaltabitur honore. The horn shall be exalted in honour. SMYTH, of Drumcree.

> This motto refers to Ps. xcii. 10, "My horn shalt thou exalt like the horn of an unicorn;" and the crest is an unicorn's head, the emblem of strength and dignity.

Corona mea Christus. Christ is my crown. CHETWODE, bt. LAPSLEY. WEBB.

Coronat fides. Faith crowns all. DALL. PRINGLE, bt.

Couper fait grandir. Cutting causes growth. COOPER.

> A play on the name.
> "Per damna, per cædes, ab ipso
> Ducit opes animumque ferro."—HOR. *Car.* iv. 4, 59.

Courage! CUMMIN. CUMING, of Reluglas. CUMMING, of Pitully. CUMMING, of Coulter, bt.

Courage à l'Ecosse. SPENSE.

> The translation of this motto is given "Courage after the manner of the Scotch;" this cannot be correct. Perhaps "Courage et l'Ecosse" ("Courage and Scotland") may have been the war-cry of the Queen of Bohemia's Scottish general, the ancestor of this family.

Courage à la mort. Courage till death. HUTCHINS.

Courage avance le home. Courage advances the man. VAUGHAN, of Littleton, kt.

Courage et esperance. Courage and hope. STORIE.

Courage sans peur. Courage without fear. AYNESWORTH. GAGE, v. WILLOUGHBY.

Cou re bu. I have broken my hold. FARRELL.

Court hope. COURTHOPE.

Court no friend, dread no foe. MALLOCH. PETER.

Craggan phithich. The rock of the raven. MACDONNEL. MACDONELL.—*Crest*—A raven perched on a rock.

Craig elachie. The rock of alarm. GRANT.

> *Crest*—A rock inflamed; this and the motto allude to those signal-fires which were lighted in time of danger on rocks, to alarm the country.

Craig ubhe. The black rock. FARQUHARSON.

Craignez honte. Fear shame. BENTINCK. DILLWYN, of Bur-roughes-Lodge. PORTLAND, b. WESTON.

Crainte refrainte. Fear restrained. POYNTZ.

Cras mihi. To-morrow for me. PARBURY.

Crede Byron. Trust Byron. BYRON, b.

Crede cornu. Trust the horn, or Trust *Hornby.* HORNBY.

> *Crest*—A bugle horn.

Crede Deo. Trust in God. ATKINSON.

Crede et vince. Believe and conquer. GILDOWRIE. TOASH.

Crede mihi. Believe me. FITZ-MARMADUKE.

Credo. I believe. KIRSOPP. SINCLAIR.

Credo Christi cruce. I trust in the cross of Christ. DARIT.

Credo Deo. Believe in God. ATKINSON.

Credo et amo. I believe and love. CROSSLEY, of Scaitcliffe.

Credo et videbo. I believe, and I shall see. CHRESLY.

Credunt quod vident. They believe what they see (or because they see). ELLIOTT.

An eye forms part of the crest.

Crescam ut prosim. I will increase, that I may do good. MITCHELSON. O. OF ST. JOACHIM.

Crescat Deo promotore. May he prosper with God as his guide. LESLIE, of Powis.

Crescent. They will increase. TATTON.

There are crescents in the arms.

Crescit sub pondere virtus. Virtue thrives beneath oppression. CHAPMAN, bt. CHAPMAN, of Whitby. DENBIGH, e. FIELDING. SEYS. SLATTER, of Chesterfield.

Crescitque virtute. And increases by virtue. MACKENZIE.

Crescitur cultu. It is increased by cultivation. BARTON, of Swinton, and Stapleton Park.

Crest — An acorn slip fructed or.

Cresco. I increase. STIVEN. MITCHAEL, of Alderstoun.

Crest — A stalk of wheat bladed and erect.

Cresco crescendo. I increase by increasing. NEVILLE-ROLFE.

Cresco et spero. I increase and hope. HANNAY.

Cresco per crucem. I increase by the cross. DAVIS. ROWAN.

Cressa ne careat. Let not Cressa (*Cresswell*) want. CRESSWELL.

Creta cruce salus. Salvation born from the cross. KINNAIRD, b. WATERHOUSE.

Crom abù. Crom (now Croom Castle) defying. GERALDINE, CO. Kildare.

This motto was altered in consequence of an Act of Parliament, into "Si Dieu plet Crom abú," If God please Crom defying.

Crom a boo. Crom for ever. FITZGERALD. LEINSTER, d. DE ROS, b.

This motto was the ancient war-cry of the clan or sept of Fitzgeralds; the Irish *A Boo*, or *Abu*, meaning in English, for ever (or lit. defying). Crom is a castle, co. Limerick, which formerly belonged to the Fitzgeralds.

This is one of the many Irish gathering cries, the use of which was forbidden, under pain of fine and imprisonment, by repeated Acts of Parliament.

Crow not, croke not. CROCKETT.

Cruce delector. I delight in the cross. SINCLAIR.

Cruce glorior. I glory in the cross. PYE.

Cruce non leone fides. My trust is in the cross, not in the lion. MATTHEW, of Coggeshall, co. Essex.

The arms are az. three lions ramp. ar. on a chief of the second three cross crosslets fitchée sable.

Cruce non prudentia. By the cross, not by prudence. TOPHAM.

Cruce quam muro tutior. Safer by the cross than in a wall.

Cruce salus. Through the cross salvation. SHEE.

Cruce spes mea. My hope is in the cross. BIRD.

Cruci dum spiro fido. Whilst I have breath I confide in the cross. DYSON. D'URBAN. GALWAY, V.

Cruci dum spiro spero. Whilst I breathe my hope is in the cross. DARLINGTON. METTERVILLE, V.

> "I'll perish at His cross;
> It cannot be—I'll not despair,
> For sinner never perished there."—RAFFLES.

Cruciata cruce junguntur. Crosses are joined to the cross. GAIRDEN, of that Ilk. GARDYNE.

Crux Christi lux cœli. The cross of Christ is the light of Heaven. PETTIWARD.

Crux Christi nostra corona. The cross of Christ is our crown. BARCLAY, bt. MERCER. MERSAR.

Crux dat salutem. The cross gives salvation. SINCLAIR.

> "Without Christ all gain is loss,
> All hope despair, that stands not on his cross."—COWPER.

Crux fidei calcar. The cross is the spur of faith. BROOKING.

Crux mihi grata quies. The cross is my pleasing rest. ADAM. EDIE. M'ADAM.

Crux nostra corona. The cross is our crown. AUSTIN.

Crux præsidium et decus. The cross is (my) guard and honour. TYLER.

Crux salutem confert. The cross confers salvation. BARCLAY.

Cubo et excubo. I sleep and watch. GRÆME.

Cui debeo fidus. Faithful to whom I owe faith. CRAW.

Cui fides fide. Place full confidence in whom you trust. PEARD.

Cuidich an high. Assist the king. M'DONNEL.

Cuimhniah bas Alpin. Remember the death of *Alpin.* M'ALPIN.

Cuinich bas Alpin. Remember the death of Alpin. ALPIN. MACALPIN, of Alpin. McALPIN.

Cuislean mo cridhe. The pulsation of my heart. M'DONNEL.

Culpari metuit fides. (HOR. *Od.* iv. 5. 20.) Faith fears to be blamed. WHITFIELD.

Cum cruce salus. Salvation with the cross. MOUNTAIN.

Cum corde. With the heart. DRUMMOND, of Cultmalundy.

Crest— A hand grasping a heart.

Cum Deo. With God.

Cum magnis vixisse. To have lived with the great. SWIFT.

This motto was borne by the celebrated Dean Swift.

Cum plena magis. Rather when she is full. SMITH, of Giblston. The crest is a crescent.

Cum prudentia sedulus. Diligent with prudence. BEATSON. BETSON. *Crest*—A bee erect, wings expanded, all ppr.

Cuncta mea mecum. My all is with me. STEDMAN.

Cunctanter tamen fortiter. Slowly yet resolutely. HUTCHINSON.

Cur me persequeris. (Acts, ix. 4.) Why persecutest thou me? Eustace. Eton.

Cura atque industria. By carefulness and industry. Vair.

Cura dat victoriam. Caution gives victory. Denham.

Cura et candore. With prudence and sincerity. Cunningham, bt. Forbes, of Ardo.

Cura et industria. By care and industry. Walker, of Dalry.

Cura pii diis sunt. Pious men are a care to the gods (*i.e.* under their care.) Mogg.

Curæ cedit fatum. Fate gives way to caution. Thomson.

Curæ testimonium. A testimony of caution. Taunton.

Cú ɲe bú. Or in English characters, Cu re bu, sometimes Cu reab ha. The hound broken loose. O'Farrell.
Crest — A greyhound courant, collared and chained, the latter broken.

Curre ut vincas. Run that you may conquer. Warren.
"So run that ye may obtain."—1 *Cor.* ix. 24.

Currendo. By running. Hollist.
In the arms is a greyhound courant.

Currit qui curat. He runs who takes care. Fuller.

Cursum perficio. I accomplish the race. Hunter.

Cuspis fracta causa coronæ. A spear broken in the cause of the crown or is the cause of a crown. Rolt, co. Kent.

D

Da a fydd. God will come. Jones, co. of Carmarthen.

Da gloriam Deo. Give glory unto God. Dyers' Comp.
" Give glory unto the Lord."—*Isa.* xlii. 12.

Da nobis lucem, Domine. Give us light, O Lord! Glaziers' Comp.

Dabit Deus vela. God will fill the sails. Tennant.
Crest — A sail ppr.

Dabunt aspera rosas. Rough ground will produce roses. Mushet.

Ddal gwaed Cymru. Entertain Welsh blood. Lloyd.

Danebrog. O. of Danebrog.

Dant lucem crescentibus orti. Rising from crescents they give light. Hodges.
Crest — A star rising from a crescent.

Dant priscæ decorum. Deeds of antiquity confer renown. Stewart.

Dante Deo. By the gift of God. Wolff, bt. Van Wolff.

Dare quam accipere. Rather to give than to receive. Guy.
The motto of Sir Thomas Guy, founder of the celebrated hospital which bears his name.

Dat cura commodum. Vigilance ensures advantage. MILNE.
Dat cura quietem. (VIRG. *Æn.* iv. 5.) Vigilance ensures tranquillity. MEDLICOTT, bt.
Dat Deus incrementum. God gives increase. CROFTON, b. CROFTON, bt. MUGGERIDGE.
Dat et sumit Deus. God giveth and taketh away. ETHELSTON.
Dat gloria vires. Glory gives strength. HOG. HOGG. HOGUE.
Dat tela fidelitas. Fidelity supplies weapons. TIPPING.
Data fata secutus. Following my destiny. (VIRG. *Æn.* i. 382.) ARCHDALE. PORTER. ST. JOHN, b. STREATFIELD.
> " There's a divinity that shapes our ends,
> Rough-hew them how we will."—SHAKSPEARE.

D' accomplier Agincourt. To accomplish Agincourt. DALISON.
D' en haut. From on high. WHITEFOORD.
De bon vouloir servir le roy. To serve the king with right good will. BENNET. GREY, e. GREY, bt. TANKERVILLE, e.
De Dieu tout. From God every thing. WHITE. BECKFORD.
De Dieu est tout. From God every thing. MERVYN.
De hirundine. From the swallow. ARUNDEL.
> This motto is an allusion to the name ; and the arms, six swallows, have a similar reference.

De marisco. From the (*Marsh*) bulrush. MARSH.
De mieux je pense en mieux. From better I think to better. BROOKE.
De monte alto. From a high mountain. MAUDE.
> This motto is used by the family of Maude, to show their descent from Eustace de Mont Alto, an Italian warrior, who followed the Conqueror on his expedition to England.

De præscientiâ Dei. From the foreknowledge of God. BARBERS' COMP., London. BARBERS-SURGEONS' COMP., Exeter.
De tout mon cœur. With all my heart. BOILEAU, bt. POLLEN.
De vivis nil nisi verum. Of the living speak nothing but what is true. HYDE.
Debonnaire. Graceful. BALFOUR. BETHUNE, bt. BETHUNE.
Decens et honestum. Becoming and honourable. FYFFE, of Dron.
> " Quod decet honestum est ; et quod honestum est, decet."— CIC. *de Off.* lib. i. 27, 2.

Decerptæ dabunt odorem. Plucked they will emit fragrance. AITON. *Crest*— A hand plucking a rose.
Decide. DAVIS, of Leytonstone.
Decide and dare. DYCE.
Deckan. HISLOP.
> This word is borne over the crest of augmentation for services rendered in the Deckan.

Decori decus addit avito. He adds honour to that of his ancestors. ERSKINE. KELLY.
Decrevi. I have resolved. GADESDEN. NUGENT, bt.
Decus summum virtus. Virtue is the highest honour. HOLBURNE, bt. HULBURN.

Dedit meliora dabitque. He has given better things and will give them. Or, *Debet meliora dabitque.* He owes better things and will give them. ORMEROD.

Deeds not words. DAWSON, of Low Wray. RICKFORD, of Aylesbury. SAINTHILL. PIRIE. COMBS.

Deeds show. RUTHVEN, b.

Defend. WOOD, of Boneytown. WOOD, of co. Gloucester, bt.

Defendamus. Let us defend. T. of TAUNTON.

Defendendo vinco. By defending I conquer. GRAHAM, of Braco.
> Crest — Two hands issuing out of a cloud, in each a sword, the dexter flourishing aloft, the sinister in a defensive posture.

Defend the fold. CARTWRIGHT, of co. Notts, Northampton and Suffolk. *Crest* — A wolf's head.
> " Build ye folds for your sheep."— *Num.* xxxii. 24.

Defensio non offensio. Defence not offence. MUDIE.

Deficiam aut efficiam. I will fail, or I will perform. STORIE.

Degeneranti, genus opprobrium. To a degenerate man his family is a disgrace. ASHURST.
> '' What can ennoble sots, or slaves, or cowards?
> Alas ! not all the blood of all the Howards."— POPE.

Dei dono sum quod sum. By the bounty of God I am what I am. LUMSDEN, of Pitcaple and Cushnie. LUNDIN, of that Ilk.

Dei donum. The gift of God. T. of DUNDEE.

Dei memor, gratus amicis. Mindful of God, grateful to friends. ANTROBUS, bt.

Dei omnia plena. All things are full of God. HINDS.
> "Ab Jove principium— Jovis omnia plena."— VIRG. *Ec.* iii. 60.

Dei Providentia juvat. The providence of God is our help. WELMAN, of Poundsford Park.

Delectare in Domino. (Ps. xxxvi. 4.) To rejoice in the Lord. BAMPFYLDE. POLTIMORE, b.
> " Lie silent in your graves, ye dead !
> Lie quiet in your churchyard bed !
> Ye living, tend your holy cares ;
> Ye multitude, pursue your prayers ;
> And blame not me if my heart and sight
> Are occupied with one delight ! "— WORDSWORTH.

Delectat amor patriæ. The love of country delights. SMITH, co. Meath.

Delectat et ornat. It is both pleasing and ornamental. BROWN, of Edinburgh. CREE. M'CRAE. M'CREE. MACREA. HARVIE.

Delectatio. (My) delight. FORBES, of Riris.

Delecta.io mea. My delight. POLLOCK, of Roxburgh.
> Crest — An open book.

Del fuego io avolo. I escape from the fire. BERNERS.

Deliciæ mei. My delight. DALGLEISH, of Scotscraig.
> Crest — An open book.

Demeure par la vérité. Stick by the truth. MASON.

Denique cœlo fruar. I shall enjoy heaven at last. MELVILLE.

Denique cœlum. Heaven at last. BESWICKE. BONAR, of Camden
Leven. and MELVILL, e. MELVILL. MELVILE, of Raith.
" The war-cry of the Crusaders."—BURKE.
Denique sursum. Upwards at last. MELVIL.
Denique decus. Honour at length. STODDART.
Denuo fortasse lucescat. Perchance it may become clear again.
SPURDENS.
Deo adjuvante. With God assisting. PELLEW, VISCOUNT
EXMOUTH.
> The crest of this family is on a rocky shore with Plymouth Citadel, in
> the background a ship with "Dutton" inscribed on the stern. This
> crest, with the motto, were granted to Sir Edw. Pellew, kt., in 1796,
> when he was created a baronet for his gallant conduct in saving all on
> board the Dutton transport, with the exception of a few drunken
> sailors.

Deo adjuvante. God aiding. JONES. SALMONS. WILLIAMS.
Deo adjuvante, fortuna sequatur. With God assisting, good
fortune may follow. ROBERTS, of Crofton Hall, co. Sallop.
Deo adjuvante non timendum. With God assisting we must
not fear. COYNE. FITZWILLIAMS. HAMLET. PETERS.
WILLIAMS.
Deo adjuvante vincam. God helping I shall conquer. HART.
Deo cari nihilo carent. Those dear to God want nothing.
WEEKES.
Deo date. Give unto God. ARUNDEL, of Wardour, b.
> " 'Give unto God' with conscience clear,
> The homage of a heart sincere;
> And let thanksgiving duly find
> Its seat of empire in our mind."

Deo donum. A gift from God. DARLING.
Deo duce. God my guide. HENNIDGE. RICKETTS. T. of
PITTENWEEN, Scotland. HOOPER.
Deo duce decrevi. Under God's direction I have determined.
HARNAGE, bt.
Deo duce, comite industria. God being my guide, industry my
companion. SLANEY, co. Salop. NICOLL.
Deo duce, ferro comitante. God my guide, and my sword my
companion. CAULFIELD. CHARLEMONT, e.
Deo duce, fortunâ comitante. With God as my guide, good
fortune as companion. MERCHANTS OF EXETER. SLADEN.
Deo ducente nil nocet. With God as leader, nothing can
injure. EAST INDIA COMP.
Deo et labore. By God and by labour. SEBAG.
Deo et principe. With God and the prince. LAMB, bt.
Deo et principi. For God and the prince. MONTOLIEN.
Deo et regi asto. I stand by God and the king. DEACON.
Deo et regi fidelis. Faithful to God and the king. DALY.
Deo favente. By the favour of God. ALVES. DINGWALL.
Deo favente florebo. By the favour of God, I shall prosper.
BLENSHELL.

Deo fidens proficio. Trusting to God I go forward. CHADWICK.
Deo gloria. Glory to God. GENNYS.
" Fear God and give glory to him."— *Rev.* xiv. 7.
Deo gratias. Thanks to God. SENHOUSE.
Deo honor et gloria. Unto God be honour and glory.
LEATHER SELLERS' COMP.
" To the only wise God be honour and glory."— 1 *Tim.* i. 17.
Deo inspirante, rege favente. By the inspiration of God and
the king's favour. STAHLSCHMIDT.
Deo juvante. By God's assistance. DUFF. FIFE, e. GROZE.
GRIMALDI. MAITLAND. SHATT. TAWSE. WODDERSPOON.
This motto is borrowed from the reply made by Grimoald, Duke of
Benevento, to Pepin, the son of Charlemagne, when required to submit
to him :—
" Liber et ingenuus sum natus utroque parente,
Semper ero liber credo— Deo juvante."
Free and of gentle blood was I born from either parent ;
Free will I ever be I trust— God aiding.

Deo juvante consilio et armis. By counsel and arms with the
aid of God. MAITLAND.
Deo juvante vinco. By God's assistance I conquer. STEWART.
Deo non fortunâ. By Providence, not by fortune. DIGBY, e.
HARRISON.
Deo non fortunæ. To God not fortune. GARDINERS.
Deo omnia. All things to God. HARTER.
Deo pagit. He covenants with God. PAGIT, of Hadley.
Deo, patriæ, amicis. To God, my country, and my friends.
ARUNDELL. GRENVILLE. LUTWIDGE. SCRIMGEOUR.
Deo patriæque fidelis. Faithful to God and my country.
FAGAN.
Deo, patriæ, regi. For God, my country and my king. COOPER.
Deo,patriæ,tibi. For God your country and yourself. LAIMBORO.
Deo, regi, et patriæ. To God, my king, and my country.
IRVINE.
Deo, regi fidelis. Faithful to God and the king. ATKINSON.
O'DALY.
Deo, regi, patriæ. To God, my king, my country. DUNCOMBE,
of Cassgrove. FEVERSHAM, b. IRVINE, of Kinconssie.
Deo, regi, vicino. To God, my king, my neighbour. BROMSGROVE
GRAMMAR SCHOOL. COOKES. WORCESTER COLL. OXON.
Deo regique debeo. I owe duty to God and the king. JOHNSON.
Deo regique liber. Free to serve God and the king. JOHNSON,
of Twickenham, bt.
Deo, reipublicæ, et amicis. To God, our country, and our
friends. LEVANT COMP.
Deo semper confido. In God I trust ever. JAMES, of Otterburn.
Deo servire regnare est. To serve God is to reign. ARUNDELL.
Deo volente. God willing. REEVES. PALLISER.

Depechez. Make haste. GOVAN.

Depressus extollor. I am exalted after being depressed. BUTLER.
KILKENNY.

Désormais. Hereafter. CLIFFORD.

Despair not. EAST LAND COMP.

Desperatio facit audacem. Despair makes (me) daring.

> *Crest*—A stag.

Despicio terrena. I despise earthly things. BEDINGFIELD, of
Ditchingham. M'CROBIE.

> "Animi excellentia magnitudoque, cum in augendis opibus utilitati-
> busque et sibi et suis comparandis, tum multo magis in his ipsis
> despiciendis, elucet."—CIC. *de Off.* lib. i. v. 5.

Despicio terrena et solem contemplor. I despise earthly things
and contemplate the sun. BEDINGFIELD, bt.

> In the arms an eagle displayed.

Detur forti palma. Let the palm be given to the brave.
SINCLAIR, of Brimmes.

> "Quis cuique dolor victo, quæ gloria palmæ,
> Nonne vides ?"—VIRG. *Geo.* lib. iii. 102.

Deum cole, regem serva. Worship God, revere the king. COLE,
Earl of Enniskillen. COLE, of Twickenham. TOWNSHEND,
co. Cork. COLERIDGE. JONES.

> "Reverence with lowly heart
> Him whose wondrous work thou art ;
> Keep his goodness still in view,
> Thy trust and thy example too."—BURNS.

Deum posui adjutorem. I have taken God for my helper.
KINGSTON.

Deum time. Fear God. MURRAY, of Blackbarony, bt. MUR-
RAY, of Clairemont, bt.

> "Fear God, the Lord of heaven."—*Jonah,* i. 9.

Deus adjuvat nos. God assists us. BOOTH, bt.

Deus alit eos. God feeds them. CROKER, of Trevillas, whose
crest is a raven. JAMES, crest, a chough.

> "Beneath the spreading heavens,
> No creature but is fed ;
> And he who feeds the ravens
> Will give his children bread."—COWPER.

Deus clypeus meus. God is my shield. BIDDLE.

> "God is a shield unto them that put their trust in him."— *Prov.* xxx. 5.

Deus dabit. God will give. MORE, of Innernytie.

Deus dabit vela. God will fill the sails. CAMPBELL. NORMAN,
co. Sussex. The crest of Campbell is a galley.

> "Heaven speed the canvass, gallantly unfurl'd
> To furnish and accommodate a world,
> To give the pole the produce of the sun,
> And knit the unsocial climates into one."—COWPER.

Deus est nobis sol et ensis. God is a sun and sword to us.
POWELL.

Deus est spes. God is our hope. RIDSDALE.
"Blessed is the man that trusteth in the *Lord*, and whose hope the *Lord* is."— *Jer.* xvii. 7.

Deus et libertas. God and liberty. GODFREY, bt.

Deus fortitudo mea. God is my strength. JONES, of Beal-anamore.

Deus gubernat navem. God steers the vessel. T. of RENFREW. LECKIE.
"The Lord the pilot's part performs,
And guards and guides me thro' the storms."— COWPER.

Deus hæc otia. God has given us this ease. LAMBERT.
The words of Virgil are "Deus nobis hæc otia fecit."

Deus hæc otia fecit. God hath given this tranquillity. WILLIAMS, co. Brecon and Herts.

Deus incrementum dedit. God has given increase. FIRTH.

Deus indicat. God discovers. EAST INDIA COMP.

Deus juvat. God assists. M'DUFF.

Deus major columnâ. God is stronger than a column. HENNIKER, b. There are three columns in the arms.

Deus me audit. God hears me. LAWFORD. MAUDUIT.
A rebus on the word *m' aud(u)it.*

Deus meum solamen. God is my comfort. KEIR, of Linlithgow.

Deus meus dux meus My God is my guide. ST. ALBYN.

Deus mihi adjutor. God is my helper. OCHTERLONIE.

Deus mihi providebit. God will provide for me. GOOLD, bt. KEANE, b. JERRNEY.

Deus mihi sol. God is my sun. NICHOLSON, of Ballow.

Deus nobis. God with us. PINKNEY.

Deus nobis hæc otia fecit. (Virg. *Ec.* i. vi.) God hath given us this tranquillity. BOLGER. BURROW. HIDE. T. of LIVERPOOL.

Deus nobis quis contra? God for us, who shall be against us? DE MONTMORENCY. MORRES. CARTER. ROBINS.

Deus nobiscum, quis contra? If God be with us, who can be against us? The BARON DE BLISS, Brandon Park.

Deus non reliquit memoriam humilium. God hath not forgotten the humble. MEYNELL, of North Kilvington.
"Valet ima summis
Mutare, et insignem attenuat deus,
Obscura promens."— HOR. *Car.* i. 34, 12.

Deus noster refugium. Our God is (our) refuge. BARNES.
"The eternal God is thy refuge."—*Deut.* xxxiii. 27.

Deus pascit corvos. God feeds the ravens. CORBET, bt. CORBET, JOHNES. JONES. WILLIAMS, of Temple House. CORNISH. CORBIN. CORBYN. PROTHEROE. RAVENSHAW.
Ravens are borne by these families.
"Who provideth for the raven his food."— *Job*, xxxviii. 41.
"He that doth the ravens feed,
Yea, in his providence caters for the sparrow ;
Be comfort to my age."— SHAKSPEARE.

Deus pastor meus. (Ps. xxiii. 1.) God is my Shepherd. BOGIE,
or BOGGIE.

Deus prosperat justos. God prospers the just. AVELAND, b.
HEATHCOTE.

Deus protector noster. God is my protector. O. OF THE LAMB
OF GOD, SWEDEN. EMERSON-TENNENT, of Tempo.

Deus providebit. God will provide. BURTON, bt. BOLGER, of
Wexford. DRUMMOND, of Blair. LESLY, of Aberdeen.
MARSHALL. MATHER. MEIN. MUNDY. PRIDEAUX, bt.

> " Happy the man who sees a God employ'd
> In all the good and ill that chequer life !
> Resolving all events, with their effects
> And manifold results, into the will
> And arbitration wise of the Supreme."—COWPER.

Deus refugium nostrum. God our refuge. MALCOLM.

Deus robur meum. God is my strength. WOOD, of Brownhills.

> " The *Lord* JEHOVAH is everlasting strength."—*Isa.* xxxvi. 4.

Deus solamen. God is my comfort. KER. KERR.

> " One adequate support
> For the calamities of mortal life
> Exists—one only ; an assured belief
> That the procession of our fate, howe'er
> Sad or disturbed, is ordered by a Being
> Of infinite benevolence and power."—WORDSWORTH.

Deus solus auget aristas. God alone increaseth the harvest.
RIDDELL, of Felton.

> " I have planted, but God gave the increase."—1 *Cor.* iii. 6.
> " But when the Lord of grace and power
> Has bless'd the happy field,
> How plenteous is the golden store
> The deep-wrought furrows yield."—COWPER.
> There are sheaves of rye in the arms and crest.

Deus tuetur. God defends. DAVIES, of Elmley Park.

Devant si je puis. Foremost if I can. MAINWARING, bt. MAIN-
WARING. SCROPE. JACKSON. GRINDLEY.

> There is a tradition that Ranulphus de Mesnilwaren, who accompanied
> William the Conqueror from Normandy and founded the family of
> Mainwaring in Cheshire, was one of the first that set foot on English
> ground, and that the words, afterwards adopted as the family motto,
> were uttered by him as he leapt ashore.

Devouement sans bornes. Devotion without limits. PRODGERS.

> " Yield to the Lord with simple heart,
> All that thou hast, and all thou art."—COWPER.

Dextra cruce vincit. His right hand conquers with the cross.
HURLEY. *Crest*—A hand holding a cross.

Dextra fideque. By my right hand and my fidelity. BELL.

Dhandeon co heiragh ali. In spite of who would gainsay.
M'DONALD.

ΔΙΑ ΤΗΣ ΣΤΕΝΗΣ. Through the narrow way. CLARKE.

Di ofn di ymffrost. Fearless, boastless. WYNNE, of Pengwern.

Dial gwaed Cumru. Welsh blood will revenge. LLOYD. MOS-
TYN, b.

Dias-mo-dhuthaich. For God and my country. MACKENZIE, bt.

Diciendo y haciendo. Saying and doing. PAGET, co. Somerset.

Dictis factisque simplex. Simple in words and deeds. SAWREY. GILPIN.

Die virescit. It attains vigour by time. WOOD, of Grange-haugh. *Crest*—An oak-tree.

Dieppe. HARVEY.

This word was granted to Capt. Harvey for gallant conduct at this place.

Dieu aidant. God helping. BALFOUR, of Forret.

Dieu aide au premier Chretien (sometimes written Chrestien) et baron de France. God assists the first Christian and baron of France. O. OF THE DOG AND COCK. MONTMORENCY, France ; " le premier Baron Chrestien."

Dieu aide au premier Chrestien. God assists the first Christian. MONTMORENCY.

Dieu avec nous. God with us. BERKELEY, e. BERKELEY, of Spetchley. SEGRAVE, b. CALCRAFT. CALCOTT.

Dieu ayde. God assists. DE MONTMORENCY. FRANKFORT DE MONTMORENCY, v. MOUNTMORRES, v.

Dieu defend le droit. God defends the right. CHURCHILL. b. BLENKINSOP. HUNTER. SEATON. SPENCER. e.

" And God befriend us, as our cause is just."—SHAKSPEARE.

Dieu donne. God gives. COLPOYS.

Dieu est ma roche. God is my rock. ROCHE, bt. FERMOY, b.

" God only is my Rock."—2 SAM. xxii. 2.

" O God ! whose thunder shakes the sky
Whose eye this atom globe surveys,
To thee, my only Rock, I fly,
Thy mercy in thy justice praise."—CHATTERTON.

Dieu est mon aide. God is my help. BAND, of Wookey House.

Dieu est tout. God is every thing. ALLINGTON.

Dieu et ma patrie. God and my country. MARTON.

Dieu et mon droit. God and my right. Her Most Gracious Majesty, Queen VICTORIA.

This motto, first assumed by Richard I., was dropt in the succeeding reigns until revived by Edward III., A.D. 1340.

Dieu et mon espée. God and my sword. NORTON, of Elmham, co. Norfolk, and RICKINGHALL, co. Suffolk.

There are three swords in the arms.

Dieu et mon pays. God and my country. M'KIRDY.

Dieu et mon roi. God and my king. RAWLINSON.

Dieu me conduise. God guide me ! HAYES, bt. DELAVAL.

Dieu me garde. God keep me. AGARDES.

Dieu nous aventure donne bonne. May God give us good fortune. HAMBURGH MERCHANTS.

Dieu pour la Tranchée, qui contre? (If) God (be) for the *Trenches*, who shall be against them ? LE-POER-TRENCH. CLANCARTY, e.

Dieu pour nous. God for us. FLETCHER, of Ashford. PETERS.

Difficilia quæ pulchra. Things which are beautiful are difficult,
i.e. Honour is hard to win. ELFORD, bt.

Dii moresque dabunt. The gods and (our own) habits will
give it. O'BEIRNE.

Diligenter et fideliter. Diligently and faithfully. ALLEN.

Diligentia. Diligence. DICKMAN.

Diligentia cresco. I rise by industry. MONCRIEF, of Edinburgh.

Diligentia ditat. Industry renders rich. FERRIER. NEWELL.

Diligentia et honore. With diligence and honour. GARNETT.

Diligentia et vigilantia. Diligence and watchfulness. SEMPLE.

Diligentia fit ubertas. Plenty is caused by diligence. HAY.

Diligentia fortior. Stronger by diligence. TRUELL.

Dinna waken sleeping dogs. ROBERTSON, of Lude.
Crest—A sleeping dog.

Dios mi amparo y esperanza. God is my support and hope.
GIBBS.

Dirigat Deus. May God direct us. ALLEN.

Dirige. Direct us. ALDRIGE. *Crest*—A hand holding a pen.

Diriget Deus. God will direct it. BUTTER.
Crest—Two arms drawing a bow with arrow.

Disce ferenda pati. Learn to endure what must be borne.
HOLLINGWORTH, of Hollingworth.

Disce mori mundo, vivere disce Deo. Learn to die to the world ;
learn to live to God.

Disce mori ut vivas. Learn to die that thou mayest live. UNETT.

Disce pati. Learn to endure. CAMPERDOWN, e. DONKIN, of
Ripon. DUNCAN.

Disciplina, fide, perseverantia. By discipline, fidelity, and
perseverance. DUCKWORTH, bt.

Discite justitiam. Learn justice. NISBET, of Dirletoun.
"Discite justitiam moniti, et non temnere divos."—VIRG. *Æn.* vi. 620.

Discite justitiam moniti. (Virg. *Æn.* vi. 620.) Learn justice,
being admonished. RUSSELL, bt.

Discordiâ maxima dilabuntur. The greatest things are brought
to naught by discord. TAILORS' COMP. Exeter.

Discrimine salus. Safety in danger. TRAIL.
This motto and crest, which is a column set in the sea, were assumed by
an ancestor of this family, who when shipwrecked, A.D. 1418, escaped
by clinging to a rock.

Disponendo me, non mutando me. By influencing me, not by
changing me. MANCHESTER, d. MONTAGUE.

Dissipatæ. Dispersed. SCRYMGEOUR, of Dundee. SCRIMGEOUR.
In the reign of Alexander I., when that monarch was in pursuit of
certain rebels and traitors, Sir Alexander Carron snatched the banner
from the hands of him who bore it, and carrying it across the Spey,
planted it in sight of the rebels. For this and other acts of daring,
the king made Sir Alexander hereditary standard-bearer of Scotland,
gave him a grant of lands, and assigned to him the name of Scrymgeour,
or valiant in battle, together with an honourable coat, and the motto
"Dissipatæ," referring to the scattered forces of the rebels.

Distantia jungit. It joins things that were apart. CASE.
> *Crest* — A hand holding a buckle.

Ditat Deus. God enriches. M'TAGGART.
Ditat et alit. It enriches and nourishes. GUTHRIE.
Ditat servata fides. Tried fidelity enriches. ARCHBALD. INNES, of Edinburgh. PAPILLON.
Ditat virtus. Virtue enriches. CHEAP.
Divide et impera. Divide and rule. DENISON.
Divina sibi canit. She sings divine songs to herself. LAUCHLAN. LACHLAN. LOCHLAN. LOGHLAN.
Divini gloria ruris. (Virg. *Geor.* i. 168.) The glory of the heavenly abode. FOSTER.
Divino robore. By divine strength. GALIEZ. GELLIE.
Divisa conjungo. I heal divisions. GORDON, of Glastirim.
Dixi, Dixi. I have said, I have said. DIXON.
Do ever good. DOVER.
Do good. SPENCE, of Kerbuster.
> " I never did repent for doing good,
> Nor shall not now."—SHAKSPEARE.

Do it with thyself. BUXTON.
Do no ylle, quoth D'Oylle. D'OYLEY, bt. D'OYLEY, co. Norfolk.
> The name was originally spelt D'oylle.

Do not for to repent. BOTELER.
Do or die. DOUGLAS, of Springwood, bt. DOUGLAS, of Cavers.
Do that ye come fore. BROUGHTON.
Do well and doubt not. BLAKESTON, bt. BRUCE. HOUSTON.
Do well and let them say. ELPHINSTON. SCOT, of Orkney. SCOTT.
Do well, doubt not. KINGSMILL. BRUCE.
Do well, doubt nought. BRUCE, of Killroot.
Dolce nella memoria. Sweet in the memory. O. OF AMARANTA.
Dolore lenio dolorem. By suffering I alleviate pain. PALMER.
Domat omnia virtus. Virtue conquers all things. GOUGH, of Perry Hall. FFARINGTON, of Ffarington.
Domine, dirige nos. O Lord, direct us. (Eccles. xxxvi. 19.) CITY OF LONDON. BROME, of West Malling.
Domini factum est. It is the Lord's doing. (Ps. cxviii. 23.) CORBET. SCOTT, of Moreton. SIBBALD, co. Berks.
Domino quid reddam ? (Ps. cxvi. 12.) What shall I render unto the Lord ? BLOFIELD.
Dominus a dextris. The Lord is on my right hand. BATT.
> There are three dexter hands in the arms.

Dominus bonus *propitiabitur.* Our God will be propitious. BONUS.
Dominus dedit. The Lord hath given. HARRIES.
Dominus dux noster. The Lord is our guide. STUART.
Dominus exultatio mea. The Lord is my delight. STUBS.

Dominus fecit. The Lord hath done it. BAIRD. JACKSON.

> An ancestor of the Baird family rescued William the Lion of Scotland from a wild boar, who attacked him when alone and unarmed. Besides large lands, the grateful king conferred upon him a Boar passant as a bearing, with the above motto.

Dominus fortissima turris. The Lord is the strongest tower. DETTAVILLAND. TOWER.

> In the arms are three towers.

Dominus illuminatio mea. The Lord is my light. UNIVERSITY OF OXFORD. LEYCESTER, of White Place.

Dominus petra mea. The Lord is my rock. DAMPIER.

Dominus providebit. (Gen. xxii. 8.) The Lord will provide. BOYLE. BURTON, of Burton Hall and Longner. GLASGOW, e. MASSON. M'LAWS. M'VICAR.

Dominus salus mea. The Lord is my safety. SMITH.

Domum antiquam redintegrare. To resuscitate an ancient house. HEPBURN, of Smeaton, bt.

Donec impleat orbem. Until it fill its orb. KIDD. KYD, of Craigie. *Crest* — An increscent.

Donec rursus impleat orbem. Until it again fill its orb. SCOTT, bt. SOMERVIL. SOMMERVILLE.

Donec totum impleat orbem. Until it fill the whole world. O. OF THE CRESCENT.

Dove andate ? Whither are you going ? BARCHARD.

Dread God. CARNEGIE, bt. CARNEGIE, of Kinnard. GORDON, of Earlston, bt. GORDON, of Aston and Craighlaw. HAY. HODGSON. MONRO, bt. MACDOUGAL.

Dread shame. LEIGHTON, bt. LEIGHTON, of Shrewsbury.

Drogo nomen, et virtus arma dedit. Drogo is my name, and valour gave me arms. DREW, who is descended from the family of DROGO.

Droit. Right. TUNSTALL, of Durham Hartley.

Droit à chacun. To each his right. DODEDE.

Droit et avant. Just and forward. SYDNEY, v.

Droit et loyal. Just and loyal. DUDLEY, earl of Leicester, temp. Queen Elizabeth. HUNTINGFIELD, b.

Droit et loyalté. Justice and loyalty. VANNECK.

Drop as rain, distil as dew. DISTILLERS' COMP., London.

Droyt et devaunt. Right and forward. DRURY.

Drwy rynwedd gward. In this cause I would bleed. WALWYN.

Ducat amor Dei. Let the love of God lead us. BATTYE.

Duce et auspice. Under guidance and auspices (of the Holy Ghost). O. OF THE HOLY GHOST, France.

Ducit amor patriæ. Patriotism leads me. BLADES. PHILIPPS, bt. PHILIPPS, of Dale Castle. LECHMERE, of Rhyd, co. Worcester, bt.

> " Monstrat amor verus patriæ."—VIRG. *Æn.* xi. 892.

Ducit Dominus. The Lord leads. DEZOM.

Ducitur hinc honos. Hence honour is derived. BUCHANAN, of Miltown.

Ducitur, non trahitur. He is led, not drawn. ALEXANDER.
Crest—A horse's head bridled.

Ductus, non coactus. Led, not forced. ROBERTSON.

Dulce periculum. Danger is sweet. M'ALLA. M'CALL. MACAULEY, b.

Dulce pro patriâ periculum. Danger is sweet for one's country. KER, of Moristoun.

Dulce quod utile. That is agreeable which is useful. STRANG. STRONG, bt.

Dulcedine capior. I am captivated by sweetness. HOWLASTONE.
There is a violin in the arms.
" How sweet the moonlight sleeps upon the bank !
Here shall we sit, and let the sounds of music,
Creep in our ears."—SHAKSPEARE.

Dulces ante omnia Musæ. The Muses are delightful above all things. LOWES, of Ridley Hall.
" Tale tuum carmen nobis, divine poëta,
Quale sopor fessis in gramine, quale per æstum
Dulcis aquæ saliente sitim restinguere rivo."—VIRG. *Ec.* v. 45.

Dulcis amor patriæ. The love of one's country is sweet. CLIFFORD. FITZWYGRAM, bt. ROBINSON.

Dulcis pro patria labor. Labour for one's country is sweet. M'KERRELL, of Hill House.

Dulcius ex asperis. The sweeter because obtained by hardships. FERGUSSON, bt. FERGUSON.
Crest—On a thistle leaved and flowered ppr., a bee or.

Dum clarum rectum teneam. May I keep the line of right as well as of glory. PENN, of Stoke Park.

Dum cresco spero. While I increase I hope. RIDER.
The crest a crescent.

Dum exspiro spero. While I die I hope. LACE.

Dum in arborem. Until grown into a tree. HAMILTON.
Crest—An oak-plant.

Dum memor ipse mei. While I am mindful of myself. IRVINE, bt.

Dum sedulo prospero. While engaged industriously I prosper. SWINTON.

Dum sisto vigilo. Whilst I stand still I watch. GORDON, bt.
Crest—A stag at gaze.

Dum spiro cælestia spero. While I have breath I hope heavenly things. JONES, of Thurston.

Dum spiro spero. While I have breath I hope. ASCHMATY. ASSCOTTI. AUCHMUTY, of Brianstown. BAINBRIDGE. BAKER. BANNATYNE, of Newhall. BLOXAM. BROOKE. BUSHELL. ARITON. COLQUHON. COMPTON. COTTEE. COTTER, bt.

DAVIES, of Marrington Hall. DEARDEN. DEARDON. DILLON, v. DORAN. DRUMMOND. ELRICK. GLAZEBROOK. GOING. GORDON. GURNEY. HOARE, bt. HOARE, (see also "Venit Hora.") HUNTER. LEARMOUTH. LEE. MONK-MASON, of Mason-Brook. MOORE. MORICE. MORRIS. OLDFIELD. O'REILLY. PARTRIDGE, of Hockham, co., Norfolk. PEARSON. PRICE. ROBERTS, of Beechfield. RODWELL. SHARP. SMITH. STANTON. STRETTON. SPEARMAN, of Thornley. SPRY. SYMONDS. TATLOCK. THOMPSON, CO., Durham. WALKER. WESTERMAN.

Dum varior. Until I am changed. RAMSAY, of Idington.

A crescent forms part of the crest.

Dum vigilo tutus. While I am vigilant I am safe. GORDON, of Knockespoch.

Dum vivimus, vivamus. While we live let us live. DODDRIDGE. HEWITT. VYVYAN.

" Live while you live, an epicure would say,
And snatch the pleasures of the present day;
Live while you live, the sacred preacher cries,
And give to God each moment as it flies.
Lord ! in Thy view let both united be !
I live in pleasure when I live to Thee !"—DR. DODDRIDGE.

Dum vivo, spero. While I live I hope. STUART-MENTEITH, bt. MONTEATH. THOM. LATTA. WHITEWAY.

Dum vivo, vireo. While I live I flourish. LATTA.

Crest — An oak-tree ppr.

Durat, ditat, placet. It endures, it enriches, and it pleases. GED, of that Ilk.

Dureté. Hardness. EVELYN, of Wotton.

Duriora virtus. Virtue tries harder things. WYATT.

Duris non frangor. I am not disheartened by difficulties. MURE, of Caldwell. MUIR. MOORE, of Corswall.

Durum sed certissimum. Hard but most sure. GILLANDERS.

𝔇𝔲𝔱𝔶. BROUNCKER, of Boveridge.

" *Stern* daughter of the voice of God !
O Duty ! if that name thou love,
Who art a light to guide, a rod
To check the erring and reprove ;
Glad hearts ! without reproach or blot ;
Who do thy work and know it not :
May joy be theirs while life shall last !
And thou, if they should totter, teach them to stand fast !
WORDSWORTH.

Duw fyddo ein cryfdwr. God be our strength. EDWARDS.

Dux mihi veritas. Truth is my guide. HAGGARD.

Dux vitæ ratio. Reason is the guide of life. BENNETT. BOULTON. WEST.

Duw a darpar ir brain. God provides for the crows. HUGHES, of Plas Coch. *Crest*—A Cornish chough.

Duw a Digon. God is enough, *i.e. Deus sufficit.* VAUGHAN. PRYTHERCH. NICHOLL, of Dimlands.

Duw by Ras. God thy grace. KEMEYS-TYNTE, of Haleswell.
Duw ydi (sometimes *ydyw*) *ein cryfdwr.* God is our strength.
  EDWARDS, of Manchester.
Duw yn digon. God is sufficient.

E

E labore dulcedo. Pleasure arises out of labour. BOYLE. INNES.
  M'INNES.
E mare. From the sea. HUGHAN.
E perseverantia honor. Honour from perseverance. DAVEY.
E spinis. From among thorns. DELAP. DUNLOP, of Garnkirk.
  There is a rose in the crest.
῾Η σου χειρ, Κυριε, δεδοξασται εν ισχυι. Thy hand, O Lord,
  hath been glorified in strength. EMERSON. O. OF THE
  REDEEMER, Greece.
E tellure effodiuntur opes. Our wealth is dug out of the earth.
  ASTON, of Bescot, who made a fortune by coal-mining.
E tenebris lux. Light out of darkness. LIGHTBODY.
  In allusion to the name and to the crest, an estoile rising from a cloud.
> " Hail, holy Light, offspring of heaven, firstborn,
>   Whose fountain who shall tell? Before the Sun,
>   Before the heavens thou wert, and at the voice
>   Of God, as with a mantle, didst invest
>   The rising world of waters dark and deep,
>   Won from the void and formless infinite."—MILTON.
E vive en esperance. And live in hope. AKERS.
Ea nostra voco. I call these things our own. PECHELL, bt.
Eamus quo ducit fortuna. Let us go where fortune leads. ATTY.
  JAMES.
Early and late. WILKINSON.
Ecce Agnus Dei, qui tollit peccata mundi. (John, i. 29.) Behold
  the Lamb of God, which taketh away the sin of the world.
  TALLOW-CHANDLERS' COMP.
Efficiunt clarum studia. Studies make him illustrious. MILNE,
  of Muretoun.
Effloresco. I bloom greatly. CAIRNS, of Pilmor.
  Crest—A cinquefoil.
Efflorescent cornices dum micat sol. Rooks will flourish while
  the sun shines. ROOKE, of Carlisle, Akenhead and Wigtoun.
  Crest — A rook feeding on a wheatsheaf.
E'en do. M'HUD.
E'en do, but spare nocht. MURRAY, bt. MACGREGOR, bt.
E'en do, boit spair nocht. MURRAY. M'GREGOR, of that Ilk.
E'en do and spare noighte. M'ALPINE.
E'in do and spare not. GREGORSON. M'GREGOR. PETERS.
  MAC PETER.

Ει μη εν τω σταυρω. Except in the cross. SCALTER. THORP.

El hombre propone, Dios dispone. Man proposes, God disposes. DAVY.

El rey y la patria. King and country. O. of ST. FERDINAND.

Eloquentia sagitta. Eloquence (is) my arrow. BLAND.
There are pheons (arrows) in the arms.

Elvenaca floreat vitis. May the vine of *Elvion* flourish. ELVIN, of East Dereham.
The crest is a demi-lion holding a vine-branch.
" The vine luxuriant cleaves
Tender in shoot, yet large in leaf and high ;
Its purple fruit delicious to the taste
Producing wine to cheer the heart of man."

Emergo. I emerge. GLASS. WEBSTER.
The crest of Webster is the sun rising out of the sea.

Emeritus. I have served my country. EMERIS, of Louth, co. Lincoln. This has a punning reference to the name.

En avant. Forward. D'EYNCOURT. LUCY.

En bon espoir. In good hope. NICHOLAS, of East Love. WILLOUGHBY.

En bon et poyer. In right and might. COCKAYNE.

En bon foy. In good faith. CHADWICK. SACHEVERELL.

En ! dat Virginia quartum. Lo ! Virginia gives a fourth. VIRGINIA MERCHANTS.

En Dieu est ma fiance. In God is my trust. LUTTRELL.

En Dieu est ma foy. In God is my faith. CHEEVERS. LEGH-KECK. MAULEVERER, co. York. STAUNTON, co. Warwick.

En Dieu est mon esperance. In God is my hope. GERARD, bt. GERARD, of Prescot. WALMSLEY.

En Dieu est mon espoir. In God is my hope. SMITH, bt. TREVANION, of Caerhays.
"In him whose promise never yet has fail'd
I place my confidence."—HANNAH MORE.

En Dieu est tout. In God is everything. DAVIES. CHAMBRE. CONOLLY, of Castletown. WENTWORTH, co. York. WATSON. WATSON-WENTWORTH, m. of Rockingham.

En Dieu ma foy. My faith is in God. (Gal. iii. 22.) STAUNTON. SAMPSON.

En Dieu ma foi. My faith is in God. FAVILL.

En esperanza. In hope. MACK.

En espoir je vive attendant grace. I live in hope awaiting grace. SCROPE.

En foi prest. Ready in faith. BARLOW, of Ryde, Isle of Wight.

En grace affie. On *grace* depend. BRUDENEL. CARDIGAN, e. GRACE, bt.

En la rose je fleurie. I flourish in the rose. LENNOX. RICHMOND, d.
The arms of Lennox, duke of Richmond, have a bordure componée or and gu. charged with eight roses of the second ; to these the motto refers.

En parole je vis. I live on the word. LEGGE. STAWELL, b.

En pure foi. In pure faith. HEWITT.

En suivant la vérité. By following truth. PORTSMOUTH, e. WALLOP. WILLIAMS, co. Monmouth.

En tout loyale. In all loyal. CARNE.

En vain espère, qui ne craint Dieu. He hopes in vain, who fears not God. JANSSEN.

Endure and hope. WRIGHT. WYATT.

Endure fort. Endure boldly. CRAWFORD and BALCARRES, e. LINDSAY.

Enfans du roy. Children of the king. INFANTLEROY.

There are three children's heads in the arms, and a fleur-de-lis in crest.

Enough in my hand. CUNNINGHAME.

Ense animus major. The mind (*i.e.* reason) is more powerful than the sword. RYMER.

Crest — A hand holding a sword.

Ense et animo. With sword and courage. GRANT, bt.

Crest — A hand holding a sword.

Ense libertatem petit. He seeks liberty by his sword. CALD-WELL.

Eo altius quo profundius. The higher the deeper. LLOYD.

Equanimiter. With equanimity. SUFFIELD, b.

Er codiad y caera. From the foundation of the fortress. HEATON.

Erectus, non elatus. Exalted, but not elated. BEAUMONT, bt. BEAUMONT, of Barrow. CLARKE. PHILLIPS.

This motto was assumed by Henry de Beaumont, who, temp. Edw. I., was made king of the Isle of Man for life, and summoned to Parliament as a baron. It asserts that his pride had not increased with his fortune.

Ero quod eram. I will again be what I was. LANDEN. SCROGIE.

The crest of Scrogie is the trunk of an oak-tree, sprouting out branches and leaves.

Errantia lumina fallunt. Wandering lights deceive. KINNAIRD.

" I see that all are wanderers, gone astray
Each in his own delusions; they are lost
In chase of fancied happiness, still woo'd
And never won."— COWPER.

Eryr eyrod eryri. The eagles of the eagles of Snowdon. WYNNE, of Pengwern.

There is a tradition that the crest (an eagle) and motto, were adopted by an ancestor of the Wynnes of Eroydis, who either caught or killed an eagle of extraordinary size, on the north side of Snowdon ; and a grave-stone was found near the Chapel of Eroydis, inscribed " Bedd yr Eryr," Grave of the Eagle.

" The eagle soars,
And maketh his nest on high ?
The rock is the place of his habitation :
He dwells on the crag, the place of his strength."—*Job*, xxxix. 27.

Esperance. Hope. WALLACE, bt. ELLIS. O. OF THE THISTLE OF BOURBON.

Esperance en Dieu. Hope in God. BULLOCK. BEVERLY, e. GREATHEAD. NORTHUMBERLAND, d. PRUDHOE, b. PERCY.

> This motto, although borne by other families beside that of Percy, was first adopted by them from their family having experienced such vicissitudes of fortune that at last they learned to trust to no human strength, but to hope in God alone.

Espère le bien. Hope for good.
Espère mieux. Hope for better. HEATH.
Esperez en Dieu. Hope in God. GALE.
Espoir me comfort. Hope comforts me. TILNEY. STRAINGWAYS.
Essayez. Try. DUNDAS, bt. DUNDAS. ZETLAND, e.
Essayez hardiment. Try boldly. DUNDAS, of Keukevi[1].
Esse et videri. To be and to seem to be. WILKINSON.
Esse quam videri. To be rather than seem to be. ADDENBROOKE. BEADON. CRAWLEY-BOEVEY, bt. BONHAM. BROWNLOW. BUNBURY. COLLETT. COUTS. CROFT, bt. DELINE. FLINN. GRATTEN. HAMMERTON. HILL. HOOD. LONGLEY. LURGAN, b. MAITLAND. MARIS. MATHIL. OAKES. ROUND. SHERIFF. ST. PAUL, bt. ST. PAUL. SWIRE, of Cononley. THURSTON, of Weston, co. Suffolk. THURSTON, of Talgarth. TURNER. TURNOUR, of Swaffham, co. Norfolk. WINTERTON, e. WOODCOCK, of Coventry.

> The words of this motto were used by Sallust in praise of Cato, when comparing that patriot with Cæsar, after he has described their respective speeches in the history of the Catilinarian conspiracy.

Est concordia fratrum. Harmony becomes brothers. BROWN, of Brandon.

> Alexander Brown who settled in Baltimore in 1800, had four sons whom he united in partnership with himself. From this circumstance he chose the above motto, which is still borne by his representatives.

Est Deo gratia. Thanks are to God. SEARLE.
Est meruisse satis. It is sufficient to have deserved. MASSINGBERD, co. Lincoln.
Est nulla fallacia. There is no deceit. CARR, of Cocken.
Est pii Deum et patriam diligere. It is the part of a pious man to love God and his country. ATKINSON.
Est voluntas Dei. It is the will of God. BALDWIN. OLIFFE.
Esto. Be it so. HILL.
Esto fidelis. Be faithful. AUBERTIN. WHITTER.
Esto fidelis usque ad finem. Be faithful even to the end. FYDELL.
> Evidently intended as a play upon the name.

Esto miles fidelis. Be thou a faithful soldier. MILES.
Esto perpetua. Be perpetual. AMICABLE LIFE INSURANCE SOCIETY.
Esto quod audes. Be what you dare. DELWAY.
Esto quod esse videris. Be what you seem to be. AUFRERE.

BARKWORTH, of Wyton. COLE. HOOKE. MILLS. MILLES.
SONDES, b. WATSON.
"Men should be what they seem."—SHAKSPEARE.

Esto semper fidelis. Be ever faithful. DUFFIELD, of Coverdale,
co. York. YEA, bt.
"Fundamentum enim est justitiæ fides, id est dictorum conventorumque
constantia et veritas."—CIC. *de Off.* 1. 7. 6.

Esto sol testis. Let the sun be witness. JONES, co. Salop, bt.

Esto vigilans. Be vigilant. LLOYD, of Dolobran. OKEOVER.

Estote fideles. Be ye faithful. DE WINTON.

Estote prudentes. Be ye prudent. WILKINS.

Et agere et pati fortiter, Romanum est. Both to do and to endure
bravely is (a) *Roman(s)* part. ROMER.

Et arma et virtus. Both arms and virtue. DUNDAS. HAMILTON,
of Westburn.

Et arte et Marte. Both by skill and valour. BAIN.

Et custos et pugnax. Both a preserver and a champion. MAR-
JORIBANKS.

Et decerptæ dabunt odorem. Even when plucked they will give
out scent. AITON, of Kippo.
The Aitons of Kippo being, as it were, plucked from the main stem,
elegantly compare themselves to roses, plucked, yet fragrant; and
they bear for crest a rose-branch.

Et decus et pretium recti. Both the honour and the reward of
rectitude. FITZ - ROY. GRAFTON, d. SOUTHAMPTON, b.
DISNEY.
"Aut virtus nomen inane est,
Aut decus et pretium rectè petit experiens vir."—HOR. *Ep.* i. 17, 42.

Et Dieu mon appui. And God my support. HUNGERFORD.
"He firm as stands the rock's unshaken base,
Yet panting for a surer resting-place,
The human hurricane unmoved can see,
And say, 'O God, my refuge is in Thee!'"—BOWLES.

Et domi et foris. Both at home and abroad. MACK. LIVINGSTONE.

Et juste et vrai. Both just and true. RAY. WRAY.
I have no doubt this motto is intended as a play on the name.

Et manu et corde. Both with hand and heart. BATES.

Et Marte et arte. Both by valour and skill. BAIN. BAYN.
BAYNE. DRUMMOND, of Pilkellanie.

Et mea messis erit. My harvest will also arrive. DENNY, bt.
Crest—A hand holding five ears of rye.

Et neglecta virescit. Even though neglected, it flourishes.
HAMILTON, of Kilbrackmont.

Et nos quoque tela spar*simus.* And we also have hurled our
javelins. HASTINGS, m.
Those letters of the word "sparsimus" which are printed in Roman, form
the Latin word 'pars,' and are equivalent to the Greek μοιρα (*moira*),
which was the title of the Marquis of Hastings at the time he assumed
the motto.

Et patribus et posteris. Both for our ancestors and our posterity. LYDALL.

Et regem defendere victum. To defend the king even in his defeat. WHITGREAVE, of Moseley Court.

> This motto was first borne by Thomas Whitgreave, of Moseley, celebrated as having after the disastrous issue of the battle of Worcester, mainly contributed to the preservation of King Charles the Second.

Et servata fides perfectus amorque ditabunt. Both tried faith and perfect love will enrich. YOUNGE.

Et suivez moi. And follow me. HAWLEY.

Et vi et virtute. Both by strength and virtue. BAIRD, bt. BURROWES, bt. STANNUS.

Et vitam impendere vero. (Juv. Sat. vi. 91.) To sacrifice even life to truth. HOLLAND, b. ROUSSEAU.

Eternitatem cogita. Think on eternity. BOYD, of Trochrig.

Ἦτοι τὸν λογὸν ἄφετε, ἢ καλῶς αὐτῷ προσστῆτε. Either discard the word, or becomingly adhere to it. MORES.

Ette weel. Aim well. SMART.

Crest — A hand holding a dart.

Εὐγένεια καὶ Ἀρέτη. Gentle birth and virtue. NICHOLL.

Ever faithful. GORDON, of Tacachie.

Ever ready. BRYSON. BURN.

Evertendo fœcundat. It renders fruitful by turning over. IMBRIE. *Crest*—A plough.

Every bullet has its billet. VASSALL, of Milford, co. Southampton.

> These words were used by Col. Spenser Vassal, when leading on his troops to the assault of Monte Video, in order to encourage them under a severe fire. Scarcely had he spoken when a bullet struck and killed him. His family in consequence assumed the sentence for their motto, and received as an augmentation the breached bastions of a fortress with the words Monte Video above.

Ewch yn uchae. Go well. WYNN-WILLIAMS.

Ex armis honos. Honour gained by arms. OGILVY, of Logie.

Ex bello quies. Peace arises out of war. MURRAY.

Ex caligine veritas. Truth out of darkness. CLAVERLY.

> "Cognitionem rerum aut occultarum, aut admirabilium, ad beate vivendum necessariam ducimus."— CIC. *de Off.* lib. i. iv.
>
> "Darkness shows us worlds of light
> We never saw before."— MOORE.

Ex campo victoriæ. From the field of victory. CAMPBELL.

Ex candore decus. Honour from sincerity. KEITH, of Craig.

Ex candore virtus. Virtue from candour. WHYTE.

Ex concordia victoriæ spes. Hope of victory through union. BARNARD.

Ex duris gloria. From suffering ariseth glory. BENTHAM.

Ex fide fortis. Strong through faith. BEAUCHAMP, e. LYGON. PINDAR.

Ex flamma lux. Light from flame. INGLEDEW.

Ex hoc victoria signo. Victory (is gained) from the sign. RATTARY, of Scotland.

Crest — A hand holding a cross crosslet fetchée.

Ex industria. Through industry. MILNE, of Edinburgh. MYLNE.

Ex merito. Through merit. CHESTON. THARROLD.

Ex recto decus. Honour through rectitude. DURNO.

Ex seipso renascens. Born again from its own ashes. FRASER.

Crest — A phœnix in flames.

The phœnix, a bird reported to dwell in the deserts of Arabia, was said after living for several hundred years, to build for himself a funeral pile, the fire of which he fanned with his wings until it burst into a blaze and consumed him. From the ashes another phœnix arose with renewed youth and beauty.

Ex sese. From himself. ELKIN.

Ex sudore vultus. By the sweat of the face. SWETTENHAM, of Swettenham and Somerford.

This motto, which is intended as a play upon the name, refers to th spades in the arms and to Gen. iv. 19, " In the sweat of thy face shalt thou eat bread."

Ex undis aratra. Ploughs from the waves. DOWNIE, of Edinburgh.

Crest — A ship under sail, with a plough upon deck.

Ex unitate incrementum. Increase from unity. GUTHRY. GUTHRIE.

Ex uno omnia. All things are from one. ASHMOLE.

Ex urna resurgam. I shall rise again from the urn, *i.e.* the tomb. BLANDY.

Ex usu commodum. Advantage from its use. SMITH, of Dirleton. *Crest* — A hand holding a writing quill.

Ex vile pretiosa. Valuable things out of a base one. PATTINSON.

In allusion to his having discovered a method of separating silver from lead, — 1851.

Ex virtute honos. Honour from virtue. JARDIN.

Ex vulnere salus. Health from a wound. BORTHWICK.

Exaltabit honore. It will exalt with honour. SMYTH, of Graybrook.

Exaltavit humiles. He hath exalted the humble. HOLTE, of Erdington.

Excitari non hebescere. To be spirited, not inactive. DE GREY. WALSINGHAM, b.

Excelsior. Higher. STEINTHAL.

Excitat. He rouses. FORD.

Exegi. I have accomplished it. LEES, bt.

Exempla suorum. The examples of his ancestors. INNES, bt.

Exemple brave et louable. A brave and praiseworthy example. PALLISER.

Exitus acta probat. The result tests the act, or the end proves the deed. BISET. NISBET. NIVISON. STANHOPE.

Expecta cuncta supernè. Expect all things from above. WILSON, of Inverness.

Expectes et sustineas. Thou mayest hope and endure. GWYN, of Ford Abbey. WHARTON.

Expertus fidelem. Having found him faithful. LEWIS, bt.

Extant rectè factis præmia. The rewards of good deeds endure. COFFIN, bt.

Extinguo. I extinguish. DUNDAS.

> *Crest*—A salamander in flames. This animal was anciently supposed to be insensible to the effects of fire, and to extinguish it.

Extremos pudeat rediisse. Let it shame us to have come back last. WESTMACOTT.

F

Fabula sed vera. A *story*, but a true one. STORY.

Fac et spera. Do and hope. ASKEW. AYSCOUGH. CALDWELL. CAMPBELL, Lawres. CROMMELIN. DONALD. DELACHEROIS. FEA. HEATHCOTE. HYATT. LEDSAM. MACKNIGHT. M'GEE. MATHERSON. MYNORS. SCEPTER.

Fac justa. Act justly. NEWINGTON.

Fac simile. Do thou the like. SICK AND HURT OFFICE, London.

Fac similiter. Do likewise. OLIVER.

Face aut tace. Do or be silent. VEEL.

Facie tenus. Even to the face. WHELER, co. Warwick.
> In the arms are three leopards' faces.

Facies qualis mens talis. As the face so is the mind. BLAIR, of Balmill. *Crest*—A Roman's head.
> "Laudo te, et fortunatam judico,
> Id cum studuisti ; ibi formæ mores ut consimiles forent."
> TER. *Heaut.* 2, 4, 2.

Facta non verba. Deeds not words. HOYLE, co. York. DE RINZEY. DE RENZEY. WELLS, of Sporle, co. Norfolk. WILSON, of Beckenham.
> "With empty and selfish pretences away !
> By your actions you're judged, be your speech what it may."—COWPER.

Factis non verbis. By deeds not words. DUMERGUE. MONEY.

Facto non verbo. By deed not word. DAY.

Factum est. It is done. PLASTERERS' COMP.

Faded, but not destroyed. PAVER, of Braham Hall, co. York.
> *Crest* — A tree ppr.

> This motto doubtless refers to the crest as well as to the old barony of Percy, of which this family is co-heir.

Faire mon devoir. To do my duty. JOCELYN. RODEN, e.

Faire sans dire. To do without speaking, *i.e.* Deeds not words. FOX. FIELDER. HEYES, co. Chester. ILCHESTER. e. PAR. TODD. KINGSFORD. WARR, of Grappenhall.

Fais qui doit, arrive qui pourra. Do your duty, happen what may. CURE, of Blake Hall.

" Ratio postulat, ne quid insidiose, ne quid simulate, ne quid fallaciter."
CIC. *de Off.* lib. iii. 17, 1.

Fais bien, crains rien. Do well, fear nothing. JORNLIN. ZORNLIN.

" Possessions vanish, and opinions change,
And passions hold a fluctuating seat ;
But, by the storms of circumstance unshaken,
And subject neither to eclipse nor wane,
Duty exists."– WORDSWORTH.

Faith and hope. LINDSEY.

Faith and works. NELSON, e.

Faithful in adversity. HAMILTON, of Barns, Scotland.

Faithful to my unhappy country. MOLYNEUX.

Faitz proverount. Deeds will prove. GRIMSTON.

Fal y gallo. As I can. GREENLY, of Titley Court, co. Hereford.

Fama candidâ rosâ dulcior. Fame is sweeter than the white rose. TAYLOR.

There are three white roses in the arms.

Fama perennis erit. Thy fame shall be enduring. WYBORN.

Fama semper vivet. Our renown shall live for ever. LIDDELL. RAVENSWORTH, b.

" Semper honos, nomenque tuum laudesque manebunt."—VIRG. *Ec.* v. 7, 6.

" Still shall thy name, conspicuous and sublime,
Stand in the spacious firmament of time,
Fixed as a star : such glory is thy right."—WORDSWORTH.

Fama semper vivit. Fame lives for ever. GASON.

Famæ studiosus honestæ. Desirous of honourable fame. BROWNE.

Famæ venientis amore. With the love of future fame. STARKY, of Spye Park and Bromham.

" Incenditque animum famæ venientis amore."—VIRG. *Æn.* vi. 889.

Famam extendere factis. To extend fame by deeds. GALWAY, v.

" Stat sua cuique dies ; breve et irreparabile tempus
Omnibus est vitæ ; sed famam extendere factis,
Hoc virtutis opus."—VIRG. *Æn.* x. 467.

Famam extendimus factis. We extend our fame by our deeds. VACH, of Dawyck. VEITCH.

Familias firmat pietas. Piety strengthens families. RAMSAY. WARDLAW, bt. WARDLAW, of Tillycoultry.

Fare et age. Say and do. SAY, of Swaffham, co. Norfolk.

Fare fac. Speak, do, *i.e.* Say it and do it. FAIRFAX, b. FAIRFAX.

Fari quæ sentiat. To speak what he may think. BARKAS. ORFORD, e. WALPOLE.

" Ubi sentire quæ velis, et quæ sentias dicere licet."—TACITUS, *Hist.* i. 1.

Fari quæ sentient. To speak what they think. BRETARGH. WALPOLE.

" Quid voveat dulci nutricula majus alumno,
Quam sapere et fari ut possit quæ sentiat."—HOR. *Ep.* lib. i. 4, 8.

Fast. GRAY, of Cartyne.

Fast without fraude. BROOKE, of Norton Priory, bt.

Fata viam invenient. The fates will find a way. SPANGE. VAN SITTART.

Fatti maschi, parole femmine. Deeds are masculine, words feminine. CALVERT.

> " Let women, Edward, war with words ;
> With curses monks, but men with swords."

Fato non merito. By fate not desert. FITZ-GEORGE.

Fato prudentia major. (Virg. *Geor.* i. 416.) Prudence is greater than fate. CHENEY. LOMAX, of Clayton.

> " Wisdom and fortune combating together,
> If that the former dare but what it can,
> No chance may shake it."—SHAKSPEARE.

Faugh a bollagh. Clear the way. GOUGH, v.

Faut être. It must be. MUMBEE.

Faveat fortuna. Let fortune favour. NEWTON.

Favente Deo. By God's favour. PAWSON. REYNOLDS, of Great Yarmouth and Necton, co. Norfolk. WILKIE. FISHER.

Favente Deo et sedulitate. God and assiduity favouring. COLLINS.

Favente Deo supero. By God's favour I conquer. MITCHELL.

Favente Numine. By the favour of Providence. DYCE-SOMBRE. MICKLETHWAYT. PECKHAM.

Favente Numine regina servatur. By the favour of the Deity the Queen is preserved. MICKLETHWAIT, bt.

> This motto was assumed by Sir S. B. P. Micklethwait, when he was created a baronet for an important personal service rendered by him to Her Majesty and the Duchess of Kent, at St. Leonard's, co. Sussex, Nov. 1832.

Faventibus auris. By favourable gales. STIRLING, of Dundee.

> *Crest*—A ship under sail.

Fax mentis honestæ gloria. Glory is the light of a noble mind. FORBES, bt. LANDER. MOLLESON. THE NOVA-SCOTIA BARONETS.

> The favourite motto of Henry, Prince of Wales, eldest son of King James the First ; founder of the order of the Scottish branch of the baronetage, by which branch it was accordingly adopted.

Fax mentis incendium gloriæ. The torch of glory inflames the mind. FORBES. GRANARD, e.

Fayth hathe no feare. RYCROFT, bt.

Feal pero desdecado. Faithful though fallen. CHURCHILL.

ꝼᴇᴀꞃ ᴃuᴊᴓ ᴀᴃu. The yellow (haired) man defying. FITZ MAURICE, Kerry Geraldines.

> This motto alludes to the complexion of the first settler.

Fear God. CROMBIE. CHEYNE. BRISBANE, bt. GORDON. HUDDART. M'ANDREW. M'DOWELL. M'DOUGAL. MUNRO.

Fear God and live. SINCLAIR.

Fear God, fear nought. LOCKER.

Fear God in life. SOMERVILLE, b. SOMERVILLE, of Drum.

> " Silence hath a tongue ; the grave,
> The darkness, and the lonely waste, have each

A tongue that ever saith, Man ! think of God !
Think of thyself ! think of eternity !
Fear God, the thunders say ; Fear God, the waves.
Fear God, the lightnings of the storm reply ;
Fear God, deep loudly answers back to deep."—POLLOK.

Fear not friendship. THOMPSON.

" Friendship which, once determined, never swerves,
Weighs ere it trusts, but weighs not ere it serves."— HANNAH MORE.

Fear one. COZENS-HARDY, co. Norfolk.

Fear to transgress. CLONMEL, e. SCOTT.

Feed ye my sheep. (John, xvi. 17.) SHEPHERD.

Felicem reddet religio. Religion will render happy. MILLAR

Felicior quo certior. Luckier as it is surer. ORMISTON.

Crest — An anchor.

Felicitate restituta. With happiness restored. O. OF THE TWO SICILIES.

Felis demulcta mitis. A stroked cat is gentle. KANE. KEANE, bt.

Crest — A cat rampant.

Felix qui pacificus. He is happy who is peaceful. SPENCE.

Fe med'um buen hidalgo. Faith measures a good gentleman. BOCKENHAM.

Ferant mea serta columbœ. Let doves bear my garland. HODGSON. *Crest* — A dove holding an olive-branch.

Ferar unus et idem. I will pass along one and the same. MICHELL. COLLINGWOOD, b.

Ferendo et feriendo. By bearing and striking. HARRISON, of Copford Hall.

" *King Richard.* Norfolk, we must have knocks ; ha ! must we not ?
Norfolk. We must both give and take, my loving lord."— SHAKSPEARE.

Ferendo feres. Thou wilt bear it by endurance. IRVINE, of Cairnfield.

The crest is a cross crosslet gu., and a holly-branch with leaves vert. in saltier.

"Depend
Upon no help of outward friend ;
Espouse thy doom at once, and cleave
To fortitude without reprieve."

Ferendo non feriendo. By bearing not by striking. DEANE.

Ferendum et sperandum. We must endure and hope. MAC-KENZIE, of Redcastle.

Feret ad astra virtus. Virtue will bear us to the skies. KELLET, bt.

Ferio, tego. I strike, I defend. HAWDON. HERKLOTT. HOWDON. M'AUL. M'CALL. SIMS. SYME.

Feroci fortior. Bolder than the ferocious (boar). The head of which is borne in the arms. LOCKHART, of Birkhill.

Feros ferior. I strike the fierce. THE CHISHOLM.

Ferox inimicis. Fierce to his enemies. SYKES, of Leeds.

Ferré va ferme. The shod horse goes surely. FARRER.

There are horseshoes in the armorial bearings.

Ferro comite. My sword my companion. MORDAUNT, bt. TOLSON, of Bridekirk, co. Cumberland.

Ferro consulto. I argue with the sword. TREGOSE.

Crest — An arm in armour brandishing a sword.

Ferro non gladio. By iron, not by the sword. GUEST, bt.

This motto asserts that the fortune of the family was acquired from their iron works not by military achievements.

Ferro tego. I cover with iron.

F. E. R. T. THE ROYAL SARDINIAN O. OF THE ANNUNCIATION.

These four letters have been variously interpreted. Favin says that they signify, Frappés, entrés, rompés, tout. Others explain them by "Fortitudo ejus Rhodum tenuit," in memory of Amadeus the Great, who compelled the Turks to raise the siege of Rhodes. Ashmole says that both these opinions are wrong, and that the word ought to be written without stops between the letters, in which case it signifies "he bears," or "endures."

Fert lauream fides. Faith bears the laurel. HAY, of Lethim.

Fert palmam mereat. He bears the palm, let him deserve it. BATES.

Fertur discrimine fructus. Profit is gained by danger. GORDON, of Aberdeenshire.

Fervet opus. The work is urged on vigorously. TREWEEKE.

Arms — Ar. a beehive beset with bees diversely volant ppr.

" Fervet opus, redolentque thymo fragrantia mella."— VIRG. *Geor.* iv. 169.

Fest. Firm. DE LA FIELD.

Festina lente. Be quick without impetuosity ; or, as it may be punningly translated for the Onslow family, "On slow." BARNARD. BLAAUW. BROOKES. CAMPBELL. COLQUHON. DUNSANY, b. EVERETT. FINGALL, e. FLETCHER. LOUTH, b. MEWBURN, of Darlington. ONSLOW, bt. ONSLOW. PLUNKET, b. RIGGE. RAWLINSON, knt. ROTHERY. SWIFT, of Rotherham: TROTTER, bt. TROTTER. WESTCOMBE. WHITTAKER.

This motto is originally a Greek maxim, σπευδε βραδιως, assigned by Aulus Gellius to Augustus, to whom the former gives great credit, for having found means so briefly to express a maxim of a very peculiar nature, including, as he expresses it, both "industriæ celeritas," and "diligentiæ tarditas," a quickness of application with wariness of proceeding.

Ffyddlawn beunydel. Always faithful. WATKINS, of Woodfield, near Droitwich.

This motto is in allusion to the crest, a talbot's head.

Ffyddlon at y gorfin. Faithful to the end. JAMES.

Fiat Dei voluntas. God's will be done. MEREDYTH, bt.

Fiat justitia. Let justice be done. BRYCE. COKER.

Crest — Out of a cloud in the sinister, a dexter hand holding a pair of scales, all ppr.

Fiat voluntas Dei. The will of God be done. SALWEY.

Fide et amore. By fidelity and love. CARDEN, bt. CONWAY, DICEY. GARDINER, of Ely. HEART. HERTFORD, m. SADLER. CHADWICK, of Lynn, co. Norfolk, by whom this motto is borne is a descendant of the Lancashire branch of the

family; one of his ancestors, Sir Andrew Chadwick, saved
Queen Anne in 1709 from a fall from her horse, for which
service he is said to have been knighted.

Fide et caritate laboro. I labour with faith and charity. BOVIER.

Fide et clementia. By faith and clemency. MARTIN, co. Sussex.

Fide et constantia. By fidelity and constancy. JAMES, co.
Kent. DIXON.

Fide et fiducia. By fidelity and confidence. BLACKMAN.
GILCHRIST. HARNAGE, bt. PRIMROSE. ROSEBERRY, e.
THORLBY. WATT.

Fide et firme. Faithfully and firmly. FAIRHOLM.

Fide et fortitudine. With faith and fortitude. AUBERT.
BRICKDALE. COX. CAPEL. ESSEX, e. FARQUHARSON, of
Invercauld. HICKSON. LAWRENCE, of Llanelweth. M'FAR-
QUHAR. NOBLE, of Reresbie. MADAN. LLOYD, of Coedmore.

Fide et in bello fortis. Strong in faith and in war. CARROT.

Fide et industria. By faith and industry. WHITTINGHAM.

Fide et integritate. By fidelity and integrity. VENNING.

Fide et labore. By faith and labour. ALLEN.

Fide et Marte. By fidelity and military service. RALSTON.

Fide et opera. By faith and work. M'ARTHUR. STEWART.

Fide et sedulitate. With faith and diligence. ELWOOD.

Fide et spe. With faith and hope. BORTHWICK.

Fide et vigilantia. By faith and vigilance. STEPNEY, bt.

Fide et virtute. By fidelity and valour. BRANDLING. GLAD-
STONE, bt. GOODWIN. RAMSBOTTOM. ROCHEAD.

Fide, labore, et virtute. By faith, labour, and virtue. MARYOTT.

Fide laboro. I labour with faith. BOVIER.

Fide non armis. By faith not arms. GAMBIER.

Fide parta, fide aucta. By faith obtained, by faith increased.
M'KENZIE, of Kilcoy, bt. MACKENZIE, of Fairburn.

Fide, sed cui vide. Trust, but in whom take care. ASTLEY, bt.
ASTELL. BEAUMONT, of Whitley. COYNEY, of Weston Coyney.
BIRKBECK. ASTLEY, of Everleigh. BANKES, of Winstanley.
GREENSUGH. HOLME. PRICKETT. REYNOLDS. STAPLETON.

Fide sed vide. Trust but take care. PETRIE. REYNOLDS.

Fidei coticula crux. The cross is the test of truth. CHEVALLIER.
CLARENDON, e. BAKER, bt. JERSEY, e. VILLERS. WHATTON.

Fidei signum. The emblem of faith. MURRAY, of Deuchar.

Fidelè. Faithfully. ROUPELL. ROUSSELL.

Fideli certa merces. To the faithful there is certain reward.
BOTTOMLY. BOTTOMLEY. MORLEY, e. PARKER.

Fideli certe merces. To the faithful man there is assuredly a
reward. SAUL or SAULE.

> " He who is faithful, honest, just,
> True to his word and to his trust,
> Shall, if from these he never swerves,
> Meet the reward which he deserves."

Fideli quod obstat ? What hinders the faithful ? FIREBRACE.
Fidelis. Faithful. CRICHTON. HILL, of Oxon. KENAH. SHEPHERD.
WALDY.
Fidelis ad urnam. Faithful to the tomb. MALONE.
Fidelis et audax. Faithful and bold. RUSSELL.
Fidelis et constans. Faithful and steadfast. BRAGGE.
Fidelis et in bello fortis. Faithful and brave in war. GILLESPIE.
Fidelis et suavis. Faithful and gentle. EMERY.
Fidelis in omnibus. Faithful in all things. COLLINS.
Fidelisque ad mortem. And faithful to death. TAYLOR.
Fidelis usque ad mortem. Faithful even unto death. SUTTON,
of Elton.
Fidelitas. Fidelity. PURDIE. SCOT. SCOTT, of Edinburgh.
Fidelitas regi et justitia mihi. Fidelity to the king and justice
to myself. DAWSON.

This motto is now borne by Dawson-Duffield, of Coverdale, co. York,
who represents the family.

Fidelitas vincit. Fidelity prevails. COTTON. DUNSCOMBE.
Fidelitate. By fidelity. NEWMAN.
Fidélité est de Dieu. Fidelity is of God. MELLOR. POWERS-
COURT, v. WINGFIELD.

" 'Tis faith, holy faith, that, like springs underground,
By the gifted of heaven alone can be found."—MOORE.

Fideliter. Faithfully. CUNLIFFE, bt. HAMILTON. HAVELOCK,
bt. HENRY. MUCKLESTON. RALPH. OGILVY. SYMONDS.
TEALE.
Fideliter et constanter. Faithfully and constantly. O. of
ERNEST SAXE-COBURG-GOTHA.
Fideliter et diligenter. Faithfully and diligently. GRAHAM, bt.
Fideliter et recte. Faithfully and uprightly. PITCHES.
Fideliter serva. Perform faithfully. NORRIS, co. Norfolk.
Fidem meam observabo. I will keep my faith. SHEDDON.
Fidem meam servabo. I will keep my faith. SHEDDON.
Fidem parit integritas. Integrity produces confidence. KAY.
KAYE, bt.

" Fides autem ut habeatur, duabus rebus effici potest : si existimabimur
adepti conjunctam cum justitia prudentiam."—CIC. *de Off.* i. ix. 8.

Fidem rectam qui colendo. Who by cultivating right faith.
HIBBERT.
Fidem servabo genusque. I will preserve, (*i.e.* be true to) my
faith and my race. MASSEY, of Watton, co. Norfolk.
Fidem servo. I keep faith. ALEXANDER, of Boghall.
Fideque perennant. And they endure through faith. IRVINE.

Crest — A sheaf of holly ppr. banded gu.

Fides. Faith. MAXTON. PETREE. ROSTER. WYLLIE, of
Forfar.

Fides culpari metuens. Fidelity fearful of blame. YELDHAM.

Fides invicta triumphat. Invincible loyalty triumphs. C. of GLOUCESTER.

Fides montium Deo. The trust of the *Hills* is in God. HILLS.

Fides non timet. Faith fears not. HARVEY. LEE. MONTEAGLE, b. RICE.

Fides præstantior auro. Faith is more estimable than gold. CLAPPERTON. GIBB.

Fides probata coronat. Tried faith crowns. CAMPBELL, of Purvis, bt. LAIDLAW. ROCH.

Fides servata secundat. Tried fidelity makes prosperous. NAPIER, bt. STIRLING.

Fides Stephani. Stephen's faith. STEPHENS.

Fides sufficit. Faith sufficeth. HALKET, bt. HALKETT, co. Fife. HALKET, co. Warwick.

Fidus ad extremum. Faithful to the last. LEITH, of Whitehaugh.

> "Master go on, and I will follow thee
> To the last gasp, with truth and loyalty."—SHAKSPEARE.

Fidus amicus. A faithful friend. CAMPBELL, of Islay.

Fidus et audax. Faithful and bold. CALLAGHAN. LISMORE, v. SLADE, bt.

Fidus in arcanis. Faithful in secret affairs. STEVENSON.

Fidus in arcanum. Faithful in a secret affair. STEVENSON.

Fiel pero desdichado. Faithful, though unfortunate. MARLBOROUGH, d. THANET, e. TUFTON.

Fier et fort. Proud and strong. SHELTON.

Fier et sage. Proud and wise. BRADFORD, Sir Thomas, G.C.B.
Crest—A peacock's head, in its mouth a serpent, entwined round the neck.

Fier sans tache. Proud, without blemish. GOFF.

Fight. ASHE, of Ashfield. ORKNEY, e. ROSSLYN, e. SINCLAIR, b. ST. CLAIR.

Fight on, quoth Fitton. FITTON.

Finem prospiciens. Looking to the end. TURNER.

Finem respice. Consider the end. BLIGH. BROOKE. COLLIS. DARNLEY, e. HALL, of Grappenhall. PATTENSON.

Fingit premendo. He shapes by (re)pressing. CUTCLIFFE.
In allusion to the pruning-hooks in the arms, and to the name.

Finis coronat opus. The end (or *Finnis*) crowns the work. FINNIS.

Finis coronat opus. The end crowns the work. BAKER, of Ashcombe, bt. BARNET. BAYLEY. CROSTHWAITE.

Finis dat esse. Death gives us (real) being. BURGRAVE. BROGRAVE.
This motto is an allusion to the name, the *grave* being the end of our mortality.

Firm. DALRYMPLE, bt. DALRYMPLE, of Cranstoun, North Berwick, &c. DALRIMPLE. LAING, of Lindertis. STAIR, e. WALL, of Wortley Park. MEASON. WALSH, bt. REID, bt.

Firm en foi. Firm in faith. CHICHESTER, v.

Firm to my trust. GLYN, bt.

Firma durant. Strong things last. LESLY, of Finrassie.
Referring to the buckles in the arms.

Firma et ardua. Solid and and lofty objects. MACKENZIE, of Rosehaugh.

Firma nobis fides. Faith is strong to us. VILANT. WATERHOUS.

Firma spe. With strong hope. LESLY, of Kincraige. LESLIE.

Firma spes. Hope is strong. MONCRIEF.

Firmè. Resolutely. DALRYMPLE. ELPHINSTONE.

Firmè dum fide. Firmly while faithfully. HEIGNIE.

Firmè durans. Firm to the last. LESLIE, of Wardes.

Firmior quo paratior. The more prepared, the stronger. DUNBAR. SELKIRK, e.

Firmitas et sanitas. Strength and health. GRIFFITH.

Firmitas in cœlo. Stability in heaven. ST. GEORGE, bt. MAHER.

Firmitas in cœlo, stabilitas in terra. Firmness in heaven, stability on earth. St. GEORGE.

Firmiter maneo. I last steadily. LINDSAY, of Culsh.

Firmor ad fidem. I am true to the faith. CHIPPENDALL.

Firmum in vita nihil. Nothing in life is permanent. BUNBURY, bt. DOLPHIN. RICHARDSON.

Firmus in Christo. Firm in Christ. FIRMIN.

Firmus in firmis. Firm among the firm. RICHARDSON.

Firmus maneo. I remain steadfast. BREEK. LINDSAY.

Fit inde firmior. Hence it is made stronger. SKIRVIN.
Crest—A hand holding a buckle.

Fit via vi. A *way* is made by labour. CAMPBELL. WAY.

Fixus adversa sperno. Firm I despise adversity. HAMERTON, of Hellifield.

Fixus ac solidus. Firm and substantial. STEWART, of Rosling.
" Fortis et constantis est, non perturbari in rebus asperis, nec tumultuantem de gradu dejici, ut dicitur."—CIC. *de Off.*

Flecti non frangi. To be bent not to be broken. PALMERSTON, v. PHILLIPS.

Floreat crux. May the cross flourish. LADBROOKE, Lynn, co. Norfolk. Crest—A hand holding a cross.

Floreat majestas. Let majesty flourish. BROWN, bt.

Floreant lauri. May the laurels flourish. LOWRY.

Floreo in ungue leonis. I bloom in the lion's claw. KING.
Crest—A lion ramp. holding in its claw a rose, the emblem of strength and beauty.

Flores curat Deus. God careth for the *flowers.* FLOWERS.
Crest—A hand holding a rose and thistle.

Floret qui laborat. He is prosperous who labours. ROSS.

Floret qui vigilat. He is prosperous who is vigilant. SMITH.

Floret virtus vulnerata. Wounded virtue flourishes. FLOYER.

Flourish. ROSE. *Crest*—A rose.

Fluminis ritu ferimur. We *rush* on like a *brook.* RUSHBROOKE.

Foi, roi, droit. Faith, king, right. LYNES.

Foi en loyalté. Faith in loyalty. D'ANVERS.

Follow me. BREADALBANE, m. CAMPBELL, bt. GURWOOD.

Fons et origo. The *Fountain* and source. LA FOUNTAINE, bt.

For aedel daad. For a noble action.

> Inscription on the reverse of the Danish medal granted for noble actions.
> The obverse contains a portrait of the king.

For-d-ward. STRACHEN, bt.

For liberty. MACRE.

> " The land we from our fathers had in trust,
> And to our children will transmit or die :
> This is our maxim, this our piety ;
> And God and nature say that it is just."—WORDSWORTH.

For my country. JOBLING.

For my Duchas. GRANT.

For right. STIRLING, of Denchray.

For right and reason. GRAHAM. KING.

For security. ROBERTOUN, of Ernock. STEEDMAN.

For sport. ROSE-CLELAND. *Crest*—A falcon on a glove.

Force avec vertu. Strength with virtue. LEIGH, of West Hall.

ꝼorꝺꞷarꝺ. BALFOUR.

Foresight. HAMBROUGH, of Steephill Castle, Isle of Wight.

Foresight is all. LIDDERDALE, of St. Mary Isle, Scotland.

Forget me not. CAMPBELL.

Forget not. CAMPBELL, of Auchinbreck, bt.

Forma flos, fama flatus. Beauty is a flower, fame a breath.
BAGSHAWE, of Wormhill, co. Derby.

> There is a bugle-horn between three roses in the arms, to which bearing
> this motto refers, as well as to the crest, a cubit arm, issuing out of
> clouds, ppr. holding a bugle-horn, sa. garnished or, within the strings
> a rose both gules.

Fors non mutat genus. Fortune does not change race. MAUGHAN.

Fort et fidèle. Bold and faithful. HEATON-ELLIS.

Fort et loyal. Bold and loyal. SELBY.

Forte escu. Strong shield. FORTESCUE.

Forte en loyauté. Strong in loyalty. DACRE.

Forte et fidèle. Brave and faithful. TALBOT DE MALAHIDE, b.

Forte scutum salus ducum. A strong shield is the safety of
generals. FORTESCUE, e. FORTESCUE. CLERMONT, b.

> Sir Richard, surnamed the Strong (le Fort), saved the life of the Con-
> queror at Hastings, by covering him with his shield (*escu*). In re-
> membrance of this the motto was granted him.

Fortem fors juvat. Fortune favours the bold. MENZIES.

Fortem posce animum. (Juv. Sat. x. 35.) Wish for a strong
mind. CRAMPTON, bt. FYNNEY. PHILLIMORE. HERIOT.
TWISLETON. SAY and SELE, b.

> " Let peace ne'er leave me, nor my heart grow cold,
> Whilst life and sanity are mine to hold."— BLOOMFIELD.

Fortes adjuvat ipse Deus. God himself aideth the brave. DAVENPORT.

Fortes fideles. Brave and faithful. STENHOUSE.

Fortes fortuna juvat. Fortune favours the bold. BLENNERHASSET, bt. BLOOMFIELD, b. DICKSON. DOLLER. MURRAY. TROYTE.

> " Fortes fortuna adjuvat."—TER. *Phor.* i. 4, 26.
> " Fortune th' audacious doth juvare,
> But lets the timidous miscarry."—HUDIBRAS.

Fortes semper monstrant misericordiam. The brave always show mercy. BALDWIN.

Forti et fideli nihil difficile. To the brave and faithful man nothing is difficult. DEANE. M'CARTHY. MUSKERRY, b. O'KEEFE.

Forti favet cœlum. Heaven favours the brave. OSWALD.

Forti fors bona. Fortune is favourable to the bold. WATSON.

Forti nihil difficile. Nothing is difficult to the brave. DISRAELI.

Forti non ignavo. To the brave man, not to the dastard. LYELL. LYLE. LYELL. LYDE.

Fortior leone justus. The just man is stronger than a lion. GOODRICKE, of Ribstone Hall.

> Crest—A demi-lion erm., issuing from a ducal coronet or, holding a battle-axe.

Fortior qui melior. He is the stronger, who is the better man. BUCHAN.

Fortior qui se vincit. He is strongest who conquers himself. POLEY, of Boxted Hall. MADDEN.

Fortiorum fortia facta. The brave deeds of brave men. STARK. STORK.

Fortis atque fidelis. Brave and faithful. SAVAGE, of Dublin.

Fortis cadere, cedere non potest. The brave man may fall, but cannot yield. DROGHEDA, m. MOORE, bt. MOORE, co. Kent and Berks.

> " Call not the royal Swede unfortunate,
> Who never did to fortune bend the knee ;
> Who slighted fear,—rejected steadfastly
> Temptation ; and whose kingly name and state
> Have 'perished by his choice and not his fate !' "—WORDSWORTH.

Fortis cadere, non cedere potest. The brave man may fall, but cannot yield. MOORE.

> " They dare the death, unknowing how to yield ;
> And falling in their rank, still keep the field."—DRYDEN.

Fortis est qui se vincit. He is brave who conquers himself. WOODS.

Fortis est veritas. Truth is strong. ANGUS. BARTON, of Threxton, co. Norfolk. C. of OXFORD. HUTCHON.

Fortis esto, non ferox. Be brave, not ferocious. WINTRINGHAM, bt.

> " This is true courage, not the brutal force
> Of vulgar heroes, but the firm resolve
> Of virtue and of reason."—WHITEHEAD.

Bortis et æquus. Brave and just. LIVINGSTONE, of Aberdeen.
Fortis et astutus. Bold and crafty. POTT, of Bentham.
Fortis et egregius. Bold and excellent. DOWLING.
Fortis et fide. Brave and faithfully. CARFRAE, of Edinburgh.
Fortis et fidelis. Brave and faithful. CLOSE. BETON. BRYAN.
DOUGLAS. DUNBAR. D'ALTON. FINLAY. FINDLAY. FLETCHER.
MAY. HIND. FITZGERALD. ORME. LALOR. MIDDLETON.
Fortis et fidus. Brave and trusty. FLINT. LOUGHNAN.
M'CLAUCHLAN. M'LACHLAN, of Kilchoan. M'LAUCHLAN.
Fortis et hospitalis. Brave and hospitable. MURPHY.
Fortis et lenis. Brave and gentle. CURRY.
Fortis et placabilis. Brave and placable. SCOT, of Bonholm.
Fortis et velox. Strong and swift. WALDRON.
Fortis in arduis. Brave under difficulties. M'DOUGALL.
M'DOWALL. MIDDLETON. LORD. THOMPSON. BEATON.
BETUNE. FINDLAY.

" Vivite fortes ;
Fortiaque adversis opponite pectora rebus."—HOR. *Sat.* ii. 2.

Fortis in bello. Brave in war. CANTILLON DE BALLYLUGE.
Fortis in procella. Strong in the storm. WOODS.

Referring to the oak-tree in the arms.

Fortis in teipso. Brave in thyself. OGLE.
Fortis qui prudens. He is brave who is prudent. ORMSBY.
Fortis si jure fortis. Strong if strong in right. STOCKENSTROM, bt.
Fortis sub forte. The brave under the brave. FITZ-PATRICK.

Crest—A dragon vert, surmounted by a lion, tail extended, sa.

Fortis sub forte fatiscet. The brave shall grow weary beneath
the brave. ROBECK.
Fortis turris mihi Deus. God is my strong tower. O'KELLY.

There is a tower in the arms.

Fortis valore et armis. Strong in courage and arms. HATCH.
Fortissima veritas. Truth is most powerful. KIRKALIE.
KIRKALDY.
Fortiter. Bravely. BEAUMAN, of Wexford. BOSWELL.
CLIPSHAM. ELLIOT, of Harwood. LONGBOTTOM. M'CRAY.
M'ALISTER. M'LACHLAN. WRIGHT. WARRAND.
Fortiter ac sapienter. Bravely and wisely. HORDERN.
Fortiter defendit, triumphans. Triumphing, it bravely defends.
T. OF NEWCASTLE-UPON-TYNE.
Fortiter et celeriter. Boldly and quickly. MATHER, of Lauton.
Fortiter et feliciter. Boldly and fortunately. WHITE.
Fortiter et fide. Boldly and faithfully. BUNTEN, of Kilbride.
Fortiter et fideliter. Boldly and faithfully. ARMITAGE. BRIGGS.
BROWNE, of Browneshill. COX. FALLOUS. NORTON, of
Kings-Norton. O'FALLON. PENNYMAN, bt. PEPERRELL.
WILSON, of Knowle Hall. ORANMORE and BROWNE, b.

Fortiter et honestè. Boldly and honourably. ABNEY.

Fortiter et rectè. Boldly and rightly. DRAKE, bt. RANKIN. ANDERSON.

Fortiter et strenuè. Boldly and earnestly. DEMPSTER. M'LEAN.

> " The brave man is not he who feels no fear,
> For that were stupid and irrational ;
> But he, whose noble soul its fear subdues,
> And bravely dares the danger nature shrinks from."— BAILLIE.

Fortiter et suaviter. Boldly and mildly. OGILVIE, of Milltoun.

> " What would you have ? Your gentleness shall force
> More than your force move us to gentleness."— SHAKSPEARE.

Fortiter, fideliter, feliciter. Boldly, faithfully, successfully. HUTCHINSON. JACKSON. MONCK, v. RATHDOWNE, e.

Fortiter gerit crucem. He bravely supports the cross. ALLAN. DONOUGHMORE, e. HUTCHINSON, bt. TRITTON.

> These families have crosses in their armorial bearings.

Fortiter in re. Bravely in action. NUNN.

Fortiter in re, et suaviter in modo. Firmly in act and gently in manner. BEAUFORT.

Fortiter qui fidè. He acts bravely, who acts faithfully. HAMILTON.

Fortiter qui sedulo. He acts bravely, who acts carefully. KEITH, of Craig.

Fortiter, sed aptè. Boldly, but appropriately. FALCONER.

Fortitudine. With fortitude. BARRY. D'WARRIS. DUERRY-HOUSE. ERSKINE, bt. FAIRLIE-CUNNINGHAME, bt. M'CRAY. M'CRAE. HOBSON. HALL. MOWBRAY. O. OF MARIA THERESA.

> " The martial courage of a day is vain —
> An empty noise of death the battle's roar —
> If vital hope be wanting to restore,
> Or *fortitude* be wanting to sustain,
> Armies or kingdoms."— WORDSWORTH.

Fortitudine et decorè. By boldness and gracefulness. BALLING-HALL.

Fortitudine et ense. By valour and the sword. CROSSDELL.

Fortitudine et fidelitate. By fortitude and fidelity. BROWN. STUCKEY.

Fortitudine et labore. By fortitude and exertion. REID.

Fortitudine et prudentiâ. By fortitude and prudence. HARGREAVES. HERBERT. HACKET. LIGHTON, bt. O'REILLY, of Knock Abbey. POWIS, e. YOUNGE, of Bassingbourn.

Fortitudine vincit. He conquers by fortitude. DOYLE, bt.

Fortitudo. Fortitude. CLARK, of Belford, and Werk.

Fortitudo et fidelitas. Fortitude and fidelity. T. of DUMBARTON.

Fortitudo et justitia invictæ sunt. Fortitude and justice are invincible. MAGUIRE.

Fortitudini. For courage. HOSTE, bt. MILITARY O. OF MARIA THERESA.

Fortuna audaces juvat. Fortune favours the bold. CLEVELAND. COLMORE. CREGOE. BARRON, of Kilkenny.

Fortuna et honos ab alto. Fortune and honour are from above. RYDON.

Fortunâ et labore. By good fortune and exertion. SYM.

Fortunâ favente. With fortune in my favour. FALKINER, bt. PUDSEY.

Fortuna juvat audaces. Fortune favours the bold. BARON.

Fortuna sequatur. Let fortune be attendant. ABERDEEN, e. GORDON. WARREN.

Fortunâ, virtute. By good fortune and valour. BEATH. BEITH.

Fortuna virtuti comes. Fortune the companion of valour. FERGUSON.

Fortunam honestent virtute. Let them make honourable their fortune by their virtue. BRANDRETH.

Fortune and opportunity for ever. O'MULLOY.

Fortune de guerre. The fortune of war. CHUTE.

Fortune helps the forward. CARMICHAEL.

Fortune le veut. Fortune so wills it. CHAYTOR, bt.

> " The power that ministers to God's decrees,
> And executes on earth what Heaven foresees,
> Call'd providence, or chance, or fatal sway,
> Comes with resistless force, and finds or makes her way.
> Nor kings, nor nations, nor united power,
> One moment can retard the appointed hour."— DRYDEN.

orward. CASTLE-STEUART, e. STEWART, of Athenry, bt. QUEENSBURY, m. KER. OGILVIE. OGILVY, bt. CARREL. DOUGLAS. SANDBY. HOWALES. STRACHAN. STIRLING, bt. CAMPBELL. BALFOUR. SPEIR. WEMYSS, e. WARD.

Forward in the name of God. LOTHIAN, m.

> This motto, otherwise spelt "Fordward," is the one originally used by the family of Kerr, which is that of the Marquis of Lothian. However for the last 200 years or thereabouts, and until very lately, "Sero sed serio" has been adopted instead of it, as may be seen in most Peerages. The present Marquis has resumed the ancient motto.

Forward, kind heart. BELL. *Crest*—A winged heart.

Forward ours. SETON, of Culbeg and Tough, Scotland.

Forward without fear. GORDON, of Embo, bt.

Foy. Faith. GILPIN, of Bungay, Suffolk.

Foy en tout. Faith in everything. YELVERTON. SUSSEX, e. SUTCLIFFE.

Foy est tout. Faith is everything. RIPON, e. ROBINSON. BABINGTON.

> This is an expression used by an ancestor of the Babington family, when he was sent by King Henry IV., with six other young knights, on an expedition of danger, and adopted by his descendants as a motto.

Foy pour devoir. Faith for duty. SOMERSET, d. SEYMOUR.

Foy, roi, droit. Faith, king, duty. LYNES, of Tooley Park.

Fragrat, delectat, et sanat. It smells sweet, is pleasing, and healthful. CLELLAND. *Crest*—A rose gules.

Fragrat post funera virtus. Virtue smells sweet after death. CHIESLY.

Frangas non flectes. Thou may'st break, but shalt not bend me. COLLINS. GOWER. GRANVILLE, e. JONES. KIMBER. OWEN. LEVESON. SUTHERLAND, d. WHIMPER.

Frango. I destroy. M'LAREN. *Crest*—A mortar piece.

Frango dura patientia. I break hard things by perseverance. COOPER.

Frappe fort. Strike hard. THACKWELL. WODEHOUSE, b. WODEHOUSE.

Frappez fort. Strike hard. NETHERWOOD.

Fratres habitent inter se concordes. (Ps. cxxxiii.) Let brethren dwell together in unity. JOSEPH.

Free. SCOTT.

Free for a blast. CLERK, bt. CLARK, of Courie Castle. PEN-NYCOCK. RATRAY, of that Ilk.

> The barony of Penicuik, the property of Sir G. Clerk, bt., is held by the following tenure. The tenant is bound, whenever the king comes to hunt on the Borough Muir, near Edinburgh, to sit upon a large stone, called the Buckstone, and blow three blasts on his horn. Hence the motto.

Frere *ayme* frere. *Frere* love thy brother. FRERE.

Fronti nulla fides. There is no trusting a countenance, or appearances. CRIPPS.

Fructu arbor cognoscitur. (Matt. vii. 16.) The tree is known by its fruit. PURTON.

Fructu noscitur. It is known by its fruits. NEWBIGGING.

> *Crest*—A date-tree fructed ppr.

Fructum habet charitas. Charity hath fruit, *i.e.* satisfaction or pleasure. BUCKSTON.

Fugit hora. The hour flies. FORBES. *Crest*—An hour-glass.

> " Quod adest, memento
> Componere æquus. Cætera fluminis
> Ritu feruntur."—HOR.

> " Improve the present hour, for all beside
> Is a mere feather on a torrent's side."—COWPER.

Fugit irrevocabile tempus. Irrevocable time flies. SHADFORTH.

> *Crest*—A lion resting his paw upon an hour-glass.

> " Ille potens sui
> Lætusque deget, eum licet in diem
> Dixisse, Vixi ; cras vel atrâ
> Nube polum pater occupato,
> Vel sole puro : non tamen irritum
> Quodcunque retrò est, efficiet ; neque
> Diffinget, infectumque reddet,
> Quod fugiens semel hora vexit."—HOR. *Car.* iii. 29, 41.

Fugite fures omnes. Fly all ye thieves. JOHNSON, of Wilmslow.

Fuimus. We have been. AILESBURY, m. BRUCE. ELGIN, e. SANFORD. KENNEDY. WERE, of Wellington. EVERS.

> We have been glorious in another day."—BYRON.

Fuimus et sub Deo erimus. We have been, and we shall be under God. COHAN. HOLLAND.

Fulget virtus. Virtue shines bright. BELL.

Fulget virtus intaminata. Unspotted virtue shines bright. BELCHES.

Furor arma ministrat. (Virg. *Æn.* i. 150.) Rage furnishes arms. BAYNES, bt.

Furth fortune. MURRAY, of Edinburgh.

Furth fortune, and fill the fetters. ATHOL, d. DUNMORE, e. GLENLYON, b. MURRAY, bt. MURRAY. STEWART.

> During the reign of one of the early Scottish kings a robber was in the habit of plundering the country. One of the Murrays, ancestor of the Duke of Athol, undertook to put a stop to the annoyance, and, as he was setting out, the king is reported to have said to him, "(Go) forth, (good) fortune (attend you), and (may you) fill the fetters (with your captive)."

Futurum invisibile. The future is inscrutable. BEVILLE.

> " Prudens futuri temporis exitum
> Caliginosâ nocte premit Deus :
> Ridetque, si mortalis ultra
> Fas trepidat."—HOR. *Car.* iii. 29, 29.

Fy ngobaith sydd yn nuw. My hope is in God. CARNE.

Fy nhy'n unig. My house alone. POWELL.

Fy nuw a chymru. My God and Wales. PHILIPPS. WALTERS.

G

Galea spes salutis. Hope is the helmet of salvation. CASSELS. DUDLEY.

> " Let us, who are of the day, be sober, putting on the breast-plate of faith and love; and for an helmet, the hope of salvation."—1 *Thess.* v. 8.

ᵹall njabaᴄ abu, sometimes ᵹall nuaᴅ abu. The swarthy stranger defying, or the red stranger defying. BURKE. DE BURGOS.

> Many of the Burkes took the name of Gall or Gauls, *i.e.* Stranger. The second form of the cry is the more likely to be correct, and to be adopted from Richard the red earl.

Game to the bone. NIXON. *Crest*— A game-cock.

Gang forrit. KENNEDAR.

Gang forward. STIRLING, bt. STIRLING, of Achoyle. KEIR, &c.

Gang through. STERLING.

Gang warily. DRUMMOND.

Garde. Watch. M'KENZIE.

Garde bien. Watch well. CARRICK. MONTGOMERY.

Garde la foi. Keep the faith. KENSINGTON, b. RICH, bt.

Garde la foy. Keep the faith. DE LA BECHE.

Garde la loi. Keep the law. SLATOR.

D

Garde le roy. Defend the king. LANE, of King's Bromley.

> This motto was assumed by Col. John Lane of Bentley and Hyde, in commemoration of the distinguished services rendered by his father, himself, brother, and sister, to Charles II., whom they concealed and helped on his way after the battle of Worcester. For these services a special augmentation to their arms was granted to the family, and pensions assigned to the two brothers and sister, which however soon fell into arrear.

Garde ta bien aimée. Protect thy well-beloved. MAZE.

> Ma-z-Aimée in the Romance tongue signifies "My well beloved," and of this *maze* seems to be a contraction, as is also *mse,* which in Provence means mistress. To this derivation the motto appears to refer.

Gardez. Beware. CAVE, bt.

> This motto has the same signification with "Cave," the imperative of *caveo,* alluding to the name.

Gardez bien. Watch well. EGLINTON, e. LIVERE. MONT-GOMERY, co. Donegal, bt. MONTGOMERY, of Stanhope, bt.

Gardez la croix. Keep the cross. WARD, co. Wilts.

Gardez l'honneur. Preserve honour. BROADLEY, bt. HANMER.

Gardez la foy. Keep the faith. POULETT, e. DYMOCKE, temp. Hen. VIII.

Gardez le capron. Preserve Capron. HOLLIST.

> In allusion to the former name of this family, which was Capron.

Gare la bête. Beware of the beast. GARBETT.

> A play on the name, and in allusion to the griffin in the arms.

Gaude, Maria Virgo ! Rejoice, O Virgin Mary. COOPERS' COMP.

Gaudebunt campi, et omnia quæ in iis sunt. (Ps. xcvi. 12.) Let the fields rejoice and all that therein is. CAMPI.

Gaudeo. I rejoice. BROWN, bt. BROWNE, of Westminster.

Gaudere et epulari oportet. It is fitting to rejoice and feast. STALYING.

Gaudet luce. He rejoices in the light. GALTON, co. Warwick.

> *Crest* — On a mount vert an eagle em., looking up at the sun or, its claw resting on a fleur-de-lis gu.

Gaudet tentamine virtus. Virtue exults in the trial. DART-MOUTH, e. LEGGE.

Gaudium adfero. I bring good tidings. CAMPBELL.

> *Crest* — A dove with olive-branch.
> "The dove her resting-place hath found ;
> Glory to God,—deliverance to mankind!"

Gauge and measure. EDMINSTON.

> *Crest* — A hand drawing a semicircle with a compass ppr.

Generositate. By generosity. NICOLSON, bt. NICHOLSON.

Generosus et animosus. Generous and courageous. GLENNON.

Generosus et paratus. Generous and prepared. HARWOOD.

Generosus nascitur non fit. The gentleman is born not made. WHARTON.

Genitum se credere mundo. To believe oneself born for the world. SAUNDERS.

Genti æquus utrique. Worthy of both families. BOOTH-GORE, bt.

This motto asserts that the head of this family is the worthy representative of the two families of Gore and Booth.

Gesta verbis præveniunt. Their deeds go before their words. ECKLEY. HARCOURT. SWANSTON. WOODCOCK.

Ghuznee. KEANE, b.

The first baron of this family commanded the forces which captured Ghuznee during the expedition of the British into Cabul.

Ʒſlla an a-naɱaſb abú! In Latin "Vir super hostes." The literal English is, "A youth over his enemies defying" or in "defiance." O'DONOVAN.

In the family of O'Donovan of Banlaghan, an ancient Irish dagger, much resembling a dirk, and called a Dadagh, is preserved as an heirloom, and to the successful use of this by the chief of the O'Donovans allusion is made in the motto. The circumstances were as follows: Clancarty, M'Carty Reagh, and O'Donovan went with their forces into Limerick to plunder as was their wont, and brought back a considerable booty to Clancarty's castle of Blarney. Clancarty wished to treat his two companions as he had treated M'Carty Reagh on a former occasion, and to drive all the cattle into his own bawn. This was immediately opposed by O'Donovan, who in the scuffle which ensued, threw down Clancarty, and wresting from his hand the Dadagh, which he had drawn against him, slew him on the spot, and then divided the spoil with M'Carty

Give and forgive. ANDREWS.

" Æquum est
Peccatis veniam poscentem reddere rursus."—HOR. *Sat.* i. 3, 74.

Give the thankys that are due. PLUMER, of Gilston.

Giving and forgiving. BIGGAR, of Wolmet.

Gladio et arcu. With sword and bow. STUBBER.

Gladio et virtute. By the sword and by valour. GARSTIN.

Gloria Deo! Glory to God. CHALLEN, of Shermanbury. HENN.

Gloria Deo in excelsis. (Luke, ii. 14.) Glory to God in the highest. LEAKE.

Gloria calcar habet. Glory has a spur. KNIGHT, of Clopton.

This motto is an allusion to the golden spurs assumed by the esquire when the order of knighthood was conferred upon him as a mark of honour; and asserts by implication that glory (*i.e.* the man who has done glorious deeds) is spurred, or, in other words, is a knight. In the arms is a golden spur.

Gloria in excelsis Deo. Glory to God on high. KILLOCK.

Gloria finis. Glory is the end. BROOKE.

Gloria non præda. Glory, not plunder. MURRAY, of Lochnaw.

Gloria Patri. Glory to the Father. DEWAR.

Gloria virtutis merces. Glory is the reward of virtue. ROBERTSON, of Auchleeks.

" Vix invenitur, qui, laboribus susceptis periculisque aditis, non quasi mercedem rerum gestarum desideret gloriam."—CIC. *de Off.* 1, xx. 13.

Gloria virtutis umbra. Glory is the shadow of virtue, *i.e.* its constant attendant. ETERS. LONGFORD, e. PAKENHAM.

Gloria sat Deus unus. God alone is sufficient glory. WESTON.

Gloria soli Deo. Glory to God alone. PENRUDDOCKE, of Compton Park.

> This motto, attributing all honour to God, is borne by the Penruddocke family, well known for its piety and valour. Another motto "Deus meus esto in pace prælioque" (Be thou my God in peace and in battle), is found under the Penruddocke arms on a portrait still preserved at Compton Hall, and denotes a disposition to rely upon, as the other does to praise, the Divine being.

Gnaviter. Skilfully. ANDERSON, of Broughton, bt.

Go, and do thou likewise. (St. Luke, x. 37.) COLSTON.

> This motto is borne by the Colston family in commemoration of the eminent philanthropist Edward Colston, of Bristol, of whom it may be said, in the words of Shakspeare,—
>
> > " His life was gentle, and the elements
> > So mixed in him, that Nature might stand up
> > And say to all the world, 'This was a man!'"

Go on, and persevere. NICHOL.

Go on, and take care. THOMPSON, co. York.

Go straight, and fear not. LE HART.

Go through. BRENTON, bt.

God be guide. KENNEDY.

God be my bede, i.e. God be my aide. BEEDHAM.

God be my guide. BLAIR. BUTLER. GLENGALL, e.

God be our friend. STAPLE MERCHANTS' COMP.

God be our good guide. RUSSIA MERCHANTS' COMP.

God can raise to Abraham children of stones. PAVIOURS' COMP.

> Ὅτι δύναται ὁ Θεὸς ἐκ τῶν λίθων τούτων ἐγεῖραι τέκνα τῷ Ἀβραάμ.
> — *St. Luke*, iii. 8.

God careth for us. MITFORD, of Pitshill.

> " Who art thou that doubtest to cast all thy care, all thy burthen upon God who is wiser than thou to provide, kinder to show pity, mightier to save?"—JEREMY TAYLOR.

God caryth for us. PITS.

God feeds the crows. (Job, xxxviii. 41.) CRAWFURD.

God for us. DOUGLAS.

God fried. (Gott-friede.) The peace of God. GODFREY, bt.

God give grace. TAIT.

God gives increase. (1 Cor. iii. 6.) BALFOUR, bt.

God giveth the victory. SIMON.

> " Thine, O Lord, is the victory and the majesty."—1 *Chron.* xxix. 11.

God grant grace. GROCERS' COMP.

God grant unity. WHEELWRIGHTS' COMP.

> > " Have mercy, Lord, on each
> > And all, for all men need it equally!
> > May peace, and industry, and commerce, weld
> > Into one land all nations of the world,
> > Rewedding those the deluge once divorced."—BAILEY.

God guide all. LESLY, of Aberdeen.

God in his least creatures. SILK TROWERSTERS' COMP.

God is all. FRASER, of Fraserfield.

God is love. (1 John, iv. 8.) WESLEY.

God is my defender. BREAME.
" Yea, the Almighty shall be my defence."—*Job*, xxii. 25.

God is my safety. CRAW, of Nether-Byer.

God is our spring.

God is our strength. IRONMONGERS' COMP.

God me guide. CRICHTON, of Easthill.

God my trust. MASON, of Necton Hall, co. Norfolk.
" I plant my foot upon this ground of trust,
And silence every fear with —God is just."—COWPER.

God send grace. ERNE, e. DALRYMPLE. CRICHTON.

God send me wel to kepe. ANNE OF CLEVES, fourth wife of
Henry VIII.

God shaw the right. CRAUFURD, of Newfield, Drumsog, &c.

God shield the right. CRAWFURD.

God the only founder. FOUNDERS' COMP.

God will provide. (Gen. xxii. 8 and 14.) STEWART.

God with my right. BRYSON. BUCHANAN, of Drumakill.

God with us. (Isa. vii. 14.) GORDON. MOODIE.

Good God increase. GOODALLE.

God's providence is my inheritance. BOYLE.
This motto was adopted by Robert Boyle, who, in the reign of Elizabeth,
raised himself from very humble beginnings to the earldom of Cork.

Gofal dyn duw ai gwared. God will release man from care.
PARRY.

Gogoniant y cleddyf. Glory to the sword. GWYN. GWYNNE.
In the arms are two swords; and the crest is an arm embowed in
armour, holding a sword by the blade-point downwards in bend
sinister.

Good deeds shine clear. MINSHULL.

Goojerat. GOUGH, v.
For an account of this motto see "Barrosa."

Gott mit uns. God with us. H.S.H. LE PRINCE DE PRUSSIA.

Grace me guide. FORBES, b. POWNALL, of Hounslow.

Grace my guide. FORBES.

Gradatim. By degrees. ANDERSON. HOPWOOD. KILGOUR.

Gradatim plena. Full by degrees. BURNSIDE, of Whitlaw.
GORDON. *Crest —* A crescent argent.

Grassagh abú. Graces defying. GRACE (also GERALDINES), of
Courtstoun.

Gradatim vincimus. We conquer by degrees. BROWNE.
CURTIS, bt. DUKE, bt,
The arms of Browne are sa three mallets argent. *Crest —* A mallet, as
in the arms.

Gradu diverso via una. The same way by different steps.
CALTHORPE, b.

Grandescunt aucta labore. The acquirements of industry
render illustrious. A'COURT. HEYTESBURY, b.

Gratâ manu. With a grateful hand. CALL, bt.

Grata quies. Rest is grateful. BEXLEY.
> "Quandoque licebit
> Nunc veterum libris, nunc somno et inertibus horis
> Ducere sollicitæ jucunda oblivia vitæ."—HOR. *Sat.* ii. 6. 60.

Grata sume manu. Take with a grateful hand. BRISCO, of Coghurst. WINNINGTON, bt.
> "The willow that droops by the side of a river,
> And drinks all its life from the stream that flows by,
> In return spends that life in the cause of the giver,
> And shadows the stream from the heat of the sky."—EDMESTON.

Gratia Dei grata. The grace of God is grateful.

Gratia naturam vincit. Grace conquers nature. EDWARDS, bt.

Gratis a Deo data. Given freely by God. SKEEN. SKENE.

Gratitude. BIGLAND, co. Lancaster.

Grato animo. With grateful mind. BARKER. BLAYDS.
> "A grateful mind
> By owing owes not, but still pays, at once
> Indebted and discharged."—MILTON.

Graves *disce mores.* Learn serious manners, or *Graves* learn manners. GRAVES, co. Gloucester.

Gravis *dum suavis.* Grave yet gentle. GRAVES.

Graviter et pié. Gravely and piously. PARK.

Grind well. MARBLERS' COMP., London.

Grip fast. LESLIE, bt. LESLIE, co. Antrim, and Aberdeen. ROTHES, e.
> When Margaret, queen of William I. of Scotland, was crossing a swollen river, she was washed from her horse, and on being seized by the girdle by Bartholomew de Leslyn, the ancestor of the Leslie family, continued to exclaim, as he bore her towards the bank, "Grip fast;" which words she afterwards gave him as a motto.

Gripe griffin hold fast. TRAFFORD, of Trafford Park, bt.
> For account of this, see the other motto of this family, "Now thus."

Grossos qui rodit roditur. GROWSE, of Beldeston, co. Suffolk.
> This motto is thus rendered by the family :—
> "Who biteth sour grapes is bit,
> Who smiteth the Grouse is smit."

Growi hil Gwernimon. Gronow's of the race of princes. Rev. THOS. GRONOW, M.A., Ash Hall, co. Glamorgan.

Guard yourself. MIDDLETON, of Kill Hill.

Gud og Kongen. God and the king. O. OF THE DANEBROG, Denmark.

Guarde la foy. Keep the faith. RICH.

Gwell angau na cywilydd. Better death than shame. LLOYD, of Ferney Hall. MACKWORTH. bt.
> "Here on my bended knee I beg mortality,
> Rather than life preserved with infamy."—SHAKSPEARE.

Gwell angau na gwarth. Death before disgrace. FENTON.

Gwell angeu na chwylydd. Death is preferable to shame. WILLIAMS.

Gwell marw. Better die. PRICE.

H

Ha persa la fide, ha perso l'honore. Faith lost, honour is lost. LEWIS, of St. Pierre.

Habeo non habeor. I hold but am not held. BOOTH.

Habere et dispertire. To have and to share with others. AVELAND, b.

Habet et suam. He hath also his own. SETON VISCOUNT KINGSTOUN.

> This motto was adopted by that branch of the Setons who were created Viscounts Kingstoun in 1650, to denote that, besides their ancestral honours, they had fresh ones of their own.

Hâc ornant. With this they adorn. SCOUGALL.

Crest — A pen.

Hactenus invictus. Hitherto unconquered. CRAWFURD. GALLIGHTLY. GELLATLY.

Hæc aspera terrent. These hardships terrify. MOUBRAY.

Hæc generi incrementa fides. Fidelity (gave) these honours to our race. TOWNSHEND, m.

Hæc lucra laborum. These are the advantages of industry. ROWAND.

Hæc manus inimica tyrannis. This hand is hostile to tyrants. BURRELL, of Knepp Castle, co. Sussex, bt.

> " . . . . Manus hæc inimica tyrannis,
> Ense petit placidam sub libertate quietem."
>
> " This hand, to tyrants hostile ever,
>   Grasps the sword that makes it free,
> And seeks intent their bonds to sever,
>   Gentle rest in liberty."

Hæc manus ob patriam. This hand for my country. MACTIER. SHUCKBURGH, bt.

Hæc olim meminisse juvabit. It will hereafter delight us to remember these things. LEWIS.

Hæc omnia transeunt. All these things pass away. BOURNE.

Hæc præstat militia. This warfare excels. BANNERMAN.

Hallelujah. AYLMER, bt. AYLMER, of Lyons, co. Kildare.

Hallelujah! Hallelujah! Hallelujah! TUITE.

Hardiment et bellement. Boldly and handsomely. STUCKLEY, bt.

Hastings. HERON. HORN, of Bishopwearmouth.

Haud facile emergunt. They do easily rise up. BENNETT.

Haud inferiora secutus. Not having mean pursuits. GERARD.

Haud lege peritior. Not more skilful than the law. READ.

Haud nomine tantum. Not in name alone. BEST.

In allusion to the name.

Haud ullis labantia ventis. Yielding under no winds. IRWIN, of Calder Abbey. IRVING.

Haut et bon. High and good. DONERAILE, v. ST. LEGER.

Have at all. DRUMMOND, of Carlourie.
    Crest— A dexter hand with a curling-stone.

Have faith in Christ. GLENDONING, of Partoun. GLENDONWYN.

Have mercy on us, good Lord ! SITLINGTON, of Wigton.
    "He that made them will have mercy on them."—*Isa.* xxvii. 11.

Have patience and endure. RUSHTON.

Hazard warily. SETON, of Abercorn, bt.

Hazard, zet forward. SETON. WINTON, e.
    This ancient motto of the Seton family (variously written, yet, yit, zet, zit,) is borne by the Lords Seaton and Earls of Winton, of old,—the chiefs of the name—and by many junior branches of the same family. Douglas's *Peerage,* and Wood's edition of it, unaccountably omit this motto in describing the Earl of Winton's arms ; but there is abundant evidence in old engravings, sculptures, &c., to show that it was the favourite motto of the family.

He who looks at Martin's ape, Martin's ape will look at him.
    MARTIN. *Crest*—An ape looking in a mirror.

Health and happiness. KAYE, of Dalton Hall.

Heart and hand. MATHESON.

Heart of oak. WEYLAND, of Woodrising, co. Norfolk.

Heb Dduw heb ddim, Duw a digon. Without God without anything, God is enough. DAVIES. EDWARDS, co. Wicklow. HOPKINS. HUGHES, of Kinmel. JONES, of Ystrad. LLOYD, of Dan-yr-alt, &c. MEREDITH, bt. MEYRICK. MORGAN. MOSTYN, b. WILLIAMS.

Heb Duw heb ddim. Without God we have nothing. PRICE.

Heb nefol nerth, nid sicr saeth. Without heavenly aid no arrow is sure. JONES, of Hartsheath, co. Flint.

Help. FOUNDLING HOSPITAL.
        "Oh ! 'tis a godlike privilege to save,
        And he that scorns it is himself a slave."—COWPER.

Help at hand, brother. MUIRE.

Hic fidus et roboreus. He is trusty and strong. STIRLING.

Hic fructus virtutis. This is the fruit of valour. WALLER, bt.
    Sir Richard Waller, of Groombridge, having taken Charles Duke of Orleans prisoner at Azincour, detained him, during twenty-four years, until his ransom of 400,000 crowns was paid. In remembrance of the friendship which sprung up between the prince and his captor, and possibly of the profit which the latter gained from his prize, the crest of Waller, "a walnut-tree fructed ppr.," received on one of its boughs the fruit of valour, that is, the addition of a shield with the arms of France, viz. az. three fleur-de-lis or, differenced with a label of three points.

Hic labor. This is the difficulty. DEE.

Hic labor, hoc opus. (Virg. *Æn.* vi. 129.) This is the difficulty, this the task. MORTLAKE.

Hic murus aheneus. Let this be your wall of brass. MACLEOD.
    In the arms is a castle triple towered.
        " Hic murus aheneus esto,
    Nil conscire sibi, nulla pallescere culpâ."—HOR. *Ep.* i. 1. 60.

Higher. GALLOWAY.

Hinc ducitur honos. Hence honour is derived. NISBET.

Hinc fortior et clarior. Hence the stronger and more illustrious. MARTIN.

Hinc garbæ nostræ. Hence our sheaves. CUMMIN, of Brunthill.

Arms—Az. a fleur-de-lis between three garbs (sheaves) or. Crest—A hand holding a sickle all ppr.

Hinc honor et opes. Hence honour and wealth. HAY, of Cardenie.

In allusion to the crest, an ox-yoke, erect, in pale with two bows gu.

Hinc illuminabimur. Hence we shall be enlightened. OLIPHANT, of Clasbury, Langtoun, &c.

Crest—The sun in splendour.

Hinc incrementum. Hence comes increase. HAY, of Woodcockdale.

Crest—A cubit arm, ppr. holding an ox-yoke with bows gu.

This motto, as well as "Hinc honor et opes," alludes to the profit derived from agriculture, of which the ox-yoke is an emblem.

Hinc mihi salus. Hence comes salvation to me. PEVERELL, of Hants. MABERLY. SPALDING.

This motto is in allusion to the cross in the armorial bearings of each of these families.

Hinc odor et sanitas. Hence fragrance and health. LIDDEL, of Edinburgh.

Crest—A rose gu. stalked and leaved, ppr.

Hinc origo. Hence our origin. BALNAVES.

Hinc orior. Hence I rise. CAMERON. HERVIE. HOWIE. PATERSON. STEWART, of Dalguise.

Hinc spes affulget. Hence hope shines upon us. INNHOLDERS' COMP.

Hinc spes effulget. Hence hope shines forth. ABERDOUR.

Crest—An anchor and sword in saltire.

Hinc usque superna venabor. Henceforth I will follow after heavenly things. MURRAY, of Philliphaugh, Danesfield, &c.

Hinc vigilo. Hence I watch. PHILIP II. OF SPAIN.

Hindostan. HUSSEY, of Wood Walton, co. Huntingdon.

His calcabo gentes. By these I will trample on the nations. COLCLOUGH.

His fortibus arma. Arms to these brave men. NISBET.

His gloria reddit honores. Glory confers honour on these men. DRUMMOND.

His nitimur et munimur. We are supported and strengthened by these. MACONOCHIE, of Meadowbank.

Alluding to the supporters, two Highlanders attired ppr. in Campbell tartan, each holding in the exterior hand a bow and arrow.

His regi servitium. With these we render service to the king. NEILSON.

Crest—A dexter hand holding a spear erect, to which this motto refers.

His Saladinum vicimus armis. We conquered Saladin with these arms. MINSHULL.

His securitas. In these is safety. BARTON. BARSANE.
Both these families bear an anchor in their arms, to which the motto refers.

His utere mecum. Use these things with me. TWOGOOD.
" Si quid novisti rectius istis,
Candidus imperti ; si non, his utere mecum."—HOR. *Ep.* i. 6. 67.

Hoc age. Do this. PARIS.

Hoc ardua vincere docet. This teaches us to overcome difficulties. WINCHESTER.

Hoc in *loco Deus rupes.* Here God is a rock. HOCKIN.

Hoc majorum virtus. The valour of my ancestors won this.
LOGAN.

Hoc opus. This is the task. DEE, of Mortlake.

Hoc securior. Safer by this. GRIESON, of Lagg, bt. GRIER.
GRIEVE. COLLISON. LOCKHART.
Fetterlocks are borne by all these families.

Hoc virtutis opus. This is the work of virtue. BULWER-
LYTTON, bt.

Hodie non cras. To-day, not to-morrow. MOSTYN. VAUX, b.
BOWYER-VAUX, Great Yarmouth.

Hodie mihi, cras tibi. To-day for me, to-mo. row for thee.

Hold fast. ANCRAM (crest an anchor). DOWNIE. FROME bears
also an anchor. LESLY, a buckle. MACLOIDE. M'LEOD,
SMITH.

Hold fast, sit sure. SADDLERS' COMP.

Holme *semper viret.* Holme always flourishes. HOLME, of
Paull-Holme. *Crest*—A holly-tree.

Hominem te esse memento. Remember that thou art a man.
WYBERGH, of Clifton Hall.

Homo homini vulpes. Man is a fox towards his fellow-man.
WOLSELEY, of Wolseley, bt.

Homo proponit, Deus disponit. Man proposes, God disposes.
STARKEY.

Homo sum. I am a *man.* HOMAN, bt. MANN. MANNS.
Me. —— "Tantumne ab re tua est otii tibi,
Aliena ut cures. eaque nihil quæ ab te attinent ?
Ch. Homo sum : humani nihil à me alienum puto."—TER. *Heaut.*

Hone*sta libertate.* By honourable liberty, or *Hone* support
liberty. HONE.

Honesta peto. I seek honourable things. OLIPHANT.
" Querimus honestum : quod etiam si nobilitatum non sit, tamen
honestum sit ; quodque vere dicimus, etiam si a nullo laudetur,
naturâ esse laudabile."—CIC. *de Off.* i. 4. 9.

Honesta quam magna. How great are honourable things.
WALKER.

Honesta quam splendida. Honour rather than splendour.
BARRINGTON, v. HINE. DICKENS, knt.

Honestas. Honesty. FAAL. GOADIE. GOUDIE
Crest of Faal—A pair of scales.

Honestas et fortitudo.   Honour and courage.   DUNCKERLEY.

Honestas optima politia.   Honesty is the best policy.   GOFF.
GRANGER.   OWEN, bt.   SPARROW, of Redhill.

Honestate vetustas stat.   Ancestry is established by honour.
STEWART, of Edinglassie.

Honestæ gloria fax mentis.   Glory the firebrand of the honourable mind.   PILKINGTON, bt.

Honeste audax.   Honourably bold.   EDINGTOWN.   PARKYNS.
RANCLIFFE, b.   WOLLEY, of Allen Hill.

Honeste, fortiter.   Honourably and bravely.   SMITH.

Honestè vivo.   I live honestly.   HALKET, bt.   HALKETT.

Honesto vivo.   I live by honesty.   HALKET.

Honestum præferre utili.   To prefer the honest to the profitable.
RAIKES, of Welton.

> "Cum id, quod utile videtur cum eo, quod honestum est, comparatur,
> jaceat utilitatis species, valeat honestas."—CIC. *de Off.* iii. 11. 18.

Honestum prætulit utili.   He has preferred honour to profit.
EMLINE.

Honestum pro patriâ.   What is honourable for my country.
HAMILTON.

Honestum utili prefero.   I prefer honour to profit.   M'GELL.

Honestum utili præfer.   Prefer the honourable to the agreeable.
HAMBROUGH, of Steephill Castle, Isle of Wight.

Honesty is better than riches.   RAY-CLAYTON, of Norwich.

Honesty is good policy.   THOMSON, of Edinburgh.

Honesty is the best policy.   THOMAS, of Yapton, bt.

Honi soit qui mal y pense.   Dishonoured be he who thinks ill
of it.   O. OF THE GARTER.

> The story of the foundation of the Order of the Garter has been too often
> recited to need repetition here. Its truth has been questioned by
> Ashmole and many others, on account of its being a mere rumour,
> and because of its intrinsic improbability. Now, although many
> stories founded on rumour are absolutely false, it by no means follows
> that no rumour is founded on fact; and although the authority of
> Polydore Virgil, when unsupported, is of little value, yet there is
> reason to believe that this particular rumour, if a pure invention of
> the worthy chronicler, would have been contradicted both by heralds,
> who doubtless, had they possessed it, would have put forth a more
> sounding tale, and by his numerous noble readers, who, if they
> possessed no other knowledge, were "well up" in all that related to
> arms and chivalry.
>
> As to the strange nature of the ensign of the Order, it may be argued
> that many of the garbs and devices, assumed by knights in honour of
> their elected fair ones, were not less fantastic. Thus, one of the
> heroes of the "Mort d'Artus" figured in a tournament, like Scott's
> Thomas-a-Kent, "in the garb of a lady when boune to her rest," and
> hence, for some time, bore the title of "Knight of the night-gear,"
> and tales of this sort were founded on actual fact. When we consider
> that the fair Chatelaine of Salisbury must have been not a little com-
> promised by the very evident symptoms of that "spark of fine love"
> which Edward manifested for her; it seems noways improbable that
> the chivalrous monarch might, after the awkward accident reported
> to have occurred at the famous ball, give to his new order a motto
> which, while it rebuked those who dared to impugn the fame of the

Countess, might bind all wearers of the garter to defend that fame,
while they defended the legend which their garter bore.

Honneur et patrie. Honour and my country. O. OF THE
LEGION OF HONOUR.

Honneur me guide. Honour guides me. LOUSADA.

Honneur pour objet. Honour for object. PAGE.

Honneur sans repos. Honour without repose. MONTGOMERY.

Honor. Honour. LAWTON.

Honor Deo. Honour be to God. MERCERS' COMP.

" Honour the Lord with thy substance and first-fruits."— *Prov.* iii. 9.
" I extol and honour the King of Heaven."— *Dan.* iv. 37.

Honor et amor. Honour and love. NIBLIE.

Honor et honestas. Honour and honesty. PATRIARCHE.
TREMAYNE.

" Say, what is honour? 'Tis the finest sense
  Of *justice* which the human mind can frame,
  Intent each lurking frailty to disclaim,
  And guard the way of life from all offence
  Suffered or done."— WORDSWORTH.

Honor et veritas. Honour and truth. WALLER, bt.

Honor et virtus. Honour and virtue. AKINS. GROGAN, bt.
MORGAN.

Honor fidelitatis præmium. Honour is the reward of fidelity.
BOSTON, b. IRBY.

Honor post funera vivit. Honour lives after death. BROADLY.

Honor potestate honorantis. Honour is in the power of him
who honours. EDWARDS. KYNASTON.

Honor probataque virtus. Honour and approved valour. FITZ-
GERALD, of Turlough. MACDERMOTT.

Honor sequitur fugientem. Honour follows him who shuns
it. DONEGALL, m.

Honor virtutem coronat. Honour crowns virtues. DAVIES.

Honor virtutis præmium. Honour is the reward of virtue, or
valour. BELL. BOYLE. CORK AND ORRERY, e. HAWTIN.
HAWTYN. HOLE. FERRERS, e. FIELDING. SHIRLEY.

" For gold the merchant ploughs the main,
  The farmer ploughs the manor ;
  But glory is the sodger's prize,
  The sodger's wealth is honour."— BURNS.

Honor virtutis pretium. Honour is the reward of virtue.
MILLS.

Honorantes me honorabo. I will honour those who honour me.
ATTHILL, co. Norfolk. HUNTINGDON, e. MANNSELL.

Honorate, diligite, timete. Honour, love, fear. MOSELEY.

Honorat mors. Death confers honour. BRAGGE. BROIGG.

Honore et amore. With honour and love. RICHARDS.
GRANTHAM, of Ketton. HAMMERSLEY. SOLOSBOROUGH.

Honore et virtute. With honour and virtue. GILLBANKS.

Honore pietas. Piety with honour. WATERS.

Honos alit artes. Honour nourishes arts. GREENHILL.
Hope. Rhode Island, North America.

> Hope—"is heaven all heaven, descending on the wings
> Of the glad legions of the King of kings;
> 'Tis more—'tis God diffused through every part,
> 'Tis God himself triumphant in the heart."—COWPER.

Hope and not rue. OLIPHANT. PRINLIS.
Hope for the best. SISON. SISSON.
Hope on, hope ever.

> 'Εν ίλπισιν χρη τους σοφους ίχειν βιον.—EURIPIDES.

Hope to share. RIDDELL.
Hope well and love all well. BOWER.
Hora è sempre. Now and always. DENYS, bt. FARMER. POMFRET, e.
Hos gloria reddit honores. Glory confers these honours. DRUMMOND, bt.
Hostis honori invidia. Envy is an enemy to honour. DICKENS. HARBOROUGH. PATTISON. SHERRARD. WEGG.
Huic generi incrementa fides. Faithfulness caused the increase of this family. TOWNSHEND, co. Denbigh.
Huic habeo non tibi. I hold it for him, not for thee. BURROUGHS. ELLIS. NEWTON.
Humani nihil alienum. (Ter. *Heaut.* i. 1, 25.) Nothing that relates to man is indifferent to me. TALBOT, e. TALBOT, bt. YOUNG, kt., Garter king-at-arms.
Humilitate. With humility. CARLYSLE.
Hwy peri clod na golud. Fame lasts longer than riches. LLOYD, of Rosindale and Aston.
Hyeme exsuperata. When winter (or the storm) is overpassed. WRANGHAM.

> Evidently alluding to the crest, a dove volant, with an olive-branch in its beak.

Hyeme viresco. I flourish (or am green) in winter. STRODE, of Strode. *Crest*—A savin tree ppr.

I

I abide my time. PENNEFATHER.
I am, I am. RICKETSON.
I am alone. LONE.
I am ever prepared. MACBREID. M'LEVRARD.
I am readie. FRASIER, of Pitcallain.
I am ready. FAIRLEY. FRAZER. MAXWELL, bt. SCOT, of Hundilshope.

I beare in minde. CAMPBELL, of Barbreck.

I beare the bel. BELL, of Rammerscales.

I byde. TAYLOR-GORDON.

I byde it. NISBET, bt. NISBETT, of that Ilk.

I byde my time. CAMPBELL, of Auchmannock. CRAWFURD, of Newfield.

I conquer or die. LUMSDEN.
". . . Horæ
Momento cita mors venit, aut victoria læta."—HOR. *Sat.* i. 47.

I dare. CARNWARTH, e. ADAIR. DALZIELL. DALSIEL. DALYELL.
When the Picts had hanged one of the friends of Kenneth II. of Scotland, he being grieved thereat, offered a reward to whoever would dare to take the body down. A gentleman replied "Dal zell," which in Gaelic means "I dare," and, having succeeded, assumed the body for his arms, and took his own words for his motto.
"I dare do all that may become a man."— SHAKSPEARE.

I Dduw bo'r diolch. To God be thanks. LLOYD, of Bronwydd.

I desire not to want. CRANSTON.

I die for those I love. PATTERSON. STACPOLE. STEWART.

I force no friend, I fear no foe. FARQUHARSON.

I gain by hazard. HAMILTON, of Edinburgh. *Crest*— A ship.

I grow and wither both together. WITHER.

I hope. GORDON. STRALOCH.

I hope for better. BOSWELL, of Dowen.

I hope in God. MACNAGHTEN. M'NAUGHTEN. NAUGHTEN.
"How happy those whose hopes depend
Upon the Lord alone,
For those that trust in such a friend
Can ne'er be overthrown."

I hope to share. NISBET. RIDDELL, bt.

I hope to speed. CATHCART, e. CATHCART.

I live in hope. KINNEAR.

I make sicker. KIRKPATRICK, bt.
Bruce, while yet engaged in the struggle which ended in his obtaining the throne of Scotland, chanced to meet the Red Comyn, a zealous partisan of the English, in the cloisters of the Greyfriars' Church at Dumfries. High words ensued between them, and at length Bruce in his passion felled Comyn to the ground with his dagger. As he was rushing hastily out of the sacred edifice he was met by Kirkpatrick, one of the staunchest of his adherents. who, seeing his agitation, asked him what was the matter; "I doubt," replied Bruce, "that I have slain the Red Comyn." "Doubtest thou?" rejoined the other, "I will make sicker;" and immediately entering the church, despatched the wounded man. So little disgrace was supposed to attach to the deed, that Kirkpatrick's descendants adopted his words for their motto.

I make sure. ESCOTTS. JOHNSTONE. KIRKPATRICK.

I mean well. SHAW, bt. STEWART, bt. SUTCLIFFE. CALLENDER.

I renew my age. GARSHORE. *Crest*— An eagle.
"Thy youth is renewed like the eagle's."—*Ps.* ciii. 5.

I rest to rise. BLAYNEY.

I rise by industry. FOULIS, of Edinburgh.

I saved the king. TORRANCE.
The following explanation of this motto is taken from the Heraldic

Library in Edinburgh :—"Two men of this name saved King Robert Bruce when hard beset by his enemies in the west of Scotland, by rowing him across a river or arm of the sea, hence the motto." The family of Torrance also bears two oars in the arms as commemorative of the same event. This service was rendered to King Robert previously to the battle of Bannockburn, fought in June 1314.

I soar. EDIDGE.

I trow aught. TROWER, of St. Albans.

I trow aright. TROWER.

I trust in God. RICHARDSON. WHEATLY.

"I trust in the mercy of God for ever."—*Ps.* lii. 8.

I wait my time. PORTEOUS.

I will. DAVIS.

I will follow. CAMPBELL.

I will not forget. CAMPBELL, of Ballochyle.

I will secure him. KIRKPATRICK.

For origin of this motto see "I make sicker."

Ich Dien. PRINCE OF WALES.

"The King of Bohemia, who fell at the battle of Crecy, had three ostrich-feathers for crest, and ICH DIEN for motto. The ensign and legend were adopted by the Black Prince of Wales; the words probably on account of their apt allusion to the good service he did on the day of that victory to his royal father and his country; and they have been continued by his successors as a lasting memorial of his triumph."
—BURKE.

Randle Holme deduces the three ostrich-feathers from a totally different source; he asserts that they were the ensign of the Prince of Wales during the independence of that country prior to the invasion of the English. After this event (he adds) the eldest sons of the Kings of England as Princes of Wales, continued the badge ensigned with a coronet, with the motto ICH DIEN, I serve; to express the sentiment that, although of paramount dignity in that country, they still owed allegiance to the crown of England."—*Harl. MS.* 2035.

Ichthys (ἰχθυς, Greek for fish). A word found on many seals, rings, lamps, urns, and tombstones, belonging to the earliest Christian times. Each character forms an initial letter of the following words, Ιησους Χριστος Θεου Υιος Σωτηρ : *i.e.* Jesus Christ the Son of God the Saviour. The picture of a fish is also sometimes engraved in similar works having a mystical meaning.

If God will. SAMSON.

If I can. CAMPBELL COLQUHON, of Killermont.

If need be.

Ignavis nunquam. Never for the idle. JENYNS.

Igne constricto, vita secura. Fire being restrained life is secure. DAVY.

Assumed by Sir Humphry Davy, inventor of the safety-lamp.

I.H.S. (Jesus Hominum Salvator). Jesus the Saviour of men. O. OF THE SERAPHIM, Sweden.

Il buon tempo verra. Bright days will come. JENNINGS, of Hartwell.

Il suffit. It sufficeth. DARKER.

Il tempo passa. Time flies. BOYNTON, bt.

> " Redeem thine hours — the space is brief,
> While in my glass the sand-grains shiver,
> And measureless thy joy or grief
> When Time and thou shall part for ever."—SCOTT.

I'll be wary. FINLAY.

I'll bide Broadalbine. MAXWELL, of Teylling.

I'll deceive no man. HAMILTON, of Somelston.

> " I will tell truth : by grace itself I swear."—SHAKSPEARE.

I'll stand sure. GRANT.

I'll try. NEWBIGGING.

Illœso lumine solem. To behold the sun with sight unhurt.
ROSSLYN, e. WEDDERBURN.

> In allusion to the eagle's head which is the crest.

Illumino. I enlighten. FARQUHARSON, of Houghton.

> *Crest*—The sun rising out of a cloud.

Illustrans commoda vitæ. Illustrating the conveniences of
life. ROYAL INSTITUTION OF GREAT BRITAIN.

Illustribus et nobilitati. For the illustrious and the ennobled.
O. OF THE LION OF LEMBOURG.

Il y a de ma vie. My life is at stake. LIEVRE.

> As "Lièvre" in French means "hare :" this motto connects the name
> with the crest, which is a hare.

Imitari quam invidere. To imitate rather than to envy. CHILD,
of Newfield Hall, Bigelly House, &c. PLEYDELL.

Immaculata gens. An unspotted race. VAUGHAN.

Immersabilis. Not to be overwhelmed. HAMILTON, of Bangour.

Immersabilis est vera virtus. True virtue cannot be overwhelmed. CODRINGTON.

Immersi tremor Oceani. The trembling of the ocean which
flows around. O. OF ST. MICHAEL.

> This motto refers to an old legend, that whenever the enemies of France
> approached the rock of St. Michael, that archangel excited a storm
> which scattered them.

Immota fides. Immoveable faith. THE DUCAL ORDER OF
BRUNSWICK, of HENRY THE LION.

Immota triumphans. Triumphing unmoved. FORNEAULEX.

Immotus. Immoveable. ALSTON, of Herts and Suffolk.

Immutabile, durabile. Immutable, lasting. ROLLAND, of Disblair.

Impavide. Fearlessly. B. BOND-CABBELL.

Impavidum ferient ruinæ. Dangers shall strike me unappalled.
MUNDELL.

> " Si fractus illabatur orbis
> Impavidum ferient ruinæ."— HOR. *Od.* iii. 3, 7.
> *Crest*—A broken orb.

Impegerit fidus. The faithful man may have stumbled.
CONSTABLE.

Impelle obstantia. Thrust aside obstacles. ARTHUR.

Impendam expendar. (2 Cor. xii. 15.) I will spend and be
spent. BURKETT.

Imperat æquor. He rules the sea. MONYPENNY.

Crest—A Neptune on a dolphin.

Imperio. By command. MURRAY, of Broughton.

Imperio regit unus æquo. One only rules with unbiassed
sway. GUNNING, bt.

" Divosque mortalemque turbam
Imperio regit uuus æquo."—HOR. *Od.* iv. 3. 47.

Impetueux. Impetuous. POYNTZ.

Impromptu. In readiness. DUNBAR, of Mochrun.

In alta tende. Aim at things on high. WEBB.

In altum. Toward heaven. ALSTONE.

In ardua. On high. HOARE.

In ardua nitor. I contend against difficulties. HALKERSTON.

In ardua petit. He searches after things difficult of attainment. MALCOLM, of Poltalloch.

In ardua tendit. He reaches towards things difficult of
attainment. M'ALLUM. M'CALLEM. MALCOLM, of Burnfort.

In ardua virtus. Virtue against difficulties. LEATHES, of
Herringflcet. WOLSTENHOLME.

In arduis fortis. Strong in adversity. FORDYCE.

In arduis fortitudo. Fortitude in adversity. HAMILTON.

In arduis viget virtus. Virtue flourishes in adversity. GURDON,
of Letton, Cranworth, and Barnham Broom, co. Norfolk.
GURDON-REBOW. DORIEN. MAGENS.

" Victory is most sure
For him, who, seeking faith by virtue, strives
To yield entire submissiou to the law
Of conscience,—conscience reverenced and obeyed,
As God's most intimate presence in the soul."— WORDSWORTH.

In bello quies. There is peace (*i.e.* it is obtained by) in war.
MURRAY, of Ochtertyre, bt.

In bivio dextra. In a forked path choose the right hand.
ROKEBY.

In caligine lucet. It shines in darkness. BAILLIE, bt.

Crest— An estoile rising out of a cloud.

In candore decus. There is honour in sincerity. CHADWICK,
of Pudleston Court.

In Canopo ut ad Canopum. *i.e.* On board the Canopus, (which
ship he commanded), as at Canopus, (*i.e.* Aboukir, where
was the Canopic mouth of the Nile.) LOUIS, bt.

In certa salutis anchora. On a sure anchor of safety. GILLESPIE.

In cœlo confidemus. We will trust in heaven. HILLS.

In cœlo quies. There is rest in heaven. BEWICKE. BOSCAWEN.
COLDHAM. DOLPHIN, of Eyford. HORLOCK.

This motto, as well as " Resurgam," is frequently used on hatchments
instead of the family motto.

In cœlo spes mea est. My hope is in heaven. MICKLETHWAITE.

> " The grove, the sky-built temple, and the dome,
> Though clad in colours beautiful and pure,
> Find in the heart of man no natural home :
> The immortal mind craves objects that endure :
> These cleave to it ; from these it cannot roam,
> Nor they from it : their fellowship is secure."— WORDSWORTH.

In constantia decus. (There is) honour in constancy. COPPARD.

In copia cautus. Careful amid plenty. DOD, of Edge.

In cornu salutem spero. I trust to the horn for safety. HUNTER.

In cruce confido. I trust in the cross. THRALE.

> " Let the unerring Gospel be your guide ;
> Regard not man, in Christ alone confide."—MARRIOTT.

In cruce et lachrymis spes est. There is hope in the cross and in tears. HINCKS, of Breckenbrough.

> *Crest*—A demi-lion gu. guttée de larmes (i.e. tears) gorged with a collar dancettée ar. the sinister paw resting on an annulet or.

In cruce fides. Faith in the cross. RUDGE. GLENDENING.

In cruce glorior. I glory in the cross. CLIFFE, co. Wexford. DOUGLAS, of Rosehill. PYE.

In cruce salus. In the cross is salvation. AIKEN. ABERCROMBY. BRIGHAM. BOURKE. LANGHOLME. MOUNTEM. MARR. LAWRENCE. TAILOUR. TAILYOUR.

> " The cross !
> There, and there only, is the power to save.
> There no delusive hope invites despair ;
> No mockery meets you, no deception there."— COWPER.

In cruce spero. I trust in the cross. ALLARDIC. BARCLAY.

In cruce spes mea. In the cross is my hope. DE LA FIELD.

In cruce triumphans. Triumphing in the cross. RAFFLES.

In cruce vincam. I shall conquer in the cross. OLDFIELD.

In cruce vinco. Through the cross I conquer. COPLEY.

In crucifixa gloria mea. My glory is in the cross. KNATCH-BULL, bt.

In defence. WILLIAMSON. ALLARDICE, of Dunotter.

In defiance. MACBRAIN. MACBRAIRE, of Tweedhill, &c.

In defence of the distressed. ALLARDICE.

In Deo confido, nil desperandum. Trust in God, nothing is to be despaired of. KELLY.

In Deo confido. I trust in God. KIRKMAN. TOVY. LAWFORD. MOORE.

In Deo est mihi omnis fides. In God is my whole trust. PALMER, bt.

> " I trust in the mercy of God for ever and ever."—*Ps.* lii. 8.

In Deo fides. My trust is in God. CHAPPLE.

In Deo fides, lux in tenebris. Faith in God is light in darkness. HARE.

In Deo fido. I trust in God. MEDLEY.

In Deo mea spes. (Jer. xvii. 19.) My hope is in God. HESKETH, of Gwyrch Castle. NEATE.

In Deo omnia. In God are all things. BLUETT. HUXLEY. REED.

In Deo salutem. Salvation in God. SCOBELL.
"Salvation is of the Lord."—*Jonah*, ii. 9.

In Deo sola salus. The only salvation is in God. GRUNDY.
"Truly in the Lord is the salvation of Israel."—*Jer.* iii. 23.

In Deo solo salus est. Salvation is in God alone. SPARROW.

In Deo solo speravi. In God alone have I trusted. ALLEN.

In Deo solo spes mea. My hope is in God alone. KAY. KEY.

In Deo spero. I place my hope in God. DE SAUMAREZ, b.

In Deo spes mea. In God is my hope. COURAN.

In do bait spair nocht. GRENWOOD.

In Domino confido. (Ps. xi. 1.) I trust in the Lord. ASHETON. CARGILL. COCKBURN. ERSKIN. ERSKINE. NEWDIGATE. M'GILL. WILLIAMS. WALKER. WILLYAMS.
"Yet, then, from all my griefs, O Lord,—
Thy mercy set me free,
Whilst in the confidence of prayer,
My soul took hold of thee."—ADDISON.

In Domino et non in arcu meo sperabo. I will rest my hope on the Lord, and not in my bow. MOLONY, co. Clare.
There is a bow and arrows in the arms, and the crest is an arm embowed in armour, in the gauntlet a dagger.
"I will not trust in my bow, neither shall my sword save me."—*Ps.* xliv. 6.

In dubiis constans. Firm amid dangers. COCKBURN.

In earnest. MARSHALL, of Steadingly, Leeds.

In ferrum libertate ruebant. Through liberty they rushed to the sword. GARDNER.

In fide et in bello fortis. Strong both in faith and war. BAGWELL, of Marlfield. CARROLL, or O'CARROLL, of Ballymore.

In fide, justitia, et fortitudine. Through faith, justice, and fortitude. O. OF ST. GEORGE, of Bavaria.

In God I trust. (Job, xiii. 15.) FRAZER. THOMPSON.

In God is all. FRASER. FRAZER. SALTOUN, b.

In God is all my trust. (Ps. lxxi. 5.) GRANT. PEWTERERS' COMP.

In God is all my hope. PLUMBERS' COMP.

In God is all our trust. BREWERS' COMP. BRICKLAYERS and TILERS' COMP.

In his pride of place. COWIE. *Crest*—A falcon towering.

In hoc plenius redibo. Through this I shall become fuller. MINSHULL, co. Chester.
This alludes to the crescent which is in the crest.

In hoc signo. Under this sign. WOODHOUSE, co. Stafford.
Alluding to the cross which is the crest.

In hoc signo spes mea. In this sign is my hope. D'URBAN. TAAFFE, v.

In hoc signo vincam. Under this sign I shall conquer. O. OF ST. MARY THE GLORIOUS.

In hoc signo vinces. Under this sign thou shalt conquer. ARRAN, e. AISCOUGH. BURTEE, bt. BERRIE. BOOTH, bt. BURKE. CAVAN. D'URBAN. DICKENS. GORE, bt. GLASHAM. GLASBERN. IRONSIDE. KUYFTON. LANGTON, of Newton Park. KNOX, of Belleck Abbey. MACADAM. M'CARLIE. M'KERLIE. MOSSE. NEWLING. O. OF ST. CONSTANTINE. STANHOPE, bt. TAYLOR. TURNEY. WATSON. O'DONNELL, bt.

It is related by Eusebius in his life of Constantine, that when that emperor was about to engage in battle with his opponent Maxentius, A.D. 312, and was putting up earnest prayers for success, he saw, about noon, with his own eyes, in the heavens the trophy of the cross, placed above the sun, consisting of light, with an inscription annexed, *ιν τουτῳ νικα,* "In this conquer." The sign was also seen by his army and greatly encouraged them. The same night Christ appeared to him in a vision, and commanded him to make a standard resembling the sign which he had seen in the heavens. This he accordingly did, adorning the standard with gold and jewels, and terming it the "Labarum." The motto variously modified is used by many families, most of whom also have a cross as part of their armorial bearings.

In hoc spes mea. In this is my hope. GORDON, of Beldorney.

In allusion to the crest, a cross crosslet fetchée or.

In hoc vinces. In this shalt thou conquer. CROSS.

In Jehovah fides mea. In Jehovah is my trust. BRAILSFORD.

In labore quies. In labour is rest, *i.e.* obtained by it. HELYER.

In libertate sociorum defendenda. In defending the liberty of our companions. MACGREGOR.

In lumine luceam. I may shine in the light. THOMPSON.

In malos cornu. My horn against the bad. DADLEY.

There are attires (horns) in the arms.

In medio tutissimus. In the middle path safest. SMITH, of Lydiate.

Safest when you keep the mean, the advice of Apollo to Phaeton.

In medio tutissimus ibis. Thou wilt go safest in the middle. HARRIS.

In medio vitæ summus in morte. In the midst of life we are in death.

"There is but a step between me and death."—1 *Sam.* xx. 3.

In meliora spera. Hope for better things. DONKIN.

In memoriam majorum. In remembrance of our ancestors. FARQUHARSON.

In moderation placing all my glory. FITZHUGH.

In monte Cöeli castra Cöli. On the hill of Cöel (Heaven ?) is the camp of Cöel. KELLY.

Here Cöeli may either denote the ancient name of O'Kelly, or may mean heaven.

In multis, in magnis, in bonis. In many, in great, in good things. BOWES, of Bradley.

In multis, in magnis, in bonis expertus. Experienced in many, in great, in good things. BOWES.

In omnia paratus. Ready for all things. DUNALLY, b. REAY.

In omnia promptus. Ready for everything. RAE, bt.

In pace ut sapiens. In peace as a wise man. SLOPER.

In periculis audax. Bold in danger. MAHER.

In portu quies. There is rest in port. SKELMERSDALE, b. WATKINS. WILBRAHAM, of Cheshire. WILBERFORCE.

In pretium persevero. I persevere for my reward. JENNER.

In promptu. In readiness. DUNBAR, bt. TROTTER.

> According to a family tradition of the Trotters, a brother of Lord Giffard being suddenly sent for by James II. of Scotland, rode from his mansion, which lay at a considerable distance from court, on a fast trotting horse. Having presented himself before the king sooner than he was expected, James asked in surprise how he came there so quickly. "I trotted," said Giffard ; and in remembrance of this reply, and of his zeal, the monarch gave him the name of *Trotter*, with the motto "ready."

In recto decus. Honour in acting right. FERRIER. SCOTT. BRUNSWICK and LUENBURG. SYME. SIMMONS. HOSEASON.

In recto fides. Faith in rectitude. DIXON.

In sanguine fœdus. A covenant by blood. O. OF THE TWO SICILIES. O. OF ST. JANUARIUS, of Naples.

In sanguine vita. Life in the blood. COBBE.

> *Crest* — A pelican's head vulning itself.

In season. WALKINGSHAW, of that Ilk.

In seipso totus teres. Fully furnished in himself. SMITH.

> "Totus teres atque rotundus."— HOR.

In silentio fortitudo. Courage in silence. HARDRESS. THORESBY.

In solo Deo salus. Salvation is in God alone. HAREWOOD, e.

In spe erigi. To be exalted in hope. M. PEDRO DE ZULUETO.

In spe et labore transigo vitam. I pass my life in hope and exertion. MACK.

In sublime. Upwards. REID.

In te, Domine, speravi. (Ps. xxx. 2.) In Thee, O Lord, have I put my trust. ABBS. GREENHILL. HAIRE. LYON, of Auldabar. PRESTWICH. ROUSE. STRATHMORE, e. VALE.

In te fido. I trust in thee. M'LARTY.

In tempestate floresco. I flourish in the tempest. COFFIN. PINE.

> Crest of Pine,— A pine-tree.

In tenebris lucidior. The brighter in darkness. INGLIS.

> *Crest* — A star environed by clouds.

In tenebris lux. Light in darkness. SCOTT.

In the defence of the distressed. ALLARDICE.

In the Lord is all our trust. (Job, xiii. 15.) MASONS' COMP. London.

In the name of God try. WOOLNOUGH, of London.

In the sweat of thy brow shalt thou eat thy bread. (Gen. iii. ver:
19.) GARDENERS' COMP.

In time. HOUSTON, b. HOUSTON. *Crest* — A sand-glass.

> " Redeem thine hours—the space is brief—
> While in my glass the sand-grains shiver,
> And measureless the joy or grief,
> When time and thou shalt part for ever !"— SCOTT.

In trau vast. Firm in fidelity. O. OF THE HOSPITALLERS OF
ST. HUBERT.

In utraque fortuna paratus. Prepared for either good or bad
fortune. COTTON. COMBERMERE, v.

> " Whatever sky's above me.
> Here's a heart for every fate."— BYRON.

In utroque. In both. VALANGE. WALLANGE.

In utroque fidelis. Faithful in either case. CAREY. FALK-
LAND, v. NASH.

In utroque paratus. Prepared in either case. DEACON. BLOME.
ELPHINSTON. MACKENZIE. MURRAY, of Clarendon. AKROYD.

In utrumque. For both. RANKEN.

In utrumque paratus. Prepared for either. MACKENZIE, of
Delvin, bt. CALDECOTT, of Rugby Lodge. LAWFORD.

> " In utrumque paratus ;
> Seu versare dolos, seu certæ occumbere morti."— VIRG. Æn. ii. 61.

In veritate triumpho. I triumph in the truth. BIDDULPH.
GREAVES. MYDDLETON.

In veritate victoria. Victory is in truth. AKROYD, of Bank-
field. HUNTINGDON, e. HASTINGS, bt. ABNEY. HASTINGS,
of Willesley Hall. INGHAM.

> C. F. Abney Hastings also bears the motto, "Fortiter et honeste," for
> Abney. The motto, "In veritate victoria," has been used by many of
> the Hastings family. Sir E. Hastings, younger brother of the Earl of
> Huntingdon, Baron Hastings (ancestor of the present Marquis of
> Hastings, and of Lady Edith Abney Hastings), who joined Queen
> Mary at Framlingham with 6000 horse, and was subsequently created
> Lord Loughborough, bore " Vi sua vincit veritas." " Vincit veritas,"
> and "Victor veritas," have also all been used by members of the
> family ; but gradually the present motto, "In veritate victoria," has
> been principally used.

In via virtuti pervia. In the road which is accessible to
valour. HAMILTON.

In victos. Against the conquered. CRACKNELL.

In virtute et fortuna. In valour and fortune. GARDNER.

In well beware. WOMBWELL, bt.

Incepta persequor. I persevere in what I undertake. WILKINSON.

Incidendo sano. I cure by cutting. KINCAID, of that Ilk.

> Alluding to the bistoury, which forms part of the crest.

Incipe. Begin. BRANTHWAITE.

Inclytus perditæ recuperator coronæ. The famous recoverer of
a lost crown. SETON.

> *Crest*— A man in complete armour on horseback at full speed, holding
> on the point of a sword an imperial crown.

Inclytus virtute. Renowned for virtue. KYAN.
Incoctum pectus honesto. A bosom deeply imbued with honour. SMEDLEY, of Revesby, co. Lincoln.
Inconcussa virtus. Unshaken virtue. BENSON. LANE.
Incorrupta fides. Uncorrupted faith. WHITMORE.
Incorrupta fides, nudaque veritas. Uncorrupted faith and the naked truth. FORDE. MYERS, bt. WASKETT, of Hingham.
Incrementum dat Deus. God gives increase. MOSELEY, of Owsden.
Inde securior. Hence the safer. MURRAY, of Livingston.
    Crest — A hand ppr. holding a fetterlock.
Indignante invidia florebit justus. The just man will flourish in spite of envy. CROSBIE.
Indocilis pauperiem pati. Untaught to suffer poverty. MERCHANTS OF BRISTOL.
Indubitata fides. Undoubted faith. REYNELL.
Indulge fortune. BOVER.
Indure furth. LINDSEY.
Industria. By industry. CALROW. CRIERIE. FETTES. FIDDES. GENTLE. KELTIE. M'CRIRE. OGILVY. PEEL, bt.
    "*Industry!* rough power!
    Whom labour still attends, and sweat and pain;
    Yet the kind source of every gentle art,
    And all the soft civility of life!
    Raiser of human kind!"—THOMSON.
Industriâ atque fortunâ. By industry and good fortune. LAWRIE.
Industria ditat. Industry enriches. SIDESERF; *Crest* — A cornucopia. REATH. WAUCHOP, of Niddry; *Crest* — A garb. WAUGH. VANDERPLANT.
Industria et labore. By industry and labour. M'GASSOCK.
Industria et probitate. By industry and probity. HIVES. WASHBOURNE. BROWNE, of Ebbw Vale, co. Monmouth.
Industria et spe. By industry and hope. BARGE. CLAXTON. FENOUILLET. HORROCKS. SAGE. WARDEN.
Industria et virtute. By industry and virtue. BEAVER.
    This motto refers to the name and to the beaver in the crest, the well-known emblem of industry.
Industria murus. Industria is a protection. THOMSON.
Industria permanente. By unremitting industry. NEAVE.
Industria, virtus, et fortitudo. Industry, valour, and fortitude. SMELLIE, of Slindon, co. Sussex.
Industriæ munus. The gift of industry. LEECHAMAN.
Industry the means, plenty the result. MARYLAND, North America.
Inébranlable. Not to be shaken. ACLAND.
Inest clementia forti. Mercy is inherent in the brave. GENT. MAULE.
Inest jucunditas. There is cheerfulness in it. ELLIOT.
    Crest — A hand holding a flute.

Ingenio et merito. By ability and desert. GROUT.

Ingenio et viribus. By skill and strength. HUDDLESTONE.

Ingenium innumerata labi. My disposition is to glide along unnoticed. LAWRIE.

Ingenuas suscipit artes. He fosters the polite arts. LONG, of Carshalton.

Ingratis servire nefas. It is impossible to serve the ungrateful. MARTIN.

Inimicus inimico. Hostile to an enemy. NAGLE.

Initium sapientiæ est timor Domini. The fear of the Lord is the beginning of wisdom. MARTIN, of Long Melford, bt. (Prov. i. 7. Ps. cxi. 10.)

Innixus vero validus. He that rests upon the truth is strong. LYON.

Innocence surmounts. GULLAND.

Innocens non timidus. Innocent but not fearful. ROWE.

Innocent and true. ARBUTHNOT, bt.

Innocentia securus. Secure in innocence. JACKSON, bt.

> " Majorum facta fortia, mihi spes omnes in memet sitæ quas necesse est et virtute et innocentia tutari : nam alia infirma sunt."—SALL. *Bell. Jug.*
>
> " The silence often of pure innocence
> Persuades, when speaking fails."—SHAKSPEARE.

Innocue ac provide. Harmlessly and providently. ARBUTHNOT, of Montrose. LAPINGTON.

Insperata floruit. It has flourished unexpectedly. WATSON.

> This motto refers to the tree torn up, yet sprouting again, which forms part of the crest.

Inservi Deo et lætare. Serve God and rejoice. HOWARD, bt. WICKLOW, e.

> " Remote from man, with God he passed the days,
> Prayer all his business, all his pleasure praise."—PARNELL.

Insignia fortuna paria. My desire and my fortune are matched. DE LA FIELD.

> This motto, as well as an honourable coat, is said to have been given to an ancestor of this family, who was created a count of the Holy Roman Empire after the battle of Zenta.

Insiste firmiter. Persevere resolutely. MOORSIDE.

Insolitos docuere nisus. (Hor. *Car.* iv. 4. 8.) Taught unwonted exertions. BABINGTON.

> *Crest*—Out of a ducal coronet a demi-eagle.
>
> Horace, in the ode from which this line is taken, compares the courage of the youthful Drusus to that of a recently-fledged eagle.

Insontes ut columbæ. Innocent as doves. FRANCIS.

Instat vi patriæ. He rushes on with the strength of his country. TICHBURN.

Insult me not. M'KENZIE, of Applecross, co. Ross.

Intaminatis fulget honoribus. (Hor. *Car.* iii. 2, 17.) He shines with unstained honours. SETON. WINTON, e.

Intaminatis honoribus. With unstained honours. Fitz-
Herbert. St. Helens, b.

" Virtus repulsæ nescia sordidæ
Intaminatis fulget honoribus."—Hor. *Car.* iii. 2, 17.

Integra mens augustissima possessio. An honest mind is the
most glorious possession. Blayney, b.
Integritas semper tutamen. Integrity is always a safe-guard.
Harries.
Integritas tuta virus non capit. A safe integrity does not take
poison. Holl.
Integritate et fortitudine. By integrity and bravery. Jones.
Integritate sola. By integrity alone. Marrable.
Intemerata fides. Faith undefiled. Aberdeen. Robertson.
Intento in Deum animo. With mind intent on God. Bosvile.
Inter cruces triumphans in cruce. Amongst crosses, triumphing
in the cross. Dalton.

Arms—Az. semée of cross crosslets, a lion ramp. guardant ar.

Inter hastas et hostes. Among spears and enemies. Powell.
Inter lachrymas micat. It shines amidst tears. Blunt.

Crest—The sun in glory, charge on the centre with an eye issuing tears.

Inter primos. Among the first. Hopkins.
Inter utrumque tene. Keep between the two. Jemmett.
Interna præstant. Inward things are best. Arbuthnot.
Interno robore. By internal strength. Mytton.
Intrepidus et benignus. Intrepid and benign. Mackennal.
Invia virtuti via nulla. No road is inaccessible to virtue.
Seton.
Invia virtuti pervia. Pathless ways may be trodden by valour.
Hamilton.
Invicta labore. Unconquered by labour. Armstrong.
Invicta veritate. By invincible truth. Abell.
Invicta fidelitas præmium. The reward of invincible fidelity.
Hereford, e.
Invictus. Unconquered. Cracknell.
Invictus arduis. Unconquered in difficulties. Harrison.
Invictus maneo. I remain unconquered. Armstrong, of
Gallen. Brockett. Ballycumber, of Garry Castle. Inglis.
Invidia major. Superior to envy. Drago. Inwards.

" Invident honori meo : ergo invideant labori, innocentiæ, periculis etiam
meis : quoniam per hæc illum cepi."—Sall. *Bell. Jug.*

Invidere sperno. I scorn to envy. Davies. Saunders.
Invigila sic vinces. Watch, so shalt thou conquer. Price.
Invita fortuna. Though fortune be unwilling. Knightley, bt.
Invitum sequitur honor. Honour follows one who desires it
not. Donegal, m. Chichester. Templemore, b.
Ipse amicus. I am my own friend. Baron.
Ira leonis nobilis. The anger of the lion is noble. Croome.

Iram leonis noli timere. Fear not the anger of the lion. LONG.
　　In allusion to the lions in the arms.

Irrevocabile. Irrevocable. BRUCE, of Kinross. BENNETT.

Irrideo tempestatem. I laugh at the storm. WOOD, of Mount
　　House. *Crest*—An oak-tree on a mount.

Irrupta copula. The tie unbroken. MORRIS.

Ita. Thus. COCKBURN.

Iterum, iterum, iterumque. Again, again, and again. FOOTE.
　　This motto was used by the celebrated Samuel Foote, on his carriage,
　　when he luckily came into the possession of a third fortune after
　　having squandered away two.

Iterum virescit. Again it grows green. BISSET.
　　　　Crest—The stump of a tree sprouting.

Ito tu et fac similiter. Go thou and do likewise. (St. Luke, x.
　　37.) OLIVER.

It's good to be loun. FORRESTER.

J

J'ai bonne cause. I have good reason. BATH, m. THYNNE.

J'ai bonne esperance. I have good hope. CRAIG. M'KEAN.

J'ai espoir mieux avoir. I hope for better things. DINE.

J'ai la clef. I have the key. GRIEVE. GRIVE.
　　　　There are fetterlocks in the arms.

J'aime à jamais. I love for ever. JAMES.
　　　　Crest—A dolphin.
　　This motto evidently contains a play upon the name, as well as in all
　　probability an allusion to the crest, for, according to the ancient poets
　　and writers of natural history, the dolphin entertained a deep and
　　enduring affection for the human species.

J'aime l'honneur qui vient par la vertu. I love the honour
　　which is attained through virtue. O. OF THE NOBLE PASSION.

J'aime la liberté. I love liberty. MUSSENDEN. RIBTON, bt.

J'aime mon Dieu, mon roi, et ma patrie. I love my God, my
　　king, and my country. KIRVIN.

J'aspire. I aspire. DEVIZMES.

J'avance. I advance. BARTRAM. EAST. KER, of Abbot Rule.

J'ay bonne cause. I have good reason. BOTFIELD.

J'ay ma foi tenu à ma puissance. I have kept my faith as far
　　as I am able. CROKER.

J'ayme à jamais. I love for ever. JAMES, bt.

J'espère. I hope. SWINTON, of Swinton. HAMILTON.
　　　　" Unfading hope ! when life's last embers burn,
　　　　When soul to soul, and dust to dust return,
　　　　Heaven to thy charge resigns the awful hour !
　　　　O ! then thy kingdom comes, immortal power !"—CAMPBELL.

J'espère bien. I hope well. CREW, of Crew, Crewcombe, &c.
Jam jam. Now now, *i.e.* forthwith. BUXTON.
Jamais abattu. Never beaten down. LINDOE.
Jamais arrière. Never behind. DOUGLAS, b. DOUGLAS, bt.
 DOUGLAS, of Whitriggs. FRYER. HAMILTON. SELKIRK, e.
Jam transit hyems. Now winter is passing. HAGUE.
 There is a primrose in the arms.
Je crains Dieu. I fear God. WHITEHURST.
Je defie fortune. I defy fortune. DELVES.
Je dis la vérité. I tell the truth. PEDDER, of Ashton Lodge.
 " I am as true as truth's simplicity,
 And simpler than the infancy of truth."— SHAKSPEARE.
Je feray ce que je diray. I'll do what I say. JEFFERAY.
Je gardye bien. I am careful. PICKERING.
Je le feray durant ma vie. I will do it so long as I live. FAIR-
 FAX, of Gilling Castle.
Je le tiens. I hold it. AUDLEY, b. TOUCHET.
Je les maintiendrai. I will maintain them. BISS.
Je luis imperceu. I shine unseen. LEY.
Je maintiendrai. I will maintain. WILLIAM III. and MARY.
 MALMESBURY, e. NESBITT, of Lismore.
Je me fie en Dieu. I trust in God. BLOIS, bt. PLYMOUTH, e.
 WINDSOR.
Je me souviendrai. I will remember. TATTNALL.
Je me tourne vers l'occident. I turn towards the west. WESTROPP.
Je m'en souvien-dray. I will remember it. AVERQUERQUE.
Je mourrai pour ceux que j'aime. I will die for those I love.
 BLENKINSOPP. COULSON.
Je ne change qu'en mourant. I change but in death. SALVIN.
Je ne cherche qu'ung. I seek but one. COMPTON, Northampton, m.
 The crest is on a mount vert, a beacon or inflamed ppr., on it a label
 inscribed " Nisi Dominus." Thus the mottoes and the crest together
 denote that the Lord is the only light that their owner seeks.
Je ne puis. I cannot. DELVES, of Cheshire and Lancashire.
Je n'oublierai jamais. I will never forget. BRISTOL, m. HER-
 VEY, bt. HERVEY, of Killiane.
Je n'oublierai pas. I will not forget. BALDWIN.
Je pense. I think. WEYMISS, e.
Je pense à qui pense plus. I think of him who is the most
 thoughtful. ROSE.—CLELAND.
Je pense plus. I think the more. MARR, e.
Je recois pour donner. I receive to distribute. INNES.
Je suis petite, mais mes picqûres sont profondes. I am small,
 but my sting strikes deep. O. OF THE BEE.
Je suis prest. I am ready. FRASER, bt. TYTLER.
Je suis prêt. I am ready. FARNHAM, b. FRASER. LOVAT.
 MAXWELL. SIMPSON.

Je suis veillant à plaire. I am watchful to please. SAUNDERSON.

Je tans grace. I have mercy. SIR F. BRYAN, temp. Hen. VIII.

Je tiendray ma puissance par ma foi. I will maintain my power by my faith. CROKER.

Je trove bien. I find well. BARNARDISTON.

Je veux de bonne guerre. I wish fair play. WENLOCK, b.

Je veux bonne guerre. I wish fair play. THOMSON. THOMPSON.

Je veux le droit. I desire that which is just. DUCKETT.

Je veux le droict. I desire that which is just. DUCKETT, bt.

> Ducket, of Coningsby, co. Lincoln, bt. bears also the motto, "Malo mor quam fœdari," "Rather death than disgrace," which he gets from the Jacksons, of Richmond, Yorkshire.

Je vive en esperance. I live in hope. AKERS.

Je vive en espoir. I live in hope. ROUS. STRADBROKE, e. STEPHENS.

Je voil droyt avoyre. I will have justice. WHARTON.

Je voil droit avoir. I will have right. HUNTLEY.

Je voys. I see. JOSSEY, of Westpans. *Crest*—An eye.

Jehova portio mea. The Lord is my portion. MERCER.

> "God is my portion," *Ps.* lxiii. 10. "Thou art my portion, O Lord!" *Ps.* cxix. 57. "The Lord is my portion," *Lam.* iii. 34.

Jehovah-Jireh. The Lord will provide. GRANT, of Monymusk, bt.

> יְהוָה יִרְאֶה. *Gen.* xxii. 14. "And Abraham called the name of that place Jehovah-jireh, The Lord will see," *i.e.* The Lord will take care that everything necessary shall be done for those who trust in Him.

Jesu, esto mihi Jesus. Jesus, be Jesus unto me. SWALE.

Jesus seul bon et bel. Jesus alone good and fair. BREARY.

Jesus. CHIPPENHAM. CHIPMAN.

> "*Jesus* calls us, o'er the tumult
>   Of our life's wild, restless sea,
> Day by day his sweet voice soundeth,
>   Saying, 'Christian, follow Me.'"

Jesus hominum Salvator. Jesus the Saviour of mankind. LEGAT. O. OF THE SERAPHIM.

Join truth with trust. JOINERS' COMP., London.

Jouir en bien. To enjoy innocently. BECKWITH, of Thurcroft.

Jour de ma vie. Day of my life, *i.e.* "Most glorious day of my life." WEST, Earl of Delawarr.

> This motto is supposed to have been assumed by Roger de la Warre (ancestor of the present earl) in commemoration of the share which he had in the capture of King John of France at the battle of Poictiers, 19th September, 1356, and for which he received on the field, as a badge of honour (still borne by the family), a crampet, or chape of the sword, given to him by King Edward III.

Jovis omnia plena. (Virg. *Ecl.* iii. 60.) All things are full of Jove. WESTBY. GODDEN.

Joy sans fin. Joy without end. WIDDINGTON.

Jubilee. STAMER.

Sir William Stamer, being created a baronet in the year of the jubilee, 1809, assumed this word as one of his mottoes.

Jucunda oblivia vitæ. It is pleasant to forget (the calamities of) life. BALGUY.

Judge. MENZIES.

Gilbert Menzies, an ancestor of this family, bore the standard of Montrose at the battle of Philiphaugh. On that standard was depicted the headless body of Charles I., with the words, "Judge and avenge my cause, O Lord!" To commemorate this, his descendants bear for crest "a knight armed cap-a-pied, holding the royal standard, inscribed with the word 'Judge.'"

Judge and avenge my cause, O Lord. MENZIES.

Judge not. ERSKINE.

"Judge not, that ye be not judged."— *Matt.* vii. 1.

Judge nought. BUCHAN, e. ERSKINE. STUART. TRAQUAIR, e.

Judicium parium, aut leges terræ. The judgment of our peers or the law of the land. CAMDEN, m. RAINES.

This motto, which was adopted by the first Lord Camden, is an extract from Magna Charta.

Juncta arma decori. Arms united to merit. M'GOUAN.

Juncta virtuti fides. Fidelity joined to valour. MURRAY.

Juncti valemus. Being joined we are powerful. WALKER.

Jungor ut implear. I am joined that I may become full. MEIK.

Crest — A decrescent and increscent uniting.

Junxit amicos amor. Love hath united friends. O. OF ST. JOACHIM.

Juravi et adjuravi. I have sworn, and sworn solemnly. MOORES.

Jure, non dono. By right, not by gift. FOULKES. LLOYD.

Jus meum tuebor. I will defend my right. REYNOLDS.

Jus suum cuique. To every man his own. NOEL. PERROTT.

Jussu regis India subacta. India subdued by the king's command. MUNRO, bt.

This motto was assumed by the first baronet for services rendered at the siege and storm of Seringapatam.

Justa sequor. I follow honourable things. KEITH.

Juste et droit. Just and frank. WHICHCOTE, bt.

Justi germinabunt. The just shall shoot forth. SMITHSON.

Justitia. Justice. NURSE. SIBBALD, of Balgony.

Crest of Nurse— A pair of balances ppr.

Justitia et fortitudo invincibilia sunt. Justice and fortitude are invincible. MAGUIRE.

Justitia et pax. Justice and peace. PLUMBERS' COMP.

Justitia et veritas. Justice and truth. LAWRISTON. CHARLES I.

Justitia et virtus. Justice and virtue. CHARLESWORTH.

Justitia virtutum regina. Justice is the queen of the virtues. GOLDSMITHS' COMP.

Justitiæ soror fides. Faith is the sister of justice. THURLOW, b. THURLOW.

"Justis autem et fides hominibus, id est bonis viris, ita fides habetur, ut nulla sit in his fraudis injuriæque suspicio."—CIC. *de Off.* ii. x. 10.

Justitiæ tenax. Persevering in justice. ASTLEY. HASTINGS, b.
Justi ut sidera fulgent. The righteous shine as the stars. M'COLL. SANDILANDS, whose crest is an estoile issuing from a crescent.

"They that be wise shall shine as stars for ever and ever."—*Dan.* xii. 3.

Justum et tenacem. Just and firm of purpose. COLTHURST, bt. MACKNIGHT or M'KNIGHT.

" Justum et tenacem propositi virum
Non civium ardor prava jubentium,
Non vultus instantis tyranni
Mente quatit solidâ."—HOR. lib. iii. Od. 3.

Justum et tenacem propositi. Just and firm of purpose. HOLMES.
Justum perficito, nihil timeto. Act justly, and fear nothing. ROGERS, of Yarlington Lodge.

" The virtuous man who leads
Invincibly a life of resolute good,
And stands amid the silent dungeon-depths
More free and fearless than the trembling judge."—SHELLEY.

Justus esto, et non metue. Be just, and fear not. ROBSON.

" Be just and fear not."—SHAKSPEARE.

Justus et fidelis. Just and faithful. BOMFORD.
Justus et propositi tenax. Just and firm of purpose. CHEDWORTH. HOW. PENRICE, of Gt. Yarmouth.
Justus et tenax. Just and firm. HUNT-GRUBBE.
Justus propositi tenax. The just is firm of purpose. FERRAND.
Justus ut palma. The righteous man is as the palm-tree. PALMES.
Justus ut palma florebit. The righteous man shall flourish as the palm-tree. O. of ST. GEORGE, of Bavaria.
Juvant arva parentum. The lands of my forefathers delight me. CASSAN, Queen's Conuty.

" . . . . Where'er we roam,
Our first best country ever is at home."—GOLDSMITH.

Juvant aspera fortes. Difficulties delight the brave. STEUART.
Juvant aspera probum. Misfortunes benefit the good man. DENHAM, bt. STEUART, of Coltness, bt. STEWART.
Juvante Deo. By God's assistance. LAYARD.
Juvant Deus impigros. God assists the diligent. STRACHAN.
Juvat dum lacerat. It helps while it tears. KROYE.

Crest — A plough.

Juvat lacerat. It helps (while) it tears. KNOYE. KOEHLER.

The arms and crest both have plough coulters in them.

Juxta Salopiam. Near to Shropshire. CHADWICK.

K

Κἀν θελη ὁ Θεος. If God will. SCHEFFELD, kt. of Rhodes, temp.
Hen. VIII.

Karanza wheelas karanza. Love worketh love. POLWHELE,
of Polwhele, Cornwall.

> The following lines form a portion of some verses written by Mrs. Abdy
> on reading the above motto :—
>
>   " ' Love worketh love,'—these words may well
>   The gentle spirit cheer,
>   That strives to weave love's tender spell
>   In daily doubt and fear.
>   Droop not! your wish to soothe and bless,
>   Successful yet may prove ;
>   Scan not each failure in distress,
>   Love ever worketh love.
>
>   And, tho' the love we bear our kind
>   May blamelessly be shown,
>   In kindling in another's mind
>   Affection like our own.
>   Let us our heart's best thoughts resign
>   To Him who reigns above :
>   'Tis only meet for love divine
>   To waken perfect love."

Kars. WILLIAMS, bt.

> This motto was granted to its gallant bearer for his protracted defence
> of the city of Kars against the Russians.

Ke ne dune ke ne tiens ne pret ke desire, or, *Qui non dat quod
habet non occupat ille quod optat.* He who does not give
what he has, does not gain what he desires. KING
HENRY III.

Keep fast. LESLY, of Burdsbank. *Crest*—A buckle.

Keep firm in the faith. O. OF HUBERT.

Keep traist. HEPBURN.

Keep tryst. BELCHES. HEPBURN, bt.

Keep tryste. SEMPILL. SEMPLE, of Cathcart, &c. HEPBURN,
of Colquhalzie.

Keep watch. BRYDEN, of Berwick.

Kensol tra Tonkein ouna Diu mathern yn. Before all things,
Tonkin, fear God in the king. TONKIN.

Khelat. WILLSHIRE, bt.

> This motto is borne by Sir T. Willshire, bart. K.C.B., in commemoration
> of his gallantry at the capture of Khelat ; and for his services at the
> Cape, he takes for crest a Caffre, with the word "Caffraria" over.

Kunst, Macht, Kunst. Art, might, art. PAPWORTH.

Kur, deu, res, pub, tra. For God and the commonwealth.
HARRIS, of Hayne, co. Devon.

ΚΥΡΑ. SMITH, R.N.

> This is an abbreviation of "ΚΥΡΑΝΑ," the Doric form of Cyrene, and
> is found upon a celebrated coin of that colony.

Kymmer-yn Lydeirnon. HUGHES.
   This is the name of the lordship which this family has held for many
   generations.

Kynd kynn knawne kepe. Keep your own kin-kind. KAYE,
   of Denby Grange, bt.

L

L'amour de Dieu est pacifique. The love of God is peaceful.
   O. OF MARY MAGDALEN.
L'amour et l'amitié. Love and friendship. DAY, of Kirby,
   Bedon, co. Norfolk.
L'amour et loyauté. Love and loyalty. SWAYNE.
L'esperance du salut. The hope of salvation. GRABHAM.
L'esperance me console. Hope consoles me. DE CARDONNEL.
L'esperance me comfort. Hope comforts me. NAIRNE, b.
   NAIRN, of St. Ford.
L'espoir est ma force. Hope is my strength. TUPPER.
L'homme vrai aime son pays. The true man loves his country.
   HOMFRAY, co. Stafford.
     " Patriots have toiled, and in their country's cause
       Bled nobly ! and their deeds, as they deserve,
       Receive proud recompense."— COWPER.
L'honneur me guide. Honour guides me. LOUSADA.
L'honneur nous unit. Honour unites us. FURNIVAL.
L'union fait la force. Union makes strength. LEOPOLD, king
   of the Belgians.
La bondad para la medra. Goodness produces success.
   LENNARD.
La fin couronne les œuvres. The end crowns the works.
   YARKER, of Leyburn.
La fortune passe par tout. The vicissitudes of fortune are
   common to all. LEWIS. ROLLO, b.
La générosité. Generosity. O. of GENEROSITY.
La liberté. Liberty. ACKERS.
     " Freedom's battle once begun,
       Bequeathed by bleeding sire to son,
       Though baffled oft, is ever won."— BYRON.
La liaison fait ma valeur, la division me perd. Union makes
   me valuable, division destroys me. O. OF THE FAN.
La mayor victorio de ellas es el bien merecellas. The greatest
   victory is in having deserved it. GUEVERA.
La merle aime la liberté. The blackbird (or *merle*) loves
   liberty. MERLE.

La mort me suit. Death follows me. BOLTON.
Referring to the bolts or arrows in the arms and crest.

La paix. Peace. LENDRUM. *Crest*—A dove with olive-branch.

La tête plus que l'argent. The head is better than riches. RAVEN.

La vertu est la seule noblesse. Virtue is the only nobility. GUILDFORD, e. NORTH.
" Les hommes sont égaux ; ce n'est point la naissance,
C'est la seule vertu qui fait la différence."—VOLTAIRE.

La vertu surmonte tout obstacle. Virtue overcomes every obstacle. ROWLEY.

La vie durante. During life. AYMAND. CORNEWALL, bt. CORNWALL, of Shropshire. LEIGH, co. Chester.

Labile quod opportunum. That which is opportune is quickly gone, or opportunity soon slips by. HOWMAN, of Bexwell, co. Norfolk.
The meaning of this motto is, perhaps, best expressed, either by the well-known adage, "There's many a slip between the cup and the lip," or by "Take time by the forelock."

Labor et industria. Labour and industry. TANE.
Crest—A plough.

Labor et prudentia. Labour and prudence.

Labor improbus omnia vincit. Extraordinary labour surmounts all difficulties. MITCHELL, of Landath.

Labor ipse voluptas. Toil itself is pleasure. LOVELACE, e. J. G. NICHOLS, F.S.A.
This motto was adopted by John Nichols, F.S.A., the author of the *History of Leicestershire*, and the *Literary Anecdotes of the Eighteenth Century*; and for forty years editor of the *Gentleman's Magazine*; nor could any have been more expressive of his own literary character.

Labor omnia superat. Labour conquers all things. LAING.

Labor omnia vincit improbus. (Virg. *Geor.* i. 145.) Incessant labour conquers all things. BUTLER.

Labor omnia vincit. Perseverance overcomes all difficulties. BROWN. CUTLER. CHAPLIN. BURDER. DANIEL, co. Stafford. EDDINGTON. M'NAIR. PRATTMAN.

Labor vincit omnia. Labour conquers all things. RICHARDSON.
Formerly borne by the family of Ffarington.

Labora. Labour. M'KIE. MACKIE.
"The labour of the righteous tendeth to life."— *Prov.* x. 16.

Labora ut in æternum vivas. Strive that you may live for ever. APREECE, bt.
" Every man shall receive according to his labour."—1 *Cor.* iii. 8.

Laboranti numen adest. God is with him that endeavours. MACFARLANE.

Labore. By labour. ABBOT. TENTERDEN, b. WALMESLEY.
Assumed by the first Lord Tenterden to commemorate his rise by industry.

Labore et fiducia. By industry and confidence. LITSTER.

Labore et honore.   By industry and honour.   BOWDEN.   REND-
    LESHAM, b.   THELLUSON.   PEMBERTON, of Barnes.   VINER.
Labore et perseverantia.   By labour and perseverance.   CAMPBELL.
    WOODS.
Labore et prudentia.   By labour and prudence.   BARTOLOZZI.
Labore et scientia.   By industry and science.   WYLIE, bt.
Labore et virtute.   By industry and virtue.   GARDNER.   PIGOTT.
Labore omnia florent.   All things flourish with industry.   DRINK-
    WATER.
Labore vinces.   You will overcome by toil.   SUGDEN.   ST.
    LEONARDS, b.
Lædere noli.   Be unwilling to hurt.   STEWART.
Læti acie florent.   They flourish joyful in their keenness of
    mind.   EYRE.
Lætitia per mortem.   Joy through death.   LUTHER.
Lætitia et spe immortalitatis.   With joy and hope of immortality.
    LYTE.   SHAW.

> " The men were gladsome ; for their moral sense
> They fortified with reverence for their gods,
> And they had hopes that overstepped the grave."— *The Excursion.*

Læto aere florent.   They flourish in glad *air.*   AYRE.
Laissir ronam aboo.   The torch that leads to victory.   MAHONEY.
Lam beaṅṡ abu, or modernly, Lamh dearg Eirinn abu, meaning,
    " The red hand in defiance," and " The red hand for Ireland
    in defiance."   O'NEILL.

> In the latter form of the motto the abú is often left out, and the cry is
> only "The red hand for Ireland."   This cry, of course, alludes to the
> bearing of the clan, the red hand, now the badge of a baronet.   There
> is a legend that an ancestor of the O'Neills was, with other adventurers,
> approaching the coast of Ireland in a boat, and that, they having
> agreed that whoever touched the land first should be ruler, he chopped
> off his left hand and threw it ashore.   Now, the earliest examples of
> the coat of the O'Neills do not contain the salmon over which the
> hand is said to have been thrown, and the hand is invariably a dexter
> one ; nor are the O'Neills the peculiar proprietors of a hand as their
> cognizance ; on the contrary, several families of Milesian descent in
> Ireland or Scotland, bear, as part of their armorials, a dexter hand,
> *e. g.* O'Daly, O'Donovan, McDonald, &c.

Lam laṡoiṅ abu.   The strong hand defying, or modernly, Lamh
    laider a-n-nachter.   The strong hand from above, or the
    strong hand uppermost.   O'BRIEN.

> This latter form of the motto, by the alteration of one letter, may be
> rendered " Vigueur de dessus," Strength from above, and is so used
> by the Marquis of Thomond.

Lam Foiṅṫeṅac abu.   The open hand defying.   O'SULLIVAN.

> This motto alludes to the arms ; to the descent from Finglim (Anglice,
> "Florence," a man's name) of the generous hand ; to the traditional
> origin of the surname ; and to the old proverb,—
>> " Nulla manus tam liberalis
>> Atque generalis atque universalis
>> Quam manus Sullivanalis."

Lamh derg aboo.   The red hand defying.   MAGAWLY.

Lamh foisdineach an næchtar. What we gain by conquest we
secure by clemency. SULLAVAN, of Thames-Ditton, bt.

Lampada tradam. I will pass on the torch. WHEWELL.

The crest is a dexter hand in bend, couped at the wrist, in the act of
conveying to another dexter hand, issuant from the wreath argent, a
torch gules.

This motto alludes to certain Greek races where the runners passed a
torch from hand to hand; thence Lucretius says of the generations of
mankind,—

". . . et, quasi cursores, vitai lampada tradunt."—lib. ii. 76.

Laram nomhiam a buaah. It blazes before us to victory.
MAHONEY.

Lassez dire. Let them say. MIDDLETON.

Latet anguis *in herba.* The snake lurks in the grass. ANGUISH.

Crest — A snake nowed in grass, all ppr.

Laudans invocabo Dominum. I will call upon the Lord with
praise. PALGRAVE.

" I will call on the Lord who is worthy to be praised."—2 *Sam.* xxii. 4.

Laudes cano heroum. I sing the praise of heroes. DAILIE.

Laudo manentem. I praise him that waits. ONSLOW. STAN-
HOPE.

Laugh lader an aughter. Laugh harder and louder. KENNEDY.

Lauro redimita quiescam. I will rest crowned with laurels.
LYON.

The crest is a demi-lady ppr. attired or and az., holding in the dexter
hand a thistle, in the sinister a chaplet of laurel ppr.

Lauro scutoque resurgo. I rise again with laurel and shield.
LORAINE, bt.

Crest — A laurel-tree couped, two branches sprouting out ppr., and fixed
to the lower part thereof with a belt gu., edged and buckle or, an
escutcheon az.

Laus Deo. Praise be to God. ARBUTHNOTT, v.

Law. BOWEN.

Le bon temps viendra. The prosperous time will come.
GRIFFITH, of Llwynduris. FARRINGTON. HARCOURT, of
Aukerwycke. WREY, bt.

Le jour viendra. The day will come. DURHAM, e. LAMBTON.

Le nom, les armes, la loyauté. My name, my arms, my loyalty.
NEWLAND.

These are a portion of the memorable words used on the scaffold by
Roger Newland, of Newlands, co. Southampton, who was executed for
aiding the attempt of Charles I. to escape from Carisbrooke Castle.
"Deprived," said he, " of my life and property, I leave to posterity
my name (which none can assail), my arms (which traitors, ignorant
alike of gentility and heraldry, cannot efface), and my loyalty, which
none can impugn."

Le roy et l'église. The king and the church. ROGERS.

Le roy et l'estat. The king and the state. ASHBURNHAM, e.
SHERARD.

Le roy, la loy, la foy. King, law, faith. GROVER.

Le roy le veut. It is the king's pleasure. DE CLIFFORD. LORD
DACRE, temp. Hen. VIII.

Lead on. HOTHAM, b.

Legale judicium parium. The legal judgment of my peers.
YATES.

Lege et labore. By law and labour. BELL.

Lege, sapere aude. Read, dare to be wise. TATTERSHALL.

Leges arma tenent sanctas. Arms cause laws to be respected.
BENSON.

Leges juraque serva. Observe the laws and ordinances. GRANT,
of Kilgraston. SIR WM. HERNE, Knt.

Leges juraque servat. He observes the laws and statutes.
HEARNE.

" Vir bonus est quis
Qui consulta patrum, qui leges juraque servat."—HOR. *Ep.* i. 16, 40.

Leges juraque servo. I observe the laws and ordinances. LEIGH,
of Belmont, co. Chester.

Legi regi fidelis. Faithful to the king and law. BARRY. SAUTRY.

Legibus antiquis. By the ancient laws. LEIGH, of Bardon.

Legibus et armis. By laws and arms. GORDON, of Gordonbank.

Legite et discite. Read and learn. ASHLEY.

Leniter sustineo. I support gently. SHEATH.

Lente in voto. Slowly (is) in my power, *i.e.* is what I wish.
THOMSON.

Lente sed attente. Slowly but carefully. ROBERTS.

Lente sed opportune. Slowly, but opportunely. CAMPBELL.

Lento sed certo et recto gradu. With a slow but sure and
straight step. KNOWLYS, of Heysham.

Leo de Juda est robur nostrum. The Lion of Judah is our
strength. BORLASE. WARREN.

Leoni non sagittis fido. I trust to the lion not to my arrows.
EGERTON.

Lesses dire. Let speak. MIDDLETON. WHARTON.

Let brotherly love continue. PLASTERERS' COMP. PIPE-MAKERS'
COMP.

Let Curzon hold what Curzon held. CURSON. HOWE, e.

Let the deed shaw. ADDISON. FLEMING. MOWBRAY.

Let the hawk shaw. PORTEOUS.

Let them talk. HEWETSON.

Let us love one another. BASKETMAKERS' COMP.

"Let us love one another, for love is of God."—1 *John,* iv. 7.

Leve et reluis. Rise and shine. LAWSON, co. York, bt. LAWSON.

Crest — Two arms embowed, couped at the elbow, vested erm., cuffs ar.
supporting in the hands ppr. a ring or, gemmed gu., within the ring
the sun in splendour gold.

Levius fit patientia. It is rendered lighter by patience. BUR-
GESS. GLOSTER.

". . . levius fit patientia
Quicquid corrigere est nefas."— HOR. *Car.* i. 25, 20.

Lex et justitia. Law and justice. CLARKE.

Liber et audax. Free and bold. FREEMAN, of Castle Cor.

Liber et erectus. Free and erect. GRAHAM.

Libera terra, liberque animus. A free earth and a free mind, or a *Frankland* and a free mind. FRANKLAND, bt.

Liberalitas. Liberality. FURLONG.

Libertas. Liberty. CARBERY, b. CHATTERIS. BIRCH, bt. EVANS, of Ash Hall. EVANS, Lyng, co. Norfolk. BAILEY. GREGORY. LEWIS.

> " We must be free or die, who speak the tongue
> That Shakspeare spake, the faith and morals hold
> Which Milton held."—WORDSWORTH.

> " . . . everything that is and will be free,
> Bear witness for me, wheresoe'er ye be;
> With what deep worship I have still adored
> The spirit of divinest Liberty."—COLERIDGE.

Libertas et natale solum. Liberty and my native soil. ADAMS of Bowden. FREEMAN. SANDERSON.

> " Breathes there the man, with soul so dead,
> Who never to himself hath said,
> This is my own, my native land ?"—SCOTT.

Libertas in legibus. Liberty in the law. WYNFORD, b. BEST.

Libertas pretiosior auro. Liberty is more precious than gold. SOUTHBY.

Libertas sub rege pio. Liberty under a pious king. ADDINGTON. PACKE. SIDMOUTH, v.

> " Fallitur egregie quisquis sub principe credit
> Servitium ; nunquam libertas gratior exstat
> Quam sub rege pio."—CLAUDIAN, lib. iii. v. 114.

> " They err indeed who think, if single sway
> Should rule the land, 'tis slavery to obey !
> A good king's subjects cherish liberty,
> No other freemen are so safely free."

Libertas virtus sunt summa potestas. Liberty and virtue are the highest power. RICHARDS.

Libertate quietem. Quiet in liberty. WOODFORD, bt.

These words form part of the lines which the Latin poet puts in the mouth of Cato,—

> " Manus hæc inimica tyrannis,
> Ense petit placidam sub libertate quietem."

Liberté toute entière. Liberty unfettered. BUTLER-DANVERS. LANE. LANESBOROUGH, e.

> " The discipline of slavery is unknown
> Amongst us,—hence the more do we require
> The discipline of virtue ; order else
> Cannot subsist, nor confidence, nor peace."—WORDSWORTH.

Licet esse beatis. It is allowed to men to be happy. WARDE.

Light on. LIGHTON, of Ullishaven.

Lighter than air. AYRE.

Lissa. HOSTE, bt.

This name was inscribed on a medal given by the Prince-Regent to Sir William Hoste, for the brilliant victory achieved by him, at the head of four frigates, over the combined French and Italian squadrons off the island of Lissa on the coast of Dalmatia, 13th March, 1811. The medal is represented in the arms of the family as pendent from a naval crown in chief. "Cattaro" is also borne by the Hoste family on their crest of augmentation, in memorial of the services of Sir William before the Dalmatian fortress of that name.

Littora specto.   I view the shores.   HAMILTON.

Live but dread.   LINDSAY, of The Byres, Scotland.

Live in hope.   COLDSTREAM.

> " We live by Admiration, Hope, and Love ;
> And, even as these are well and wisely fixed,
> In dignity of being we ascend !"— WORDSWORTH.

Live to live.   SUTTON.   WITELEY, or WHITELEY.   DUNDAS.

> " In realms of changeless gladness,
> Where friendship's ties are never crushed and broken,
> We still shall meet : Heaven, who beholds our sadness,
> Hath to the trusting heart assurance spoken
> Of that blest land, where, free from care and pain,
> Fond friends unite again."— STANLEY.

Lock sick.   Be sure.   ERWIN.

Lock sicker.   Be sure.   DOUGLAS, bt.   MEGGET.   MORTON, e.

Loisgim agus soilleirghim.   I will burn and enlighten.   M'LEOD.
    MACLEOD, of Cadboll.   *Crest*—The sun in splendour.

Look to the end, saith Kennedy.   KENNEDY.

Look to the past.   JONES.

Loquendo placet.   He pleases when he speaks.   FAIRFOWL.

> *Crest* — A parrot.

Lord, have mercy ! (Matt. xvii. 15.) DRUMMOND. STRATHALLAN, v.

Lord, let Glasgow flourish.   T. of GLASGOW.

Love.   M'LEISH.   M'CLEISH, of Maryfield.

> " Love is indestructible :
> Its holy flame for ever burneth ;
> From heaven it came, to heaven returneth :
> Too oft on earth a troubled guest,
> At times deceived, at times opprest,
> It here is tried and purified,
> Then hath in heaven its perfect rest :
> It soweth here with toil and care,
> But the harvest-time of Love is there."— SOUTHEY.

Love and dread.   BAKER.

Love and loyalty.   CROMPTON.   STANSFIELD.

> " And steady loyalty and faithful love."— GOLDSMITH.

Love as brethren.   COOPERS' COMP., London.

" Love one another."— *John,* xiii. 35. These words of our blessed Saviour contain the germ of all duty, virtue, and charity.

Love as you find.   TEMPEST.

Love, but dread.   LINDSAY.

Love, serve.   COOPER.   SHAFTESBURY, e.

> " O Love, thou sternly dost thy power maintain,
> And wilt not bear a rival in thy reign,
> Tyrants and thou all fellowship disdain."— DRYDEN.

Loyal à mort.   Loyal to death.   ADAIR.   CHATTERTON, bt.
    ELY, m.   HEPWORTH, of Pontefract.   LAFOREY, bt.   LOFTUS.

Loyal à la mort. Loyal to death. LOFTUS, bt. LYSTER, of Rowton Castle. LOFTUS, co. Norfolk. SHADWELL.

Loyal au mort. Loyal to the dead. ADAIR, bt. ATTERBURY, bt. BARWELL. DRUMMOND, of Innermay. LAFOREY. LANGTON. BELSHER. LOFTUS. ROBERSON. LYSTER. PENDRILL.

Loyal devoir. Loyal duty. CARTERET, b. GRENFELL.

Loyal en tout. Loyal in every thing. BROWN. KENMARE, e.

Loyal in adversity. GERRARD.

> ". . . he that can endure
> To follow with allegiance a fallen lord,
> Does conquer him that did his master conquer."—SHAKSPEARE.

Loyal, secret. Loyal, confidential. LAWSON.

This motto was adopted, on his appointment to office, by Sir George Lawson, knt., who, temp. Hen. VIII., was made treasurer of Berwick-upon-Tweed.

Loyal je serai durant ma vie. I will be loyal as long as I live. STOURTON, b.

Loyal suis je. Loyal am I. SHIRLEY.

Loyal until death. WHITE, bt.

Loyalle à mon amy. Loyal to my friend.

Loyalment je sers. I serve loyally. JEPHSON. NORREYS.

Loyalté me lie. Loyalty binds me. MARGESSON. RICHARD III.

Loyaulte n'a honte. Loyalty knows no shame. CLINTON. NEWCASTLE, d.

Loyauté m'oblige. Loyalty binds me. BERTIE. LINDSEY, e.

Loyauté sans tache. Loyalty without defect. DARE.

Loyouf as thow fynds. TEMPEST, of Broughton. GREENLY.

Luce. With light. LUCY.

Luceat et crescat. Let it shine and grow. BLACKWOOD.

Crest — An increscent.

Lucem amat virtus. Virtue loves the light. STRACHEY.

Lucem spero. I hope for light. KEMP, bt.

Luceo boreale. I shine at the north. SELON.

Crest — A star of six points.

Luceo non uro. I shine, but do not burn. MACKENZIE, bt. M'KENZIE. M'LEOD, of Colbeck. SMITH.

Crest — A mountain inflamed.

> "Soon a score of fires I ween
> From height and hill and cliff were seen —
> Each after each they glanced to sight,
> As stars arise upon the night."—SCOTT.

Lucerna pedibus meis. A lamp unto my feet. MANT.

> "Thy word is a lamp unto my feet, and a light unto my path."—*Ps.* cxix. 105.

Lucet. It shines. SCOT. *Crest* —a star.

> "Heaven's ebon vault,
> Studded with stars unutterably bright,
> Through which the moon's unclouded grandeur rolls,
> Seems like a canopy which love had spread
> To curtain her sleeping world."—SHELLEY.

Luctor, at emergam. I struggle, but I shall recover. MAITLAND.

Luctor, non mergor. I struggle, but am not overwhelmed. GLASS.

Lumen accipe et imperti. Receive the light and communicate it. HOLLINGSWORTH.

The following extract from Ennius illustrates this motto :—

" Homo, qui erranti comiter monstrat viam,
Quasi de suo lumine lumen accendat, facit.
Nihilo minus ipsi lucet, cum illi accenderit."

Lumen cœleste sequamur. May we follow heavenly inspiration. BEATIE.

Lumen sevimus antique. We sowed light of old. REDWOOD.

Lumen umbra Dei. Light is the shadow of God. GLAZIERS' COMP.

Lux Dei ibi salus. In the light of God there is safety. DIXWELL.

Lux et salus. Light and safety. BRUNTON.

Crest—A beacon with flames of fire ppr.

Lux in tenebris. Light in darkness. FULLERTON, of Westwood.

" Thou art gone to the grave, but we will not deplore thee,
Tho' darkness and shadows encompass thy tomb ;
For thy Saviour has passed thro' its portals before thee,
And the lamp of His love is thy light thro' the gloom."

Lux mea Christus. Christ is my light. NEWMAN. ROGERS.

"Sun of my soul ! Thou Saviour dear,
It is not night if thou be near ;
Oh, may no earth-born cloud arise,
To hide thee from thy servant's eyes."—KEBLE.

Lux mihi laurus. The laurel is my light. CHAMBERS.

Lux tua via mea. Thy light is my way. BLOUNT, bt. BLOUNT.

"The way which from this dead and dark abode
Leads up to God :
Away where you might head the sun, and be
More bright than he."

Lux tua vita mea. Thy light is my life. BLOUNT, of Maple Durham.

Lux venit ab alto. Light comes from above. DALLAS, bt.

" Fountain of light and living breath,
Whose mercies never fail nor fade,
Fill me with life that hath no death,
Fill me with light that hath no shade ;
Appoint the remnant of my days
To see thy power, and sing thy praise."—QUARLES.

Lux vitæ. The light of life. BURTON, of Lindley and Bedworth.

Lȳbba pu ϸ pu lȳbbe, or *Lubba bu te bu Lybbe.* Live that you may live. AYLOFFE, bt.

Lybia. Africa. DOYLE, bt.

Lyræ nervos aptavi. I fitted, or tuned, the strings of my lyre, *i.e.* harp ; in allusion to the harp in the arms. SIRR.

M

Ma force d'en haut. My strength is from above. LANDON.
MALET.

Ma joye en Dieu seulement. My joy is in God alone. MOM-
PESSON, co. Norfolk.

Ma volonté. My will. CHARLES DUKE OF ORLEANS, father of
Louis XII. of France.

Mack all sicker. ALMACK.

Macte. Go forward. SMITH.

Macte virtute patrum. Go on in the valour of your fathers.
MACKRELL.

Madripore. HISLOP, bt.

> This word is inscribed on the standard of the Indian chief, Holkar, which
> the lion in the arms of Hislop is represented in the act of tearing. It
> commemorates the services of the first baronet at that place.

Magistratus indicat virum. The magistracy shows the man.
LONSDALE, e. LOWTHER, bt.

> This motto aaserts that high office when won, serves as a touchstone to
> show the real character of him who has obtained it.

Magna est veritas. Great is truth. STILLINGFLEET.

> "Great is the truth and stronger than all things."— 1 *Esdras*, iv. 35

Magna est veritas et prevalebit. Truth is great and will prevail. RODEN.

Magna vis fidelitatis. The force of fidelity is great. NEWMAN.

Magnanimiter crucem sustine. Sustain the cross (*i.e.* support
afflictions) with magnanimity. KENYON, b. WHITNEY.

Magnanimus esto. Be great of mind. INGRAM. IRVINE.

Magni animi pretium. The reward of magnanimity. O. OF THE
WHITE ELEPHANT.

Magnum in parvo. Much in *little.* LITTLE. CONGILTON.

Magnus Hippocrates ; tu nobis major ! Great Hippocrates !
thou art greater than we. DIMSDALE.

Maharajpore. LITTLER, G.C.B.

Maintien le droit. Support the right. BRYDGES, of Denton
Court, bt. BRIDGES. LEATHAM.

Major opima ferat. Let the more worthy carry off the
honours. MOIR, of Stonniewood. MORE.

Major virtus quam splendor. Virtue is preferable to splendour.
AULD. BAILLIE, of Jerviswood.

Majora sequor. I pursue greater objects. HALIBURTON.

Majora tenta præsentibus æquus. When equal to the present,
attempt greater things. LYNCH.

Majores sequor. I follow my ancestors. GORDON.

Make a clean heart and a cheerful spirit. PORTMAN, b.

Make all sure. ARMOURERS' AND BRAZIERS' COMP., London.

Mal au tour. Misfortune to the tower. PATTEN.

Crest — A tower inflamed.

Mala prævisa pereunt. Evils foreseen are destroyed. HODGES.

Malgré l'envie. In spite of envy. THIRLEY.

Malgré le tort. Despite of wrong. DAVIS. HOUGHTON, bt. JAMES.

Malim esse probus quam haberi. I had rather be honest than be thought so. KENNEDY, of Kirkmichael.

Malis obsta. Resist misfortunes. URMSTON, of Warrington.

Mallem mori quam fœdari. I would rather die than be disgraced. GILBERT, bt.

"Here on my knee, I beg mortality,
Rather than life preserved with infamy."— SHAKSPEARE.

Malo mori quam fœdari. I would rather die than be disgraced. ATHLONE, e. BARNEWELL, bt. BEALE. BOUCHER. CASLEY. CARSON, of Scarning, co. Norfolk. CHETHAM STRODE, of South Hill. DAEG. DE FREYNE, bt. ESMOND, bt. O. OF ERMINE. FFRENCH, b. FRENCH. GINKELL. GINGLE. HARTY, bt. HIGGINSON. JACKSON, of Preston. KINGSLAND, v. LISTER. MULLOY. MENZES. MURRAY. O'MULLEY. PRIOR, of Rathdowney. POE, of Harley Park. PAYNE, bt. PAYNE, of Jersey. PAIN. RYAN, of Inch. SURTEES. STRODE, of Shipton Mallet. TRIMELSTOWNE, b. TENISON.

"For life I prize it
As I weigh grief, which I would spare for honour,
'Tis a derivative from me and mine;
And only that I stood for."— SHAKSPEARE.

Malo pati quam fœdari. I prefer suffering to disgrace. DUCKETT.

"This I must do, or know not what to do,
Yet this I will not do, do how I can."— SHAKSPEARE.

Malum bono vince. Subdue evil by good. HAY, of Linplum.

"Be not overcome of evil, but overcome evil with good."— *Rom.* xii. 21.

Man do it. EDGAR, of Wadderly.

Mane diem. Await the day. MAYNE.

Mane prædam, vespere spolium. Game in the morning and a feast at night. HURT.

This motto which alludes to the crest, a stag wounded (*Hurt*), and to the bearer's name, may be thus explained,—(The stag when hurt supplies to the hunter) game in the morning, and a feast at night.

Manent optima cælo. The best things await us in heaven. MILLER, of Glenlee, bt. MILLER, of Collierswood.

"Comfort's in heaven: and we are on the earth,
Where nothing lives but crosses, care, and grief."— SHAKSPEARE.

Maneo, non fugio. I stand firm and do not fly. GORDON.

Manet in æternum. It endureth for ever. SPREWELL. WARNER, of Ardeer, co. Ayr. *Crest*—An open Bible.

"The word of the Lord endureth for ever."—1 *Pet.* i. 25.

Manners makyth man. HOOD, of Barton Park, co. Lancaster.

WICKHAM. WYKEHAM, Bishop of Winchester and Lord Chancellor of England, who in 1379 founded New College, Oxford.

"Manners maketh man, the want of them the fellow."

Manu et corde. With heart and hand. BATES, of Denton.

Manu forti. With a strong hand. BOYD, Clinkskales. JESHAM. MACKAY. M‘CAY. M‘CASKER. REAY, b.

Manuque. And by the hand. JOSSEY. *Crest*—An eye ppr.

This motto possibly has reference to the crest, and denotes that the family were ready both with eye and hand.

Manus hœc inimica tyrannis. This hand is hostile to tyrants. CARYSFORT, e. DOSSEY. HEMSWORTH, of Shropham, co. Norfolk. MANLEY. PROBYN. RIVERSDALE, b. TONSON.

"Manus hæc inimica tyrannis
Ense petit placidam sub libertate quietem."

Manus justa nardus. A just hand is a precious ointment. MAYNARD, v. MAYNARD, of Harlesey Hall.

The name, Maynard, is here supposed to be compounded of "Manus, hand," and "nardus, ointment."

Marbu mhiann leinn. As we would desire. CAMPBELL.

Mare ditat, rosa decorat. The sea enriches and the (Mont-) rose adorns. T. OF MONTROSE.

Mars deni*que* victor es. Thou *Mars* (*den*) at length art the conqueror. MARSDEN.

Marte et arte. By valour and skill. DRUMMOND, of London. MAGUIRE. NEVOY.

Marte et arte. By valour and skill. JONES, of Cranmer Hall, co. Norfolk, bt.

These words refer to the bravery and great scientific skill, shown by Lieut.-General Sir John Thomas Jones, K.C.B. during the Peninsular War. For his services he was created a baronet, and besides the above motto, had the word " *Netherlands*," (which see) inscribed beneath the castle, on his chief of augmentation ; and " *Badajoz*" on the medal suspended from the neck of the lion in the crest.

Marte et clypeo. By war and the shield. METHEN, of Craiglownie.

Marte et industria. By arms and industry. OGILVY.

Marte et ingenio. By war and wit. SMITH, co. Essex, bt.

Marte et labore. By arms and toil. NEWGILL.

Marte et mari faventibus. War and wave favouring. MORRIS.

This motto refers, as well to the name of this ancient family, which in the British language signifies " powerful in war " (Mawr rwyce), as to the various gallant actions on land and sea performed by several members of it, especially in America and the last general war.

Marte non Arte. By arms not art. NEASMITH.

Martis non Cupidinis. Of Mars not Cupid. FLETCHER, bt.

Maturé. In good time. SMITH.

Maturus cœlo non˙ cadit ante diem. He who is ripe for heaven falls not before his day. ELISS

Maya. CAMERON, bt. See " Acre."

Me certum mors certa facit.   Certain death makes me resolute.
SIBBALD, of Kips, Scotland.

> *Crest*—A mort (death's) head ppr.

Me duce carpe viam.   With me for leader hasten on your way.
BURDETT.

Me fortem reddit Deus.   God makes me strong.   SCOTT.

Me meliora manent.   Better fortunes await me.   MOSSMAN.

Me stante virebunt.   While I exist they shall flourish.   TIRWHIT.
TYRWHITT, of Ketilly, co. Lincoln.

Me vincit, ego mereo.   He hath conquered me I am the gainer.
SINCLAIR.

Mea anchora Christus.   Christ is my anchor.   MAYOR.

> " Which hope we have as an anchor of the soul."—*Heb.* vi. 19.

Mea dos virtus.   Virtue is my dower.   MEADOWS, co. Suffolk.

Mea fides in sapientia.   My trust is in wisdom.   FRYER.

Mea gloria crux.   The cross is my glory.   HEALD.

Mea gloria fides.   Faith is my glory.   GILCHRIST.   WATSON.

Mea spes est in Deo.   My hope is in God.   SMITH.   MILLER.

Mea virtute me involvo.   I wrap myself in my virtue.   WILLIAMS,
of Clovelly Court, bt.

> " . . . Meâ
> Virtute me involvo, probamque
> Pauperiem sine dote quæro."—HOR. *Car.* iii. 29. 54.

Meæ memor originis.   Mindful of my origin.   MANSON.

Mean, speak, and doe well.   URQUHART, of Cromarty.

Mean, speak, and do well.   URGUHART, of Meldrum.

Mecum habita.   Dwell with me.   DUN.

Mediis tranquillus in undis.   Tranquil in the midst of waters.
SMYTH, co. Perth.

Medio tutissimus.   Safest in the middle.   LANGTON, of
Fransham, co. Norfolk.

> "Who moves within the middle region shares,
> The least disquiets, and the smallest cares."—POMFRET.

Medio tutissimus ibis.   The middle path is safest.   BUSFIELD.
SENIOR.

> These words are taken from the caution given by Phœbus to his son
> Phaeton. See Ovid. *Met.* lib. ii. 137.

Mediocria firma.   Mediocrity is safe.   BACON, bt.   GRIMSTON.
LAWDER.   LOWNDES-STONES.   VERULAM, e.

Mediocriter.   With moderation.   MOIR.   MURISON.

> "Go, search among your idle dreams,
> Your busy or your vain extremes!
> And find a life of equal bliss,
> With that which moderation gives."

Meditatio Christi meditatio.   The meditation of Christ is (the)
meditation (of a Christian).

Meliora speranda.   Better fortunes in expectancy.   DOUGLASS.

Meliora sperando.   By hoping better things.   DOUGLAS.

Meliora spero. I hope for better things. WALSH.

Meliora spero sequorque. I hope and strive for better fortunes. RAIT.

Meliora supersunt. Better things remain. ANNESLEY.

Meliore fide quam fortunâ. With better fidelity than fortune. GRESLEY, bt.

Melitæ amor. Love of Malta. RUTTER.

Melior fortunâ virtus. Virtue is better than fortune. MELLOR.

Memini. I remember. CAMPBELL.

Memento Creatorem. (Eccles. xii. 1.) Remember thy Creator. KEITH.

Memento mei. Remember me. L'ESTRANGE, of Moystown.

Memento mori. Remember that thou must die. GUMBLETON. O. OF DEATH'S HEAD.

> "Pale Death with equal foot strikes wide the door
> Of royal halls, and hovels of the poor."—COWPER.

Memor. Mindful. RUSSELL.

Memor esto. Be mindful. CAMPBELL. GRAHAM, of Killern. HUTCHINSON, of Edinburgh. M'FELL. M'PHAIL.

Memor esto brevis ævi. Be mindful that time is short. MILNES.

> "Think on thy home, my soul, and think aright
> Of what's yet left of life's wasting day:
> Thy sun posts westward, passed is thy morn,
> And twice it is not given thee to be born."—DRUMMOND.

Memor esto majorum. Be thou mindful of thine ancestors. FARQUHARSON.

Memor et fidelis. Mindful and faithful. SELSEY, b. REED. PEACHY.

> "Many sounds were sweet,
> Most ravishing, and pleasing to the ear;
> But sweeter none than voice of faithful friend—
> Sweeter always, sweetest heard in loudest storm."—POLLOK.

Memorare novissima. To remember death. HANFORD.

Memoria pii æterna. The memory of the pious man is eternal. SUDELEY, b. TRACY.

> "———— The memory of the just
> Lives in everlasting fame."—MONTGOMERY.

Mens conscia recti. A mind conscious of rectitude. ASHBROOK, v. BOULTON. COLLIS. CRISP. CHRISOP. FLOWER. JARY, of Burlingham. KIRSOP. NIGHTINGALE. PHILLIPS. MACARTNEY, bt. SILLIFANT. WRIGHT. WESTMORE. WATLINGTON.

> "One self-approving hour whole years outweighs,
> Of stupid starers and of loud huzzahs."—POPE.

Mens cujusque is est quisque. As the mind of each, so is the man. COTTENHAM, b. LESLIE, of Surrey. PEPYS, bt.

> "He that has light within his own clear breast,
> May sit i' th' centre and enjoy bright day;
> But he that hides a dark soul and foul thoughts,
> Benighted walks under the mid-day sun—
> Himself is his own dungeon."

Mens et manus. Heart and hand. DUNCANSON.

Mens flecti nescia. A mind that cannot be bent. HULTON.

Mens immota. A constant mind. SHAW.

Mens pristina mansit. The original mind hath remained. POPHAM, of Littlecott.

Mens sibi conscia recti. A mind conscious to itself of rectitude. CRESPYNY. WRIGHT, bt.

Mente et manu. With heart and hand. GLASSFORD. PATRICKSON.

Mente manuque. With heart and hand. FARQUHAR, bt. BENSHAW. BORTHWICK, of Stow.

Mente manuque præsto. Ready with heart and hand. FOULIS, bt.

Mentis honestæ gloria. The glory of an honest mind. GREY.

Merces hæc certa laborum. This is the sure reward of industry. SETON, bt.

Merci, fortune. Thank you, fortune. The Lord AUDLEY, temp. Henry VIII.

Mercy is my desire. ABERCROMBIE. LAING. LANG. WISHART.

> " No ceremony that to great ones 'longs,
> Not the king's crown, nor the deputed sword,
> The marshal's truncheon, nor the judge's robe,
> Becomes them with one-half so good a grace
> As mercy does."—SHAKSPEARE.

Merere. To deserve. CURRER, of Cliften House. ROUNDELL.

Meret qui laborat. He is deserving who is industrious. STORIE.

Merite. Merit. CURRIER.

Meritez. Deserve. WALTHAM.

Merito. Deservedly. DUNLOP, bt. DELAP. DELOP.

Merses profundo pulchrior evenit. Sink him in the sea he comes out fairer. DAVISON, of Lanton, co. Northumberland.

Meruisse manu. To have merited by the hand. WILLS.

Messis ab alto. Our harvest is from the deep. ROYAL FISHERY COMP. WHITTUCK.

Metuenda corolla draconis. The dragon's crest is to be feared. LONDONDERRY, m. STEWART.

Crest—A dragon statant or.

Metuo secundis. I am fearful in prosperity. HODGESON. UPPLEBY, of Wootton.

Mi camokah baalim Yehowah. (Exod. xv. 11.) Who is like unto thee of the gods, O Jehovah? GOLDSMID.

This was the motto borne by the Asmonean family, and from the initial letters of the Hebrew words which compose it, the name "Maccabee" was formed.

Micat inter omnes. He shines amongst all. HAGGARD, of Bradenham, co. Norfolk. *Crest*—A star of six points.

Mieux être que paraître. Better be than seem. BARCLAY.

Migro et respicio. I come forth and look back. RAMSAY.

Crest—An eagle reguardant.

Mihi consulit Deus. God careth for me. BENNETT.

Mihi cœlum portus. Heaven is my haven. BRUGES.
This motto is borne on a ribbon entwined round the crest, an anchor.
"Tired with vain life, we close the willing eye;
'Tis the great birthright of mankind to die."—THOMSON.

Mihi et meæ. For me and for mine. ANNE BOLEYN, Queen of Henry VIII.

Mihi cura futuri. My care is for the future. ONGLEY, b.

Mihi jussa capessere. To execute my commands. MASHAM.

Mihi lucra. My gains. SCOTT.

Mihi lucra pericula. Dangers are profitable to me. SUTTIE.

Mihi parta tueri. To defend the things acquired by me. NORTH. STYLEMAN-LE STRANGE.

Mihi robore robor. My strength is in the oak. CUNNINGHAM.
An oak-tree forms part of the crest.

Mihi solicitudo futuri. I have a care for the future. THACKWELL.

Mihi terraque lacusque. Mine are the land and the pools. FULLARTON. Alluding to the otters in the arms.

Mihi tibi. To me and to you. POPE, co. Shropshire.
Crest—A hand holding a pair of scales.

Mihi turpe relinqui. It is base for me to be left.

Mihi vita Christus. Christ is my life. KAYE.

Miles et fortis. A soldier and a brave one. ORD.

Militia mea multiplex. My warfare is manifold. TOKE, of Godinton. TOOKE.

Mind your own business. REMNANT, of Billericay.

Minorca. DUCKWORTH, bt.
This word is inscribed in gold letters on a flag held by one of the supporters, and refers to the services of the first baronet at the capture of that island. ST. DOMINGO, in letters of gold on the chief of augmentation, commemorates the signal defeat of the French fleet by the squadron under the command of Vice-Admiral Sir J. T. Duckworth, K.B., in the Bay of St. Domingo, Feb. 6th, 1806.

Mirabile in profundis. A wonderful object in the deep. WHALLEY, co. Somerset and Hants.
Crest—A whale's head.

Miserere mei Deus, secundum magnam misericordiam tuam. (Ps. li.) "Have mercy on me, O God, according to thy great mercy."
This is borne on the rim of the coronet of the King-at-arms.

Misericordia temperet gladium. Let pity moderate the sword. MULES.

Miseris succurrere. To help the miserable. PRINCE. SMYTH, co. Clare.
'Tis not enough that we with sorrow sigh,
That we the wants of pleading man supply,
That we in sympathy with sufferers feel,
Nor hear a grief without a wish to heal:
Not these suffice—to sickness, pain, and woe,
The Christian spirit loves with aid to go;
Will not be sought, waits not for wants to plead,
But seeks the duty—nay prevents the need."—CRABBE.

Miseris succurrere disco. I learn to succour the unfortunate.
DRAMOND. HINDE. HODGSON. MACMILLAN. SOLTAU.
" Non ignara mali, miseris succurrere disco."—VIRG. Æn. i. 630.

Miserrima vidi. I have seen most miserable things. ZEPHANI.
Misnach. Courage. CAMPBELL.
"Cowards die many times before their death ;
The valiant never taste of death but once."

Mitis et fortis. Gentle and brave. ORD.
Moderata durant. Moderate things are lasting. BUSHE. IRVINE,
of Bieldside. STAUNTON, of Longbridge.
Modeste conabor. I will attempt moderately. HAGGARD.
Mœnibus crede ligneis. Trust to wooden walls. CLARKE.
" Britannia needs no bulwarks,
No towers along the steep ;
Her march is o'er the mountain wave,
And her home is on the deep :
With thunders from the native oak
She quells the floods below."

Modice augetur modicum. A little is increased by degrees.
WILLIAMSON, of Hutchinfield.
Modicum modice erit magnum. A little will be much by
degrees. WILLIAMSON, of Kirkaldy.
Mon Dieu est ma roche. My God is my rock. ROCHE. FERMOY, b.
"The Lord is my rock."—2 *Sam.* xxii. 2.

Mon Dieu, mon roi, et ma patrie. My God, my king, and my
country. KERWAN, co. Galway.
Mon privilege et mon devoir. My privilege and my duty. SHEVILL.
Mon tresor. My treasure. MONTRESOR.
Monachus salvabor. I a *monk* (*house*) shall be saved. MONK-
HOUSE, of Newcastle-on-Tyne.
Mone sale. Advise with wit. MONSELL, of Tervoe.
Moneo et munio. I advise and defend. DALRYMPLE. ELPHIN-
STONE, bt. ELPHINSTONE, of Horn and Logie.
Moniti meliora sequamur. (Virg. *Æn.* iii. 188.) Let us, being
admonished, follow better things. MAHON, bt.
Monitus, munitus. Forewarned, forearmed. HORN, of Westerhall.
This motto refers to the notes of alarm given by the horn which forms
the crest, as well as to the owner's name.
Monstrant astra viam. The stars show the way. OSWALD.
Crest — A hand pointing to a star.
Monstrant regibus astra viam. Stars show the way to kings.
O. OF THE STAR OF SICILY.
Monte alto. From a high hill. MOWAT, of Inglistoun.
Crest — On the top of a hill an oak-tree.
Monte de alto. From a high hill. ATTHILL.
Monte dessus. Soar upward. BUNNY.
Montez toujours. Aspire always. WALSHAM, bt.
Monte Video. LUMLEY. VASSALL.
See "Every bullet has its billet."

Montjoye St. Denys. French cri-de-guerre.
This may either denote that their patron saint was the Frenchmen's delight ; or to the hill near Jerusalem, whence the pilgrim's eye was first gladdened with a view of the Holy City, or to a place which lies between Paris and St. Denis.

Mora trahit periculum. Delay brings danger. SUCKLING.
Moribus antiquis. With ancient manners. THROCKMORTON, bt.
Moriendo modulor. Dying I sing. MITCHELL.
Moriendo vivo. In dying I live. YALDWYN.
Moriens cano. Dying I sing. COBBE.
In allusion to the swans in the arms which are said by the ancient poets to utter when dying certain melodious but sad strains.
"He makes a swan-like end,
Fading in music."—SHAKSPEARE.

Moriens, sed invictus. Dying, but unconquered. GAMMELL.
Mors, aut honorabilis vita. Death, or life with honour. JOYCE.
Mors aut vita decora. Either death or honourable life. DEMPSTER.
Mors ærumnarum requies. Death is rest from afflictions. RUMNEY.
"Look up, my soul, pant tow'rd the eternal hills;
Those heavens are fairer than they seem ;
There pleasures all sincere glide on in crystal rills,
There not a dreg of guilt defiles,
Nor grief disturbs the stream
That Canaan knows no noxious thing,
No cursed soil, no tainted spring,
Nor roses grow on thorns, nor honey wears a sting."—WATTS.

Mors Christi mors mortis mihi. Christ's death is to me the death of death. BOOTHBY, bt.
"By him recalled to breath,
Who captive led captivity,
Who robbed the grave of Victory,—
And took the sting from death !"—CAMPBELL.

Mors crucis mea salus. The death of the cross is my safety. BLOUNT, of Orletory.
Mors in vita. Death in life. SMITH.
Mors janua vitæ. Death is the gate of life. BROGRAVE.
Mors lupi agnis vita. The death of the wolf is life to the lambs. OUSELEY, bt. RENDELL.
Mors mihi lucrum. Death is gain to me. JONES. LLUELLYN.
"His faith, in death unshaken, tower'd on high,
And show'd succeeding Christians how to die."

Mors non timenda est. Death is not to be feared. COLEMAN.
"Let recreant yield, who fears to die."—SCOTT.

Mors potior macula. Death rather than infamy. CHAMBERLAYNE.
"Here on my knee, I beg mortality,
Rather than life preserved with infamy."—SHAKSPEARE.

Mort en droit. Death in the right. DRAX. EARLE-DRAX.
Morte leonis vita. Life by the death of the lion. VAUX, b.
Mortem aut triumphum. Death or victory. CLIFTON, of Lytham and Clyfton.
This motto alludes to the crest, an arm embowed in armour holding a sword. It is very old, appearing under the arms of the family in the

tower of the parish church at Kirkham, which tower was built by an ancestor of this family in the reign of Hen. V. or Hen. VI. The tower has been replaced by a new one within the last fifteen years, but the coat-of-arms is still preserved.

Mortua vivescunt. The dead revive. LINDSAY, of Blackholm.

Crest — A withered branch of oak sprouting forth green leaves.
" Life is real ! Life is earnest !
And the grave is not its goal ;
' Dust thou art, to dust returneth,'
Was not spoken of the soul."—LONGFELLOW.

Mos le*gem regit.* Custom rules the law. MOSLEY, bt.

Mouguerre. BYNG. STRAFFORD, b.

This word is borne on an escroll, which accompanies the crest of augmentation commemorative of the services of the first Lord Strafford.

Moveo et propitior. I move and am appeased. KNOX. RANFURLEY, e. WELLS.

Mullac a boo. Victory for the Duns, or inhabitants of the Hills. Or the inhabitants, *i.e.* the Duns, defying. DUNNE. DOYNE.

This motto is sometimes written "Mullher a boo."

Multa tuli fecique. I have endured and done much. ARKWRIGHT.

Multa in parvo. Much in *little.* LITTLE. HEPBURN.

Munifice et fortiter. Bountifully and bravely. HANDYSIDE.

Munit hæc et altera vincit. This defends, that conquers. NOVA SCOTIA KNIGHTS.

Munus et monumentum victoriæ Spures, 1513. A reward and remembrance of the victory of Spurs, 1513. LONGEVILLE-CLARKE.

Murus aheneus. A wall of brass. M'LEOD. NIELSON.

Murus æneus esto. Be thou a wall of brass. REYNELL, bt. MACLEOD.

Arms of Reynell, ar. masonry sa. a chief indented of the second.
"Hic murus aheneus esto,
Nil conscire sibi, nulla pallescere culpa."—HOR. *Ep.* i. 1. 60.

Murus æneus, conscientia sana. A sound conscience is a wall of brass. LUMLEY. SCARBOROUGH, e. WILLIAMSON.

Murus æneus mens conscia recti. A mind conscious of rectitude is a brazen wall. FIELD.

"True conscious honour is to feel no sin ;
He's arm'd without that's innocent within;
Be this thy screen and this thy wall of brass."—POPE.

Murus æneus virtus. Virtue is a wall of brass. WALTON, of Clifton, Gloucestershire.

An allusion to the name Wal-ton.

Mutare fidem nescio. I cannot break faith. OUTRAM, bt.

Mutare non est meum. It is not mine (*i.e.* my nature) to change. FREWEN, of Northiam.

Mutare sperno. I scorn to change. HOBHOUSE. LEFROY. SINGLETON, co. Clare.

Anthony Lefroy, a Protestant, emigrated from Flanders to England during the Duke of Alva's persecution, and took this motto to denote his constancy to his faith.

Mutare vel timere sperno. I scorn to change or to fear.
BEAUFORT, d. BARNES. BYTHESEA. SOMERSET.

Mutas inglorius artes. (To exercise) unambitious of glory, the
silent arts. HALFORD, bt.

> This motto is a quotation from the description of the physician Japis,
> in Virgil's *Æn.* lib. xii. 397, and was assumed by the first Baronet who
> was an eminent physician.
>
> "Japis ——
> Preferr'd the powers of plants, and silent praise
> Of healing arts, before Phœbean bays."—DRYDEN

Mutuo amore cresco. By mutual love I grow. LINDSAY.

My defence. ALLARDICE.

My hope is constant in thee. MACDONALD.

> These words were used by Robert Bruce to the Lord of the Isles at the
> battle of Bannockburn, and are expressive of the confidence which he
> placed in that chief in spite of the insinuations of his nobles. Sir
> Walter Scott alludes to this in the "Lord of the Isles" when Bruce
> says,—
>
> "Lord of the Isles, my trust in thee
> Is firm as Ailsa rock."

My hope is in God. MIDDLETON.

> "Lord, what wait I for? my hope is in thee."—Ps. xxxix. 7.

My king and country. TYLER.

My prince and my country. HARRIS, b.

My trust is in God alone. CLOTH-WORKERS' COMP., London.

> "Such trust have we through Christ to God-ward."—2 *Cor.* iii. 4.

My trust is in the Lord. (Ps. lxxi. 5.) UNWIN.

My word is my bond. SMALLMAN.

N

N'oublie. Do not forget. GRAHAM. MOURE. MOIR. MOIL.

Na bean d'on chat gun lamhainu. Touch not a cat but a glove.
MACPHERSON, of Cluny. *Crest*—A cat sejant.

Na fyno Duw na fyd. What God willeth not will not be. PRICE.

Nagpore. JENKINS. Commemorative of services at that place.

Natale solum dulce. Our native soil is sweet. TAYLOR, of
Todmorden Hall, co. Lancaster, and Burghfield, co. Berks.

> "Man, through all ages of revolving time,
> Unchanging man, in every varying clime,
> Deems his own land of every land the pride,
> Beloved by heaven o'er all the world beside;
> His home the spot of earth supremely blest,
> A dearer, sweeter spot than all the rest."—MONTGOMERY.

Nativum retinet decus. He retains his native honour. LIVING-
STONE.

Naturæ donum. The gift of nature. PEACOCK.

Naturæ minister. A servant of nature. HELHAM.

Naufragus in portum. Shipwrecked I got into haven. HEARD.

> Sir Arthur Heard, formerly Garter King-at-Arms, was in his early days a midshipman in the navy. Having on the coast of Guinea been carried overboard with the yard on which he was standing when his vessel, the Blandford, was dismasted in a tornado, he at a later period obtained a grant of arms with motto as above, to commemorate his almost miraculous rescue from the waves.

Nautis stella refulsit. The star has shone on sailors, *i.e.* seamen. SEAMAN.

Nautæ fida. Faithful to the sailor. SIRR. *Crest*—An estoile.

Navarin. CODRINGTON.

> This motto was borne by Sir Edward Codrington, G.C.B., who commanded the English forces at Navarino.

Ne cadam insidiis. Lest I fall into snares. CLELAND.

Ne cede malis. Yield not to misfortunes. ALBEMARLE, e. DOIG. KEPPEL.

> " Be thou secure of soul, unbent with woes,
> The more thy fortunes frown, the more oppose."—DRYDEN.

Ne cede malis; sed contra. Yield not to misfortunes; on the contrary, meet them with fortitude. CANNING, v. GARVAGH, b. STRATFORD, b.

> " Tu ne cede malis; sed contrà audentior ito,
> Quam tua te Fortuna sinet."—VIRG. *Æn.* vi. 95.

Ne cuiquam serviat ensis. Let not your sword be the slave of any one. PEACHY.

Ne doubtero. I will not doubt. STRANGWAYS, of Well.

Ne m'oubliez. Forget me not. CARSAIR.

Ne nimium. Not too much. ABERDEEN, e. GORDON.

Ne obliviscaris. Do not forget. CAMPBELL, bt. M'TAVISH.

Ne oubliez. Do not forget. MONTROSE, d. GRAHAM.

Ne parcas nec spernas. Neither spare nor scorn. LAMOND. LAMONT.

Ne quid falsi. Nothing false. WOLLASTON, of Shenton.

Ne quid nimis. Not too much of anything. AUSTEN, of Shalford. DRINKWATER, of Irwell. FOULER.

> " Id arbitror
> Adprime in vita esse utile, Ut *ne quid nimis.*"—TER. *And.* i. 1, 34.

Ne supra. Not beyond. CATSZNELLAGE.

Ne supra modum sapere. Be not over wise. NEWPORT, bt. NASSU.

> "Quid æternis minorem
> Consiliis animum fatigas?"—HOR. *Car.* ii. 11, 12.

Ne te quæsiveris extra. Seek nothing beyond your sphere. HEWETT, bt. HEWITT.

> " Let none presume
> To wear an undeserved dignity."—SHAKSPEARE.

Ne tenta vel perfice. Attempt not or accomplish. HILL.

Ne tentes aut perfice. Attempt not or accomplish. Down-
SHIRE, m. ELECTRIC TELEGRAPH COMP. FAUNCE. HILL,
bt. HILL.

Ne timeas recte faciendo. Fear not when acting right.
HADDERWICK.

Ne vi, sed virtute. Not by violence, but by virtue.
Ne vile. Not vile. NEVILE.

Ne vile fano. Bring nothing base to the temple. FANE.
WESTMORELAND, e. STAPLETON.

Ne vile *velis.* Wish nothing base. ABERGAVENNY, e. BRAY-
BROOKE, b. NEVILE, of Thornley. NEVILL.

Ne vous importer jamais. Never be too eager. DOWNING.

Nec ab ordine cedunt. Nor do they depart from their rank.
BUCKWORTH, of Cley, co. Norfolk, and Spalding, co. Lincoln.

Nec ab oriente, nec ab occidente. Neither from the east nor
from the west. BOTESHAM. JERMYN.

Nec abest jugum. Nor is a yoke wanting. HAY, of Leith.
This family, which is an offset from that of Errol, while it takes for
its crest an ox-head, adds the foregoing motto, in which it asserts,
that the yoke which at Loncarty did such good service in the hands
of Hay of Errol, would not in case of need be found wanting in those
of his collateral descendants. See " Serva jugum."

Nec arrogo, nec dubito. I neither arrogate nor hesitate, *i.e.* I
neither claim too much, nor do I hesitate to claim my due.
ASSHERTON.

Nec aspera terrent. Difficulties do not daunt. TYLER. O.
OF THE GUELPH.

Nec beneficii immemor injuriæ. Forgetful of an injury, not
of a kindness. WALROND.

Nec careo, nec curo. I have neither want nor care. CRAW.

Nec cito, nec tarde. Neither swiftly nor slowly. BALLANTINE.

Nec cupias, nec metuas. Neither desire nor fear. HARDWICKE,
e. YORK. YORKE, of Erddig.

Nec deerit operi dextra. Nor shall my hand be wanting to
the work ; *i.e.* It shall be done with heart and hand. In
allusion to the heart in the arms. BROTHWICK, of Mayshiels.

Nec deficit. (Virg. *Æn.* vi. 143.) Nor is another wanting.
GREGORY. RODDAM, of Roddam. SMITH.

Nec degenero. I do not degenerate. LANE.

Nec desit virtus. Nor let valour be wanting. FURSE.

Nec devius unquam. Never varying,—lit. Never wandering
from the way. WALLACE.

Nec elata, nec dejecta. Neither overjoyed nor dejected. NORTH-
MORE.

Nec ferro, nec igne. Neither by sword nor fire. M'KAILE.

Nec flatu, nec fluctu. Neither by wind nor wave. EDWARD.
UDWARD.

Nec fluctu, nec flatu. Neither by wave nor wind. BURNET, of Dalleladies.

Nec habeo, nec careo, nec curo. I have neither property, want, nor care. BOWSTRING-MAKERS' COMP. WITHERS.

Nec invideo, nec despicio. I neither envy nor despise. RAYMOND.

Nec lusisse pudet, sed non incidere lusum. It does not shame me to have played, but that I have not left off playing. BOND.

Nec male notus eques. A knight not badly known. SOUTH-WELL, v. SOUTHWELL.

Nec me meminisse pigebit. Nor shall I regret to remember. WYNNE, bt.

Nec metuas, nec optes. Neither fear nor desire. CODDINGTON.

Nec minus fortiter. Not less bravely. CUTHBERT. CUTHBERTSON.

Nec mireris homines mirabiliores. Wonder not at wonderful men. LAMBERT.

Nec mons, nec subtrahit aer. Neither does the mountain diminish, nor the wind cease to blow. FORBES, of Brux.

Nec obscura, nec ima. Neither obscure nor low. LAW, of Burntoun.

Nec opprimere, nec opprimi. Neither to oppress nor be oppressed. SNEYD, of Ashcomb. KYNNERSLEY.

Nec parvis sisto. I do not continue in obscurity. DE BATHE, bt. DE BURGH, of West Drayton.

Nec placida contenta quiete est. Nor is content with quiet repose. MORDAUNT. SHIPLEY.

Nec prece, nec pretio. Neither by entreaty nor reward. BATE-MAN, b. HANBURY.
> " Nor will I barter Freedom's cause
> For England's wealth or Rome's applause."—SCOTT.

Nec pretio, nec prece. Neither by bribery nor prayer. BATEMAN.

Nec quærere, nec spernere honorem. Neither to seek nor to despise honour. BOLINGBROKE, v. BOUGHEY, bt. ST. JOHN.

Nec rege, nec populo, sed utroque. Neither for king nor people, but for both. ROLLE, b. WILKINSON.

Nec sinit esse feros. It (education) does not suffer them to be brutal. GRAZEBROOK, of Pedmore, co. Worcester. LANGHAM, bt.
> The crest of both these families is a bear's head muzzled.
> " Ingenuas didicisse fideliter artes,
> Emollit mores. nec sinit esse feros."—OVID. *de Ponto,* eleg. 9.

Nec sorte, nec fato. Neither by chance nor destiny. RUTHER-FORD, of Edgerston.

Nec sperno, nec timeo. I neither despise nor fear. ELLAMES.

Nec temere, nec timide. Neither rashly nor timidly. ABBOTT, Fellow of St. John, Cambridge, 1750. ALDWORTH. BARNE. BENT. BLAIR. BLOSSE. BRADFORD, e. BRIDGEMAN. BUCKE-LEY, bt. BUCKLEY. CHINNERY, bt. CLEVELAND, d. COTTEREL,

of Hadley. FORBES. GUEST. GRAHAM. HOLDEN. LUDLOW.
MILWARD. MITCHELL. MUNSTER, e. OWEN. PURVIS.
RICHARDS. SANDFORD. SIMEON, bt. VANE. WAKEMAN, bt.
WALKER. WESTERN, b.

Nec tempore, nec fato. Neither by time nor fate. M'DONALD.

Nec timeo, nec sperno. I neither fear nor despise. BOYNE, v.
GLOVER. GREEN, of Lichfield. PAGEN. SHIPPARD, bt.

Nec timidus, nec ferus. Neither fearful nor brutal. TROTTER.

Nec timidè, nec temerè. Neither timidly nor rashly. FORBES.

Nec timet, nec tumet. He is neither timid nor arrogant. LLOYD.

Nec triste, nec trepidum. Neither sad (*trist*) nor fearful. TRIST.

Nec vi, nec astutia. Not by force nor by cunning. WARING.

Nec vi standum, nec metu. We must stand neither by force
nor fear. RAWLINS.

Nec volenti, nec nolenti. For one neither willing, nor for one
unwilling. WESTBY, of Thornhill.

Neminem metue innocens. Being innocent fear no one. EYRE.

Nemo me impune lacessit. No one provokes me with impunity.
IRWIN, co. Sligo. NETTLES, of Nettleville, &c. co. Cork.
O. OF ST. ANDREW OF SCOTLAND.

> This motto refers to the holly-leaves in the armorial bearings of Irvin.
> The thistle in the badge of the Order of St. Andrew, and its allusion
> to the name, and to the nettle-leaves in the arms of Nettles, is obvious.

Nemo sibi nascitur. No one is born for himself alone. COLES.
SCOTT.

Nemo sine cruce beatus. No one is happy but by the cross. BAKER.

> *Crest* — A hand holding a cross calvary.
> " . . For thyself in meekness,
>   A blessing humbly claim ;
>   And link with petition,
>   Thy great Redeemer's name."—ANON.

Nemo solus sapit. No one is wise by himself. SIR JOS.
PAXTON, Knt.

Nescit abolere vetustas. Antiquity cannot abolish it. OUGHTON.

Nescit amor fines. Love knows no end. SCOT, of Vogry.

> " Is virtue aught but sympathy and love
>   For all that lives beneath us or above,
>   Aye, all that is — the mountain stream and wood,
>   For all God's works are beautiful and good.
>   Men but in this each other's worth o'ercome :
>   They all love some one, and are good to some ;
>   The bad love few, and them with fervour small ;
>   The good love many much ; the best love all."— MOILE.

Nescit occasum. It knows not setting. O. OF THE POLAR STAR.

Nescit vox missa reverti. When a word is once spoken it cannot be recalled. HAISEY.

Netherlands. JONES, of Cranmer Hall, co. Norfolk, bt.

> This motto was adopted by Sir John T. Jones, under the following cir-
> cumstances. At the Congress of Vienna it was determined to erect
> fortresses on the northern frontier of France, in what was then the
> kingdom of the Netherlands, and six and a half millions sterling were

contributed by France and the Allies for the purpose. The Duke of Wellington had charge of the erection, and under him Sir John T. Jones. When Sir John was made a baronet, he asked the Duke what addition to the family coat-of-arms he should assume : the Duke wrote. "I should say a castle and the word Netherlands would be the right thing," referring to the great works. The Duke's suggestion was at once adopted.

Never fear. STEWART, of Castlestewart, and St. Fort.

Never give in. LAWRENCE, bt,

New Ross. JOHNSON, of Bath, bt. See "Vicisti et vivimus."

Ni dessus, ni dessous. Neither above nor below. GROVE.

Ní ᴅíoᴄlᴀɪᴛɴɪȝᴄᴇᴀɴ Sᴇᴀɴᴄᴜɼ lé ʜ-ᴀɪᴍꝟɪɴ, or Ní ᴅíoᴄlᴀɪᴄɴᴇᴀɴ Sᴇᴀɴᴄᴜɼ le ʜ-ᴀɪᴍꝟɪɴ ; in English characters, *Ni diothlaithrightear Seanchus le h-aimsir.* History is not destroyed by time. CONROY, of Llanbrynmair, Montgomeryshire, and of Bettifield, co. Roscommon, bt.

This motto of Sir Edward Conroy, bt. refers to the hereditary office of Senachie, *i. e.* historian, bard, and herald to the kings of Connaught, which vested by hereditary right in the Bardic Sept of O'Mulconry. The motto alludes to history symbolised by the book in the arms; to the hand in the crest grasping the laurel wreath with which the poet's verse and the herald's voice crown martial glory; and to the bards with their ancient harps who appear as supporters. This family having been obliged to fly from Ireland to France in the 17th century by Cromwell, thus paraphrased their Irish motto ; "L'antiquité ne peut pas l'abolier," *i. e.* l'histoire ; or, as it is otherwise written in a rhyming manner :—

" Si Dieu plait
L'antiquité
Ne peut pas nous abolir."

Ni plus, ni moins. Neither more nor less. KNYVITT.

Nid cyfoeth ond boddlonrwydd. No wealth without contentment. GARNONS, co. Denbigh, and co. Herts.

Ni ddaw da o hir arofyn. No good comes of long intending. LLANOVER, b., of Llanover and Abercarn.

This motto is found in "Chwedlau y Doethion" (the Sayings of Wise Men), a Welsh MS. believed to have been written by Geraint Fardd Glâs A.D. 900. It forms the last line of the following stanza :

" A glywaist ti chwedl aderyn
O ganol y llwyn Celyn ?
Ni ddaw da o hir arofyn."

(Hast thou heard the saying of the bird,
From the midst of the holly-bush,
No good comes from long intending ?)

As some of these wise axioms occur also in the poems of Llywarch Hên, the celebrated bard of the sixth century, it is a proof that the proverbs themselves are considerably older, or they could not have been regarded as established popular sayings in his time, if they had not existed at a much earlier date, and it is probable that many of them are of Druidic origin.

Nid meddyg ond meddyg enaid. No physician but Physician of the soul. FRASER. PUGHE, of Ty Gwyn.

Nihil alienum. Nothing foreign. DYNEVOR, b.
See "Nihil humani alienum."

Nihil desperandum. Never despair. WALLEY.

Nihil habere sine labore. To have nothing without labour. COOKE.

Nihil hoc triste recepto. This being received, sorrow is at an end. O. OF OUR REDEEMER.

> " Chase from our minds the infernal foe,
> And peace, the fruit of love, bestow ;
> And lest our feet should step astray,
> Protect and guide us in the way."—DRYDEN.

Nihil humani alienum. Nothing relating to man is foreign to me. HUTCHINSON, of Whitton.

> "Tantumne ab re tua est otii tibi,
> Aliena ut cures, eaque nihil quæ ad te attinent?"
> "Homo sum : humani nihil à me alienum puto."—TER. *Heaut.* i. 1. 23.

Nihil invitâ Minervâ. Nothing contrary to one's genius. ACADEMY OF THE MUSES.

> "Nihil decet invita, ut *aiunt, Minerva,* id est, adversante et repugnanto natura."—CIC. *de Off.* i. 31. 3.

Nihil obstabit eunti. Nothing shall oppose him as he goes. ARDEN.

Nihil quod obstat virtuti. Nothing which is opposed to virtue. HIGGINS.

Nihil sine cruce. Nothing without the cross. BERESFORD.

Nihil sine Deo. Nothing without God. PETERSON.

Nihil sine labore. Nothing without labour. BERRY. EATOR. TEMPLER. THEARLE, of London.

Nihil utile quod non honestum. Nothing dishonest or dishonourable is useful. DOVERS. MOOR. MOORE, of Fawley.

> A maxim of the Stoics often quoted by Cicero.
>
> "Est nihil utile, quod idem non honestum : nec quia utile, honestum est; sed quia honestum, utile."—LIB. iii. 30. 10.

Nihil verius. Nothing more true. WEIR.

Nihil virtuti invium. Nothing is inaccessible to virtue. COLDRIDGE. COLERIDGE.

Nihilo nisi cruce. With nothing but the cross. BARBOUR.

> *Crest*—A cross calvary on three grices.

NIKΩ ΛΑΟΣ. I the people am victorious. NICOLAS, of London.

> As the septinsular lion is a supporter of the arms of Nicolas, and represents the freed population of the seven islands, he as the embodied people says, "I the people am victorious."

Nil actum si quid agendum. Nothing has been done if any thing remains to do.

Nil admirari. Not to admire. BOLINGBROKE. CLARE, e. CAREW, b.

> "Nil admirari propè res est una, Numici,
> Solaque, quæ possit facere et servare beatum."—HOR. *Ep.* i. 6. 1.

Nil æquo plus. Nothing more than my due. HAWKINS.

Nil agit, litem quod lite resolvit. He does no good, because he settles strife by strife. FIELD.

Nil amplius oro. I pray for nothing more. COX.

Nil arduum. Nothing is difficult. GORDON, of Banff.

Nil clarius astris. Nothing is brighter than the stars. BAILLIE.

> There are stars in the arms and crest.

Nil conscire sibi. To have a conscience free from guilt. *Lit.* To be conscious of nothing of one'self, *i. e.* against one's self. (See next motto.) Biss. Bullock, of Faulkbourn. Carew, bt. Collingwood. French. Michel, of Dewlish. Rothwell. Rogers. Sibthorp. Winchelsea, e. Walker. Webb.

> " Be this thy brazen bulwark of defence,
> Still to preserve thy spotless innocence."—Francis.

Nil conscire sibi nulli pallescere culpæ. To be conscious of (no guilt) to oneself, to grow pale for no crime. Sanders.

> " Hic murus aheneus esto,
> Nil conscire sibi, nulli pallescere culpæ."—Hor. *Ep.* i. 1. 60.

Nil desperandum. Never despair. Anson, bt. Anson. Chard. Chawner. Cookson, of Whitehill. Crosbie. Gardiner. Hay. Horn. Hawkins. Hawkswell. Heron, bt. Heron. Imry. Jones. Lichfield, e. Musgrove, bt. Ogilvy, of Ruthven. Parry. Stewart. Simpson. Silver. Walker, bt.

Nil desperandum. Never despair. Tucker.

> " Nil desperandum Teucro duce et auspice Teucro."—Hor. *Ep.* i. 7. 27.

Nil desperandum auspice Deo. Nothing to be despaired of under the auspices of God. Anderson.

Nil desperandum est. We must never despair. Stewart, bt.

Nil extra numerum. Nothing out of time. Randall.

Nil falsi audeat. Let him dare nothing false. Nicholl.

Nil impossibile. Nothing is impossible. Du Bisson.

Nil indigne. Nothing unworthily. Wordie.

Nil invita Minerva. Nothing contrary to one's genius. Prime.

> See " Nihil Minerva."

Nil magnum nisi bonum. Nothing is great unless good Cooper, bt.

Nil moror ictus. I heed not blows. Money. Kyrle, of Much Marcle. Muney, of Whettam. *Crest* — A hedgehog.

Nil nequit amor. Love can do everything. Reidheugh.

Nil nisi cruce. Nothing unless by the cross. Beresford, bt. Beresford, v. Decies, bt. Gully. Waterford, m.

Nil nisi patria. Nothing without one's country. Hindmarsh.

Nil penna, sed usus. Not the quill, but its use. Gilmer.

> There are three pens in the arms.

Nil sine causa. Nothing without a cause. Brown.

Nil sine Deo. Nothing without God. Reeves.

Nil sine labore. Nothing without labour. Atkinson. Dax.

Nil sine magno labore. Nothing without great labour. Kidd.

Nil sine numine. Nothing without the Deity. Blundell. Banner. Weld, of Lulworth.

> " . . . Sure, whate'er we mortals hate or love,
> Or hope or fear, depends on powers above ;
> They move our appetites to good or ill,
> And by foresight, necessitate the will."— Dryden.

Nil sistere contra. Nothing to oppose us. Nicolson, of Carnock. Stewart, of Greenock.

Nil solidum. There is nothing unchangeable. Goldie.
Williams, co. Dorset.

> " So fleets the world's uncertain span,
>   Nor zeal for God, nor love for man,
>   Gives mortal monuments a date,
>   Beyond the power of time and fate."

Nil temere. Nothing rashly. Balfour. Tennyson. Tenny-
son-D'Encourt.

Nil temere, neque timore. Nothing rashly, nor with fear.
Berney, bt.

Nil temerè tenta, nil timidè. Attempt nothing either rashly or
timidly. Buckle, co. Sussex.

Nil time. Fear nothing. Man.

Nil timeo. I fear nothing. Drummond.

> "Nil me fatalia terrent."— Virg. Æn. ix. 133.

Nil veretur veritas. Truth fears nothing. Napier.

Nile. Thompson, bt.

> This word is inscribed on a flag charged with a cross which is borne by
> one of the supporters of the arms of Thompson of Hartsbourne, in
> memorial of the distinguished services of the first baronet at the
> battle of the Nile.

Nisi Christus nemo. Christ or no one. Parkin.

Nisi Dominus. (Ps. cxxvii. 1.) Except the Lord. Compton,
bt. Compton, of Carham. Hartbury, &c.

Nisi Dominus frustra. It is vain without the Lord. Hinde.
City of Edinburgh. Inglis. Towers.

Nisi paret imperat. Unless he obeys, he commands. Bernard.

Nisi virtus vilior alga. Without virtue viler than the sea-weed.
(*mosses*). Moises. Algar.

Niti facere, experiri. To strive to do is to experience.
Caldwell, of Lindley Wood.

Nitamur semper ad optima. Let us always strive for the best.
Bigsby.

> The motto over the crest of Bigsby, which is an eagle displayed or armed
> gu., is " Ad astra."
> The name of Bigsby has been at different periods variously written by
> the family as Bigbury, Bigbery, Bigby, and Bigsby ; upon the subject
> of which changes Sir William Dugdale makes the following remarks :
> "And that this is the same and no other, though the appellation it
> now hath sound not like it, I shall sufficiently manifest ; *Byrig* in our
> old English signifieth *civitas* or *burgus* in Latine ; which, being now
> changed into *Bye*, alters not the meaning of the word, inasmuch as *Bye*
> with the Saxons is no other than *habitatio* in Latine ; neither is it out
> of use with us at this day in that sense, those orders and rules that
> are usually made at our Court Barons being called *Bye* laws, *id est,
> Town* laws ; Byan, the verb in the same tongue signifying to dwell."
> The addition of the letter *s* to the first syllable of the name as in many
> similar instances, may be supposed to have been adopted *euphoniæ
> gratiâ*.

Nitimur in vetitum. We struggle against what is forbidden.

Nitor donec supero. I strive until I overcome. RUSSELL, of Charlton Park, co. Gloucester, bt.

Nitor in adversum. I contend against adversity. GOODING. HORNER.

No force alters their fashion. KING STEPHEN, of England.
> This king bore a plume of ostrich-feathers as his device, to which the motto alludes.

No heart more true. HAMILTON, of Daichmont.

No sine periculo. I swim without danger. WALKER, of New-castle-on-Tyne. *Crest*—A swan swimming in a loch.

Nobilis ira. Noble in anger. CREIGHTON-STUART. STEWART, of Tillicoultry, bt.

Nobilis est ira leonis. The wrath of the lion is noble. INGLIS, bt. INGLIS, of Stewart, Buchanan, &c. BROOME.
> Lions are borne by these families.

Nobilitas est sola virtus. Virtue is the only nobility. THACKERAY.
> " He whose mind
> Is virtuous, is alone of noble kind;
> Though poor in fortune, of celestial race:
> And he commits the crime, who calls him base."—DRYDEN.

Nobilitas unica virtus. Virtue is the only nobility. STEWARD, of Nottingham.
> " Oh that clear honour
> Were purchased by the merit of the wearer—
> How much low peasantry would then be gleaned
> From the true seed of honour."—SHAKSPEARE.

Nobilitat. It ennobles us. HOUGHTON.

Nobilitatis virtus non stemma character. Virtue, not pedigree, should characterise nobility. FRESHFIELD, of Stoke New-ington. WESTMINSTER, m.
> " Les hommes sont égaux; ce n'est point la naissance,
> C'est la seule vertu qui fait la différence."—VOLTAIRE.

Nocentes prosequor. I prosecute the bad. DUMBRECK. SAVARY.
> "Continuo ferro culpam compesce, priusquam
> Dira per incautum serpant contagia vulgus."—VIRG. *Geor.* iii. 468.

Noctes diesque præsto. Ready by night or day. MURRAY.

Nodo firmo. In a firm knot. HARRINGTON, bt. HARRINGTON.
This has reference to the badge, which is a knot, termed a Harrington knot.

Noli altum sapere. Desire not to be overwise. CLARKE.

Noli irritare leonem. Irritate not the lion. ABBS. UNDER-WOOD.
> By a fine metaphor Macaulay applies this idea to the Lion of England : —
> " Look how the lion of the sea lifts up his ancient crown,
> And underneath his deadly paw treads the gay lilies down !
> So stalked he when he turned to flight, on that famed Picard field,
> Bohemia's plume, and Genoa's bow, and Cæsar's eagle shield :
> So glared he when, at Agincourt, in wrath he turned to bay,
> And, crushed and torn, beneath his claws the princely hunters lay."

Noli irritare leones. Do not exasperate the *lions.* LYONS, b. LYONS, of Ledestown.

Noli me tangere. Touch me not. GRAHAM. GRÆME.

Noli mentiri. Do *not lie.* NOTLEY.

Nolo servile capistrum. I am unwilling (to bear) the slavish halter. MARSH, bt.

Non ad perniciem. Not to destruction. CARLETON.

Non abest virtuti sors. Fortune deserts not virtue. NISBET.

Non arbitrio popularis auræ. Not by the caprice of popular applause. DALE, of Ashborne.

> "Virtus, repulsæ nescia sordidæ,
> Intaminatis fulget honoribus :
> Nec sumit, aut ponit secures
> Arbitrio popularis auræ."—HOR. *Car.* iii. 2. 17.

Non aliunde pendere. Not to rely on others. COKE.

> "We rejoice in Christ Jesus, and have no confidence in flesh."—*Phil.* iii. 3.

Non arte sed Marte. Not by science but by war. NASMYTH, bt.

Non aspera juvant. Rough things do not delight. LOWIS.

Non cantu sed actu. Not by singing but by acting. GILLMAN.

Non civium ardor. Not the ardour of the citizens. MOORE, of Appleby. SPURGEON, of Gressenhall, co. Norfolk.

> " Justum et tenacem propositi virum
> Non civium ardor prava jubentium,
> Non vultus instantis tyranni
> Mente quatit solida."—HOR. *Car.* iii. 3. 1.

Non credo tempori. I do not trust to time. O. OF ST. NICHOLAS.

Non crux, sed lux. Not the cross, but its light. BLACK. BLAIR. CRAMER. GRIFFITHS.

Non deest spes. Hope is not wanting. FORBES, of Alford.

Non deerit alter aureus. Another golden fruit will not be wanting. DON, bt. *Crest*—A pomegranate.

> " Primo avulso, non deficit alter
> Aureus ; et simili frondescit virga metallo."—VIRG. *Æn.* vi. 143.

Non deficit. He is not wanting. FOULIS. HAMILTON.

Non deficit alter. (Virg. *Æn.* vi. 143.) Another is not wanting. AULDJO. ALJOY. SMITH, of Berdodc. STAINFORTH. WALWYN, co. Herts.

Non degener. Not degenerated. GRINDLEY. KINLOCK, of that Ilk. KINGLAKE, of Saltmoor. KINLOCK. WEDDERBURN, bt.

Non deludere. Not to delude. DE LUDERS.

Non desistam. I will not desist. Row.

Non dormio. I sleep not. MAXWELL.

Non dormit qui custodit. The sentinel sleeps not. COGHILL, bt. GULLIVER. M'KELLIP. M'KILLOP. MYERS, CO. ESSEX. LOUTHIAN. SHORE, of Norton Hall.

Non eget arcu. He does not need a bow. ELLIOT. KYNYMOUND. MINTO, e.

> The crest of Elliot and Minto is a hand throwing a dart.
> " Integer vitæ, scelerisque purus
> Non eget Mauri jaculis neque arcu,
> Nec venenatis gravidâ sagittis,
> Fusce, pharetrâ."—HOR. *Car.* i. 22. 1.

Non eget Mauri jaculis. (Hor. *Car.* i. 22. 1.)   He needs not
the Moorish javelins.   MILLER.

Non eget integer.   The pure of life wants not.   ESPINASSE.

Non ego sed gratia Dei.   Not I but the grace of God.   M'GREA.

Non est sine pulvere palma.   The palm is not obtained without toil.   YARBURGH, of Heslington.

Non est vivere sed valere vita.   Not living, but health is life.
WALKER.

> " The things that do attain
>   The happy life, ———
>   The equal friend ; no grudge, no strife ;
>   No change of rule, nor governance ;
>   Without disease, the healthful life,
>   The household of continuance."—HOWARD.

Non extinguar.   I shall not be extinguished.   FRASER.   THE
ANTIQUARIAN SOCIETY, London.

Non fallor.   I am not deceived.   KENNEDY, of Clowburn.

Non fecimus ipsi.   We have not done these things ourselves.
DUNCOMBE, of Brickhill.

Non fluctu nec flatu movetur.   He is not moved by either wave
or wind.   PARKER, of Browsholme.

Non fraude sed laude.   Not by deceit but with honour.
GORDON, co. Aberdeen and Terpersey.

Non frustra.   Not without a purpose.   BARROW.

> *Crest* — A squirrel cracking a nut.

Non generant aquilæ columbas.   Eagles do not beget doves.
LEMPRIERE.   RODNEY, b.

> " Nec imbellem feroces
> Progenerant aquilæ columbam."—HOR. *Car.* iv. 4. 31.

Non gladio, sed gratia.   Not by the sword but by kindness.
CHARTERS or CHARTRES, of Hempsfield and Kingfauns.

Non hæc sed me.   Not these things, but me.   SCROPE.

Non hæc sine numine.   These things are not without the
Deity.   BAKER.   CLIFDEN, v.

Non his insignitus.   Distinguished not by these.   SYDENHAM.

Non ignarus mali miseris succurrere disco.   Not unacquainted
with misfortune, I learn to succour the wretched.   SAVAGE.

Non in vita.   Not in life.   SMITH.

Non immemor beneficii.   Grateful for kindness.   BROADLEY.
FITZGERALD.   GRAHAM.   QUANTOCK.   LEINSTER, d.

> Thomas Fitzgerald, father of the first Earl of Kildare, was an infant
> when his father and grandfather were killed at the battle of Callan.
> Having been left in his cradle at Tralee by his attendants, who fled on
> hearing of the battle, he was carried by a baboon kept in the family to
> the top of the abbey steeple, exhibited round the battlements, and safely
> restored to his cradle. In remembrance of this the Offaley Fitzgeralds
> took a monkey for their crest with this legend, which may either refer
> to God's blessing which saved, or the monkey's kindness which spared,
> the child.

Non inferiora.   Not mean pursuits.   MONRO, of Bearcroft.

Non inferiora secutus.   Not having followed mean pursuits.

BUCHAN, of Kelly. COUNT ST. ALDERGOUDE. BROMLEY.
GRANT. MONTFORD, b.

Non invita. Not by constraint. SMITH.

Non invita Minerva. (Cic. de. Off. i. 31. 3.) Not against the
bent of your genius. SCOTT.

Non jure deficit. He is not wanting in right. FOULIS, bt.

Non lumen effugio. I shun not the light. HEWSON. HEWSON,
of Emusmore.

> The crest of the first is a bull's head with a lighted torch in the mouth.
> The crest of the last, The sun in splendour.

Non metuo. I do not fear. HAMILTON, of Little Ernock.

Non mihi, sed Deo et regi. Not for myself, but for God and the
king. BOOTH, of Salford.

Non mihi sed patriæ. Not for myself, but for my country.
HIPPISLEY, co. Berks, bt. SPRING. SPRINGE.

Non minima sed magna prosequor. I follow not trivial, but
important things. DOBIE.

Non minor est virtus quam quærere, arte tueri. Nor is it less
valour to defend by art than to obtain. MASTER.

Non minor est virtus quam quærere parta tueri. To defend
what you have gained is no less valour than to gain.
MASTER.

Non moritur cujus fama vivit. He dies not whose fame
survives. CONGREAVE, bt. CONGREAVE.

> "Bear witness, Greece, thy living page,
> Attest it, many a deathless age !
> While kings in dusty darkness hid
> Have left a nameless pyramid,
> Thy heroes, though the general doom
> Hath swept the column from their tomb,
> A mightier monument command,
> The mountains of their native land !
> There points thy muse to stranger's eye
> The graves of those who cannot die !"—BYRON.

Non multa sed multum. Not many, but much. CASWALL.

Non mutat fortuna genus. Fortune does not change the race.
OLIPHANT.

Non mutat genus solum. Country does not change the race.
HAMILTON.

Non nobis. Not unto us. WOODD.

> This, and the six following mottoes, are on the idea contained in the
> celebrated line,
>
> " Non sibi sed toti genitum se credere mundo."

Non nobis nascimur. We are not borne for ourselves. LUCY.
WEBB.

Non nobis sed omnibus. Not for ourselves, but for all mankind. ASHE, of Ashfield, &c.

Non nobis solum. Not for ourselves alone. BLAYNEY. EARDLEY.
FARDELL. JACOB. LAWLESS. MOSS. WILSON.

Non nobis solum nati sumus.   We are not born for ourselves
alone. BRADSHAW.

"Non nobis solum nati sumus, ortusque nostri partem patria vindicat,
partem amici."—CIC. *de Off.* i. 7. 5.

Non nobis solum, sed toti mundo nati.   Born not for ourselves
alone, but for the whole world. ROKEBY, b.

Non nobis tantum nati.   Born not for ourselves alone. LEE
WARNER, of Walsingham Abbey. LEE WARNER, of East
Dereham, co. Norfolk.

Non obliviscar.   I will not forget. COLVIL.

Non obscura nec ima.   Neither obscure nor very low. LAW.

Non omnibus nati.   Not born for all. FRANK.

Non opes, sed ingenium.   Not wealth, but mind. ROSS.

Non ostento, sed ostendo.   I boast not, but give proof. FOWELL.

Non parvum est seipsum noscere.   It is not a little thing to know
oneself. COOPER.

Non præda, sed victoria.   Not plunder, but victory. CHAMBERS.

Non pas l'ouvrage, mais l'ouvrier.   Not the work, but the
workman. WORKMAN. WORKMAN-MACNAGHTEN, bt.

Non quo, sed quo modo.   Not by whom, but in what manner.
HOWARD DE WALDEN, b. SUFFOLK, e. SEAFORD, b. THOMP-
SON, bt. GRIFFIN, LORD HOWARD DE WALDEN, 1784.

Non rapui, sed recepi.   I have not taken by violence, but
received. COTTERELL, bt.

Non recedam.   I will not go back. NEWALL.

Non revertar inultus.   I will not return unrévenged. LISBURNE, e.

" For time at last sets all things even—
And if we do but watch the hour,
There never yet was human power
Which could evade, if unforgiven,
The patient search and vigil long
Of him who treasures up a wrong."—BYRON.

Non robore, sed spe.   Not by strength, but by hope. TIPPET.

Non robore, sed vi.   Not by strength, but by force. TIPPET, of
Truro.

Non semper sub umbra.   Not always under the shade.
FARQUHARSON.   *Crest*—The sun rising out of a cloud.

Non sibi.   Not for himself. CLELAND. CONNELL. CONNELY.
CULLEN. LYDE. SAGE.

'Αλλὰ κάκιῖνο δῖ σι ἰνθυμιῖσθαι, ὅτι ἴκαστος ἡμῶν οὐχ αὐτῷ μόνον
γίγονιν.—PLAT. *ad Archytam.*

Non sibi, cunctis.   Not for himself, for others also. MOIR.

Non sibi, patriæ.   Not for himself, for his country. TOMLINSON.

Non sibi, sed patriæ.   Not for himself, but for his country.
BAKER. HEPPESLEY. ROMNEY, e. MARSHAM. THOMLINSON.

Non sibi, sed patriæ natus.   Not born for himself, but for his
country. JODRELL, bt.

Non sibi, sed toti. Not for oneself, but for all. VYNNE.
This is the beginning of the line to which allusion has been already made at "Non nobis."

Non sibi solum. Not alone for self. DEVAN.

Non sine anchora. Not without an anchor. DRYSDALE.
DRURY. *Crest*—An anchor.

Non sine causa. Not without a cause. JUSTICE.

Non sine Deo. Not without God. ELIOT.

Non sine jure. Not without right. CHARTER.

Non sine numine. Not without the Deity. GIFFORD, b.

Non sine oliver. Not without *oliver.* OLIVER.

Non sine præda. Not without booty. ECHLIN.

Non sine periculo. Not without danger. M'KENZIE. FRASER.
"Non fit sine periculo facinus magnum et memorabile."—TER. *Heaut.* ii. 3. 73.

Non sine pulvere palma. A reward not without labour. PEIRSE.

Non sine usu. Not without use. MAXWELL.

Non sino, sed dono. I do not permit, but I give. SIDDON.

Non solum armis. Not by arms only. LINDSAY, of Cairnie.

Non sufficit orbis. The world does not suffice. BOND.

Non temere. Not rashly. BALFOUR. FORBES, of Edinglassie, bt.

Non temere, sed fortiter. Not rashly, but boldly. BLOXSOME.
WALLINGTON.

Non terra, sed aquis. Not by land, but by water. DUNNET.

Non timeo, sed caveo. I fear not, but am cautious. HEWITSON.
OAKELEY. STRACHAN, bt. STRACHAN. SYMMONDS.

Non tua te moveant, sed publica vota. Let not thy own, but the public wishes actuate thee. ALLEYNE, bt.

Non vi, sed virtute. Not by violence, but by virtue. ELPHIN-STONE. RAMSBOTTOM.

Non vi, sed voluntate. Not by force, but by good will. BOUCHER.

Non vi, virtute. Not by force, but by virtue. BORROWS, bt.

Non videri, sed esse. Not to seem, but to be. HARE, bt.
"Men should be what they seem."—SHAKSPEARE.

Non vox, sed votum. Not the voice, but the wish. NAGLE, bt.
"Cultus Dei nullus est, nisi ab animo volente procedat."—GROT. *de Veritat.*

None is truly great but he that is truly good. PACKWOOD.

Norma tuta veritas. Truth is a safe rule. MORRALL.

Nos aspera juvant. Difficulties benefit us. LOUIS. LOWIS.

Nos non nobis. We not for ourselves. WILBERFORCE.

Nos nostraque Deo. We and ours to God. ROGERS, bt.

Nosce teipsum. Know thyself. BUCK. FRAZER. JAMES.
MURRAY. PRINGLE. PENDRED. STANFIELD, of Esholt and Burley Wood. TINDAL. TREGONWELL. WALFORD.
"Know then thyself, presume not God to scan,
The proper study of mankind is man."—POPE.

Not in vain. AYLET, co. Essex. BRANFILL. BRANDON.

Not too much. MACKINLAY.

F

Nothing hazard, nothing have. SUTTIE, bt.
Nothing venture, nothing have. BOSWELL.
Nous maintiendrons. We will maintain. SUFFOLK, e.
Nous travaillerons en esperance. We will labour in hope.
BLACKETT, bt. BLACKETT, of Wylan, Matson, &c.

> "Let us, then, be up and doing,
> With a heart for any fate;
> Still achieving, still pursuing,
> Learn to labour and to wait."—LONGFELLOW.

Now thus ! TRAFFORD, of Trafford Park, Lancashire, bt.

The ancestor of this family who, at the time of the Conquest, had an estate in Lancashire, disguised himself as a thrasher to escape the Norman soldiers; and, as in thrashing he crossed the staff of his flail to the right or left, exclaimed, "Now thus." This expression his descendants assumed for their motto, placing it above the crest, which is "A husbandman thrashing out a garb of wheat." Their other motto "Gripe Griffen, hold fast," is addressed to the Griffen segreant in the *Trafford* arms, who in the ancient form of these arms, as given in Gregson's Testa de Nevill, is represented as griping or holding fast in his fore-paws a heater-shaped shield charged with an eagle displayed, the date 1557.

Now thus, now thus. PILKINGTON, co. Lancaster.

A legend similar to that connected with the motto and crest of Trafford, as given above, is frequently, but in my opinion wrongly, assigned to this motto of the Pilkingtons. The words cannot apply to the mower in their crest, to whom however allusion is obviously made in their other motto, "Pylkington polledowne," which see.

Nubem eripiam. (Virg. *Æn.* ii. 606.) I will dispel the cloud.
SHIPPERSDON, of Pidding Hall, and Murton, co. Durham.

Crest—A hand issuing from a cloud, and there are three suns in the arms.

Nul q'un. None but one. Anciently used by the Lord Digby's.
Nulla fraus tuta latebris. No fraud is safe in its hiding-place.
ELLACOMBE.
Nulla pallescere culpa. To turn pale from no crime. FORBES.
PATTEN. PULLEINE. MITCHELL. WAYNFLETE.
Nulla retrorsum. (Hor. *Ep.* i. 1. 74.) None backwards. FERRERS.
Alluding to the horse-shoes in the arms.
Nulla rosa sine spinis. No rose without thorns. ILBERT, co.
Devon. There are three roses in the arms.
Nulla salus bello. No safety in war. LORIMER.
Nulla vestigia retrorsum. (Hor. *Ep.* i. 1. 74.) No steps back-
ward. LEVINGE.
Nulla inimicus ero. I will be an enemy to no one. DONALDSON.

> "For wisest he whose sympathetic mind
> Exults in all the good of all mankind."—GOLDSMITH.

Nulli præda. A prey to no one. M'CABIN. M'CALLE. ARUNDEL.
Nulli præda sumus. We are a prey to no one. MARLEY.
Nullius in verba. At the dictation of no man. BANKS. GABB.
ROYAL SOCIETY. SIR CHARLES YOUNG, Garter King-at-arms.

This motto is an abbreviation from the well-known line of Horace, *Ep.* Lib. i. 1. 14.

> "Nullius addictus jurare in verba magistri."

Numen et omnia. Providence and all things. GRAHAM.

Numero, pondere, et mensura. By numbers, weight, and measure. WREN-HOSKYNS, Harewood House, Herefordshire.

This motto which is borne by C. Wren-Hoskyns, Esq., who represents the family of Sir Christopher Wren, asserts that the triumphs of the architect are gained by a knowledge of mathematics and geometry, as well as of the weights and pressures of bodies according to their densities and positions, and that he who would deal with matter successfully must master all its properties. This family also bears the motto, "Vincula da linguæ, vel tibi lingua dabit," which see.

Numine et virtute. By God's providence and by virtue. YULE.

Numini et patriæ asto. I stand by God and my country. ASTON, b.

Nunc aut nunquam. Now or never. HAMPSON, bt. KILMOREY, e. NEEDHAM.

> "Trust no future, howe'er pleasant!
> Let the dead past bury its dead!
> Act—act in the living present!
> Heart within, and God o'erhead!"—LONGFELLOW.

Nunc et semper. Now and ever. WHORWOOD.

Nunc ut olim. Now as formerly. LONGCROFT.

Nuncia pacis. A messenger of peace. WHANNELL.

Crest — A dove with olive-branch.

Nunquam deorsum. Never downward. GRAHAM, of Monargan.

Nunquam fallentis termes olivæ. A branch of the never-failing *olive.* OLIVER.

Nunquam libertas gratior. Never was liberty more agreeable. SCOTT, of Stourbridge.

Nunquam nisi honorificentissimè. Never unless most honourably. FREELING, bt.

Nunquam non fidelis. Never unfaithful. MOULTRIE. MOULTRAY. MOUTRAY. MOUTRIE.

Nunquam non paratus. Never unprepared. GIBBS. JOHNSON, of Newcastle. JOHNSTONE, of Westhall, bt. JOHNSTONE, of Alva, Galabank, Gratney, &c. KNIGHT. KERRICK, of Gelderston. BETTON. SKINNER.

Nunquam obliviscar. I shall never forget. M'IVER. SIMPSON, of Sittingbourn.

Nunquam præponens. Never preferring. DUNTZ, bt.

Nunquam tentes aut perfice. Never attempt or accomplish. BENNET.

O

Ob ducem, ob patriam. For our leader, for our country. WADDY.

Ob patriam vulnera passi. Having endured wounds for their country. BURNES, of Montrose.

For illustration of this motto see "Cabool."

Obdurum adversus urgentia. Resolute against oppression. BOTHWELL, b. BOTHWELL, of Gleneorse.

Obey and rule. LOADES.

" Diis te minorem quod geris, imperas,
Hinc omne principium, huc refer exitum."—HOR. *Car.* iii. 6, 5.

Oblier ne puis. I cannot forget. SIR HENRY WYAT, temp. Henry VIII.

Obligatam redde Jovi. Pay his due to Jove. WARD.

"Obligatam redde Jovi dapem."—HOR. *Car.* ii. 7, 17.

Obsequens non servilis. Courteous not servile. HENSLOWE. WHITE.

Obsequio non viribus. By courtesy not by force. HAMILTON.

" Facile omneis perferre, ac pati,
Cum quibus erat cunque una ; iis sese dedere,
Forum obsequi studiis, adversus nemini,
Nunquam præponens se aliis."—TER. *And.* i. 1, 36.

Observe. ACHIESON. ATCHESON. *Crest*—An astrolabe ppr.

Occultus non extinctus. Hidden, not extinguished. TYTLER.

Crest—Rays of the sun issuing from a cloud.

Occurrent nubes. Clouds will intervene. ST. GERMAINS, e.

Odi profanum. I hate whatever is profane. HARE. LIS- TOWEL, e.

Odor vitæ. The sweet breath of life. HUTTON, of Marske.

These words are inscribed on the edge of an open Bible, which forms part of the crest.

Officium præsto. I perform my duty. POWNALL, of Pownall.

Ofner na ofno angau. As borne by the family of LEWIS, of Greenmeadow, co. Glamorgan, together with the motto "Patriæ fidus" over the crest. The motto in the Welsh characters is borne by the Rev. John Williams ab Ithel, A.M. Rector of Llanymowddwy. The sense of the motto in English is, " Let him be feared who fears not death."

Both these families are descended from Gwaethvoed, Lord of Cibwyr and Ceredigion, and from the noble answer made by that prince to Edgar, the Saxon king, their motto is taken. When Edgar summoned him, with the other Welsh princes, to Chester, in order to row his barge on the Dee, Gwaethvoed replied that he could not row, and that, if he could, he would not, except to save a person's life, whether king or vassal. Upon this Edgar sent a second messenger, to whom the Welsh prince vouchsafed at first no answer at all, but when the man submissively begged to be informed what reply he should bear to his master, "Let him," said Gwaethvoed, "be feared who fears not death." On hearing these words, Edgar, delighted with the spirit of the prince, went to him, gave him his hand in kindness, and entreated him to become his friend and relation, and so it was ; and since that time the motto of all descended from Gwaethvoed has been " OFNER NA OFNO ANGAU."

Ofwn yr arglwydd. We fear the Lord. WILLIAMS, co. Cardigan.

Olet et sanat. It smells sweet and heals. DUNBAR, of Hillhead.
 Crest—A rose slipped gu.
Olim sic erat. Thus it was formerly. HOOD.
Omine secundo. With favourable omen. MAC-MURDOCH.
 Referring no doubt to the ravens in the arms, they being considered
 birds of omen.
Omne bene. All's well. HARVEY.
Omne bonum Dei donum. Every good is the gift of God.
 BOUGHTON, bt. EDWARDS. POWELL.
 " Enjoy good, it is the gift of God."—*Eccl.* iii. 13.
Omne bonum desuper. Every good is from above. BURNEY,
 Honeywood, bt.
 "Every good and every perfect gift is from above."—*James,* i. 17.
Omne meum, nihil meum. Every thing mine, nothing mine.
 GRAHAM.
Omne solum forti patria. Every land is a brave man's country.
 BALFOUR, of Burleigh. BRUGES, co. Wilts. D'OYLY, bt.
 TOUNLEY-BALFOUR, of Tounley Hall.
 " All places that the eye of heaven visits
 Are to a wise man ports and happy havens."—SHAKSPEARE.
Omne solum viro patria est. Every country is a home for a
 man. MATTHEWS.
Omne tulit punctum qui miscuit utile dulci. He has gained
 every point who has mixed the useful with the agreeable.
 WARREN, of Shipperton.
Omnes arbusta juvant. Groves (*Underwood*) delight all men.
 UNDERWOOD.
Omni violentia major. Too strong for any violence. DONELAN.
Omni liber metu. Free from every fear. BIRLEY.
Omnia bene. All's well. HARVEY.
Omnia bona bonis. All things are good to the good. WEN-
 MAN. WAINMAN.
Omnia bona desuper. (Jam. i. 17.) All good things are from
 above. GOODLAKE.
Omnia debeo Deo. I owe all things to God. GRENEHALGH.
Omnia desuper. All things are from above. EMBROIDERERS'
 COMP.
Omnia fert ætas. Time brings all things. CHEESE. LUCADON.
Omnia firmat. It secures all things. COULQUHOUN.
 Crest — A hand holding a buckle.
Omnia fortunæ committo. I commit all things to fortune.
 DUFF. M'NAUGHT. MACKNYGHTE.
Omnia mundana turbida. All things of earth are troublous.
 WHITE.
Omnia pro bono. All things for good. MURDOCH. MURDOCK.
Omnia pro Christo. All things for Christ. CARDINAL WISEMAN.
Omnia Providentiæ committo. I commit all things to Provi-
 dence. DEVENISH. MEARES.

Omnia providentia Dei. All things by the providence of God. GRAHAM.

Omnia subjecisti sub pedibus,—oves et boves. Thou hast placed all things under our feet—sheep and oxen. BUTCHERS' COMP.

Omnia superat diligentia. Diligence surmounts all difficulties. MITCHELL.

Omnia vincit amor. Love subdues all things. BRUCE, of Mowance. RODERICK, of Gateacre.

 " Omnia vincit amor : et nos cedamus amori."—VIRG. *Ec.* x. 59.

 " In Hell, and Earth, and Seas, and Heaven above,
  Love conquers all, and we must yield to Love."—DRYDEN.

Omnia vincit labor. Labour conquers all things. COOK.

Omnia vincit veritas. Truth conquers all things. MUNN. NASH.

 "Then all the people cried and said, Great is truth and prevaileth over all."—1 *Esdras,* i. 41.

Omnium rerum vicissitudo. All things are subject to change. FORD, bt.

 " Omnium rerum heus ! vicissitudo est."—TER. *Enn.* ii. 2, 45.
 See also, OVID, *Met.* lib. xv. 177.
   " Even as the mists
   Of the grey morn before the rising sun,
   That pass away and perish."—SHELLEY.

On in the right. CAWARDINE.

On things transitory resteth no glory. ISHAM, bt.

 " For sure, from hour to hour we ripe and ripe,
  And then from hour to hour we rot and rot."—SHAKSPEARE.

 " The boast of heraldry, and the pomp of power,
  And all that beauty, all that wealth e'er gave,
  Await alike th' inevitable hour ;
   The paths of glory lead but to the grave."—GRAY'S *Elegy.*

One faith, one king, one law. BOURK.

Onus sub honore. There is a burthen to sustain under honour. JOHNSON.

Onwards, upwards. COX.

 Crest—Two arms in the act of shooting an arrow upwards from a bow.

Ope solis et umbræ. By help of sun and shade. IRVINE.

Opera Dei mirifica. The works of God are wonderful. BARNISTON. GARMSTON. HUSTWICK, of Hull.

Opera illius mea sunt. His works are mine. BROWNLOW, e. CUST.

Opera mundi. The works of the world. SANDERSON.

Opes industria parit. Industry produces riches. TOMLIN.

Opes parit industria. Industry produces riches. BENSON.

Opes regum, corda subditorum. The riches of kings are the hearts of their subjects. O. OF LEOPOLD.

 This motto is engraven on the reverse of the cross worn by the knights of the Austrian Order of Leopold, as well as on the gold medal which hangs round the neck of the heralds and other officers of the Order.

The obverse of the cross bears the letters **F.I.A.** (Franciscus Imperator Austriæ), and the words "Integritati et merito" (For integrity and merit).

Opiferque per orbem dicor. I am called a bringer of help throughout the world. APOTHECARIES' COMP. KADIE. KADLE. KEDDIE.

Apollo, who said this of himself, is the principal bearing in the arms of the Apothecaries' Comp., and a lancet is the crest of Kadie.

Opitulante Deo. By God's help. BRERETON, co. Norfolk.

Oportet vivere. It behoves us to live. TODD, of Tranby.

Optima cælo. The best things are in heaven. MILLAR.

Optima est veritas. Truth is best. THOMPSON. THOMSON.

Optima revelatio stella. A star the best revelation. REVELEY, of Bryn y Gwin. *Crest*—An estoile.

> "Deep horror then my vitals froze,
> Death-struck, I ceased the tide to stem;
> When suddenly a star arose,—
> It was the Star of Bethlehem.

> "It was my guide, my light, my all,
> It bade my dark forebodings cease;
> And through the storms and dangers' thrall,
> It led me to the port of peace."—KIRKE WHITE.

Optima sapientia probitas. Probity is the best wisdom. SALMOND.

Optima sperando spiro. By hoping for the best I breathe. HUMPHREYS.

Optime merenti. To the best deserving. WITHAM.

Optime merito de rege. To him who has deserved of the king. O. OF FRANCIS OF THE TWO SICILIES.

Optimum pati. It is best to suffer. SHELDON.

Optimum quod primum. That is best that is first. KIRK, of Aberfoil.

The crest is a crosier and dagger in saltire. The motto points out that the kirk, symbolised by the crosier, is the best, and therefore to be preferred to the dagger.

Optimus est qui optime facit. The *best* is he who does the best. BEST.

Optivo cognomine crescit. (Hor. *Ep.* iii. 2. 101.) He flourishes under his adopted name. LARPENT, bt.

The name was originally Hochepied.

Ora et labora. Pray and labour. DALHOUSIE, e. HOLBURTON. PATRICK. RAMSAY. MURE. SIBBALD. WESTHEAD.

Orando te aspiciam. In praying I will look to thee. FOSTER, bt.

Ore lego, corde credo. I read with my face (*i.e.* eyes), I believe with my heart. HAMILTON, of Cairness.

Crest—The Holy Bible expanded ppr.

Oriens sylva. Rising from the wood. EASTWOOD.

This motto is a literal translation of the name Eastwood.

Orna verum. Honour the truth. WEDDELL. WADDELL.

Ornat fortem prudentia. Prudence adorns the brave. DUNBAR.

Ornatur radix fronde. The root is adorned by the foliage. INNES.

Crest — A palm-branch slipped ppr.

Orthes. WALKER, bt. HARVEY, of Thorpe, near Norwich.

This word is inscribed on a tricolor flag, held by the lion, which forms one of the supporters of the arms of Sir G. Walker, in memory of the services of his father, Sir G. T. Walker, K.C.B., in the Peninsula. The ostrich, which is the other supporter, holds the colours of the 50th Regiment, with the word "Vimiera" inscribed thereon. "Orthes" is also borne by Sir R. T. Harvey, C.B., K.T.S., inscribed beneath a representation of the medal presented to him for his services at that battle.

Ostendo non ostento. I show, not boast. ISHAM, bt. BETTS. RITCHIE.

Otium cum dignitate. Repose with dignity. KELSO. MONTAGU.

Ου τεθνηκε θανων. Though he has died he is not dead. MORRELL, D.D., F.R.S., & S.A.

Oublier ne puis. I cannot forget. COLVILLE, b. COLVIL.

Our hope is on high. RIPPON, co. Northumberland.

> "We soon shall see our God,
> The hour is waxing on,
> The dayspring from on high has risen,
> And the night is past and gone;
> The light of earth has had its birth,
> And it shall have its doom;
> The Church on earth are few in birth,
> But many in the tomb."—ALFORD.

Our trust is in God. SADLERS' COMP. London.

"Trust in the Lord."—*Ps.* xxxvii. 5; xl. 3; lxii. 8; cxv. 9.

Over fork over. CONYNGHAM, m. CUNNINGHAME, bt. CUNNING-HAME, of Kilmaurs, Milucray, Corshill, &c.

Malcolm Mac Friskin, an ancestor of this family, aided Malcolm, the son of Duncan, afterwards called Malcolm Canmore, to escape from Macbeth, the murderer of his father. The prince, being closely pursued, took refuge in a barn, where the faithful Malcolm covered him up with straw, which he kept tossing about with a fork. Hence the motto.

P

Pace et bello paratus. In peace and war prepared. FRAZER.

"Domesticæ fortitudines non sunt inferiores militaribus."—CIC. *de Off.*

Pacem amo. I love peace. COLUMBALL, co. Derby. SCOT, of Broadmeadows. SCOTT, of Highchester.

> "Peace, thy olive wand extend,
> And bid wild war his ravage end,
> Man with brother man to meet,
> And as a brother kindly greet."—BURNS

Pacem, sed coronatam pacem. Peace, but crowned peace. NOTT.

In allusion to that peace by which victory and honours have been won by Sir W. Nott, G.C.B., who received the thanks of both houses of

Parliament, for the "intrepidity, skill, and perseverance," manifested by him during the operations in Candahar and Cabool, in 1841-2.

Pacis. Of peace. SLOPER. *Crest*—A dove with olive-branch.

Pacis nuncia. A harbinger of peace. MURRAY, of Stanhope, bt.
   Crest—A dove with an olive-branch in her mouth.
      "And the dove came in to him in the evening; and, lo, in her mouth was an olive-branch plucked off"—*Gen.* viii. 11.

Paix et peu. Peace and a little. MAITLAND. WALROND.

Palma non sine pulvere. The palm is not obtained without labour. ARCHBALD. DOUGHTY. LA MB. LIVERPOOL, e.

Palma virtuti. The palm to virtue. PALMER, of Wingham, bt. PALMER, of Fairfield, bt. PALMER.
      " Let skill. let enterprise, and spirit,
      Bear, as they ought, the palm of merit."

Palmam qui meruit ferat. Let him who has earned it bear the palm. NELSON, e.
   This motto is borne by the Nelson family, and was most appropriately granted to the illustrious Horatio, the first earl. The word "Trafalgar" inscribed across the arms commemorates that illustrious victory: "San Josef" on the stern of a Spanish line-of-battle ship, which forms the second crest of the family, refers to the daring capture of the San Josef, and another vessel of equal force, by Nelson, at the battle of Algesiras; while "Faith and Works" above this second crest, may point out his faith to his God and to his country, and his daring in action.
   The following is taken from Burke's *Peerage:*—
   "The words of this motto are from an Ode to the Winds in the *Lusus Poetici* of Dr. Jortin, the author of the *Life of Erasmus*, and were applied by Lord Grenville to Nelson. The whole of the passage is,—
      " Et nobis faciles parcite et hostibus:
      Concurrent paribus cum ratibus rates;
         Spectent numina ponti, et
         Palmam qui meruit, ferat."
   " O winds ! breathe calmly o'er us and our foes !
   Let ship with ship alone contending close.
   And while the sea-gods watch above the fray,
   Let him who merits bear the palm away."—MRS. T. K. HERVEY.

Pandite. Open. GIBSON. There are keys in the arms.
      " Open to me the gates of righteousness."—*Ps.* cxviii. 19.

Pandite, cœlestes portœ. Open, ye heavenly gates ! GIBSON, of Durie.

Par ce signe à Azincourt. By this sign at Agincourt. ENTWISLE, of Foxholes.
      " Sir Bertin Entwisle, an ancestor of this family, participated in the glory of Agincourt."—ELVEN's *Heraldry of Crests.*

Par commerce. By commerce. FRENCH.
      Crest—A ship in full sail.

Par fluctus portui. The wave is equal to the haven. WILBRAHAM.

Par l'amour et la fidélité envers la patrie. By love and fidelity towards our country. O. OF ST. CATHARINE.

Par la volonté de Dieu. By the will of God. GUNMAN. WYVILL, bt.

Par pari. Equal to my equal. SICKLEMORE, of Wetheringsett.

Par sit fortuna labori. Let the success be equal to the labour. PALMER, of Carlton, bt. PALMER, of Kilmare. BUCHANAN, of Drumhead. LOWMAN.

> Hugh de Palmer, the ancestor of this family, attended Richard I. in his expedition to Palestine, and, having slain a Saracen chief in single combat, and taken a standard, received from that prince permission to bear on his shield a chevron between three crescents, as a token of his valour, together with the above motto.

Par ternis suppar. A pair more than a match for three. NORTHWICK, b. RUSHOUT, bt.

Parat et curat. He prepares and is cautious. STEWART, of Blacaskie. *Crest*—A bee ppr.

Parat usum. It prepares to use it. HART.
> *Crest* —An arm holding a scimetar.

Paratus. Ready. SWORD.

Paratus ad œthera. Prepared for heaven. FALCONER.

Paratus ad arma. Prepared for war. JOHNSON, co. Berks, bt.

Paratus et fidelis. Ready and faithful. CARRUTHERS. HAMOND, bt. WALFORD.

> This motto of Sir G. Eden Hamond, bt. G.C.B. was assumed as a second one in 1783 by Capt. Sir Edward Snape Hamond, for twelve years Comptroller of the Navy, when he was created a baronet for his good services during the American war, and was specially granted a naval coronet, issuant therefrom an eagle's head, sa.

Paratus sum. I am prepared. CAMPBELL, bt. FAIRLIE. M'LURE.

Parcere prostratis. To spare the fallen. LE HUNTE.

Parcere subjectis. To spare the conquered. LONGFIELD.
> " Hæc tibi erunt artes ; pacisque imponere morem,
> Parcere subjectis, et debellare superbos."—VIRG. *Æn.* vi. 852.

Pareo, non servo. I am obedient, not servile. JENKINSON, bt.

Parere subjectus. To obey when subject. GLASGOW.

Pares *cum paribus.* Like to like, *i.e.* pairs ; in allusion to the name—PARES, of Hopewell, co. Derby. FIRTH.

Pari animo. With equal mind. LEAKE.
> " In adverse hours an equal mind maintain,
> Nor let your spirit rise too high,
> Though Fortune kindly change the scene."—FRANCIS

Paritur bello. It is obtained by war. MURRAY.

Paritur pax bello. Peace is obtained by war. BLANE, bt.

Parle bien ou parle rien. Speak well or say nothing. DOWNS.

Parlez bien, ou ne parlez rien. Speak well, or do not say anything. PARLETT, of Woodrising, co. Norfolk.

Parta labore quies. Rest attained by labour. FULTON.

Parta tueri. Defend your acquisitions. JACOB, of Bromley. LILFORD, b. POWYS.

Parum sufficit. Little sufficeth. BROWNE, bt.

Parva contemnimus. We despise small things. GERNON.

Pass forward. STEWART.

Passez avant. Pass forward. CARTER. WALDEGRAVE.

Passibus æquis. (*Walk*) With measured tread. WALKER.
Passibus citis sed æquis. With rapid but regulated steps.
TAUNTON, b.
Paterni nominis patrimonium. The patrimony of a paternal
name. OAKLEY, bt.
" Cui genus à proavis ingens, clarumque; paternæ
Nomen erat virtutis, et ipse acerrimus armis."—VIRG. *Æn.* xii. 225.
Paterno robore tutus. Safe in my ancestral strength. SCOTT.
Patience. DOW. DOWIE.
" Thou Power Supreme, whose mighty scheme
These woes of mine fulfil,
Here, firm, I rest, they must be best,
Because they are Thy will !
Then all I want (oh, do thou grant
This one request of mine !)
Since to enjoy thou dost deny,
Assist me to resign."—BURNS.
Patience and resolution. MUTERER.
" Unbounded is the might
Of martyrdom, and fortitude, and right."—WORDSWORTH.
Patience makes every thing light. LAMB.
Patience passe science. Patience surpasses knowledge. BOS-
CAWEN. FALMOUTH, e.
Patiens. Patient. DOW.
Patiens pulveris atque solis. (Hor. *Od.* i. 8. 4.) Patient of dust
and sun. FLOYD, bt.
Patienter. Patiently. BULLMAN.
Patientia casus exsuperat omnes. Patience masters all chances.
ASKEW.
Patientia et spe. With patience and hope. DUIGUID. DUNIGUID.
Patientia et magnanimitas. Patience and courage. KIRBY.
Patientia et perseverantia. With patience and perseverance.
DENT, co. York.
Patientia et perseverantia cum magnanimitate. Patience and
perseverance with magnanimity. FELLOWS.
Patientia victrix. Patience is victorious. DALTON.
Patientiâ vinces. By patience thou wilt conquer. ARDEN.
ALVANLEY, b.
Patientia vincit. Patience conquers. CHEIN, or CHEYNE. GALL.
LINDESAY, of Warmiston. NAPIER, of Tayock. NAFLEUR.
" By which we learn our hopes and fears to guide,
To bear with pain, and to contend with pride ;
When grieved to pray ; when injured to forgive ;
And with the world in charity to live."—CRABBE.
Patientia vinco. I conquer by patience. THOMPSON.
Patior, potior. I endure, I enjoy. PEYTON, bt. PEYTON.
Patior ut potior. I endure as I enjoy. SPOTTISWOOD.
Patitur qui vincit. He who suffers conquers. KENNARD, b.
Patria cara, carior fides. My country is dear, my faith dearer.
NICOLAS, SIR HARRIS, knt.

Patriæ fidelis. Faithful to my country. TIFFIN. WOOD.

" Cari sunt parentes, cari liberi, propinqui, familiares : sed omnes omnium
caritates patria una complexa est : pro qua quis bonus dubitet mortem
oppetere, si ei sit profuturus."—CIC. *de Off.* xvii. 12, lib. i.

Patriæ fidus. Faithful to my country. LEWIS, co. Glamorgan.

Patriæ infelici fidelis. Faithful to my unhappy country.
COURTOWN, e. MOLYNEUX. MONTGOMERY. STOPFORD.

Patriam hinc sustinet. Hence he sustains his country. HIGGINS.

Patriis virtutibus. By hereditary virtues. CLEMENTS. LEIT-
RIM, e.

Pauca suspexi, pauciora despexi. I have admired few things,
I have despised fewer. BERKELEY.

Paulatim. By little and little. HATFIELD. SCALES.

Pauper non in spe. Not *poor* in hope. POORE.

Pauperum solatio. For consolation of the poor. O. OF ST.
ELIZABETH, Brazil.

Pawb yn ol ei arfer. Every one after his custom. JONES, of
Idrial.

Pax. Peace. FOULIS. HATTON.
        Crest of Foulis—A dove with olive-branch.

Pax alma redit. Fair peace returns. DONVILLE, of St.
Albans, bt.

Pax armis acquiritur. Peace is acquired by arms. ARRAT.

Pax aut bellum. Peace or war. BLANE, bt. BLAIN. THESIGER.

Pax aut defensio. Peace or defence. LAUDALE.

Pax, copia, sapientia. Peace, plenty, wisdom. FLEMING, bt.
FLEMING, of Manchester. WEST.

        Crest of Fleming, bt.—A serpent nowed, holding in his mouth a garland
        of olives and vines all ppr. The emblems of Wisdom, Peace, and
        Plenty.

Pax, copia, virtus. Peace, plenty, virtue. M'ADAM. STEWART.

Pax et amor. Peace and love. HODSON, bt. JESSOP.

Pax et salus Europæ. The peace and safety of Europe. AUSTRIA.

Pax in bello. Peace in war. GODOLPHIN, b. LEEDS, d.
OSBORNE, of Newtown, bt. BERNAL-OSBORNE.

Pax potior bello. Peace preferable to war. BASTARD, of
Kitley, co. Devon. NEMEHARD.

Pax quæritur bello. Peace is obtained by war. CROMWELL, of
Cheshunt Park.
        The representative of Oliver Cromwell, the Protector.

Pax tibi, Marce, evangelista meus. Peace to thee, O Mark !
my evangelist. O. OF ST. MARK.

Pax tua, Domine, est requies mea. Thy peace, O Lord ! is my
rest. UMPHRAY.

Peace. DIXON, of Knells. HIGGA.

Peace and grace. GRAHAM, of Gartur.

Peace and plenty. BARNES.
        " For thee, sweet Peace, abundance leads along
        Her joyous train, and bards awake to song."—BLAND.

Peace with power. EDWARDS, of Roby.

Pectore non venis. With breasts, not with veins. CHILTON.

Pedetentim. Step by step (*i.e. Foot* by *Foot.*) FOOTE.

Pejus letho flagitium. (Hor. *Car.* iv. 9–50.) Disgrace is worse than death. MARTIN, of Ham Court. SAMPSON, of Henbury.

Pelasgi. The Pelasgi. STARKE.
These were the ancient inhabitants of Northern Greece.

Pelle timorem. Drive off fear. WHATLEY.

Pen awr y chalon wir. A golden head and true heart. WATKINS, of Bunigg Pennogie.

Pennsylvania. PENN, of Stoke Pogis, co. Bucks.
This motto was taken by the Penn family in commemoration of the foundation of the colony of the same name, by their great ancestor, who, contrary to the usual custom of colonists, purchased its lands and woods (*sylvæ*) from the Indians.

Penser avant parler. Think before you speak. CARBONELL.

Penser peu de soi. To think little of one's self. DAWSON.

Penses comment. Think in what manner. DAVELL. DEYVELLE.

Pensez forte. Think firmly. BROMLEY, bt. PAUNCEFORTE.

Pensez en bien. Think on good. NOEL. WENTWORTH.

Peperi. I have brought forth. PEPERELL, bt.

Per. Through. BINDLOSSE.

Per actum intentio. The intention (must be judged of) by the act. URQUHART, of Newhall.

Per acuta belli. Through the asperities of war. CARPENTER. TYRCONNEL. e.
" —— Curæ sagaces,
Expediunt per acuta belli."—HOR. *Od.* iv. 4. 74.

Per adversa virtus. Virtue through misfortunes. LIGHTON.

Per angusta ad augusta. Through difficulties to honours. CHRISTALL. MASSAREENE, v. SKIFFINGTON.

Per ardua. Through difficulties. CURTIS, of Gatcombe, bt. CLARKSON. CROOKSHANK. BERRY, bt. DRAKE, bt. M'INTYRE. M'ENTIRE. STUBBERT. MASTERTON. TAILOUR.

Per ardua ad alta. Through straits to heights. ACHANY. HANNAY, bt. HALL. HANMAN.

Per ardua fama. Through difficulties fame. WHYTE.

Per ardua surgo. I rise through difficulties. FENTON. MAHON.

Per ardua stabilis. Firm in adversity. HENSHAW. MANN, of Ditchingham, co. Suffolk.

Per ardua stabilis esto. Be firm through difficulties. DENDY.

Per ardua virtus. Virtue through difficulties. SINCLAIR. TOMLINS.

Per aspera belli. Through the hardships of war. HOPKINS. WATSON, of Ireland, who was Commander-in-chief of the marine forces on the coast of Malabar, 1767.

Per aspera virtus. Virtue through hardships. ROSS, of Craigie.
" The man of resolute and unchanging will;
Whom, nor the plaudits of a servile crowd,

Nor the vile joys of tainting luxury,
Can bribe to yield his elevated soul
To tyranny or falsehood, though they wield
With blood-red hand the sceptre of the world."—SHELLEY.

" Aspera multa
Pertulit, adversis rerum immersabilis undis."—Hor. *Ep.* i. 2. 21.

Per bellum qui providet. One who is circumspect through
war. LIDDERSDALE.

Per callem collem. By the path the hill. COLLINS, of Betterton.

Per cœli favorem. By the favour of heaven. COWIE.

Per castra ad astra. Through the camp to the stars.
NICHOLSON.

Per crucem ad coronam. By the cross to a crown. POWER,
co. of Dublin, bt. POWER, of Edinburgh. POER.

Per crucem ad stellas. By the cross to heaven. LEGARD, bt.

Per crucem confido. By the cross I have confidence. CROSLEY.

"Oh, look, my son, upon that sign
Of the Redeemer's grace divine ;
Oh, think on faith and bliss !"—SCOTT.

Per Deum et ferrum obtinui. By God and my sword have I
prevailed. HILL.

Per fluctus ad oram. Through waves to the shore. BURRELL.

Per ignem ferris vicimus. Even through fire have we conquered
with our sword. HODDER.

Crest — A fire-ship with her courses set on fire.

Per ignem per gladium. By fire and sword. WELBEY, bt.

Crest — An arm embowed in armour, issuing fesseways from clouds ppr.
holding a sword ar. pommel and hilt or, over flames of fire ppr.
issuing from the wreath.

Per il suo contrario. By its opposite. ANGLESEA, m. PAGET.

Per industriam. Through industry. ROWAN. TIBBETTS.

The crest of Tibbets is a bee.

Per juga, per fluvios. Through precipices and torrents.
HARLAND.

Per mare. By sea. ANDERSON, of Aberdeen.

Per mare, per terras. By sea and land. ALEXANDER. CALEDON,
e. DRUMMOND, of Kildies. MACALESTER. M'ALISTER.
MACDONALD, b. MACDONELL, of Glengarry.

Per mille ardua. Through a thousand difficulties. MILLERD.

Per orbem. Through the world. CLAY, bt.

Per se valens. Strong through himself. PERCEVAL.

Per sinum Codanum. Through the Baltic. GRAVES.

Per tela per hostes. Through arrows and enemies. BRYMER.

Per varios casus. By various fortunes. DOUGLAS. DRYSDALE.
HAMILTON. LAMMIE. L'AMY, co. Forfar. WALKER.

Per vias rectas. By right ways. BLACKWOOD, bt. DUFFERIN, b.

Per vim et virtutem. By strength and valour. YOUL.

Per virtutem scientiamque. By valour and knowledge. MAC-
NEIL.

Peradventure. ELLIOT, bt. COCKBURN, of Kenderland.

Percussa resurgo. Being struck down I rise again. JORDAN.
Crest — A foot-ball.

Perduret probitas. Let honesty endure. PEARSON.

Perenne sub polo nihil. There is nothing permanent under heaven. PONT.

" Since earthly joys abydis never,
Work for the joy that lasts for ever ;
For other joy is all but vain :
All earthly joy returns in pain.—DUNBAR.

Perge sed caute. Advance but cautiously. JENKINS, of Bicton.

Periculum fortitudine evasi. I have escaped danger by fortitude. HARLAND, bt. MAHON.

Periissem, ni per-iissem. I had perished, unless I had gone through with it. ANSTRUTHER, bt.

The origin of this motto is thus related by Sir Walter Scott in *Waverley.*

" One of this ancient race, finding that an antagonist with whom he had fixed a friendly meeting, was determined to take the opportunity of assassinating him, prevented the hazard by dashing out his brains with a battle-axe. Two sturdy arms brandishing such a weapon form the usual crest of the family, with the above motto, ' Periissem ni per-iissem.' "

Periissemus nisi per-iissemus. We had perished had we not persisted. BERMUDAS COMP.

Perimus licitis. We perish by what is lawful. TEIGNMOUTH, b.

The sense of this motto seems to be, that we are liable to suffer from the immoderate or objectionable use of things in themselves lawful.

Perit ut vivat. He dies that he may live. FENWICK. PHIN.
Crest — A phœnix.
See note to motto, " Ex scipso renascens."

Permitte cætera divis. (Hor. *Od.* i. 9. 9.) Leave the rest to the gods. M'CRUMMIN.

Pernicibus alis. With swift wings. CHERMSIDE.
Crest — A falcon.

Persevera. Persevere. WHITE.
" Perseverance, dear my lord,
Keeps honour bright."—SHAKSPEARE.

Persevera Deoque confido. Persevere and trust in God. BROWN.

Perseverance. BURRARD, bt. HUME. PARRY. STEEL. WEBLEY.

Perseverando. By persevering. BRINCKMAN, bt. BROOKS. COPE, co. Leicester. DUGDALE. DUCIE, e. DENDY. FRAMPTON, of Moreton. FARNELL. FLOWER, bt. HENLEY. HANROTT. HOWELL. MACGILLIVRAY. M'KELLAR. LARKWORTHY. MORTON. ROXBY. TURNLY. WOOD, of Barnsley, bt.
" He who runs may read,
That perseverance gains its meed,
And Patience wins the race."—BERNARD BARTON.

Perseveranti dabitur. It will be given to the persevering. GILMOUR. ROBERTSON. SIMPSON, co. Durham.

Perseverantia. Perseverance. BELL.

Perseverantia et labore. By perseverance and labour. PITCHER.
Perseverantia palma. By perseverance (one gains) the palm.
WILSON, of Dulwich.
Perseverantia palmam obtinebit. Perseverance will obtain the
reward. TOOTH.
Perseverantia vincit. Perseverance conquers. BURNES.
"Nil tam difficile est, quin quærendo investigari posset."
TER. *Heaut.* iv. 2, 8.
Persevere. CONGREVE, bt. COLVILE. GREIG. GARDINER.
GIBBS. FEARON. FORDYCE. FARNALL. OAKES, bt. PHILLIPS,
of Reigate Lodge, co. Surrey. SMYTHE. WHITTALL.
"Perseverance is the bridge by which man may cross his difficulties and
acquire honour."
Perspicax, audax. Quickwitted, bold. ERSKINE.
Pestis patriæ pigrities. Sloth is the bane of a country.
DUGDALE, of Merevale.
Petimus altiora. We seek loftier things. CATTLEY.
Petit alta. He seeks high things. ABERCROMBIE, bt.
Petit ardua virtus. Virtue seeks difficulties. DOUGLAS.
Phœbo lux. Light from the sun. KINNAIRD, b.
There is a crescent and star in the crest.
" Before yon sun arose,
Stars clustered through the sky,—
But, oh ! how dim, how pale were those,
To his one burning eye !
So truth lent many a ray,
To bless the pagan's night —
But, Lord, how weak, how cold were they,
To Thy one glorious light."—MOORE.
Pie repone te. Repose with pious confidence. PIERREPONT.
MANVERS, e. MORDEY.
Pie vivere, et Deum et patriam diligere. To live piously, and
to love (both) God and our country. REDMOND.
Piedmontaise. HARDINGE.
Capt. G. N. Hardinge captured a French frigate in 1808, and her name,
" Piedmontaise," was inscribed on his crest of augmentation.
Pietas et frugalitas. Piety and frugality. GUTHRY.
Pietas tutissima virtus. Piety is the surest virtue. AINSLIE.
Pietate et bellica virtute. By piety and martial valour. O. OF
ST. HENRY.
Pietate et probitate. By piety and honesty. REES.
Pie*tatis causa.* In the cause of *P*iety. PYE.
Pieux quoique preux. Pious although chivalrous. LONG.
"The calm delights
Of unambitious piety he chose,
And learning's solid dignity ; though born
Of knightly race."
Pignus amoris. A pledge of love. GRAHAM, of Douglastown.
Pilot. NICOLAS, of Cornwall.
This motto, together with augmentations to his paternal coat and crest,
was granted, 1816, to Capt. J. Nicolas of Loo, Cornwall, as a reward

for the services of himself and of his son, Capt. Toup Nicolas, who commanded H.M. Sloop Pilot on the coast of Italy, and fought in her off Toulon, a gallant action with a French three-masted vessel, La Legère, of very superior force.

Placeam. I will please. MURRAY, of Priestfield.
Plena refulget. The full moon shines. PITCAIRN.
 Crest—A full moon argent.

Πλιον ήμισυ παντος. Half is more than the whole. HILLYARD.
 This sentiment is taken from Hesiod and is thus enlarged upon by Ausonius:—
  "Incipe dimidium facti est cœpisse. Supersit
  Dimidium : rursum hoc incipe et efficies."

Plus ultra. More beyond. ELLIOTT. NAIRNE, bt. NABBS.
 In the arms of Elliott,—A castle, the gates charged with a key, on the chief under the castle the words, "plus ultra," referring to the defence of Gibraltar by General Elliott.

Plus vigila. Watch more. WHITE.
Plutot rompe que plie. Sooner break than bend. DE PONTHIEN.
Poco a poco. By little and little. RAMAGE.
Pollet virtus. Virtue excels. MARYBOROUGH, b. POOLE. POLE.
Porro unum est necessarium. Moreover one thing is needful.
 COWLEY, b. MORNINGTON, e. WELLESLEY, m.
  "One thing is needful."—*Luke,* x. 42.

Portanti spolia palma. The spoils are the palm of him who carries them off. FELTHAM.
 Crest—A hand in armour holding a broken tilting-spear. This motto refers to an old usage,—He who unhorsed a knight at a tournament claimed his arms as the prize of victory.

Portio mea quod utile. May what is useful be my portion. FLACK.
Posce teipsum. Ask thyself. HODGES.
Posse nolle nobile. To be able (but) unwilling is noble, or to be able to refuse (to do a bad action) is noble. WINGFIELD, of Tickencote.
Possunt quia posse videntur. They are able because they seem to be. GOODERE. KEIGHTLEY.
Post est occasio calva. Occasion is bald behind. CHAPMAN.
  "Rem tibi quam nosces aptam dimittere noli ;
  Fronte capillatâ, post est occasio calva."
  DIONYSIUS, *Cato Distictiorum de Moribus,* lib. ii. 6. 26.
 A Greek epigram by Posidippus (Brunck's *Anthologia*), Εἰς Ἀγαλμα του καιρου.
 Occasion was anciently represented with a forelock, but bald behind like *Time.* Lord Bacon says, "Occasion turneth a bald noddle, after she hath presented her locks in front and no hold taken."

Post funera fœnus. An interest after death. MOW.
  "Ultima semper
  Expectanda dies homini : dicique beatus
  Ante obitum nemo supremaque funera debet."
  OVID, *Met.* lib. iii. 135

  "Non omnis moriar : multaque pars mei
  Vitabit Libitinam."—HOR. *Car.* lib. iii. 30. 6.

Post funera virtus. Virtue survives death. ROBERTSON.

" Shall I be left forgotten in the dust,
  When fate relenting, lets the flower revive :
Shall Nature's voice, to man alone unjust,
  Bid him, though doom'd to perish, hope to live?

Is it for this fair Virtue oft must strive
  With disappointment, penury, and pain ?
No ! Heaven's immortal spring shall yet arrive :
  And man's majestic beauty bloom again,
Bright through th' eternal year of love's triumphant reign."—BEATTIE.

Post mortem triumpho, et morte vici ; multis despectus magna feci. I triumph after death, and in death I have conquered : despised by many, I have achieved great things. O. OF MARIA ELEONORA.

Post mortem virtus virescit. Virtue flourishes after death. TYSSEN-AMHERST, of Didlington Hall, co. Norfolk. TYSSEN, of Hackey.

Post nubes. After clouds. STOTHARD.

Post nubes lux. After clouds light. BLUNSTONE. STEDDERT.
Crest—The sun rising.

Post nubila. After clouds. JACK.

Post nubila Phœbus. After clouds sunshine. AHRENDS. CRANWORTH, b. JACK. JAFFRAY. JAFFREY. PURVIS. ROLFE. ROBINSON. PINKERTON. TARLETON, bt. TARLTON, of Collingwood. SHULDHAM.

" Non, si male nunc, et olim
  Sic erit."—HOR. *Od.* ii. 10, 17.

Post nubila sol. After clouds sunshine. PINKERTON.

Post prælia præmia. After battles honours. FELLOWS. M'INNES. NICHOLSON. ROSSMORE, b.

Post spinas palma. After difficulties a reward ; *lit.* after thorns the palm. GODFREY. PAGET.

Post tenebras lux. After darkness light. HEWATT.
Crest — The sun rising from a cloud.

Post tot naufragia portum. After so many shipwrecks a haven. SANDWICH, e. HINE.

Post virtutem curro. I run after virtue. BRISCOE.

Postera laude recens. Ever fresh in the admiration of posterity. HARDINGE, v.
Wreaths of laurel and cypress form part of the crest of augmentation.

Potior origine virtus. Virtue is better than lineage. SCOT. SCOTT.

" The faculties of intellect and will,
  Dispensed with equal hand, disposed with equal skill ;
  Like liberty indulged, with choice of good or ill.
  Thus born alike, from Virtue first began
  The difference that distinguished man from man
  He claimed no title from descent of blood,
  But that which made him noble, made him good."—DRYDEN.

Potius ingenio quam vi. Rather by skill than by force. EDGAR. YOUNG.
The crest is a sword surmounted in saltire by a pen.

Potius mori quam fœdari. Better die than be disgraced. GIFFORD.

Pour appendre oublier ne puis. I cannot forget in order to learn. PALMER.

Pour avoir fidèlement servi. For having faithfully served. O. OF CHRISTIAN CHARITY.

Pour bien désirer. For wishing well. BOLDEN. DACRE, b. BARRETT—LENNARD, bt.

Pour deservir. To deserve. CARR.

Pour Dieu et mon pays. For God and my country. DE LANTOUR.

Pour Dieu, pour terre. For God, for earth. LEIGH, co. Chester.

Pour jamais. For ever. BOLDEN. EVERS. GURWOOD.

Pour l'advenir. For the future. DUC DE BROGLIE.

Pour le merite. For merit. O. OF MERIT.

Pour le roy. For the king. MACAUL. PEATERSON.

Pour ma patrie. For my country. COOPER. DALGAIRNS.

Pour mon Dieu. For my God. PEITERE. PETER. M'PETER.

Pour parvenir à bonne foy. To obtain success with credit. CUTLERS' COMP.

Pour y parvenir. To accomplish it. CANTERBURY, V. RUT-LAND, d. MANNERS, b. MANNERS, of Goadby Marwood Park.

Poussez en avant. Push forward. BARRY.

Praise God. KERR, of Kerrislande.
    " Heralds of creation cry—
    Praise the Lord, the Lord most high !
    Heaven and earth obey the call,
    Praise the Lord, the Lord of all."—MONTGOMERY.

Praise God for all. BAKERS' COMP., of London and Exeter.

Præcedentibus insta. Press hard upon those who go before you. ST. GERMAINS, e.

Præcipitatus attamen tutus. Cast down, yet safe. DUNBAR.

Præclarius quo difficilius. The more difficult the more honourable. FOUNTAIN.

Præclarum regi et regno servitium. Honourable service to king and country. OGILVIE, of Barras, bt.

Prædæ memor. Mindful of gain. GRAHAM.

Præmiando incitat. It incites by rewarding. O. OF ST. STANISLAUS.

Præmium, virtus, gloria. Reward, virtue, glory. CROSANE.

Præmium, virtus, honor. Reward, virtue, honour. BROWN, of Blackburn. COX.

Præmium virtutis honor. Honour is the reward of virtue. CHEERE. LOVELACE. TETLOW, of Haughton.

Prænuntia pacis. Forerunner of peace. BELL.

Præsta et persta. Promise and persevere. WALKER.

Præstando præsto. By standing prominent I excel ; or while I promise I perform. HAMILTON.

Præstat opes sapientia. Wisdom excels wealth. UPCHER.

Præsto et persisto. I undertake and I persevere. HADDINGTON, e. WINCHESTER.

Præstò et præstò. Ready and ready, *i.e.* I undertake and I perform. HAWKINS.

Præstò pro patriâ. Ready for my country. NEILSON.

Præsto ut præstem. I stand prominent that I may excel: or, I promise to perform. PRESTON.

Prævide, ne præveniare. Look forward, lest you be forestalled. TIMPERLEY.

Prævisa mala pereunt. Foreseen misfortunes perish. HODGES, of Hemsted. TWYSDEN, bt. WINTERBOTHAM.

Preigne haleine, tirez fort. Take breath, pull strong. GIFFARD.

In the early part of the reign of Henry VIII., a panther which had been presented to Sir John Giffard, of Chillington, escaped from her cage, and was pursued by the knight, bow in hand, accompanied by his son. Having hurried to the top of a steep ascent, nearly a mile from his house, he overtook the beast about to spring upon a woman with an infant: and as, in his still breathless state, he was preparing to shoot at it, his son, fearing his haste might weaken the accuracy and force of his shot, called out, "Preigne haleine tire fort;" words which, modernised to "Prenez haleine, tirez fort," now form the family motto. In pursuance of this advice Sir John paused, took breath, drew his bow strongly with a sure aim, and so killed the panther and saved the woman.

Premi, non opprimi. To be pressed, not oppressed. BENNET.

Premio a la constanco militar. The reward of military fidelity. O. OF ISABEL THE CATHOLIC.

Prend moi tel que je suis. Take me as I am. BELL. ELY, m. LOFTUS. RICKETTS, bt.

Prenez en grê. Take in good will. OGLE, bt.

Prenez en ire. Take in ire. LA FOUT.

Prenez garde. Take care. ELMSLEY. EMSLIE. EMSLEY. ELMSLY. M'INTOSH. MACRITCHIE. RICHARDS.

Prenez haleine, tirez fort. See "Preigne haleine, tire fort."

Press forward. GRISSELL. MORTIMER.

Press through. BORELANDS. COCKBURN. YOUNG, of Marlow, bt.

Prest. Ready. SHEFFIELD.

Prest d'accomplier. Ready to accomplish. HEBER, co. York. SHREWSBURY, e. TALBOT.

Prest pour mon pays. Ready for my country. MONSON, b.

Prest, et, prest. Ready, ay, ready. HAMILTON.
See "Ready, aye, Ready."

Presto et spero. I perform and hope. MERRY.

Pret. Ready. ASTON.

Pret d' accomplir. Ready to accomplish. ASTON, co. Chester.

Pretio prudentia præstat. Prudence is better than profit. MORISON.

Pretiosum quod utile. That is valuable which is useful. AFFLECK, bt.

Pretium et causa laboris. The reward and cause of labour.
FREDERICK.

Pretium non vile laborum. No mean reward of our labour.
O. OF THE GOLDEN FLEECE.

Preux quoique pieux. Valiant though pious. LONG.

Prima voce salutat. He salutes with early voice. BOUCHERETT.
There is a cock in the arms.

Primi et ultimi in bello. First and last in war. O'GORMAN.

Primus è stirpe. The first from the stock. HAY, of Leys, co.
Perth.
This motto is borne by the Hays of Leys, to denote that they were the
eldest collateral branch from the main stock of the house of Errol.

Primus ultimusque in acie. First and last in battle. SKERRETT.

Principiis obsta. Meet the danger at its approach. FFOLKES,
of Hillington Hall, co. Norfolk, bt.
This is one of the aphorisms of Hippocrates, 11–29, Αϱχομινων των
νουσων ην τι δοκιη κινιιν, κινιι—thus rendered by the school of
Salerno, and quoted by Thomas à Kempis, lib. i. cap. 13 : " Whence a
certain man said, Withstand the beginning ; after-remedies come too
late."
"Principiis obsta, sero medicina paratur,
Cum mala per longas invaluere moras."

Prisca fides. Ancient faith. GLASFORD.

Pristinæ virtutis memores. Mindful of our former valour.
THE EIGHTH HUSSARS.

Pristinum spero lumen. I hope for pristine lustre. PRESTON, bt.
Crest—A crescent or. "Pristinum" seems a play upon Preston.

Prius frangitur quam flectitur. He is sooner broken than
bent. BALLANTINE-DYKES, of Dovenley, Warthole, or Ward-
hall, &c., who also bears the motto, "Nec cito, nec tarde,"
for Ballantine, which family he represents in the female
line.
Thomas Dykes, an ancestor of this family, was a staunch adherent to the
Royal cause and an active partizan of the king. After the king's
forces were subdued, he was eagerly sought for by the Republicans,
whom he eluded for upwards of twelve months by concealing himself,
when pursued, in a mulberry-tree in front of the house, part whereof
still remains (1860). He was afterwards caught and kept prisoner in
a dungeon in Cockermouth Castle, where he died. His freedom was
repeatedly offered to him by the Republicans if he would change his
principles, and when upon his refusal they threatened to increase the
severity of his treatment, he replied, "Prius frangitur quam flectitur,"
which sentence, denoting his resolution to die sooner than yield, is
still used as their motto by his descendants. The bulk of the family
estates was lost through his zeal in the cause of his master. Thomas
Dykes married Joyce Frecheville, daughter and co-heiress of John
Frecheville and cousin of the Royalist, Lord Frecheville, of Slavely, &c.
co. Derby.

Prius mori quam fidem fallere. Rather die than break faith.
DRUMMOND, of Uxbridge.

Prix de vertu. The reward of virtue. NATIONAL ORDER OF
FRANCE.

Pro aræ et regni custodia. For the guardianship of the altar and the kingdom. QUEEN MARY.

Pro aris. For our altars. HARRIS.

Pro aris et focis. For our altars and our homes. BLOMFIELD. CAMPBELL, of Shirven. HAZLERIGGE, bt. KIRKLAND. M'NAUGHT. PURDON. PHELIPS. SNELL. WAIT. WOODFORD.

> " Strike ! till the last armed foe expires,
> Strike ! for your hearths and altar-fires,
> Strike ! for the green graves of your sires,
> God and your native land."

Pro avitâ fide. For the faith of our forefathers. BROOKE.

Pro Christo et patria. For Christ and my country. GILBERT. KER. VERNER.

Pro Christo et patria dulce periculum. For Christ and my country danger is sweet. CARR. ROXBURGHE, d.

Pro cruce audax. Bold for the cross. SQUAREY.

> *Crest* — A cross crosslett or.

Pro Deo et ecclesiâ. For God and the church. BISSHOPP, bt.

Pro Deo et grege. For God and the flock. PATERSON.

Pro Deo et patriâ. For God and our country. MAGUIRE.

Pro Deo et pro patriâ. For God and my country. STACKPOLE.

Pro Deo et rege. For God and the king. BICKERTON. BLACKER. GOLDING. HAWKINS. MASTERTON. ROSSE, e.

Pro Deo, patriâ, et rege. For God, my country, and my king. BLADES, of High Paull. BEUGO. JAMES, of Dublin, bt.

Pro Deo, rege, et patriâ. For God, my king, and my country. BLAYDES, of Rawby. M'DOWALL.

> " Oh heaven ! when swords for freedom shine,
> And monarch's right — the cause is thine ;
> Edge doubly every patriot's blow,
> Beat down the banners of the foe ;
> And be it to the nations known
> That victory is from God alone."— SCOTT.

Pro ecclesia Dei. For the church of God. SWAINSON.

Pro fide ablectus. Chosen for fidelity. ABLETT.

Pro fide et merito. For fidelity and merit. O. OF ST. FERDINAND, and of MERIT.

Pro fide et patria. For faith and my country. DANIELL.

Pro fide strictus. Bound for faith.

Pro lege et patria. For law and country. DANIEL.

Pro lege, senatuque rege. For law, senate, and sovereign. DODSWORTH, bt.

Pro legibus et regibus. For laws and kings. WILSON, bt.

Pro libertate. For liberty. WALLACE, of Kelly.

> " Ego vos hortor, quod sæpe majores vestri fecere, uti contra injurias armati, eatis."—SALL. *Bell. Jug.*

Pro libertate patriæ. For the liberty of my country, EVANS. CLARINA, b. MASSY, b. MASSEY, bt. MAYSEY.

Pro libertate et patriâ. For liberty and my country, MICHIE.

Pro lusu et prædâ. For sport and prey. MACMORAN, or M'MORAN. *Crest*—A falcon, belled ppr.

Pro Magna Charta. For Magna Charta. LE DESPENCER, b. STAPLETON, bt. STAPLETON.

> " England's ancient barons, clad in arms,
> And stern with conquest, from their tyrant-king
> (Then render'd tame) did challenge and secure
> The *Charter* of thy freedom."—AKENSIDE.

Pro mitra coronam. A crown for a mitre. SHARPE.

Pro omnibus laus Deo. Praise God for all things. MANDERS.

Pro patria. For my country. BANNERMAN, bt. BETSON. BULMAN. BONSALL. COOKE. CARBERY, b. DOUGLAS, of Carnoustie, bt. DOUGLAS. GROSETH. HAY, bt. HIGGINS. HAMILTON, of Preston. HASTIE. JAMES, bt. KAY. NEW-LANDS. NEWTON, of Newton. OGILVIE. PROVAN. ROC-HEAD. SCOTT. O. OF THE SWORD. TURNER. WARRINGTON. WOOD, of Holm Hull. WIDDRINGTON.

Pro patria auxilio Dei. For my country with God's help. GROSSETT, co. Wilts.

Pro patriâ ejusque libertate. For my country and its freedom. JOY.

> " We must be free or die, who speak the tongue
> That Shakspeare spake ; the faith and morals hold
> Which Milton held."—WORDSWORTH.

Pro patriâ et rege. For country and king. JONES. THOMAS.

Pro patria non timidus perire. Not afraid to die for my country. CHAMPNEYS, bt.

> " Non ille pro caris amicis
> Aut patriâ timidus perire."—HOR. *Car.* iv. 9, 51.

Pro patria sanguis. My blood for my country. SPLATT.

> There are drops of blood (guttée de sang.) in the arms and crest.

Pro patria semper. For my country ever. CALLOW. POWER, bt.

Pro patria uro. I burn for my country. COSTERTON.

Pro patria vivere et mori. To live and die for our country. GRATTAN.

> " The land we from our fathers had in trust,
> And to our children will transmit or die,
> This is our maxim, this our piety."—WORDSWORTH.

Pro patriæ amicis. For the friends of my country. GRANVILLE.

Pro patriæ amore. For patriotism. WOLFE.

> " England with all thy faults I love thee still—
> My country ! and, while yet a nook is left,
> Where English minds and manners may be found,
> Shall be constrain'd to love thee."—COWPER.

Pro pelle cutem. Skin for fur. HUDSON'S BAY COMP.

> There are beavers, a squirrel, and bucks in the arms.

Pro prole semper. For my offspring ever. PENDOCK.

> In the crest a demi-pelican vulning herself.

Pro recto. For integrity. MEEK.

Pro rege. For the king. BURNABY, bt. CHRISTIE. GRAHAM. M'PHIE. PORCHER, of Clyffe. MACKIE.

Pro rege dimico. I do battle for the king. DYMOKE, bt. The honourable the Queen's Champion.

> This motto has an obvious allusion to the name of the family, as well as to the ancient office of Champion, which derives from the renowned family of Marmyun, together with the manor of Scrivelsby, to which the Championship is attached. Sir John Dymoke, kt. was the first who formally discharged the office, at the coronation of Richard II., and Sir Henry Dymoke, bart., the present Champion, is the seventeenth of his family who has held it.

Pro rege et grege. For king and people. GRIEVE. PATERSON.

Pro rege et lege. For the king and the law. HORTON, of Howroyde. KIDSON. MANDIT. STEWART, of Fincastle.

Pro rege et limite. For our king and the border. ELLIOT.

> This family was very numerous in the border marches.

Pro rege et patriâ. For my king and country. AINSLIE, bt. ABERHERDOUR. BELL. CARR. CAMERON, of Lochiel. DE TABLEY, b. FRANKLYN. HAMOND, of St. Albans Court. LEVEN, e. LEICESTER. LESLIE. LYON. M'CUBBIN. PODE. SMITH, of Preston, bt. STEWART. WHEATLEY.

Pro rege et patriâ pugnans. Fighting for my king and country. PASLEY, bt. SMITH.

Pro rege et populo. For king and people. BARROW, bt. BASSET, b.

> "But while we sing 'God save the king,'
> We'll ne'er forget the people."—BURNS.

Pro rege et pro patriâ semper. Always for my king and my country. LAWRENCE.

Pro rege et religione. For my king and faith. BOYCOTT, co. Salop.

> This motto was assumed by the Boycott family, when arms were assigned them by Charles II., for the loyal services rendered to Charles I. by Sylvanus and Francis Boycott, especially in furnishing him and his army with shot, grenades, and other munitions of war.

Pro rege et republica. For king and state. PAUL, bt.

Pro rege, pro patria semper. For king and country ever. LAWRENCE.

Pro rege in tyrannos. For the king against tyrants. JOHNSTON. MACDONALD. M'DOWALL, of Logan.

Pro rege, lege, et grege. For the king, the law, and the people. EDINBURGH, Royal Burgh.

Pro rege, lege, grege. For the king, the law, and the people. BESSBOROUGH, e. BROUGHAM, b. PONSONBY, b. WHITHER.

Pro rege sœpe. For the king often. WRIGHT.

Pro rege sœpe, pro patriâ semper. For the king often, for my country always. EYRE. REDINGTON.

Pro republicâ. For the state. NICHOLSON.
Pro republicâ semper. For the state always. HELLIER.
    " Every passion, ev'n the proudest, stoop'd
    To common good."—THOMSON.
Pro salute. For safety. OGILVIE, of Edinburgh.
Pro utilitate. For utility. TENNANT.
Pro veritate. For truth. KEITH, of Pittendrum.
Pro virtute. For virtue. REID, of Seabank.
    " Some lead a life unblameable and just,
    Their own dear virtue, their unshaken trust."— COWPER.
Pro virtute bellica. For military merit. O. OF MILITARY
   MERIT. O. OF THE LEGION OF HONOUR, France.
Pro virtute et fidelitate. For valour and fidelity. O. OF
   MILITARY MERIT, Hesse Cassel.
Pro virtute patria. For his valour, his country gave it. O.
   OF THE TWO SICILIES.
Proba conscientia. A good conscience. BACON.
Probando et approbando. By trying and approving. RAMSAY.
Probasti me. (Ps. xvii. 3.) Thou hast proved me. FORNEAULX.
Probitas et firmitas. Honesty and firmness. LESLY.
Probitas solo nobilitas. Probity is the only nobility. KERRISON.
Probitas verus honos. Honesty is true honour. BARRETT.
   BATESON, bt. CHETWYND, v. LACON, bt. NEWMAN. VICARY.
Probitate. By honesty. RENNIE. RENNY.
Probitate consilium perficitur. By probity counsel is made
   perfect. RENNY.
    Crest—A hand suspending a pair of scales.
Probitate et labore. By honesty and toil. GOULD.
Probitatem quam divitias. Honesty rather than riches.
   CLAYTON, of Adlington Hall, bt. CLAYDON.
    " Non possidentem multa vocaveris
    Rectè beatum. Rectius occupat
    Nomen beati, qui Deorum
    Muneribus sapienter uti."—HOR. *Car.* iv. 9, 45.
Probum non pœnitet. The honest man repents not. SANDYS, b.
Procedamus in pace. Let us proceed in peace. MONTGOMERY.
Prodesse civibus. To benefit my fellow-citizens. DENISON.
   BECKETT, co. York.
Prodesse quam conspici. To do good rather than to be con-
   spicuous. BUCK, of Agecroft. COCKS. CHAMBERLAYNE.
   GROTE, of Surrey. LEIGH. SOMERS, e.
Profunda cernit. He comprehends profound things. GOURLAY.
   SIMSON.
Progredere ne regredere. Advance, do not recede. HONYMAN, bt.
Progredior. I advance. SHARP.
Projeci. I have thrown. MAIN.
    Crest—A hand (*main*) throwing a dart.
Prompte et consulto. Quickly and advisedly. PLENDERLEITH.

Promptus. Ready. DONALDSON. KEMPT. RUSSEL. SELBY.

Promptus ad certamen. Ready for the contest. SINCLAIR.

Promptus et fidelis. Ready and faithful. CARRUTHERS. CRONDACE.

Propero sed curo. I make haste, but am cautious. GRAHAM.

Propositi tenax. Firm of purpose. BUNNY. STRUTT. SMITH.

> " Justum et tenacem propositi virum
> Non civium ardor prava jubentium,
> Non vultus instantis tyranni
>   Mente quatit solida."—HOR. *Car.* iii. 3, 1.

Propria virtute audax. Bold in his own virtue. MADDEN.

Proprio vos sanguine pasco. I feed you with my own blood. CANTRELL, co. Lancaster.

> *Arms* — Ar. a pelican vulning herself within a nest, with young ones, all ppr.

Propter obedientiam. On account of obedience. HAY.

Prosecute or perish. BUCHANAN.

Prosequor alis. I follow with speed. GRAHAM, of Dumblane.

> *Crest* — A falcon.

Prospere qui sedulo. He does prosperously who does industriously. CUNNINGHAME.

Prospere si propere. Prosperously if promptly. PEAT.

Prospice. Look forward. LUARD.

Prospice, respice. Look forward, look back. GOSSIP.

> *Crest* — Two goats, heads erased, addorsed, *i.e.* looking forward and back

Provide. STEWART, of Grandtully, bt.

Providence. CRAICK.

Providence and perseverance. FURNAVAL.

Providence with adventure. HAWKINS.

Providentiâ. By providence. ANDERSON.

Providentia Dei. The providence of God. NICHOLSON.

> " A spirit of activity and life,
> That knows no term, cessation, or decay ;
> But, active, steadfast, and eternal, still
> Guides the fierce whirlwind, in the tempest roars,
> Cheers in the day, breathes in the balmy groves,
> Strengthens in health, and poisons in disease."—SHELLEY.

Providentia Dei conservet. May the providence of God preserve. DE LA MOTTE.

Providentiâ Dei stabiliuntur familiæ. Families are established by the providence of God. LAMPLUGH.

Providentiâ divinâ. By divine providence. KEATING. KECHING. SANGSTER, or SONGSTER.

Providentiâ et virtute. By providence and virtue. RANKIN.

> " Benigno numine Jupiter
> Defendit, et curæ sagaces
> Expediunt per acuta belli."—HOR. *Car.* iv. 4, 74.

Providentia in adversis. Foresight in difficulties. TOLLET.

Providentiâ tutamur. We are protected by Providence. KENYON. NORDEN.

Providentia tutamen. Providence is my safeguard. THOMSON.

Providentiæ fido. I trust to Providence. STEWART, of Fornese.

Providentiæ me committo. I commit myself to Providence. KYLE. PARK, of Fulfordlies.

> " But why, alas ! do mortal men in vain
> Of fortune, fate, or Providence complain?
> God gives us what he knows our wants require,
> And better things than those which we desire."—DRYDEN.

Providus esto. Be thou circumspect. MAXTONE.

Prudens, fidelis, et audax. Prudent, faithful, and bold. LEIGH.

Prudens qui patiens. He is prudent who is patient. COKE. LEICESTER, e. LUSHINGTON, of Pool and Kent.

Prudens sicut serpens. Wise as the serpent. POLE.

Prudens simplicitas. A wise simplicity. AMICABLE LIFE INSURANCE SOCIETY.

Prudent comme le serpent. Prudent as the serpent. TAYLOR.

Prudenter amo. I love prudently. SCOTT, of Gala.

Prudenter qui sedulo. He does prudently who does industriously. MILNE.

Prudenter vigilo. I watch prudently. DONALDSON.

Prudentiâ et animis. By prudence and courage. STEEL.

> " In tranquillo tempestatem adversam optare dementis est ; subvenire autem tempestati quavis ratione sapientis."—CIC. *de Off.* i. xxiv. 5.

Prudentiâ et animo. By providence and courage. ANTRAM. OCHTERLONY, bt.

Prudentiâ et constantiâ. With prudence and constancy. DENMAN, b. KINGDOM OF DENMARK

Prudentia et honor. Prudence and honour. M'KINNA.

Prudentiâ simplicitate. With prudence and simplicity. WYRLEY-BIRCH, of Wretham, co. Norfolk.

> The crest is a fleur-de-lis ar. (the emblem of simplicity), entwined by a serpent ppr. (the emblem of prudence).

Prudentiâ et simplicitate. With prudence and simplicity. LANT.

Prudentia et virtute. By prudence and valour. RANKIN.

Prudentia et vigilantia. By prudence and watchfulness. PURCHON.

Prudentia, fraudis nescia. Prudence, which knows not deceit. ELPHINSTON.

Prudentia in adversos. Prudence in adversity. TOLLET, of Betley. WICKSTEAD.

Prudentia me sustinet. Prudence upholds me. BOYD.

Prudentia præstat. Prudence excels. MORISON.

> " Dii immortales, homini homo quid præstat ! stulto intelligens Quid interest."—TER. *Eun.* ii. 2, 1.

Prudentia tutus. Safe by prudence. BRODIGAN.

> *Crest*—A fox issuing from the hollow stump of a tree.

Prudhom*me* et *loyale.* Prudent and loyal. PRUDHAM.

Publica salus mea merces. The public security is my reward. DICK.

Publicum meritorum præmium. The public reward of meritorious services. O. OF ST. STEPHEN.

Pugilem claraverat. He had ennobled the champion. NEWLE.

Pugna pro patriâ. Fight for your country. DOUGHTY. TICHBORNE, bt.

Pugno pro patriâ. I fight for my country. OGILVY, of Ragel.

Pulchrior ex arduis. The brighter from difficulties. MACKENZIE, of Coul, bt.

Pulcra pro libertate. For fair liberty. VANE.

Pullis corvorum invorantibus eum. (Ps. cxlvii. 9.) When the young ones of the crows call upon him. SIR GRIFFITH AP RICE, South Wales.

Pungit, sed placet. It pricks, but pleases. ROME.
Crest — A rose-slip.

Pura sequi. To follow pure things. MILWARD, co. Worcester.

Pure foy *ma joye.* True faith (or *Purefoy*) is my delight. PUREFOY, of Leicestershire.

Pure de fonte. From a clear *spring.* SPRING. CASBORNE.

Pylkington Polledowne, i.e. Pilkington or the master polls (mows) downe (meadows). PILKINGTON, of Blackburn.
The Crest — A mower, and both motto and crest refer to the fact that the ancestor of this family, when flying from the battle of Hastings, changed clothes with a mower in order to escape the Normans.

Q

Qua pote lucet. He shines whenever possible. SMIJTH, bt.
Crest — A salamander in flames ppr.

Qua tendis? Whither do you steer? ROY.
Crest — A lymphad (a ship) on the sea.

Quæ amissa salva. What has been lost is safe. KEITH. KINTORE, e.
Referring to the Scotch regalia, which were saved from Cromwell by Sir John Keith, Earl Marshal, who buried them in Kinneff Church, and, flying to France, was supposed to have taken them with him. For this service he was raised to the peerage in 1677.

Quæ arguuntur a lumine manifestantur. What are questioned light clears up. TALLOW CHANDLERS' COMP.

Quæ fecimus ipsi. Things which we ourselves have done. FULTON.

Quæ juncta firma. Union is strength. LESLY, of Kinivie.
There are buckles in the arms.

Quæ moderata firma. Moderate things are stable. OGILVY.

Quæ prosunt omnibus artes. Arts that are beneficial to all.
SURGEONS' COMP.

Quæ recta sequor. I pursue things honourable. CAMPBELL.

Quæ serata securu. Things locked up are safe. DOUGLAS.

Crest—An oak-tree ppr. with a lock hanging upon one of its branches.

Quæ supra. What things are above. ROBERTS.

Quæ sursum volo videre. I wish to see heavenly things. DUN-
RAVEN, e. MACQUEEN. QUIN.

Quæ vernant crescent. Things which are green will grow.
BURNET.

Quæque favilla micat. Every ember shines. ROBERTSON.

Quærere verum. To seek the truth. CARLETON, v.

Quærite et invenietis. Seek, and ye shall find. (Matt. vii. 7.)
LANGDON.

Quæsita Marte tuenda arte. Things obtained by war must be
defended by art. LUTTRELL.

Qualis ab incepto. The same as from the beginning. DE
GREY, e. HAMILTON, of Abbotstown. MAJENDIE. MIRE-
HOUSE. WEDDELL.

Qualis *ero spero.* I hope what I shall be. QUAYLE.

Qualis vita finis ita. As is our life, so is our end. YONGE.

" Lives of great men all remind ns
We can make our lives sublime,
And departing, leave behind us
Footprints on the sands of time."—LONGFELLOW.

Quam non terret hyems. Which winter does not nip with
cold. CAUNTER.

Referring to the branch which forms part of the crest.

Quam plurimis prodesse. To do good to as many as you can.
WORSLEY, bt.

Quam sibi sortem. Which fortune for himself, " he made "
perhaps understood. FRASER.

Quand Dieu voldra. When God shall will.

Quantum est in rebus inane. How much insignificancy is in
human things. MINETT.

Quantum in rebus inane. What emptiness in all things
(human). OSBORNE, bt. ODELL, of Carriglea.

" This is the state of man ; to-day he puts forth
The tender leaves of hope. to-morrow blossoms,
And bears his blushing honours thick upon him ;
The third day comes a frost, a killing frost,
And—when he thinks, good easy man, full surely
His greatness is a-ripening—nips his root,
And then he falls."—SHAKSPEARE.

Quarta saluti. The fourth to health. HALLIDAY.

Quasi summ*us* magister. As though the highest master.
SOMASTER.

Que je surmonte. May I excel. CHACELER, of Shieldhill.

Que pensez. What think ye ? ST. LAWRENCE.

Quem te Deus esse jussit. What God commands thee to be. SHEFFIELD, e.

Quercus robur salus patriæ. The strength of the *oak* is the safety of our country. OAKES.

Crest — An oak-tree ppr. fructed or, encircled with pallisades.

Qui capit capitur. He who takes is taken. SMYTH, bt.

Qui conducit. One who leads. BORTHWICK.

Qui fugit molam fugit farinam. He who shuns the mill, shuns the flour. COOPERS' COMP., Exeter.

Qui honeste fortiter. He who acts honestly acts bravely. ANDERSON, of Edinburgh.

Qui invidet minor est. He that envies is inferior. CADOGAN, e. PUGH.

Qui me tanget pænitebit. Whover touch me will repent. MACPHERSON. The crest is a cat.

Qui nos vincet? Who shall conquer us? BEUGO.

Qui nucleum vult nucem frangat. Let him break the nut who wants the kernel. HASLER, co. Sussex.

Crest — A squirrel sejant, cracking a nut ppr. collared gemel az. between two branches of palm.

Qui patitur vincit. He conquers who endures. KINNARD, b. KINAIRD.

" To bear is to conquer our fate."—CAMPBELL.

Qui pense? Who thinks? HOWTH, e. LAWRENCE. WALFORD.

Qui perde la foye n'a plus de perdre. Who loses faith has no more to lose. HART.

Qui potest capere, capiat. Let him take who can take. GLEGG.

Crest — A hawk preying upon a partridge.

Qui seminant in lachrymis, in exultatione metent. (Ps. cxxvi. 5.) Who sow in tears, shall reap in joy. KEMP.

Qui sera sera. What will be, will be. EDGELL. BETTEASON, of Seven Oakes. WOLFERSTAN, co. Suffolk.

Qui s'estime petyt deviendra grand. He who thinks himself little shall become great. PETYT, of Ackworth, co. York.

Qui spinosior fragrantior. The more thorny the more fragrant. Ross, of Marchinch.

Crest — A hand holding a slip of a rose-bush ppr.

Qui stat caveat ne cadat. (1 Cor. x. 12.) Let him who standeth take heed lest he fall. DOMVILLE.

Qui trans. Who is beyond. CONNECTICUT, North America.

Qui ut Deus? Who is like God? O. OF ST. MICHAEL.

" Unde nil majus generatur ipso ;
Nec viget quicquam simile, aut secundum."—HOR. *Car.* i. 12. 17.

Qui uti scit ei bona. Be wealth to him who knows how to use it. BERWICK, b. HILL.

Qui vit content tient assez. He who lives contentedly has enough. BRADSHAW, of Barton. BRADSHAIGH.

Qui vult capere capiat. Who wishes to take let him take.
GLOAG.

Quicquid crescit in cinere perit. Whatever grows perishes in
ashes. ASHBURNER, of Cockermouth.

Evidently intended as a play upon the name.

Quid clarius astris? What is brighter than the stars? BAILLIE,
of Hoperig. There are stars in the arms.

Quid justum non quod utile. What is just, not what is useful.
PHILLIPS.

Quid leges sine moribus? What are laws without morals?
EDWARDS, of Ashill, co. Norfolk.

Quid leone fortius? What is braver than a lion? CLAYTON, bt.

Quid merui meum est What I have deserved is mine.

Quid non Deo juvante. What (can we) not (do) with God's
aid. CHALMERS, of Gaitgarth. SALT, co. York.

Quid non pro patria? What would not one do for his country?
CAMPBELL, of Perthshire. MATHEW.

Quid pure tranquillet. What purely calms. THOMAS.

Quid prodest? What does it profit? WEBB.

Quid reddam Domino? What shall I render to the Lord?
CALTHORPE.

Quid retribuam? What shall I render? PARSONS.

Quid tibi fieri non vis alteri ne feceris. Do not to another what
you wish not to be done to yourself. RAM.

Quid tibi vis fieri fac alteri. Do to another what you wish to
be done to yourself.

Quid tibi vis fieri facias. Do what you wish to be done to
you. RAM.

" And as ye would that men should do to you, do ye also to them likewise."
Luke, vi. 31.

Quid utile. What is useful. GOULDIE. *Crest*—A garb.

Quid verum atque decens. What is true and befitting. RICKETTS,
of Combe. TREVOR.

Quid verum atque decens curo et rogo. I care for and ask what
is true and befitting. LA TOUCHE.

This line is from Hor. *Ep.* lib. i. 1, 11.

Quid vult valde vult. What he wishes he very much wishes.
MOTTEUX.

Cæsar, after the triumph of Pharsalia, and in the plenitude of his
power, heard, says Plutarch, the defence of an African prince, a fol-
lower of Pompey, by Brutus. Struck with the ardour of the advocate's
feelings and language, he remarked, " I know not always what this
young man desires, but whatever he wishes he wishes intensely."
Πᾶν δὲ ὁ βούλεται σφόδρα βούλεται. PLUTARCH, *Life of Brutus.*

Quidni pro sodali? Why not for a companion? BURNET.

Quiescam. I shall have rest. STEBBING, of Woodrising.

Quiescens et vigilans. Resting and waking. FAIRNIE. FERNIE.

Quihidder will ye? Whither will ye? STEWART, of Appin.

Quidhidder will zie ? Whither will ye ? STEWART, of Appin.
Quis occursabit ? Who will encounter me ? HAMILTON.
Quis preparet corvo escam suam ? Who can prepare his food
for the *ravens ?* RAVENS.

> " Who provideth for the raven his food."—*Job,* xxxviii. 41.

> " Beneath the spreading heavens
> No creature but is fed ;
> And he who feeds the ravens,
> Will give his children bread."—COWPER.

Quis prohibeat sperare meliora ? Who can forbid to hope better
things ? PARKER.
Quis separabit ? Who shall separate us ? · O. OF ST. PATRICK.
SOUTH CAROLINE.
Quis similis tui in fortibus, Domine ? (Exod. xv. 11.) Who is
like unto Thee, O Lord, among the mighty ones ? GOLD-
MID, bt. GOLDSMID.
Quis timet ? Who fears ? PRICE, of Saintfield.
Quis ut Deus ? Who is like God ? O. OF MERIT OF ST. MICHAEL.
WING.
Quo duxeris adsum. I attend whithersoever you lead. OGILVY.
Quo fas et gloria. Whither law and glory (lead). ROBERTSON,
of Glasgow.
Quo fata vocant. Whithersoever the fates call. DE LISLE, b.
BLAND. RUSSELL, of Handsworth. SIDNEY, bt. THURLOW, b.

> " There is a divinity that shapes our ends,
> Roughhew them as we will."—SHAKSPEARE.

Quo major eo utilior. The greater the more useful. NEILSON.
Quo me cunque vocat patria. Whithersoever my country calls
me. ARDEN, of Longcroft.
Quo virtus ducit scando. I climb where virtue leads. FOLLET.
Quo virtus et fata vocat. Virtue and the fates call me.
FFOLLIOTT.
Quo virtus vocat. Whither valour calls. YATE, of Whimper,
co. Suffolk. YATE, of Bromesberrow. PEACOCK-YATE.
Quocunque ferar. Whithersoever I may be carried. SINCLAIR.
Quocunque jeceris stabit. Wherever you may cast it, it will
stand. ISLE OF MAN. M'LEOD, of Cadboll, &c.
Quod adest. That which is present. MARSHAM, of Norfolk.
Quod Deus vult fiat. God's will be done. CHETWYND, bt.
Quod dixi, dixi. What I have said I have said. DIXIE, bt.
DIXON, co. York.
Quod eorum minimi mihi. (St. Matt. xxv. 40.) What (ye do)
to the least of these (ye do) to me. CORPORATION OF THE
SONS OF THE CLERGY.
Quod ero spero. What I shall be, I hope. BOOTH, bt. BOOTH.
BARTON, of Grove and Clonelly. GOWANS. HAWORTH.
Quod facio, valde facio. What I do I do with energy. SIKES,
of Berwick. SYKES, of Highbury, Leeds, &c.

Quod honestum est decet. What is honourable is becoming. RICHARDSON.

" Quod decet honestum est; et quod honestum est, decet."—CIC. *De Off.*

Quod honestum utile. What is honest is useful. LAWSON, bt. ANNAND, of Annandale.

"Nihil honestum, quod non idem utile."—CIC. *De Off.* iii. 8. 5.

Quod justum non quod utile. What is just, not what is expedient. PHILLIPS, of Garendon Park.

Quod merui meum est. What I have deserved is mine. NOGUIER.

Quod non pro patria? What would one not do for his country? BOWIE. BOWHIE.

Quod potui perfeci. I have done what I could do. MELVILLE, v.

" As much as I can do, I will effect."—SHAKSPEARE.

Quod pudet hoc pigeat. Let that which is shameful be displeasing to you. DOBYNS.

Quod severis metes. Thou shalt reap what thou hast sown. BLISS.

"For whatever a man soweth that shall he reap."—*Gal.* vi. 7.

Quod sors fert ferimus. We have what fortune brings. CLAYTON, of Enfield.

Quod sursum volo videre. I would see what is above. DUNRAVEN, e. QUIN.

Quod tibi fieri non vis alteri ne feceris. You should not do to another what you do not wish done to yourself. BOYLE.

"Therefore all things whatsoever ye would that men should do to you, do ye even so to them."—*Matt.* vii. 12.

Quod tibi hoc alteri. (Luke, vi. 31.) Do to another what thou wouldst have done to thee. CRAWFURD, of Cartsburn. FLEETWOOD, bt. HESKETH.

Quod tibi id alii. Do that to another which thou wouldst have done to thee. LOPES.

See the Gospels of St. Matthew, vii. 12, and St. Luke, vi. 31.

Quod tibi ne alteri. What (injury) is done to thee, do not to another. ALEXANDER, of Auchmull.

" See that no man render evil for evil to any man."—1 *Thess.* v. 15.

Quod tibi vis fieri facias. Do what you wish to be done to yourself. PHILIPSE.

Quod tibi vis fieri fac alteri. (Luke, vi. 31.) Do to another what you wish done to yourself. RAM.

Quod utile. That which is useful. GOLDIE. GOULDIE.

Quod verum atque decens. What is true and befitting. DUNGANNON, v.

Quod verum tutum. What is true is safe. COURTENAY.

Quod vult, valde vult. What he wishes, he wishes fervently. MAUNSELL, bt. HOLT. HORTON.

Quondam his vicimus armis. We formerly conquered with these arms. CARLETON. DORCHESTER, b.

> Evidently an allusion to the pheons in the arms and the arrow in the crest.

Quorsum vivere mori ? Mori vita. Wherefore live to die ? To die is life. BLENCOWE.

> " Life, I repeat, is energy of love
> Divine or human ; exercised in pain,
> In strife, and tribulation ; and ordained,
> If so approved and sanctified, to pass,
> Through shades and silent rest, to endless joy."—WORDSWORTH.

Quos dedit arcus amor. The bow which love gave. HAMILTON, of Colquot.

R

Radicem firmant frondes. Branches strengthen the root. GRANT, of Darlway. *Crest*—A hand holding a laurel branch.

Radii omnia lustrant. His rays illuminate all things. BROWN-HILL. *Crest*—The sun rising from behind a mountain.

Raison pour guide. Reason for guide. GASCOYNE.

Ramis micat radix. The root glitters in its branches. ROBERT-SON.

Rapit ense triumphos. He gains victories by the sword. SMITH.

Rara avis in terris. A rarity on this earth. KETT.

> *Crest*— A peacock.

Rara bonitas. Goodness is rare. BENNET.

Rath—A'rda—Cöel. On the hill of Cöel (*i.e.* O'Kelly) is the camp of Cöel. O'KELLY.

Rather die than be disloyal. PEARSON, of Kippenrose.

Ratio mihi sufficit. The reason is sufficient for me. GRAHAM, of Drumgoon.

Ratione, non irâ. By reason, not by rage. SMALL, of Currie-hill.

Ratione, non vi. By reason, not by force. M'TAGGART, bt.

Re alta spero. I indeed hope for lofty things. RIALL.

Re et merito. By reality and merit. VASSAL-FOX. GILDEA. HEBDEN, of Appleton.

Ready. ARCHEVER. FRASER, of Farralane.

Ready, aye, ready. NAPIER, b. NICOLSON. SCOTT, of Thirle-stane.

> When the rest of his nobles, assembled at Fala, refused to follow James
> V. into England, Sir John Scott of Thirlestane alone expressed his
> readiness. Hence James granted him an honourable augmentation to
> his arms with the above motto. To this gallantry of his kinsman Sir
> Walter Scott alludes in the *Lay of the Last Minstrel :—*
> " Hence in fair remembrance worn
> Yon sheaf of spears his crest has borne ;

Hence his high motto stands revealed,
' Ready, aye Ready,' for the field."

Reason contents me. GRAHAM, of Esk and Netherby, bt.

Rebus angustis fortis. Brave in adversity. COBBOLD, of Ipswich.

Rebus justis invigilans. Watchful for justice. WALCOT.

Recipiunt fœminæ sustentacula nobis. Women receive support from us. PATTEN MAKERS' COMP.

Recreat et alit. It amuses and nourishes. DUDDINGSTOUN.

I suppose this to be an allusion to coarsing, as the crest is a greyhound.

Recreation. FORRESTER.

Recta pete. Seek for right things. FLETCHER.

Recta sequor. I follow uprightly. KEITH.

Recta sursum. Right upwards. GRAHAM, of Duntroon.

Crest — A flame of fire.

Recta vel ardua. Upright even (when) difficult. EVELICK. LINDSAY.

The crest of both these families is a sword erect in pale point upwards, on the point a pair of scales.
This denotes that your acts should be guided by the balance of justice, even when you are endangered by the point of the sword.

Recte ad ardua. Honourably throughout difficulties. MACKENZIE, of Delvin.

Recte agens confido. While acting uprightly I am confident. PERRY, of Avon Dasset.

Recte et suaviter. Justly and mildly. CURZON. SCARSDALE, b. WYBORN.

Recte faciendo audax. Bold in doing justly. GRUNDY.

Recte faciendo neminem timeas. In acting justly fear no one. HARVEY, of Ickwell Bury. ROBERTSON. SCOTT, of Betton.

" A steadfast seat
Shall then be yours among the happy few
Who dwell on earth, yet breathe empyreal air,
Sons of the morning. From your nobler part,
Ere disencumbered of her mortal chains,
Doubt shall be quelled and trouble chased away."—WORDSWORTH.

Recte faciendo, neminem timeo. Acting justly, I fear nobody. CAIRNCROSS.

Recte faciendo securus. Safe in acting justly. INGLIS, bt.

Recte omnia duce Deo. God being my guide all things will be rightly done. RODD.

Recte quod honeste. That is rightly which is honestly done. ANDERSON, of Glasgow.

Recto cursu. In a right course. CORSER.

Rectus in curvo. I keep upright in a curve, *i.e.* in a crooked path. SYMONDS, of Great Ormesby.

Reddunt commercia mitem. Social interchanges render (men) civilised. STEWART, of Dundee.

Redeem the time. HANCOCKS.

" Redeeming the time, because the days are evil."—*Eph.* v. 15.

Redoubtable et Fougueux. (Formidable and Fiery.) HARVEY, of Chigwell.

For particulars of this motto see "Temeraire."

Refero. I bring back. CAMPBELL, of Gargunnock.

Crest—A bee volant.

Refulgent in tenebris. They glitter in the dark. STODART. STUDDERT. There are three stars in the arms.

Regard bien. Attend well. MILLIGAN. MILLIKEN, of Renfrew.

Regarde bien. Look carefully. NAPIER, bt.

Regardez mon droit. Respect my right. MIDDLETON, bt.

Regem defendere victum. To defend the conquered king. WHITGREAVE.

Thomas Whitgreave, of Moseley, co. Stafford, by his zeal and loyalty contributed greatly to the preservation of Charles II. after the battle of Worcester. On this occasion he received an honourable augmentation to his arms, a second crest, and assumed the above motto.

Rege et patriâ. By my king and country. BOWER.

Regi et patriæ fidelis. Faithful to king and country. NORBURY, b.

Regi fidelis. Faithful to the king. MOULSON.

Regi legi fidelis. Faithful to king and law. BARRY.

Regi patriæque fidelis. Faithful to my king and country. SCOTT, of Great Barr, bt.

Regi regnoque fidelis. Faithful to king and kingdom. POCOCK, bt. SIMPSON.

" Hail to the crown by freedom shaped—to gird
An English sovereign's brow! and to the throne
Whereon he sits! whose deep foundations lie
In veneration and the people's love;
Whose steps are equity, whose seat is law,
—— Hail to the State of England !"—WORDSWORTH.

Regi semper fidelis. Ever faithful to the king. SMYTHE, bt.

Regio floret patrocinio commercium commercioque regnum. Commerce flourishes by royal protection, and the kingdom by commerce. AFRICAN COMP.

Regis donum gratum bonum. A king's gift is pleasant and good. KINGDON.

Regulier et vigoreux. Regular and strong. SCOTT-KER.

Remember. GAVIN. ALLEN. HOME, of Wedderburn.

Remember and forget not. HALL, of Jamaica.

Remember thy end. KEITH, of Ludquhairn.

Remember your oath. HOULTON.

Renacio el sol del Peru. The sun of Peru has risen again. PERU, America.

Renasce piu gloriosa. It is born again more glorious. ST. CLAIR.

Crest—A phœnix in flames, which bird was said to be born again from the ashes of the pile on which it had burnt itself. See "Ex seipso renascens."

Renascentur. They will rise again. AVONMORE, v. SKIFFINGTON.

Renovabitur ut aquilæ juventus tua. Thy youth shall be renewed as the eagles. BARLOW.
  There is an eagle in the armorial bearings.
  " Thy youth is renewed like the eagles."—*Ps.* ciii. 5.
Renovate animos. Renew your courage. HAY. DRUMMOND. KINNOUL, e.
Renovato nomine. With renewed name. LYTTELTON. WESTCOTE.
Reparabit cornua Phœbe. The moon will replenish her horns. POLWARTH, b. SCOTT, of Abbotsford, bt. SCOTT, of Raeburn and Harden.
  There are crescents in the arms of all these families
  " Nova crescendo reparabit cornua Phœbe."—OVID, *Met.*
Repetens exempla suorum. Following the example of his ancestors. GRANVILLE.
Republique. The commonwealth. HARRIS.
Repullulat. It buds afresh. BISSET. LAUDER, of Bellhaven. LAURIE, of Portsburgh.
  The crest of each of these families is the stump of a tree budding afresh.
Requiesco sub umbra. I rest under the shade. HAMILTON, of Dalziel. *Crest*—An oak-tree.
Res non verba. Facts not words. DUBERLY. JARRETT. M'RORIE. WILSON, bt. WILSON, of Eshton Hall.
Resolute and firm. MILBANKE, co. York, bt.
Resolutio cauta. A prudent resolution. BETHUNE.
Resolve well, persevere. COLEMAN, cos. of Norfolk, Wilts, and Gloucester. MOORE.
Respice finem. Regard the end. FISHER. LUCAS. PRIESTLY.
Respice fines. Consider the end. OVINGTON.
Respice, prospice. Look backward and forward. LLOYD, of Gloucester.
Respicio sine luctu. I look back without sorrow. DENDY.
Resistite usque ad sanguinem. Resist even to the death. KEOGH.
Retinens vestigia famæ. Keeping in the footsteps of good report. LLOYD, of Seaton. LYSTER.
Restitutor. A restorer. ORDER OF DANEBROG.
Resurgam. I shall rise again. CROSBY. STEWART, of Newhall.
  This word, or "In Cœlo quies," are legends usually inscribed on hatchments instead of the family motto.
  " God formed them from the dust, and He once more
    Will give them strength and beauty as before,
    Though strewn as widely as the desert air ;—
    As winds can waft them, or as waters bear."

Resurgere tento. I strive to rise again. STRAITON.
Resurgo. I rise again. COOPER. HAXTON. M'FALL.
Retinens vestigia famæ. Still treading in the footsteps of an honourable ancestry. LISTER, of Armytage Park. LLOYD, of Leaton-knolls. RIBLESDALE, b.

Revertite. Return ye. WARDROP. SMOLLET. HERRIES.
Revirescimus. We flourish again. BURNES. GLENELG, b.
MAXWELL, of Everingham.
Revirescit. It flourishes again. BELCHES. BELSHES, of In-
vernay.
The trunk of an oak-tree sprouting forth anew is borne by these families.
Reviresco. I flourish again. CLARKE. MACKENAN. MAXWELL,
bt. MAXWELL, of Maxwell. RUSHTON, of Elswick.
Revocate animos. Rouse your courage. HAY.
Rhad Duw a ryddid. God's grace and liberty. DINORBEN, b.
Ride through. BELHAVEN, b. HAMILTON, of Broomhill.
Rident florentia prata. The flowery meadows laugh. PRATT,
of Ryston Hall, co. Norfolk.
> This motto, which is found in the Heraldic Visitations in the British
> Museum, not only contains a punning allusion to the name of Pratt ;
> but refers also to the trefoil, pomegranate, and oak-branches which
> flourish as portions of the armorial bearings. Its words are a metrical
> rendering of part of the last verse of Psalm lxv.; while the name Pratt
> itself is found in Germany, Spain, France, and Italy, respectively,
> under the forms Pradt, Prados, Du Pré, and Prati.
>> " Oft let me wander o'er the dewy fields,
>> And see the country far diffused around,
>> One boundless blush, one white empurpled shower
>> Of mingled blossoms, where the raptur'd eye
>> Hurries from joy to joy."—THOMSON.

Rien sans Dieu. Nothing without God. KERRISON, bt. PETERS.
Right and reason. GRAHAM, of Leitchtown.
Right can never die. TOLER.
Right revere, and persevere. BERRY.
Right to share. RIDDELL.
Rinasce piu gloriosa. It rises again more glorious. ROSSLYN, e.
> Crest—A phœnix in flames.
> See " Renasce gloriosa."

Ripis rapax, rivis audax. On the banks rapacious, in the
streams daring. O'HALLORAN.
> In the arms and crest are otters.

Rise and shine. LAWSON.
Rl. ordn. Dla Reina Maria Louisa. Royal Order of Queen
Maria Louisa. O. OF MARIA LOUISA.
Robore. By strength. WEBB.
Robore et sapientia. By strength and wisdom. ROBERTSON.
Robur atque fides. Strength and faith. WHITAKER.
Robur in vita Deus. God is our strength in life. JADEWINE.
Rosa petit cœlum. The *Rose* seeks heaven. ROSE. ROUS.
Rosam ne rode. Gnaw not the rose. CASHEN. ROSS.
> The Crest of Ross—A fox with a rose in his mouth.

Rosam qui meruit ferat. Let him bear the rose who has
deserved it. PRICE.
> Crest—A lion ramp. holding a rose.

Rosario. HARVEY. For services at that place.

Rosa sine spina. The rose without a thorn. PENROSE. WADMAN.

Ros cœli. The dew of heaven. ROSKELL, co. Flint, Lancaster, and York.

Rosis coronat spina. The thorn crowns with roses. FORBES, of Corse. *Crest* — A crown of thorns.

Rubet ensis sanguine Arabum. The sword is red with the blood of the Arabs. O. OF ST. JAMES OF THE SWORD.

Ruinam salutarunt pro rege. They have hailed ruin in the cause of the king. BURNES.

> Campbell of Burnside having been obliged to fly into the north when the cause of Charles I. was ruined, gradually dropped his name, and became known by that of Burns. In allusion to the losses which he sustained and to their own repaired fortunes, his descendants took for crest "A shivered oak renewing its foliage ppr." and for motto the one above, and "Revirescimus."

Rumor acerbe, tace Cruel rumour, be still. ECHLIN. RADSTOCK, bt. ST. VINCENT, V.

Rupto robore nati. We are born from the broken oak (referring to the acorns in the arms). AIKENHEAD, of that Ilk.

Rutilans rosa sine spina. A glittering rose without a thorn. QUEEN ELIZABETH.

S

Sacra quercus. Holy oak. HOLYOAK, of Tettenhall.

> This motto is on a ribbon entwined round the stem of an oak-tree which forms the crest.

Sacrificium Dei cor contritum. (Ps. li. 17.) The sacrifice of God is a contrite heart. CORKER, of Ballimaloe.

> "Thou hast said, the blood of goats,
> The flesh of rams I will not prize;
> A contrite heart, a humble thought,
> Are mine accepted sacrifice."—SCOTT.

Sagaciter, fideliter, constanter. Sagaciously, faithfully, constantly. WARD, b.

Sae bauld. So bold. SIBBALD.

Sannid a boo. Sannid to victory. FITZGERALD, bt.

Sæpe creat pulchras aspera spina rosas. The sharp *thorn* often bears beautiful roses. THORN.

> See for an account of this motto "Ad gloriam per spinas."

Sæpe pro rege, semper pro republica. Often for the king, always for the commonwealth. VASSALL, of Milford.

Sævumque tridentem servamus. We retain the stern trident. BROKE, Sir Geo. N. Bart. C.B., of Broke Hall, Ipswich.

> This motto was granted to Admiral Sir Philip Bowes Vere Broke, bart., K.C.B., with the crest of augmentation (a dexter arm encircled with laurel and issuing from a naval crown holding a trident) for his gallant capture of the United States frigate "Chesapeake," in fifteen minutes, when in command of H.M. frigate "Shannon" off Boston.

Sail through.   HAMILTON, of Rosehill.
> *Crest* — On the sea a ship sailing.

St. Domingo.   LOUIS, bt.   DUCKWORTH, bt.   See "Minorca."
> This word is on the flag which is held by the dexter supporter of the arms, and granted for services rendered at that place by Sir Thomas Louis, K.M.T. & K.S.F.

St. Vinceut.   RADSTOCK, b.
> This motto commemorates the good service of the first baron against the Spanish fleet off Cape Lagos 14th Feb. 1797.

Sal sapit omnia.   Salt savours everything.   SALTERS' COMP.

Salamanca.   COMBERMERE, v.
> Viscount Combermere bears this word on an escroll over his crest of augmentation to commemorate his services at that battle, where he commanded the 3rd Light Dragoons.

Salus et gloria.   Our salvation and our glory.   O. OF THE STAR OF THE CROSS.

Salus in fide.   Salvation through faith.   MAGRATH.

Salus per Christum.   Salvation through Christ.   ABERNETHY. CHRISTIAN.   FORBES, of Culloden.   HARE, of Docking, co. Norfolk.   GORDON.   LEITH, of Whitehaugh.

Salus per Christum Redemptorem.   Salvation through Christ the Redeemer.   MORAY, e.   STEWART.   STUART, of Duncarn.

Salutem disponit Deus.   God dispenses salvation.   EDGAR.
> " Beauteous stand
> The messengers of peace ;
> ' Salvation by the Lord's right hand !'
> They shout and never cease."— MOORE.

Salvet me Deus.   May God help me !   SPIERS.

Salvus in igne.   Safe in fire.   TRIVETT, of Penshurst.
> This motto refers to the three trivets in the arms.

San Josef.   NELSON, e.   See "Palmam qui meruit ferat."

Sancta clavis cœli fides.   The sacred key of heaven is faith. SANKEY.   This motto appears to be a play upon the name.

Sanctus Henricus Imperator.   St. Henry the Emperor.   O. OF ST. HENRY THE EMPEROR.

Sane Baro.   A baron indeed.   The official motto of the LORD-PRIORS OF ST. JOHN OF JERUSALEM.

Sanguis et vulnera.   Blood and wounds.   SKYNNER.

Sans changer.   Without changing.   CLARKE, of Ashgate, co. Derby.   DERBY, e.   ENERY.   GROVE, bt.   LEFEVRE.   MUSGRAVE, bt.   MUSGRAVE, of Myrtle.   NIGON.   STANLEY, of Alderley, b.   STANLEY, of Dalegarth.

Sans crainte.   Without fear.   GORDON-CUMMING.   MILES. PETRE.   SANDERSON.   TYRELL, bt.

Sans Dieu le ne puis.   Without God I cannot do it.   SKIPWITH, bt.   SKIPWORTH.

Sans Dieu rien.   Without God nothing.   GODLEY, co. Leitrim. HODGKINSON.   PETRE, b.   PETER, of Harlyn.   SAUNDERSON.

Sans heure.   Without a time.   ARNELL.

Sans peur. Without fear. HOGART. KARR. SUTHERLAND.

Sans peur et sans reproche. Without fear and without reproach. BAYNARD.

Sans reculler jamais. Without ever receding. BRACKENBURY.

Sans tache. Without stain. GORMANSTON, v. LE BLANC. MARTIN, of Abercairny. MARTIN, of Colston-Basset. MICHELL. MORAY. NAPAIR, of Milliken, bt. NAPIER, of Blackstone. PRESTON. HURRY. URE. URIE.

Sans variance, et à mon droit. Without change, and for my right. BOWES.

Sans varier. Without changing. CHARLTON, of Lea Hall.

Sape et tace. Be wise and be silent. CONNELLAN.
Crest—An owl.

Sapere aude. Dare to be *wise.* AMOS. COOPER. WISE. MACCLESFIELD, e. TOWNLEY-PARKER. WISE, of Ford House.

" Knowledge for us is difficult to gain —
Is difficult to gain, and hard to keep—
As virtue's self; like virtue is beset
With snares ; tried, tempted, subject to decay."—WORDSWORTH.

Sapere aude, et tace. Dare to be wise, and hold your tongue. HESSE.

" He that attends to his interior self,
That has a heart and keeps it ; and who seeks
A social, not a dissipated life,
Has business ; feels himself engaged to achieve
No unimportant, though a silent task.
A life all turbulence and noise may seem
To him that leads it, wise, and to be praised ;
But wisdom is a pearl with most success
Sought in still water, and beneath clear skies."—COWPER.

Sapere aude, incipe. Dare to be wise, begin at once. BIRNEY. of Salin. CLAXSON. CLAXTON, of Eastgate.

" Nimirum sapere est abjectis utile nugis."—HOR. *Ep.* ii. 2, 141.

Sapere et tacere. To be wise and silent. BROADHURST.

Sapiens dominabitur astris. A wise man will govern the stars. COMBER. HUTCHINSON. The crest of Hutchinson is a star.

Sapiens non eget. The wise man never wants. DUNBAR.

" Qui ipse sibi
Sapiens prodesse non quit, necquicquam sapit."—ENNIUS.

Sapiens qui assiduus. He is wise who is industrious. HANSLER, of Eastwood. MITCHELL, bt. MITCHELL, of Barry. SPERLING.

Sapiens qui vigilat. He is wise who watches. BAGSHOT. FOWLER.

Sapienter et pie. Wisely and piously. PARK.

Sapienter si sincere. Wisely if sincerely. DAVIDSON.

Sapientia felicitas. Wisdom is happiness. UNIVERSITY OF OXFORD.

Sapientia et veritas. Wisdom and truth. DOUGLAS, of Bads.

Sapit qui Deum sapit. He is (a) *wise (man)* who has the knowledge (or " savour") of God. WISEMAN.

Sapit qui laborat. He is wise who exerts himself. DUNBAR.

Sapit qui reputat. He is wise who reflects. M'CLELLAN. M'CLELLAND. MACKLELLAN.

Sat amico si mihi felix. Enough for a friend if he be kind to me. LAW, of Lawbridge.

Satis est prostrasse leoni. It is enough to a lion to have laid low. SALUSBURY, bt.

Saturet quies. Let rest suffice. SALTER.

Save me, Lord! CORBET, of Towcross.

> " O Lord, save me, and I shall be saved."—*Jer.* xvii. 14.

Say and lo. EVERARD, of Middleton, co. Norfolk.

Scienter utor. I use it skilfully. FORBES, of Auchreddy.

Crest—A sword bendways ppr.

Scio cui confido. I know in whom I trust. AUNGIER.

Scio cui credidi. I know whom I have believed. GASKELL, of York. MILNES.

Scite, citissime, certe. I use it skilfully, most swiftly, surely. HAVERGAL.

Scopus vitæ Christus. Christ is the end of life. MENZIES.

Scribere scientes. Men skilled in writing. SCRIVENERS' COMP.

Scuto amoris Divini. By the shield of God's love. SCUDA-MORE, of Ditchingham, co. Norfolk.

The name was originally Seynte Escud'amour, The *holy* shield of love, and the bearing a cross patée fitchée gules on a shield of gold, which is still borne by some branches of the family Scudamore. Thus the arms, motto, and name had each a relation to each other, the red cross being the emblem of the Divine love. By a later grant some of the Scudamores bear gu. three stirrups or.

> " And on his breast a bloody cross he bore,
> The dear remembrance of his dying Lord,
> For whose sweet sake that glorious badge he wore,
> And dead, as living, ever Him adored :
> Upon his shield the like was also scored,
> For sovereign hope which in His help he had."
>
> SPENSER, *Faëry Queen,* b. i. c. i. St. II.

Scuto divino. With the divine shield. KAY, bt.

Scuto fidei. By the shield of faith. MORRIS, bt.

Se defendendo. In his own defence. BEEBEE, of Willey Court. ECCLES. EKLES.

Se inserit astris. He places himself among the stars. CROSSE.

Secret et hardi. Secret and bold. DYNEVOR, b. RICE.

Secundâ alite. With prosperous omen ; or rather, "By favour of the bird." LATHOM, or LATHAM.

According to a tradition of the Latham family, one of their ancestors was, when an infant, carried away by an eagle, and wonderfully spared. The story is told in several ways, but to it their crest, An eagle preying on, or rather feeding, a child, evidently refers, as does also their motto, which, although at first sight merely containing a common classical sentiment, pointing to the general luck of the family, may also refer to the favourable countenance shown by the king of birds to his prize.

Secundat vera fides. True faith prospers. OGILVY, of Banff.

Secundis dubiisque rectus. Upright both in prosperity and in perils. CAMPERDOWN, e. CLEVELAND, d. LIPPINCOTT.
" Secundis
Temporibus dubiisque rectus."—HOR. *Car.* iv. 9, 35.

Secundis usque laboribus. Continually with prosperous labours. RICHARDS.
" Secundis usque laboribus
Romana pubes crevit."—HOR. *Car.* iv. 4, 45.

Secundo, curo. I prosper and am cautious. BUCHANAN.

Secura frugalitas. Frugality is safe. MITCHELL, of Filligrige.

Secure vivere mors est. To live securely (*i.e.* without caution) is death. DAYRELL, of Lillingston.

Securior qui paratior. The better prepared the more secure. JOHNSTON, of Gormach. JOHNSON.

Securis fecit securum. My axe saved me. LUXMORE.
Crest—A battle-axe.

Securitas regni. The security of the kingdom. O. OF CYPRUS, or SILENCE.

Securitate. With security. ROBERTSTOUN, of Bedley.

Securum præsidium. A secure fortress. CRAIGIE, of Kilgraston. CRAIGDAILLIE, of Aberdeen.

Secus rivos aquarum. (Ecclus. xxxix. 17.) By *rivers* of water. RIVERS, bt..

Sed sine labe decus. Moreover an honour without stain. ELDON, e.

Sedule et secunde. Diligently and prosperously. LOCKYER.
Crest—A ship under sail, the fore and mizen topsails charged each with an ant, on the maintopsail a lion ramp.

Sedulitate. By diligence. DIVIRE. ELPHINGSTON.

Sedulo et honeste. Diligently and honestly. LYALL.

Sedulo numen adest. The deity is present with the careful man. CUNNINGHAME.

Sedulus et audax. Diligent and bold. RUTHERFURD.

Seek quiet. DEACON.

Seetabuldee. JENKINS. LLOYD.
This motto was given for services performed in India by the above, and the word " Nagpore" is also borne by them to commemorate their services at that place.

Seigneur, je te prie garde ma vie. Lord, I beseech thee save my life. BRETTELL. HENZEY. PIDCOCK. TYZACK.

Semel et semper. Once and always. ALLCARD. SWINBURNE, bt.

Semni ne semni. I can do nothing without God. DERING, bt.

Semper. Always. DUNFERMLINE, e. SETON. GRAND DUCHY OF TUSCANY.

Semper constans et fidelis. Ever constant and faithful. IRTON, of lrton. LYNCH. SPOOR.

Semper eadem. Always the same. QUEEN ELIZABETH.
" Ho ! strike the flag-staff deep, sir knight ! ho ! scatter flowers, fair maids!
Ho, gunners, fire a loud salute ! ho, gallants, draw your blades !

Thou, sun, shine on her joyously! ye breezes, waft her wide!
Our glorious *semper eadem!* the banner of our pride!"—MACAULAY.

Semper eadem. Always the same. COLLMORE. FORRESTER, bt.
FAIRBURN. HOLLINGSWORTH. HORNSEY. PANTON. REID.

Semper erectus. Always exalted. PEPPER.

Semper et ubique fidelis. Always and everywhere faithful.
FITZ-JAMES.

Semper fidelis. Always faithful. BONNER. BROADMEAD. BRUCE.
CHESTERMAN, of Wilts and Beds. DICK. EDGE, of
Exeter. FORMBY. GARRETT. HOULTON, of Farley Castle.
LYNCH, bt. MARRIOTT. NICHOLAS, bt. NICHOLLS. NEWILL.
ONSLOW, e. RICHARDSON. SMITH, of Sydling, bt. STIRLING,
of Gorat, bt. STEWART. STEUART, of Ballechin. TAYLOR.

Semper fidus. Always faithful. LEITH, of Over-Barns.

Semper hilaris. Always *merry.* MERRY.

" To sum up all, be merry, I advise;
And as we're merry, may we still be wise."—BURNS.

Semper liber. Always free. STEPHENS, of Radnorshire.

Semper paratus. Always prepared. CLIFFORD, b. CLIFFORD.
CONSTABLE, bt. DALLAS. JOHNSTONE, of Stratton. KNOWLES,
bt. LECKEY, of Londonderry. MOUNSEY. PHILLPOTTS.
ROYDES. STEWART, of Inchbrock. USTICKE. UPTON, of
Ingmire. WELLS, of Grebly Hall. WELLES.

" Uterne
Ad casus dubios fidet sibi certius ; hic, qui
Pluribus assuerit mentem corpusque superbum ;
An qui, contentus parvo metuensque futuri,
In pace, ut sapiens, aptârit idonea bello ?"—HOR. *Sat.* ii. 2, 107.

Semper paratus pugnare pro patriâ. Always ready to fight
for my country. LOCKHART, b.

Semper præcinctus. Ever ready, lit. Girt up. MULHOLLAND.

Semper præsto patriæ servire. I am ever ready to serve my
country. O'NEIL.

Semper pugnare paratus. Always ready to fight. LITCHFIELD.

Semper sapit suprema. He is always wise about (or has a
taste for) the highest (*i.e.* heavenly) matters. SELBY, of
Biddleston and Earle.

Semper sic. Always thus. BEDWELL.

Semper sidera votum. The heavens always my wish. RATTRAY.

Semper sitiens. Always thirsty. DROUGHT.

In allusion to the name.

Semper spero meliora. I constantly hope for better things.
PRINGLE.

Semper sursum. Always upwards. GRAHAM.

Crest—A flame of fire.

Semper verus. Always true. HOWE. HOME, of Kames.

Semper victor. Always conqueror. RAMSAY, of Whitehill.

Semper vigilans. Always watchful. BOURNE. ENGLAND. TODD.

WALKER. WILLIAMS. WILSON, of Edinburgh, Smeaton Castle, &c. HUGHES, of Clapham.

Semper virens. Always flourishing. BROADWOOD.

Crest — A yew-tree.

Semper virescens. Always flourishing. HAMILTON.

Semper virescit virtus. Virtue always flourishes. LIND. MARISHALL.

Semper viridis. Always flourishing. GREEN. MAXWELL.

Semper virtuti constans. Always constant to virtue. BEAVAN.

Semper virtute vivo. I always live by virtue. SIDESERF.

Sepulto viresco. I revive from my burial. ADML. SIR G. EDEN-HAMOND, bt. G.C.B.

In 1650 Sir Graham Hamond's maternal ancestor removed the head of James Graham, the noble Marquis of Montrose, from the spike on the top of the Tolbooth at Edinburgh, where it had been placed after his execution. The second crest of the Hamonds refers to that removal, and this motto (which, literally translated, means "I flourish for the buried") alludes to the palm-leaves round the crest, which flourish to honour the dead hero. For Sir G. Hamond's other motto see "Paratus et fidelis."

Sequitando si giunge. By following, he comes up. LAMBERT, bt.

Sequitur patrem non passibus æquis. He follows his father, but not with equal steps. WILSON.

Sequitur vestigia patrum. He follows the footsteps of his ancestors. IRVINE, of Inchray.

Sequitur victoria forteis. Victory follows the brave. CAMPBELL.

Sequor. I follow. CAMPBELL. MACKINRAY. MAC INROY.

Sequor nec inferior. I follow, but am not inferior. CREWE, b.

Seringapatam. BAIRD, b. CALDWELL.

In commemoration of their services at that place.

Sermoni consona facta. Deeds agreeing with words. COLLINS, co. Devon. TRELAWNEY.

Sera deshormais hardi. He will be always courageous. HARDIE.

Sero sed serie. Late but in earnest. NAIRN. SALISBURY, m.

Serpentes velut et columbæ. As serpents and doves. EMYS.

Serva jugum. Keep the yoke. ERROL, e. HAY, of Park, bt. HAY, of Glenluce, bt. NUTTALL.

In the reign of Kenneth III., A.D. 980, when the Scotch were flying from the Danes at Loncarty, near Perth, an old countryman with his two sons, armed only with the yokes of their ploughs, met and rallied them at a narrow pass, and so caused them to win the victory. As a reward for this service, Kenneth conferred on the old man, whose name was Hay, large lands, and an honourable coat with the motto "Keep (still) the yoke (which you used so well)," and the descendants of Hay have ever since continued to "*Keep the yoke*" as part of their armorial bearings.

Serva jugum sub jugo. Keep the yoke under the yoke. HAY, of Locheloy.

Servabit me semper Jehovah. The Lord will always preserve me. BARCLAY.

Servabo fidem. I will keep the faith. DUTTON. JOHNSON, of Runcorn. SHERBORNE, b.

Servare mentem. To preserve the mind. SEABRIGHT.

Servare modum. To keep the mean. FOLKE. HERNE.

> " Est modus in rebus; sunt certi denique fines,
> Quos ultra citraque nequit consistere rectum."—HOR. *Sat.* i. 1, 106.

Servare munia vitæ. To observe the duties of life. OGLANDER, bt.

Servata fides cineri. The promise made to the ashes (*i.e.* of the departed) has been kept. HARROWBY, e.

> Sir Dudley Ryder, Lord Chief Justice of the King's Bench, had kissed the king's hands on the 24th May, 1756, on his elevation to the peerage; but he dying within a few days, the patent was not completed, and the promise was not fulfilled in favour of his son Nathaniel, first Baron Harrowby, till the year 1776, when this motto was adopted to record the circumstances.

Servate fidem cineri. Keep the promise made to the ashes of your forefathers. HARVEY.

> " That fame, and the memory, still will be cherished;
> He vows that he ne'er will disgrace your renown;
> Like you will he live, or like you will he perish;
> When decay'd, may he mingle his dust with your own."—BYRON.

Servatum sincere. Kept faithfully. PREVOST, bt.

Serve and obey. HABERDASHERS' COMP., London.

Serve the king. BENNETT, of Ireland.

Serviendo. By serving. SIMEON.

Serviendo guberno. By serving I govern. O'ROURKE.

Servire Deo regnare est. To serve God is to rule. MIDDLETON, of Westerham.

Servire Deo sapere. To serve God is to be wise. SADLIER.

Servitute clarior. More illustrious by service. PLAYER.

Set on. SETON, of Fordingbridge. CAMPBELL.

Shanet a boo. Shanet to victory, or defying. FITZGERALD and VESCI, b. FITZGERALD, of Castle Ishen, bt. FITZGERALD, the Knight of Glyn, and the Knight of Kerry.

Shenichun (or *Senachie*) *Erin.* The historian of Erin. M'CARTHY.

Sherwoode. HOOD.

Shoot thus. YEOMAN.

> Crest—A hand holding a dart as if to throw.

Sibi quisque dat. Every one gives to himself. HARPER.

Si Deus quis contra? If God be with us who can be against us? BENSON, of Parkside. SPENCE. SPENS, of Lathallan.

Si Deus nobiscum quis contra nos? If God be with us, who can be against us? MAIRIS. MOUNTMORRES. OTWAY.

> The two preceding mottoes are taken from Rom. viii. 31.

Si Dieu veult. If God wills it. PRESTON, of Lancashire.

Si fractus fortis. Strong though broken. FOSTER.

> Crest — An arm holding a broken spear.

Si je n'estoy. If I were not. CURWEN.

Si je puis. If I can. COLQUHOUN, of Rossdhu, bt. COLQUHON.

When the castle of Dumbarton was occupied by certain rebels, Colquhoun of Luss was asked by his sovereign to retake it; "If I can," was the reply. He, however, collected his followers, and under pretence of a hunting-party, enticed the garrison to a distance from the castle, which he occupied during their absence. The family have ever since used the bearings and motto which on that occasion were granted them by the king.

Si je puis. If I can. CAHUN. EYRE. RADCLIFFE.

Si je pouvois. If I could. CLELAND.

Si non datur ultra. If (it is) not allowed beyond. WILLIAMS, of Colebrook.

Si non felix. (*Merry*) if not happy. MERRY.

Si possem. If I could. LIVINGSTONE, of Miltoun, &c.

Si sit prudentia. (Juv. *Sat.* vii. ver. 20.) If there be prudence. AUCKLAND, b. BROWN. EDEN, bt. HENLEY, b.

Sibimet merces industria. Industry is a recompense to itself. MILLER.

Sic cuncta caduca. All things are thus unstable. HENDERSON.

Crest—A wheel.

Sic donec. Thus until. BRIDGEWATER, e. EGERTON, of Tatton, co. Chester.

Thus, says this motto to the various branches of the noble family which bears it, *Thus* shall you ever be, prosperous, and honoured for your virtues, *until* the virtues which raised you to such prosperity pass away, for then both your fame and your fortune shall perish

Sic fidem teneo. Thus I keep faith. MOLESWORTH, bt. WELFORD.

Sic fidus ut robur. True as oak. STIRLING.

Crest—An oak-tree.

Sic fuit, est, et erit. Thus it has been, is, and will be. STEWART, of Burgh.

Sic his qui diligunt. Thus to those who love. MORRIS.

Crest—A pelican in her nest feeding her young.

Sic itur ad astra. Such is the way to immortality. DAY. BARKER. DAVIES. CARNAC, bt. KERRY. MACKENZIE, bt. MARTIN. PUGH.

" Death's but a path that must be trod
    If man would ever pass to God."—PARNELL.

Sic itur in altum. This is the way to heaven. COWAN.

Sic mihi si fueris tu leo qualisens. If thus you, lion, do to me, what a lion you will be! RANT. *Crest*—A lion sejant.

Sic olim. So hereafter. HUMFREY.

Sic nos, sic sacra tuemur. Thus we defend ourselves and sacred rights. M'MAHON, bt.

Sic paratior. Thus the better prepared. JOHNSTON, of Poulton.

Sic parvis magna. Thus great things arise from small. DRAKE, bt.

Sic rectius progredior. Thus I proceed more honourably. SINCLAIR.

Sic semper tyrannis. Thus always to tyrants. VIRGINIA, NORTH AMERICA.

Sic sustentata crescit. Thus supported it increases. GERVAIS.

Sic te non vidimus olim. We did not formerly see thee thus. PLAYFAIR, of Meigle.

Sic tutus. Thus safe. GORDON, of Park, bt. GORDON, of Craig, &c.

Sic virescit industria. Thus industry flourishes. STEWART.

Sic virescit virtus. Thus virtue flourishes. RONALD.

Sic viresco. Thus I flourish. CHRISTIE, of Craigtoun. CHRISTY.

Sic vita humana. So is human life. CAPEL.

Sic vivere vivetis. Thus you shall live, to live (hereafter). BUNCE.

Sic vos non vobis. So you not for yourselves. WALROND. FRANKS.

> Virgil, when some one had wrongly claimed a couplet in honour of Augustus, which he had written on the palace door, put up on the same door the above commencement of a verse, which, when no one else could finish it, he completed as follows,—
>
>> " Hos ego versiculos feci, tulit alter honores.
>> Sic vos non vobis nidificatis aves.
>> Sic vos non vobis vellera fertis oves.
>> Sic vos non vobis mellificatis apes.
>> Sic vos non vobis fertis aratra boves."

Sicut oliva virens lætor in æde Dei. (Ps. lii. 8.) As the flourishing *olive*, I rejoice in the house of God. OLIVER.

Sicut quercus. As the oak. CHALLONER.

Sidus adsit amicum. Let my propitious star be present. BATEMAN, co. Derby.

Signum pacis amor. Love is the token of peace. BELL.

Silentio et spe. In silence and hope. BRANDER.

S'ils te mordent, mords les. If they bite thee, bite them. MORLEY, of Marrick Park, Yorkshire.

Simili frondescit virga metallo. The twig has leaves of similar metal. CALMADY.

> The twig refers to Everitt, who took the name of Calmady, and who, according to the motto, did not degenerate from the original stock, but still bore golden fruit. The words of the motto form a portion of the celebrated lines found in Virgil, *Æn.* vi. 143 :—
>
>> " Primo avulso, non deficit alter
>> Aureus ; et simili frondescit virga metallo."

Simplex munditiis (Hor. Od. i. 5. 5.) Plain with neatness. SYMONDS, of Pilsdon. PHILIPS, co. Somerset.

Simplex vigilum veri. An honest one of the sentinels of truth. PERKINS, co. Warwick.

Simplices sicut pueri, sagaces sicut serpentes. Harmless as boys, wise as serpents. VAUGHAN.

> In the arms and for crest is a boy's head, enwrapped round the neck with a serpent.

Sincere et constanter. Sincerely and steadfastly. O. OF THE RED EAGLE.

Sincera fide agere. To act with faith sincere. BIRCH.

Sinceritate. By sincerity. FRANCKLIN.

Sine Cerere et Baccho friget Venus. Without corn and wine love grows cold. LONGE, of Spixworth.

Sine crimine fiat. Be it done without reproach. INNES, bt.

Sine cruce sine luce. Without the cross without light. CLOSE. MAXWELL.

Sine Deo nihil. Without God nothing. LITSTER.

Sine fine. Without end. CRICHTON. M'GILL. MAKGILL. MAITLAND.

Sine fraude fides. Faith without deceit. JOHNSTON.
> "Cuncta sine insidiis, nullamque timentia fraudem
> Plenaque pacis."—OVID, *Met.* lib. xv. 102.

Sine fraude fides. Faith without deceit. JOHNSTON.

Sine injuria. Without offence. WATSON.

Sine labe fides. Faith unspotted. LOCKHART, of Cleghorn.

Sine labe lucebit. He shall shine unblemished. CRAWFORD.

Sine labe nota. Known to be without a stain. CRAWFURD, of Kilburney. M'KENZIE.

Sine macula. Without spot. CARY. M'CULLOCH. M'KENZIE. SYNNOT. NORCLIFFE.
> "The purest treasure mortal times afford
> Is spotless reputation; that away,
> Men are but gilded loam, or painted clay."—SHAKSPEARE.

Sine macula macla. A mascle without a stain. CLOUGH.
> There are three mascles in the arms, I therefore take this motto to mean that the armorial bearings are without a stain.

Sine metu. Without fear. JAMESON. MERES.

Sine numine nihilum. Nothing without the divinity. JONES.

Sine sanguine victor. A bloodless conqueror. SMITH.

Sine sole nihil. Nothing without the sun. PETTIGREW.

Sine timore. Without fear. CORMACK. M'CORMACK. M'CORMICK.

Singulariter in spe. Specially in hope. LASCHER.

Sis fortis. Be thou brave. LINDSAY, of Cavill.

Sis justus, et ne timeas. Be just and fear not. WHITE.
> "Be just and fear not:
> Let all the ends thou aim'st at be thy country's,
> Thy God's, and truth's."—SHAKSPEARE.

Sis justus nec timeas. Be just, fear not. GARVEY.

Sis pius in primis. Be pious among the first. BARLOW, bt.

Sit sine labe fides. Let faith be unspotted. PETERS.

Sit laus Deo. Praise be to God. ARBUTHNOT, of Catherlan.

Sit nomen decus. May my name be an honour. WORSLEY.

Sit saxum firmum. Let the stone be firm. SAXBY.

Sit sine spina. Let it be without thorn. CAY, of Charlton.
> There is a rose in the arms.

Smite on, quoth Smith. SMITH.

So no no dea ne. COMBERFORD.

So fork forward. CUNNINGHAME, of Craigends.

So run that you may obtain. (1 Cor. ix. 24.)   BAKER.
Soho.   BRINNING.
Soies ferme.   Be firm.   MAXWELL.
Soies content.   Be content.   CHARNOCK.
Sol clarior astro.   The sun is brighter than a star.   JOHNSON.
Sol et scutum Deus.   God is our sun and shield.   PEARSON.
Sol mi re fa.   BULL.
> This motto with the arms was granted to Dr. John Bull, temp. Queen
> Elizabeth.

Sola bona quæ honesta.   Those things only are good which are
honest.   ARCHER, co. Warwick.   COLEBROOKE, bt.
Sola cruce salus.   The only salvation is through the cross.
BARCLAY.   BROOKBANK.
Sola Deus salus.   God the only salvation.   ARCHER.
> " Salvation is of the Lord."—*Jonah,* ii. 9.

Sola Deo salus.   The only salvation is in God.   ROBINSON.
> " Salvation belongeth to the Lord."—*Ps.* iii. 8.

Sola et unica virtus.   Virtue alone and without a peer.   COLLIS.
HARRIS.   HANSON.   HENLEY.
> The line in Juvenal is " Nobilitas sola est atque unica virtus," *i.e.* the
> one and only nobility is virtue.

Sola in Deo salus.   Safety alone in God.   ROBINSON, bt.
ROBINSON.   ROKEBY, b.
Sola juvat virtus.   Virtue alone delights.   BLAIRTYRE, b. OWEN.
Sola nobilitas virtus.   Virtue is the only nobility.   ABERCORN,
m.   BLAKE, of Menlo, bt.   STANDISH.
> " What profit pedigree, or long descent,
> From farre-fetcht blood, or painted monuments
> Of our great-grandsire's visage?   'Tis most sad
> To trust unto the worth another had
> For keeping up our fame ; which else would fall,
> If, beside birth, there be no worth at all."—ANON.

Sola nobilitat virtus.   Virtue alone ennobles.   HAMILTON, of
Silverton.   HILL, bt.   MOWBRAY.
> " From Virtue first began
> The difference that distinguished man from man.
> He claimed no title from descent of blood,
> But that which made him noble made him good."—DRYDEN.

Sola proba quæ honesta.   Those things only are good which
are honourable.   NEAVE, bt.
Sola salus servire Deo.   The only safe course is to serve God.
GORE, bt.   WARE, of Edinburgh.   MAGENIS.
Sola ubique triumphans.   Alone triumphant everywhere.
CARVILLE.
Sola ubique triumphat.   Alone she triumphs everywhere.
O. OF LADIES SLAVES TO VIRTUE.
Sola virtus invicta.   Virtue alone invincible.   NORFOLK, d.
HOWARD, of Greystoke.   HOWARD, of Corby Castle.   HAIGE.
HANSON.   HARRIS.   COLLIS.
> " What nothing earthly gives or can destroy,
> The soul's calm sunshine, and the heartfelt joy,
> Is virtue's prize."—POPE.

Sola virtus nobilitat. Virtue alone ennobles. HENDERSON, bt.
> See "Sola nobilitat virtus."

Sola virtus triumphat. Virtue alone triumphs. CARVILE.
> "He fixes good on good alone, and owes
> To virtue every triumph that he knows."—WORDSWORTH.

Solem fero. I bear the sun. AUBREY, bt.

Solem ferre possum. I can bear the sun. DAVIES. SANDERS.
> Referring to the eagles in the arms.

Solertia ditat. Prudence enriches. WHITELAW.
> *Crest*—A bee erect ppr.

Soli Deo. To God alone. ALLOWAY.

Soli Deo gloria. Glory be to God alone. BONTEINE. LESLY.
EUSTACE. GLOVERS' AND SKINNERS' COMP.

Soli Deo honor et gloria. Honour and glory be to God alone.
HUDDLESTON, of Sawston.
> "To the only wise God be honour and glory."—1 *Tim.* i. 17.

Solus Christus mea rupes. Christ alone is my rock. ORROCK.

Solus in pluribus. Alone among many. FORBES, of Sussex.

Solus inter plurimos. Alone among many. FORBES, of King-
erloch.
> Allusive to these being the only Forbes who were not Covenanters.

Solus minus solus. Alone, but not alone. HOSKINS.
> P. Scipio Africanus used, writes Cicero (*de Off.* iii. 1, 1), to say "that he
> was never less idle than when he was at leisure, nor less alone than
> when he was by himself."

Son comfort et liesse. His comfort and joy. T. OF DONCASTER.

Sors mihi grata cadit. A pleasant lot devolves to me. SKEEN.

Sorte contentus. Content with one's lot. WELBY.

Sorte sua contentus. Content with his lot. HARTWELL, bt.

Sorti æquus utrique. Equal to each condition. MACLEAN.

Souvenez. Remember. GRAHAM.

Soyez ferme. Be firm. CARRICK, e. HYDE. SKERRIN. FOLJAMBE.

Soyez fiel. Be faithful. YATES.

Soyez sage et simple. Be wise and simple. SPRY.
> This motto, when conjoined to the crest, which is a dove standing upon
> a serpent, forms an allusion to the well-known text (*Matt.* x. 16),
> "Be ye wise as serpents and harmless as doves."

Spare not. GIFFARD. MACGREGOR.

Spare nought. BRISBANE, bt. HAY. TWEEDDALE, m. YESTER.

Spartan. BRENTON, bt.
> The name of the ship which Vice-Adm. Sir J. Brenton, K.C.B., G.C.S.F.
> and M., commanded, who, in consideration of his gallant professional
> services, was created a baronet, 24 Dec. 1812.

Spe. By hope. HORROCKS. LOVETT.

Spe aspera levat. He lightens difficulties by hope. ROSS, of
Morinchie.
> "What future bliss he gives not thee to know,
> But gives thee hope to be thy blessing now."—POPE.

Spe et labore. By hope and exertion. JEBB.

Spe expecto. I expect with hope. FORBES. LIVINGSTONE.

Spe labor levis. Hope makes labour light. HILL, of Gressenhall Hall, co. Norfolk.

Spe posteri temporis. In hope of the latter time. ATCHERLEY.
JONES.

Spe tutiores armis. Safer by hope than by arms. LEWIS.

Spe verus. True in hope. SCOTT.

Spe vires augentur. Our strength is increased by *hope*. HOPE.
SCOTT, of Dunninald. SCOTT, of Silwood Park, bt.

Spe vitæ melioris. In the hope of a better life. LEA.

Spe vivitur. We live in hope. DOBREE.

Spectemur agendo. Let us be viewed by our actions. AGAR.
BROWN. BROWNE. DRUMSON. DUCKETT. ELLIS. ELVIN,
of East Dereham. LLOYD. MOTT. MONTAGUE, b. MONTAGUE.
MOORE. MORRIS. M'LEUR. REYNOLDS. RUTSON. SHANNON, e.
SCHOLEFIELD.

> " Quid verbis opus est ? Spectemur agendo."—OVID, *Met.* lib. xiii. 120.

Speed. JOHNSTONE. GARNOCK.

Speed, strength, and truth united. FRAME-WORK KNITTERS'
COMP.

Speed *well.* SPEID.

Spei bonæ atque animi. Of good hope and courage. MILLAR.

Spem fortuna alit. Good fortune nourishes hope. KINNEAR.
PETREE.

Spem renovat. He renews his hope. GRIERSON.

Spem renovant alæ. Its wings renew its hope. NORVILL, of
Boghall. *Crest*—A martlet rising.

Spem sequimur. We follow hope. ELLISON.

Spem successus alit. Success nourishes hope. ROSS, of Balna-
gowan, bt.

Spera. Hope. GASKELL.

> " Cease every joy to glimmer on my mind,
> But leave, oh leave the light of Hope behind."—CAMPBELL.

Sperabo. I will hope. AMAND, of Lutton. PITCAIRN, ANNAND.

Sperandum. To be hoped for. RAIT. SCOT.

Sperandum est. It is to be hoped for. WALLACE, bt. WALLACE.

Sperans pergo. I advance hoping. FLETCHER, of Kevan.

Sperantes in Domino non deficient. Those who hope in the
Lord shall not fail. NIBLETT.

Sperare timere est. To hope is to fear. RATCLIFF.

Sperat infestis. He hopes in adversity. COLBORNE. SEATON, b.

> " Sperat infestis, metuit secundus
> Alteram sortem bene præparatum
> Pectus."—HOR. *Car.* ii. 10, 13.

Sperate et vivite fortes. Hope and live bold (ly). BLAND, of
Kippax Park.

Speratum et completum. Hoped for and fulfilled. ARNET.
ARNUT.

Speravi. I have hoped. LYON. LYONS, K.C.B.

Speravi in Domino. I have placed my hope in the Lord. HAY.

Spernit humum. It despises the earth. FORBES, of Pittencrief.
MITCHELL. M'KINDLEY.

> " Invidiaque major
> Spernit humum fugiente penna."—HOR. *Car.* iii. 2, 21.

These words of Horace refer to a man who rises superior to envy and
scorns the vulgar crowd.

Spernit pericula virtus. Virtue despises danger. CARPENTER.
RAMSAY, of Banff house, bt. FORRESTER.

Sperno. I despise. ELLEIS.

Spero. I hope. ANNAND. BRISCOE. CHALMERS, of Blancraig,
and Auldbar Castle. CALDERWOOD. DOLLING, of Magheralin.
GIB. GORDON. HUTTON. LANGLANDS. LEARMOUTH.
MAKEPEACE. MENZIES. SPARROW. SHANKE, of Castlerig.
SHANK. TOOLE. WAKEFIELD. WATERS.

Spero dum spiro. I hope while I have life. CHAMBERS.

Spero et captivus nitor. I hope, and though a captive I strive.
DEVENISH.

Spero et progredior. I hope and proceed. PRINGLE, of Clifton, &c.

Spero et vivo. I hope and live. MASHITER.

Spero in Deo. I trust in God. BLACKIE.

Spero infestis, metuo secundis. I hope in adversity, I fear in
prosperity. ELLERTON. LUDLOW, e. STEWART.

Spero meliora. I hope for better things. ANSWORTH. CAR-
RINGTON. DOUGLAS. LAIRD. MOFFAT. MAXWELL. MURRAY.
PHILLIPS. RHET. RAIT. RODIE. SPARKES. SHAW, bt. SCO-
PHOLINE. STEWART. SANDERLANDS. SMITH. TORPICHEN, b.
WATSON.

> " Multa dies, variusque labor mutabilis ævi,
> Retulit in melius ; multos alterna revisens
> Lusit, et in solido rursus Fortuna locavit."—VIRG. *Æn.* xi. 425.

Spero procedere. I hope to prosper. HOPKIRK.

Spero suspiro donec. While I breathe I hope. HOPE, of Granton.

Spero ut fidelis. I hope as being faithful. MYNORS. BAS-
KERVILLE.

> " Death has its twofold aspect ! wintry—one,
> Cold, sullen, blank, from hope and joy shut out ;
> The other, which the ray divine hath touched,
> Replete with vivid promise, bright as spring."— WORDSWORTH.

Spes alit. Hope nourishes. CHILD, of Dervil. SCAIFE.

Spes alit agricolam. Hope nourishes the farmer. HUSKINSON.

Spes anchora tuta. Hope is a safe anchor. DUNMURE.

> " Hope is an anchor firm and sure, holds fast
> The Christian vessel, and defies the blast."—COWPER.

Spes anchora vitæ. Hope is the anchor of life. M'LEAY.

Spes antiqua domus. The ancient hope of the house. FORD-
BOWES.

Spes audaces adjuvat. Hope assists the brave. HOLLIS.

Spes dabit auxilium. Hope will lend aid. DUNBAR, of Durn, bt.

Spes decus et robur. Hope is honour and strength. EARDLEY-SMITH, bt.

Spes durat avorum. The hope of my ancestors endures. NASSAU. ROCHFORD. WALMESLEY.

Spes est in Deo. My hope is in God. BAGGE, of Stradsett.

> " Hope, with uplifted foot, set free from earth,
> Pants for the place of her ethereal birth,
> On steady wings sails through the immense abyss,
> Plucks amaranthine joys from bowers of bliss,
> And crowns the soul, while yet a mourner here,
> With wreaths like those triumphant spirits wear."— COWPER.

Spes et fides. Hope and faith. CHAMBERLAIN, bt.

Spes et fortuna. Hope and fortune. CHELMSFORD, b.

Spes in Deo. My hope is in God. BOULTBEE.

Spes in extremum. Hope to the last. SHORT, of Borrowstoun.

Spes infracta. My hope is unbroken. DICK.

Spes juvat. Hope delights. ROLLAND.

Spes labor levis. Hope is light labour. BIGLAND. OCHTERLONY, bt.

Spes lucis æternæ. The hope of eternal life. PITCAIRN.

Spes mea Christus. Christ is my hope. CLANMORRIS, b. LUCAN, e. BINGHAM, of Melcombe.

Spes mea Christus erit. Christ shall be my hope. POWELL.

Spes mea Deus. God is my hope. O'FARRELL. BROOKE, bt.

Spes mea in cælis. My hope is in heaven. BOYD.

> " There is a peace and joy in heaven,
> And to hope for its bliss is to mortals given."— BOYD.

Spes mea in Deo. My hope is in God. BROOKE. DEWHURST. GOSKER. GREAVES. GASKELL. GUINESS. KIRKWOOD. LEWIN. LEITHBRIDGE, bt. ROPER. TEYNHAM, b. SAUNDERS. WAINWRIGHT.

Spes mea in futuro est. My hope is in the future. ROBINSON, bt.

Spes mea, res mea. My hope is my estate. DRUMMOND, of Monedie.

Spes mea superne. My hope is from above. BRUCE, of Cowden.

Spes melioris ævi. The hope of a better age. REES.

> " The food of hope
> Is meditated action ; robbed of this
> Her sole support, she languishes and dies.
> We perish also, for we live by hope,
> And by desire ; we see by the glad light
> And breathe the sweet air of futurity ;
> And so we live, or else we have no life."— WORDSWORTH.

Spes meum solatium. Hope is my solace. CUSHNEY.

Spes non fracta. My hope is not broken. MORTON, of Scarborough.

Spes nostra Deus. God is our hope. CURRIERS' COMP. VARTY.

Spes, salus, decus. Hope, safety, honour. NESHAM, of Stockton.

Spes somnium vigilantis. Hope is the dream of a waking man. DIXON.

Spes tamen infracta. My *hope* nevertheless unbroken. HOPE, of Kers. *Crest*—A shattered globe.

Spes tutissima cœlis. The surest hope is in heaven. KING. KINGSTON, e. LORTON, v. PRICE, of Glangwilly.

Spes ultra. Hope is beyond. NAIRN, of Greenyards.
    Crest—A terrestrial globe and standard ppr.

Spes vitœ melioris. HOBHOUSE.

Spiritus gladius. The sword of the Spirit. HUTTON, of Marske.

Splendeo tritus. I shine though worn. FERRERS, of Baddesley.
    Arms—Sa. six horseshoes, three, two, and one, argent.

Sponti favos, œgro spicula. Honey to the willing, stings to the unwilling. SUTTIE. *Crest*—A bee-hive.

Spurs, 1513. CLARKE, of Kensington.
    An ancestor of this family was present at the skirmish, which, from the hasty retreat of the French cavalry, was called the Battle of Spurs.

Scrogal ma dhream. Loyal is my tribe. GREG. MACGREGOR, bt. MALLET.

Scroghal an dhream. The clan is loyal. M'ALPIN.

Scroghal mo dhream. My clan is loyal. M'ALPIN. M'GREGOR, of Camden Hill, bt. MACGREGOR.

St. Domingo. DUCKWORTH, bt.
    For particulars of this motto see "Minorca."

St. Sebastian. COLLIER, bt.

Stabit. It shall stand. GRANT. *Crest*—A mountain inflamed.

Stabit conscius œqui. Conscious of what is just he shall stand. CHARLTON. GRANT-DALTON.

Stabit quocumque jeceris. Whichever way you throw it, it will stand. The ISLE OF MAN.

Stabo. I shall stand. ACCORNE. HAWTHORNE. KINNIMOND.

Stand fast. GRANT, of Frenchie. SEAFIELD, e.
    Crest—A burning hill ppr. This represents Craigelachie, *i.e.* the mountain of the cry of distress, on which a fire was lighted to call the Grant clan together to Strathspey. When drawn up in battle the chief's word was "Stand fast," which is now used for the motto of the Grants.

Stand firm. GRANT.

Stand on. SYKES.

Stand suir. GLENELG, b.

Stand sure. ANDERSON, of Fermoy, bt. ADSON. AIRDERBECK. GRANT, of Burnside and Monymusk. PONTON.

Standard. KIDDER.

Stans cum rege. Standing with the king. CHADWICK.

Stant cœtera tigno. The rest stand on a beam. HUNTLY, m.

Stant innixa Deo. They stand supported by God. CRAUFURD.
    " God sees all suffering, comprehends all wants,
      All weakness fathoms, can supply all needs."—WORDSWORTH.

Stare super vias antiquas. I stand in the track of my ancestors. BAYNING, b.

Stat felix amico Domino. His happiness is sure when the Lord is his friend. STEUART.

Stat fortuna domûs. The fortune of the house remains. GAY, of Bath. HOWES, of Morningthorpe, co. Norfolk. WINTLE. WHITE.

> " Genus immortale manet, multosque per annos
> Stat Fortuna domûs, et avi numerantur avorum."
> VIRG. *Geor.* iv. 208.

> " Th' immortal line in sure succession reigns;
> The fortune of the family remains:
> And grandsires' grandsires the long list contains."—DRYDEN.

Stat fortuna domûs virtute. The fortune of our house endures through virtue. MOLYNEUX, bt.

Stat religione parentum. He continues in the religion of his forefathers. DE GREY. LUCAS, of Castle Thane.

Stat veritas. Truth endures. SANDERMAN.

Statio fida bene carinis. A trustworthy harbour for ships. TOWN OF CORK.

Steady. AYLMER, b. BRIDPORT, b. HOOD. M'ADAM. NORTHEN. NEILL. NORRIS. TONGE. VERELST. WELLER.

Steer steady. DONALDSON. STRACHAN, bt.

Stellis aspirate gemellis. Breathe on us with your twin stars. TWINING.

> *Crest*—The twins, Castor and Pollux, in infancy. (The stars in the shield are supposed to represent them after death.)
> " Dicam pueros Ledæ
> . . . . .   quorum simul alba nautis
> Stella refulsit . . .
> Concidunt venti, fugiuntque nubes."—HOR. *Od.* i. 12, 25.

Stemmata quid faciunt? What avail pedigrees? BAGGALAY. HICKMAN. MEYRICK, of Goodrick Court.

> " Honours best thrive
> When rather from our acts we them derive
> Than our foregoers."—SHAKSPEARE.

Stet fortuna. Let fortune be stable. CULLINGFORD, of Bays-water.

Stet fortuna domus. May the fortune of our house endure. HOLDICH, of Mardwell, co. Northampton.

See "Stat fortuna domus."

Sto cado fide et armis. I stand and fall by faith and arms. FARQUHAR.

Sto, mobilis. I stand, but am easily moved. DRUMMOND.

Sto pro fide. I stand firm for my faith. STOW.

Sto pro veritate. I stand for the truth. GUTHRIE. GUTHRY.

Strenuè et audacter. Strenuously and daringly. WOOD.

Strenuè et prosperè. Earnestly and successfully. EAMER. JEDBURGH, Royal Burgh.

Strength is from heaven. GRUBB. WHITSON.

Strike. HAWKE, b.

> " Strike! till the last arm'd foe expires;
> Strike! for your altars and your fires;

Strike ! for the green graves of your sires,
God, and your native land !"—HALLECK.

Strike alike. LAUDER.

Strike Dakyns, *the devil's in the hempe.* DAKYNS, of Derby-
shire.

Strike sure. GREIG.

Stringit amore. It binds by love. O. OF ST. STEPHEN.

Struggle. RUGGLES-BRISE, of Spains Hall.

Studendo et contemplando indefessus. Unwearied in studying
and meditation. CARDALE.

Studiis et rebus honestis. By study and honourable pursuits.
DUNNING.

Study quiet. HEAD, bt. PATRICK.

Suaviter. Gently. CAWOOD.

Suaviter et fortiter. Mildly and firmly. DAUBENEY. MINTO, e.
RATHBONE.

Suaviter, fortiter. Gently, boldly. SMITH, of Gloucestershire.

Suaviter in modo, fortiter in re. Gentle in manner, firm in act.
NEWBOROUGH, b. NUNN. WYNN.

" He's gentle and not fearful."—SHAKSPEARE.

Suaviter sed fortiter. Mildly, but firmly. BUSK. DENNIS.
WILLIAMS, of Lee.

Sub cruce candida. Under the white cross. ARDEN, b. EG-
MONT, e. PERCEVAL, co. Sligo.

White crosses patée are borne in the arms of these families.

Sub cruce glorior. I glorify under the cross. ASTELL.

Crest—A cross-crosslet entwined with a serpent.

Sub cruce salus. Salvation under the cross. FLETCHER, co.
Stafford. BANGOR, v. WARD, of Willey. CAPRON.

Sub cruce semper viridis. Always vigorous under the cross.
SHRUBB.

Sub cruce veritas. Truth under the cross. ADAMS. CROSSE.

Sub hoc signo vinces. Under this sign thou shalt conquer.
DE VESCI, v. See "In hoc signo vinces."

Sub libertate quietem. Rest under liberty. BURRELL. CAY.
CARTER. HOBLYN. KAY. KEAY, of Scotland. PETER.
PARKER. WALSHAM, bt.

Sub montibus altis. Under high mountains. SKEEN.

Sub pace copia. Under peace, plenty. FRANCE. FRANCO.

Sub pondere cresco. I grow under a weight. FLEMING.

Sub pondere sursum. Beneath my load (I look) upward.
PORTERFIELD.

Sub robore virtus. Virtue under strength. AIKIN, of Liverpool. AIKMAN, of Carnie.

Sub sole nihil. (I seek) nothing beneath the sun. MONTEITH.

Sub solo patebit. It will expand under the sun. ELLIES.

Crest—A lily close in the flower ppr.

Sub sole sub umbra crescens. Increasing both in sunshine and in shade. IRVINE, of Murthill. IRVINE.

Sub sole viresco. I flourish under the sun. IRVINE, of Artamford.

Sub spe. Under hope. DUFFAS, b. DUNBAR, of Boath, bt. DUNBAR, of Northfield, bt. DUNBAR, of Westfield. CAIRNS.

Sub tuum præsidium. Under thy protection. O. OF ST. ANNA.

Sub tutela Domini. Under the protection of God. SPODE.

Sub umbra alarum tuarum. Under the shadow of thy wings. LAWDER.

Sub umbra quiescam. I will rest under the shadow. FAIRN.

Subditus fidelis regis est salus regni. A faithful subject of the king is a preserver of the monarchy. HOPPER, of Belmont.

Col. William Carlos, one of the ancestors of this family, aided Charles II., in making his escape from the battle of Worcester, and his descendants in consequence assumed the above motto.

Subito. Promptly. CRINGAN. CRINAN.

Sublime petimus. We seek what is on high. CLEGHORN.

Sublimia petimus. We seek things on high. CLEGHORN.

Sublimiora spectemus. Let us regard loftier things. WARREN.

Sublimiora petamus. Let us seek higher things. BIDDULPH, of Ledbury, Amroth Castle, Barton, &c. BIDDULPH, bt.

Sublimiora peto. I seek higher things. JACKSON.

Successus a Deo est. Success is from God. ROBERTS.

Suffer. GLENEAGLES. HADDEN. HALDEN.

Suffibulatus majores sequor. Being buckled, I follow my ancestors, *i.e.* Having buckled on my arms I follow the example of my ancestors. HATHORN. STEWART.

Sufficit meruisse. It is enough to have deserved well. PLUMPTRE.

Sui oblitus commodi. Regardless of his own interest. ASGILE.

Suis stat viribus. He stands by his own powers. ABINGER, b.

Suivant St. Pierre. According or following St. Peter. KNIGHT.

Suivez de l'ange. Follow the angel. LONG.

Suivez la raison. Follow reason. ARMISTEAD.

Suivez moi. Follow me. BROUGH, bt. HAWLEY.

Suivez raison. Follow reason. BROWNE, of Elsing Hall, co. Norfolk. BROWNE. BARBERRIE. DIXON, of Unthank Hall. HILLASDON. KILMAINE, b. MONTAGUE, v. SLIGO, m. WYATT.

Sum quod sum. I am what I am. COLDICOTT. FORESIGHT.

Sume superbiam quæsitam mentis. Assume the pride of mind which you have acquired. SEAVER.

Summa rerum vestigia sequor. I follow the highest tracks of things. ALLAN.

Summum nec metuam diem nec optem. May I neither dread nor desire the last day. TIGHE, of Woodstock.

Sumus. We are. WEARE, of Hampton. BISHOP.

Sumus ubi fuimus. We are where we have been. WEARE.

Sunt sua præmia laudi. His rewards are his praise. BAR-
BERRIE. BROWN. PEMBERTON.

Suo se robore firmat. He establishes himself by his own
strength. GRANT.

Suo stat robore virtus. Virtue stands by its own strength.
MOWBRAY.

Super antiquas vias. Upon the ancient tracks. THORP.

Super sidera votum. My wishes are above the stars. RATTRAY,
of Craighill. *Crest*—A star ensigned with a heart flammant.

*Super*abit *omnia virtus.* Virtue shall overcome all things.
RABETT.

Superb. KEATS.

The name of a ship commanded by Sir R. Keats.

Superba frango. I destroy superb things. MACKLELLAN, of
Bombay. *Crest*—A mortar-piece or.

Superna sequor. I follow heavenly things. RAMSAY, of
Methven. WARDROP, of Strathavon.

Supra spem spero. I hope beyond hope. JEFFREYS.

Sur esperance. Upon hope. GRAVER-BROWNE, of Morley
Hall, co. Norfolk. MONCRIEFF, bt. MONCRIEFFE, bt. MOIR.

Sure. MACDONALD. *Crest*—A tower upon a rock.

Sure and steadfast. MARTIN, of Anstey Pastures.

Surgam. I shall rise. HUTCHISON.

Surgere tento. I try to rise. STRATON.

Surgit post nubila Phœbus. The sun rises after clouds.
CONSTABLE, bt. COACHMAKERS' COMP.

Sursum. Upwards. CALANDRINE. DOUGLAS. HUTCHINSON.
PRINGLE. SCOTT.

Sursum corda. Hearts upwards. HOWISON. M'GILLYCUDDY.

Suscipere et finire. To undertake and accomplish. BOLCKOW.

Sustenta la drechura. Endure misfortune. DAVYS.

Sustentatus providentiâ. Sustained by providence. ROLLAND.

Sustento sanguine signa. I support the standard with my
blood. SETON.

Crest—A man from the waist upwards in the garb of war, supporting the
ancient flag of Scotland. This motto is borne only by the Setons of
Pitmedden (baronets) and their descendants, as the Setons of Monine,
co. Aberdeen, &c.

Sustine et abstine. Bear and forbear. GARDEN. KEMEY.

Sustineatur. Let it be sustained. CULLUM, bt.

Crest—A lion sejant or, sustaining a column az. capital and base gold.

Suum cuique. To *every* man his own. EVERY, bt. DON, of
SPITTAL. GRANT, bt. GRANT, of Monymusk. THOMSON,
of Banchory. O. OF THE BLACK EAGLE OF PRUSSIA.

Suum cuique tribuens. Assigning to each his own. WALFORD.

Swift and true. FUST.

Syn ar dy hun. Know thyself. DE WINTON. WILKINS.

T

Tace. Be silent. ABERCROMBY.

Tace aut fac. Say nothing or do. BURGESS. SCOTT, bt. SCOTT.

Tache sans tâche. Strive (to be) without reproach. CARNAGIE, of North and Southesk. PATTERSON, of Kelvin Grove.

Tachez surpasser en vertue. Strive to surpass in virtue. TAYLOR.

Tais en temps. Be silent in time. TEY, of Essex.

Tak tent. Take heed. CROCKATT.

Tam animo mente sublimis. As lofty in spirit as in intellect. FORTEATH.

Tam aris quam aratris. As well by altars as by ploughs. OXLEY.

Tam arte quam Marte. As much by art as strength. M'LEA. WRIGHT.

Tam fidus quam fixus. Equally faithful as steadfast. STEWART.

Tam genus quam virtus. As much lineage as virtue. LUNDEN.

Tam in arte quam Marte. As much in skill as in force. MILNE.

Tam interna quam externa. As well internal as external (qualities). ARBUTHNOT.

Tam Marti quam Mercurio. As much devoted to Mars as Mercury. GASCOIGNE.

Tam virtus quam honos. As well virtue as honour. HAMILTON.

Tam virtute quam labore. As much by virtue as by exertion. HAMILTON.

Tandem. At length. CUNNINGHAME. FINNIE.

Tandem fit arbor. At last it becomes a tree. HAMILTON.
Crest — An oak-plant.

Tandem fit surculus arbor. A shoot (or bush) at length becomes a tree. BUSH. BURNET. BERESFORD. DOUGLAS.

Tandem justitia. Justice at length. O'DONNELLY.

Tandem implebitur. It will be full at last. SCOUGAL. SIMPSON.
Crest of Scougal — A crescent ar.

Tandem licet sero. At length though late. CAMPBELL.

Tandem tranquillus. At last tranquil. SYMMER.

Tandem vincitur. At length he is conquered.

Tanquam despicatus sum vinco. Although I am despised I conquer. GRANT.

Tant que je puis. As much as I can. DE CARDONNELL. HILTON. JOLLIFFE, bt. LAWSON, of Cramlington.

Tanti talem genuere parentes. (Virg. *Æn.* i. 606.) Such parents have produced such a man. MORAY, of Abercairny.

Tantum in superbos. Only against the proud. JACOB.

Te Deum laudamus. We praise thee, O God. HARPER. M'WHIRTER.

Te duce gloriamur. We glory under thy guidance. SINCLAIR, bt.

Te duce libertas. Where thou art leader there is liberty. CROSBY.

In allusion to the lambs in the arms, and the cross in the crest, as well as to the name. The liberty alluded to is that Christian liberty which is secured by the Lamb and Cross.

Te favente virebo. Under thy favour I shall flourish. GRANT, of Dalvey, bt.

Te splendente. Whilst thou art shining. CARSTAIRS, of Kilconquhar. BUCHAN.

The Crest of Carstairs—The sun darting its rays on a primrose.
The Crest of Buchan—The sun shining upon a sunflower.

Te stante virebo. Whilst thou endurest I shall flourish. TEMPLE. *Crest*—A pillar encircled by woodbine.

Teipsum nosce. Know thyself. SHAW, of Dublin, bt. See "Nosce teipsum."

Tela spoliis data. Weapons given by spoils. SHARPE.

Temeraire. (Rash.) HARVEY, of Chigwell.

This word "Temeraire" was the name of the ship which Sir Eliab Harvey, G.C.B., commanded at the glorious victory of Trafalgar, fought Oct. 21st, 1805. The word "Trafalgar," borne on the rim of the naval crown with which the sinister supporter (a horse) is gorged, commemorates the same event; under the arms are the names of the two French ships "Redoubtable et Fougueux" which were engaged and captured by Capt. Harvey.

Temperat æquor. He governs the sea. MONYPENNY.

Crest — Neptune bestriding a dolphin naiant in waves of the sea, holding with his dexter hand reins, and in his sinister the trident, all ppr.

Templa, quam dilecta. Temples, how beloved. BUCKINGHAM, d. NUGENT, b. TEMPLE, bt. TEMPLE.

The following is from BURKE'S *Peerage:*—
The 83d Psalm has, "Tabernacula, quam dilecta," but in the epitaph written about 1475, on John, Abbot of Croyland, who had caused the roof of his church to be gilt, the words, as in the motto, are to be found, and were probably thence derived:—

> ' Quam sibi dilecta fuerant sacra templa,
>   Laudis in exempla, demonstrant aurea tecta.' "

"The gilded roof, a monument of this holy man's worth, shows how great was his veneration for the sacred house of God."—*History of Croyland.*

Tempore candidior. Become fairer by time. MAIR.

Tempus et patientia. Time and patience. BRADBURY, co. Essex.

Tempus omnia monstrat. Time shows all things. LOVELL.

Tempus rerum imperator. Time the ruler of all things. CLOCKMAKERS' COMP.

> "Tempus edax rerum, tuque invidiosa vetustas
> Omnia destruitis : vitiataque dentibus ævi
> Paulatim lentâ consumitis omnia morte."—OVID, *Met.* xv. 234.

> "Time is the king of earth : all things give way
> Before him, but the fixed and virtuous will."—SHELLEY.

Tenax et fide. Persevering and with faith. SMITH, of East Stoke, bt.

Tenax et fidelis. Persevering and faithful. ABDY, bt. CAR-RINGTON, b. SMITH. TENNANT, of Skipton.
Tenax et fidus. Persevering and faithful. HEBBERT.
Tenax in fide. Steadfast in faith. SMITH.
Tenax propositi. Firm of purpose. GIBBES, bt. GILBERT, of Cantley Hall. GIBB. GIBBS. MORLEY. POOLE. ROUNDER.
Tenax propositi vinco. Being firm of purpose I conquer. GRIMSHAW.
Tendens ad æthera virtus. Virtue aspiring towards heaven. LEWTHWAITE.
Tendimus. We go forward. CRAIK.
Tending to peace. MUSSENDEN.
> *Crest* — A dove with olive-branch.
Tendit ad astra. He directs his gaze towards the stars. MAXWELL.
> *Crest* — A falcon gazing at a star.
Tendit ad astra fides. Faith reaches towards heaven. BURNS.
Tene fortiter. Hold firmly. BRIDGER.
> There are three crabs in the arms and the crest is a crab.
Teneat, luceat, floreat, vi, virtute, et valore. May it hold, shine, and flourish, by valour, virtue, and worth. KENNY, of Kilcloghar, and Correndos, co. Galway. KENNY, of Ballyflower, co. Roscommon.
> This motto alludes to the crest, a hand holding a roll of parchment, also to the crescents, and fleur-de-lis in the arms. The last four words of the motto are generally omitted, although registered, together with the arms and crest, in Ulster's Office, Dublin, 6th March, 1571.
Tenebo. I will hold. GRAY, of Wheatfield, M.P. for Bolton.
> Referring to the grasp of the serpent by the bear's paw in the crest, viz. on a rock ppr. a bear's paw, erect and erased, sa., grasping a snake entwined round it, also ppr.
Tenebris lux. Light in darkness. SCOTT, of Pitlochie.
Teneo. I retain. STAPLES.
> In allusion to the staple in the crest.
Teneo tenuere majores. I hold (what) my ancestors held. TWENLOW.
Tenes le vraye. Hold to the truth. TOWNLEY.
Tenez le droit. Keep the right. CLIFTON, bt. WILKINSON.
Tenez le vraye. Keep or speak the truth. TOWNLEY, of Townley.
Tentanda via est. The way must be tried. PECKHAM, of Nyton. STRONGE, bt. WILDMAN, of Newstead Abbey.
Terar dum prosim. May I be worn out provided I do good. MERRMAN, of Kensington.
Ternate. BURR.
> Granted in commemoration of the capture, in 1801, of that island by Lieut.-Gen. Burr.
Terra marique fide. With faith by land and sea. CAMPBELL, of Ardintenny. BILLING, co. Norfolk.
Terra marique potens. Powerful by land and sea. O'MALLEY, bt.

Terra marique victor. Victorious by land and sea. TRIGGER.

Terrena per vices sunt aliena. All earthly things by turns are foreign to us. FUST.

Terrena pericula sperno. I despise earthly dangers. OGILVIE, bt.

Terrere nolo, timere nescio. I wish not to intimidate, and know not how to fear. DERING, bt.

The axe is laid at the root of the tree. (Matt. iii. 10.) WOODMONGERS' COMP.

The cross our stay. PARKHOUSE.

The day of my life. WEST, of Tonbridge Wells, co. Kent.

The fruit is as the tree. KENNEDY.

> " The tree is known by its fruit."—*Luke,* vi. 44.

The grit poul. MERCER, of Aldie.

> This motto is derived from the estate of Mickloar, belonging to the above family, "Mickloar," meaning "the Great Water or Lake;" their crest is a heron, standing in or near the water, with an eel in its beak.

The noblest motive is the public good. BANTRY, e. WHITE.

The red hand of Ireland. O'NEILL, of Bunowen.

The reward of valour. MOODIE.

> The ancient motto of this family was "God with us."

The same. SKEEN.

The strongest arm uppermost. O'BRIEN. STAFFORD.

The strongest hand uppermost. KENNEDY.

The time will come. CLARKE.

They by permission shine. MURRAY, of Birmingham.

> There are three stars in the arms.

Thincke and thancke. TATE, of Burleigh Park.

Think and thank. AILESBURY, m. MONTEFIORE, bt.

Think on. MAXWELL, of Calderwood, bt. MACCLELLAN. ROSS.

Think well. ERSKINE, of Sheefield.

This I'll defend. M'FARLANE. MACFARLAN. MACPHARLIN. DURNARD.

> *Crest*—A demi-savage, grasping in the dexter hand a sheaf of arrows, and pointing with the sinister to an imperial crown which the motto asserts he will defend.

This is our charter. CHARTRES.

Thou shalt want ere I want. CRANSTOUN, b.

> This motto refers to the peculiar habits of the English and Scotch borderers of all ranks, who were accustomed to help themselves to anything of which they might stand in need, the English from Scotland and the Scots from England, as the case might be.

Thournib' creve'th. I give you the bush (*i.e.* the laurel). CREAGH.

> *Crest*—A horse's head ar. bridled ppr. a laurel-branch betw. the ears, to which the motto refers.

Through. HAMILTON, d. HAMILTON, of Silverston, bt. HAMILTON, of the Mount, co. Middlesex, bt. HAMILTON, of Woodbrook, bt. HAMILTON, of Brecon, bt. HAMILTON, co. Meath, &c. ABERCORN, m.

> In 1325, Sir Gilbert De Hamilton, who was in office at the court of

Edward II. having been struck by John de Spenser for speaking in praise of Robert de Bruce, challenged him ; and as he would not fight, slew him. To avoid the vengeance of the Spensers, he fled towards Scotland, and being hotly pursued, he and his servant changed clothes with two woodcutters who were felling an oak with a frame-saw. Seeing that his servant was disposed to notice the pursuers who soon afterwards passed by, he urged him to attend to his work by exclaim- "Through ;" this word he afterwards took for motto, and for crest— Out of a ducal coronet or an oak-tree, fructed, and penetrated trans- versely in the main stem by a frame-saw ppr., the frame gold.

Through God revived. HAMILTON, of Binning.

Thrust on. THRUSTON, of Cranbrook.

Thure et jure. By incense and justice. FOULIS, of Revelstoun.

Thus. ST. VINCENT, v. JERVIS.

Thus far. CAMPBELL, of Glenfalloch.

Thus thou must do if thou have it. SIDDONS.

Thynke and Thanke. THOS. WILLEMENT, F.S.A.

Tiburon. POYNTZ, of Bedhampton, co. Northampton.

Adm. Poyntz distinguished himself at Cape Tiburon.

Tiens firme. Hold firm. SQUIRE.

Tiens le droit. Hold or *Clench* the right. CLENCH, of Horstead.

Tiens à la vérité. Adhere to truth. DE BLAQUIERE, b. COURT-LAND. HOFFMAN. LEWTHWAIT.

Tiens ta foy. Keep thy faith. BATHURST, e. KEMP. MIGNON.

Till then thus. JONES, co. Lancaster.

Time Deum. Fear God. ROSS.

Time tryeth troth. TREVELYAN, bt.

Timet pudorem. He dreads shame. DOWNE, v.

Timor Domini fons vitæ. The fear of the Lord is the fountain of life. BUTLER. DUNBOYNE, b.

Timor omnis abest. All fear is away. CRAIGIE, of Cairsay.

Timor omnis abesto. Away with all fear. MACNAB, bt. CRAIGGE. CRAIGY.

Toute foys preste. Always ready. PIGOTT.

To God only be all glory. (Jude, 25.) GOLDSMITHS' COMP. SKINNERS' COMP.

Τῷ θεῷ δοξα. (Luke, ii. 19 and 38.) Glory to God. DOXAT.

Toleranda et speranda. We must endure and hope. WRIGHT.

Tollit peccata mundi. (John, i. 29.) He taketh away the sins of the world. FARLEY.

Toraf cyn plygaf. I'll break before I'll bend. DAVIES. OWEN.

Tot capita tot sententiæ. So many heads, so many opinions ; or, in common parlance, So many men so many minds. FITZALAN.

Του αριστευειν ενεκα. In order to excel. HENNIKER, b.

Touch not the cat bot a glove. GRANT. GILLESPIE. M'BEAN. MACKINTOSH. M'INTOSH. M'CROMBIE. MACPHERSON.

" Bot " is a word signifying " without."

Touch not the cat bot the glove. M'GILLEVRAY. GILLIES.

Toujours fidèle. Always faithful. BLADEN. BEAUCHAMP, HICKMAN. HAIRSTANES. MERCIER. MILL. PROCTOR, bt. HOLFORD, of Buckland. FENWICK. WALLINGTON. WATERS.

Toujours firme. Always firm. HENEAGE, of Hainton.

Toujours gai. Ever *gay.* GAY, of Thurning Hall, co. Norfolk.

Toujours jeune. Always *young.* YOUNG.

Toujours la même. Always the same. TAIT. O. OF THE RED EAGLE.

Toujours loyale. Always loyal. FENWICKE. PERKINS, of Sutton Coldfield. STULE.

> "Though perils did
> Abound as thick as thought could make them,
> And appear in forms more horrid, yet my duty
> (As doth a rock against the chiding flood)
> Should the approach of this wild river break,
> And stand unshaken yours."

Toujours pret, or *prest.* Always ready. ANSTRUTHER, of Elie House, bt. ABBOTT. CLANWILLIAM, e. CARMICHAEL, bt. CRAWFURD. DANIEL. DAYMAN. DEASE. DONALD. GIBON. HAWKINS. KNIGHT. MEADE. M'CONNELL. MACDONELL. OGILVIE. PETTY. PHELPS. SUTTON, bt. SMYTH, bt. TYSSEN, of Hackney and Didlington.

Toujours propice. Always propitious. DAWSON, of Castle Dawson. CREMORNE, b.

Tous jours loyal. Always loyal. FENWICK. WINFORD.

Tout bien ou rien. All well or nothing. BARHAM, b. HICKS. NOEL.

Tout d'en haut. All from above. BELLEW, bt. BELLEW.

Tout droit. All right. CARRE. CARR. CARLING. KER.

Tout en bon heure. All in good time. HICKS, bt. HICKS, of Watton, co. Norfolk. BEACH, of Oakley Hall, M.P. for North Hants.

Tout est en haut. All is above. WHITFORD.

Tout fin fait. Every thing comes to an end. ST. HILL.

Tout foys prest. Always ready. PIGOTT, bt.

Tout hardi. Quite bold. M'HARDIE.

Tout jour. Always. OGILVIE.

Tout jours prest. Always ready. SUTTON, bt.

Tout par et pour Dieu. All by and for God. DU BOIS DE FERRIESES.

Tout pour Dieu et ma patrie. Wholly for God and my country. WINN, of Nostell Priory, co. York.

Tout pour l'église. All for the church. WANDESFORD.

Tout pour l'empire. All for the empire. ORDER of RE-UNION.

Tout pourvoir. To provide for everything. OLIPHANT.

Tout prest. Quite ready. MURRAY.

Tout ung durant ma vie. Always the same during my life. BARRINGTON.

Tout vient de Dieu. All comes from God. CLINTON, b.
LEIGH, b. LEAHY, of Cork. PINCHARD. TREFUSIS.

> "There's nothing bright, above, below,
> From flowers that bloom to stars that glow,
> But in its light my soul can see
> Some features of thy Deity."—MOORE.

Toutes foys preste. Always ready. PIGOTT, of Doddershall.

Touts jours prest. Always ready. LLOYD.

Toutz foitz chevalier. Always a knight. RIDEOUT.

A play on the name.

Towton. MATHEW.

Sir David Matthew, an ancestor of this family is said to have saved the life of Edward IV. at the battle of Towton, 1461. For this service he was made Grand Standard-bearer of England.

Tractent fabrilia fabri. (Hor. *Ep.* ii. 1. 116.) Let smiths handle smiths' tools. SMITHS' COMP., Exeter.

Trade and navigation. ROYAL EXCHANGE ASSURANCE.

> "The band of commerce was design'd
> To associate all the branches of mankind :
> And if a boundless plenty be the robe,
> Trade is the golden girdle of the globe.
> Wise to promote whatever end he means,
> God opens fruitful nature's various scenes:
> Each climate needs what other climes produce,
> And offers something to the general use:
> No land but listens to the common call
> And in return receives supply from all."—COWPER.

Trade and plantations. COMMISSIONERS OF TRADE AND PLANTATIONS.

Traditum ab antiquis servare. To keep that which is handed down from ancient times. FRERE, of Roydon.

Traditus, non victus. Betrayed, not conquered. HOWDEN, b.

Traducere ævum leniter. To reform the age mildly. BROWNE.

Trafalgar. NELSON, e. NORTHESK, e. CODRINGTON. HARVEY. TYLER.

Tramite recta. By a direct path. ROE, bt.

Transfigam. I will transfix. COLT, of Gartsherrie. COULT, of Inveresk.

Treu und fest. True and faithful. THE PRINCE CONSORT.

Tria juncta in uno. Three joined in one. O. OF THE BATH.

These words denote the union of the virtues of Faith, Hope, and Charity, in Charity the greatest of them all.

Trial by jury. ERSKINE, b.

> "As long as liberty the soul delights,
> And Britons cherish and maintain their rights,
> Long as they love their country's sacred cause,
> And prize the safest bulwark of their laws,
> So long shall be with freedom's loud acclaim,
> 'Trial by jury' linked with Erskine's name."—*The Bar:* a Poem.

Trinitas in Trinitate. Trinity in Trinity. TRINITY HOUSE GUILD, or FRATERNITY.

Triumpho morte tam vitâ. I triumph equally in death as in life. ALLEN, v.

Troimh chruadal. Through hardships. M'INTYRE.
Trop hardi. Too bold. HARDIE.
Trow to you. DARELL.
True. BRUCE, of Pittarthie. HORNE.
True and trusty. HERIOT.
True as the dial to the sun. HYNDMAN.
      Crest—A sun-dial and the sun shining thereon.
True to the end. HOME, e. HOME. HUME, bt. CAMPBELL, of Powis, bt. FERGUSON. HUME, of Humewood. ORR. BINNING. FOREMAN.
True to the last. FERGUSON.
Trust in God. DAVIS. HARDNESS. HUSDELL.
Trust winneth troth. RAWDON-HASTINGS, Marquis of Hastings.

    The following is the origin of this motto. Edward IV., driven from his throne by the Earl of Warwick, king-maker, who had placed on it Henry VI., had an assembly of his nobles and friends before attempting to recover it. Going from one to the other he addressed such observations or arguments as would be most likely to induce them to join him. When, however, he came to Lord Hastings he said only to him, "I do not ask you anything, I trust to you." Lord Hastings answered, "Sire, trust winneth troth." To make the monarch's question and the noble's answer comprehensible, it must be remembered that the undertaking in which they were about to embark was nominally against Henry VI., but really against the Earl of Warwick, that Lord Hastings had married Lady Cecily Neville, the Earl of Warwick's sister, and that the daughter of the Earl of Warwick (and niece consequently, by marriage, to Lord Hastings), the Lady Anne Neville, had married the Prince of Wales, son of Henry VI. The Marquis of Hastings is Baron Hastings in direct succession from the Lord Hastings, temp. Edward IV. For the Rawdon motto see "Et nos quoque tela sparsimus."

Trustie to the end. LEITH-HAY.
Trustie and bydand. LEITH, of Craighill.
Trusty and true. SCOTT, of Hussindene.
Trusty to the end. LUMSDEN.
Truth. LEITHBRIDGE, bt.
    "The only amaranthine flower on earth
    Is virtue; the only lasting treasure, truth."—COWPER.
Truth and liberty. TYLDEN, of Milsted.
Truth is the light. WAX CHANDLERS' COMP. London.
Truth prevails. GORDON.
Truth will prevail. M'KENZIE, of Ardross.
Try. GETHIN, bt. O'HARA. PARKER, bt.
Tu, Domine, gloria mea. Thou, O Lord, art my glory. LEICESTER. BARON DE TABLEY.
Tu ne cede malis. Yield not to misfortunes. AMERY. DAMER. DE MEURON. PARRY. RIDDOCK. STEERE. TURNER.
Tu ne cede malis, sed contra audentior ito. (Virg. Æn. vi. 95.) Yield not to misfortunes, but go the more boldly against them. COOKE, of Cordangan.
Tuebor. I will defend. BYNG. TORRINGTON, v. STRAFFORD, b.
Tulloch ard. The high hill. M'KENZIE. *Crest*—A hill.

Tum pace quam prœlio.　As well in peace as in war.
GORDON.

Turn nor *swerve.*　TURNOR.

Turpiter desperatur.　Despaired is base.　HALL, bt.

Turris fortis mihi Deus.　God is a strong tower to me.　CLUG-
STONE.　KELLY.　MACQUARIE.　M'GUARIE.　O'KELLY.　PETER.

Turris *fortissima Deus.*　God is the strongest tower.　TORRE :
the name was originally DE TURRI.

Turris fortitudinis.　A tower of strength.　MANSFIELD.

Turris fortissima est nomen Jehovah.　The name of the Lord
is the strongest tower.　T. OF PLYMOUTH.

Turris mihi Deus.　God is my *tower.*　TOWERS.　KELLY.

Turris prudentia custos.　Prudence is the safeguard of the
tower.　LAUDER, SIR JOHN DICK, Bart.

> Sir Robert de Lauedre, an ancestor of this family, who was justiciary of
> all Scotland to the north of the Forth, was present at the battle of
> Halidon in 1333.　After the defeat he hastened to occupy the castle of
> Urquhart, on Loch Ness, and by his prudence, forethought, and brave
> defence of that place for David II., it stands recorded as one of the only
> four strongholds which defied the power of Edward III.　For this
> prudent act he was granted the crest, a tower with portcullis down,
> and the head and shoulders of a sentinel (Prudence) appearing above
> the battlements ppr. with the above motto, which is now borne by
> the family.

Turris tutissima virtus.　Virtue is the safest fortress.　CARLYON.

Tutamen.　A defence.　SKRINE, of Warleigh.

Tutamen Deus.　God is my defence.　BENT.　HOOPER.

Tutamen pulchris.　For the fair.　CHAMBRE.

Tutamen tela coronœ.　Our weapons are the defence of the
crown.　TISDALL.

Tutela.　A defence.　LYLE.　LYELL, of Dysart.

Tutissima statio.　The safest station.　T. of STRANREAR.

Tuto, celeriter, et jucunde.　Safely, speedily, and agreeably.
SUTTON, of Framlingham.

Tuto et celeriter.　Safely and quickly.　PENRICE, of Yarmouth.

Tutum refugium.　A safe refuge.　GILLON.　GULLON.

Tutum monstrat iter.　He shows the safe way.　COOK.

Tutum te littore sistam.　I will stop thee safely at the shore.
MURRAY.　*Crest—*A ship under sail.

Tutum te robore reddam.　I will make thee safe by my
strength.　CRAWFURD.　HINDE.

> Sir Grekan Crawfurd of Kerse, having saved David I. from a wild stag,
> assumed for arms and crest a stag's head with the above motto.

Tutus in undis.　Safe on the waves.　GRAHAM, bt.

Tutus prompto animo.　Safe in an active mind.　WEISTED.

Tutus si fortis.　Safe if brave.　FAIRBORNE.　RAEBURN.

Tuum est.　It is thine.　COWPER, e.　COOPER, of Toddington.

Tyde what may.　HAIG, of Bemerside.

Tyme tryeth troth.　TREVELLYN, bt.

Tynctus cruore Saraceno. Tinged with Saracen's blood. TYNTE.
This motto was granted by Richard Cœur-de-Lion to a young Crusader.
Tyrii tenuere coloni. Tyrian husbandmen possessed it.
M'LAURIN, of Dreghorn.

U

Ubi amor ibi fides. Where there is love there is faith.
DUCKINFIELD, bt. GARRATT. NEWMAN, co. Devon, bt.
AUBREY, co. Hereford.
Ubi lapsus? Quid feci? Whither have I fallen? What have I
done? COURTENAY. DEVON, e.
These words which express astonishment at a sudden and undeserved
fall are said to have been adopted by the Powderham branch of the
Courtenay family when they had lost the Earldom of Devon.
Ubi libertas ibi patria. Where liberty prevails there is my
country. BEVERLEY. BAILLIE. DARCH. DINWIDDIE.
GARRETT. HUGAR.
Ubique aut nusquam. Everywhere or nowhere. WHITEFOORD.
Ubique fecundat imber. Everywhere the rain fertilizes.
HIGGINBOTTOM.
The arms contain drops of rain, *i.e.* guttes-d'eau.
" The clouds consign their treasures to the fields :
And softly shaking on the dimpled pool
Prelusive drops, let all their moisture flow,
In large effusion, o'er the freshen'd world."—THOMSON.
Ubique fidelis. Everywhere faithful. HAMILTON, of Udstoun.
Ubique paratus. Everywhere prepared. FRAZER, of Fingask.
Ubique patriam reminisci. Everywhere to remember one's
country. CASS, of East Barnet. HARRIS. MALMESBURY, e.
Ultra aspicio. I look beyond. MELVILLE.
Ultra fert animus. The mind bears onwards. DURHAM.
Ultra pergere. To advance farther. LYNDHURST, b.
Unalterable. SLEIGH, of Haddington.
Un Dieu, un roi. One God, one king. D'ARCY. LYTTLETON.
Un Dieu, un roy, un cœur. One God, one king, one heart.
LAKE, bt.
Un Dieu, un roy, un foy. One God, one king, one faith. CURLE.
RUSH.
Un durant ma vie. The same while I live. BARRINGTON, bt.
Un roy, une foy, une loy. One king, one faith, one law. DE
BURGH.
Unde derivatur ? Whence is it derived? BLOXHOLME.
Une foy mesme. One same faith. GILPIN.
Une pure foi. A pure faith. HEWITT, co. Glamorgan.
Une stay. LANG.

Ung Dieu et ung roy. One God and one king. DARAY.
HATHERTON, b.
Ung Dieu, ung loy, ung foy. One God, one law, one faith.
BURKE, of St. Cleras.

" The great world shall be at last
The mercy-seat of God, the heritage
Of Christ, and the possession of the Spirit,
The comforter, the wisdom ! shall all be
One land, one home, one friend, one faith, one law,
Its ruler God, its practice righteousness,
Its life peace."—BAILEY.

Ung Dieu, ung roi. One God, one king. D'ARCY. GELL.
LYTTLETON, b.
Ung Dieu, ung roi, ung cœur. One God, one king, one heart.
LAKE.
Ung je servirai. One will I serve. CARNARVON, e. HERBERT.
Ung je serviray. One will I serve. FITZ-HERBERT, of Norbury.
BUXTON-FITZHERBERT, of Black Castle. PEMBROKE, e.
Ung roy, ung foy, ung loy. One king, one faith, one law.
BURKE, of Marble Hill, bt. BURKE, of Kilcoran, Owen,
and Clongowna. CLANRICARDE, m. DE BURGO, bt. RUSH.

The progenitor of the Clanricarde family, Baron de Tousburgh, was
governor for the Conqueror's father, Duke Robert, of many of the
chief towns in Normandy, from which circumstance he assumed the
name of De Burgo. He in all probability took his motto, with a slight
variation, from that of the town of Caen, which was, " Un Dieu, ung
foy, ung loy."
His grandson, Robert De Burgh, brought it into England with the
Conqueror.

Ung tout seul. Only one. VERNEY. VARNAY, temp. Hen. VIII.
Uni æquus virtuti. Friendly to virtue alone. MANSFIELD, e.
Unica spes mea Christus. Christ is my only hope. DISHINGTON.
Unica virtus necessaria. Only virtue is necessary, COLLEY.
WELLESLEY.
Unicus est. He is the only one. UNIACKE.
Union constitutes power. O. OF LEOPOLD.
Unione augetur. It is increased by union. MILLER.
Unita fortior. The stronger being united. RUNDALL. WOOD-
MONGERS' COMP.
Unitas societatis stabilitas. Unity is the support of society.
PARISH CLERKS' COMP.
Unitate fortior. Stronger by union. ARMY AND NAVY CLUB.
BECK.
Unite. BRODIE, bt. BRODIE, of Brodie.
Unity and loyalty. BOROUGH OF CHIPPENHAM.
Uno avulso, non deficit alter. When one is torn away another
is not wanting. AUSTRIA.
In allusion to the double-headed eagle, the bearing of that kingdom.
Uno ictu. (Cæsar *de Bell. Gall.* 1. 25.) By one blow. MORISON.
Unto God only be honour and glory. DRAPERS' COMP., London.

" Nature, attend ! join every living soul,
Beneath the spacious temple of the sky,

In adoration join ; and ardent raise
One general song ! To Him, ye vocal gales.
Breathe soft, whose Spirit in your freshness breathes ;
Oh, talk of him in solitary glooms ! "—Thomson.

Unus et idem. One and the same. Ravensworth. Siddell.

Unus et idem ferar. I will be borne along one and the same. Blundeel.

Urit fulgore suo. (Hor. *Ep.* 2. 1. 13.) It burns in its own brightness. Phœnix Insurance Comp.

Usagre. Lumley.

Usque ad aras. Even to the altars. Herne. Burchell.

Usque ad mortem fidus. Faithful even to death. Ward, of Salhouse.

Usque fac et non parcas. E'en do and spare not. Peters, of Aberdeen.

Usque fidelis. Always faithful. Napier, of Balwhaple.

Usus rectumque. Custom and right. Micklethwayte.

Ut amnis vita labitur. Life glides on like a *brook.* Brook.

Ut apes geometriam. As bees geometry. Petty.
Crest—A bee-hive with bees.

Ut crescit clarescit. As it increases, it becomes bright. Menzies. *Crest*—A crescent.

Ut cunque placuerit Deo. Howsoever it shall have pleased God. Darby. How. Howe.

" Should fate command me to the farthest verge
Of the green earth, to distant barbarous climes,
Rivers unknown to song ; where first the sun
Gilds Indian mountains, or his setting beam
Flames on the Atlantic isles ; 'tis nought to me ;
Since God is ever present, ever felt,
In the void waste as in the city full ;
And where He vital breathes, there must be joy."—Thomson.

Ut implear. That I may be filled. Mikieson.
Crest—A decrescent.

Ut mens cujusque is est quisque. As the mind of each, so is each. Pepys.

Ut migraturus habita. Dwell here as one about to depart. Lauder, of Fountainhall, bt.

" Ye noble few ! who here unbending stand
Beneath life's pressure, yet bear up awhile,
And what your bounded view, which only saw
A little part, deem'd evil, is no more ;
The storms of wintry Time will quickly pass,
And one unbounded Spring encircle all."—Thomson.

Ut olim. As formerly. Kinlock, of Couland.

Ut palma justus. The righteous is like the *palm.* Palmes.
Crest—A hand holding a palm-branch.

Ut possim. As I can. Livingston, of Glentarran.

Ut prosim. That I may be of use. Foley, b. Grigg.

Ut prosim aliis. That I may be of use to others. Greenwood. Jennings.

Ut quocumque paratus. That I may be prepared on every side. CAVAN, e. LAMBERT, co. Meath. LAMBART, co. Mayo.

Ut reficiar. That I may be replenished. ARCHBALD. ARCHI-BALD. *Crest*— A decrescent.

Ut resurgam. That I may rise again. PENNYCOCK, of Newhall.

Ut sanem vulnero. I wound to heal. HOLT.

> *Crest*— A spear-head. This motto probably alludes to the spear of Achilles, which had the power of curing as well as of inflicting wounds.

Ut sim paratior. That I may be the better prepared. CLEPHAM.

> *Crest*— A dexter hand holding a helmet.

Ut secura quies. That the rest (may be) safe. HUSKISSON.

Ut sursum desuper. I swoop down to soar again. RUMBOLD. WORSELEY. WORSLEY. There are Falcons in the arms.

Ut tibi sic aliis. As to yourself so to others. HUSSEY.

> St. Matt. vii. 12, and St. Luke, vi. 31.

Ut tibi sic alteri. As to yourself so to another. BOWLES. KINGSDON, b.

Ut vivas vigila. Watch that you may live. ARNOLD, of Ashby.

Utcunque placuerit Deo. Howsoever it shall have pleased God. DARBY.

Utere loris. Use the reins. DARLY. WADDILOVE.

> *Crest*—A horse's head in armour bridled.

Utile dulci. The useful with the agreeable. SPEDDING. SHUTTLEWORTH.

> In the arms of Spedding there are acorns and roses.
> " Omne tulit punctum, qui miscuit utile dulci."—HOR. *de A.P.* 344.

Utile et dulce. The useful and agreeable. RIDDELL, bt.

Utile primo. Useful at first. READE.

Utile secernere honestum. To separate the honourable from the useful. DAVIS.

Utilem pete finem. Seek a useful end. MARSHALL.

Utitur ante quæsitis. He uses what has been gained (or sought for) before. DRAGHORN.

Utraque Pallade. With either Pallas. BENDYSHE.

> Pallas was goddess of both Wisdom and War, and the meaning of the motto is, with wisdom and skill in war.

Utrius auctus auxilio. Increasing by help of both. RANKINE.

> Probably alluding to the Lochabar axe in the arms and the lance in the crest.

Utriusque auxilio. By the help of both. SPOTTISWOOD.

> *Crest*—Two globes the celestial and terrestrial ppr.

Utrumque. Both. KING HENRY II.

> This motto was borne with the badge a sword and olive-branch, which with the above motto declare that he was prepared for peace or war.

V

Vade ad formicam. (Prov. v. 6.) Go to the ant. ANKETEL.

Væ victis. Woe to the conquered. SENHOUSE, of Nether Hall.

Vaillaunce avance le homme. Valour advances the man.
ACTON, co. Worcester.

Valebit. He will prevail. LYSONS, of Hemsted.
    In allusion to the crest which is the sun rising from clouds.

Valens et volens. Able and willing. FETHERSTON, of Bracklyn.
FETHERSTONHAUGH.

Valet anchora virtus. Virtue our anchor is strong. GARDNER,
    b. GARDNER.

Valet et vulnerat. It is strong, and it wounds. HAY, of London.
    Crest—A hand with an ox-yoke.

Valor e lealdad. Valour and loyalty. CROFT, bt. O. OF THE
TOWER AND SWORD.

Valor et fortuna. Valour and good fortune. ROLLO, of Powhouse.

Vana spes vitæ. Worldly hope is vain. PAUL, bt.

Vanus est honor. Honour is vain. BOWDEN.

> "Some men with swords may reap the field,
>   And plant fresh laurels where they kill;
> But their strong nerves at last must yield,
>   They tame but one another still:
>   Early or late,
>   They stoop to fate,
> And must give up their murmuring breath,
> When they, pale captives, creep to death."—SHIRLEY.

Vectis. The Isle of Wight. THE ISLE OF WIGHT.

Veilliez et ne craignez pas. Watch and fear not. GURDLESTONE.

Veillant et vaillant. Watchful and valiant. ERSKINE, bt.

Vel arte vel Marte. Either by art or strength. BAINES.
DEANS, of Loeg.

Vel pax, vel bellum. Either peace or war. FRAZER, of Eskdale.
GORDON, of Rothemay. GUNN.

Velis et remis. With sails and oars. HAYNES.

Velle bene facere. To wish to do well. CURTEIS. CURTIS.

Vellera fertis oves. Sheep, ye bear the wool. ELLIOT.
    Crest—A ram.
    The whole line is "Sic vos non vobis vellera fertis oves." Can any allu-
    sion here be intended to the predatory habits of borderers?

Venabulis *vinco.* I conquer with hunting-spears. VENABLES.
    There are spears in the arms.

Venale nec auro. Not to be bought with gold. JERVIS.
    These words are part of the well-known ode of Horace which com-
    mences "Otium Divos rogat," and proceeds:—
        "Otium bello furiosa Thrace,
        Otium Medi pharetra decori,
        Grosphe, non gemmis neque purpurâ venale nec auro."
                                        HOR. *Car.* ii. 16. 1.

Venit ab astris. She came from the stars. KEITH.

This motto has reference to *Truth*, which is said to come down from heaven.

Venit hora. The hour comes. HOARE, bt. HOARE, of Cork city, Dunmanway, Annabella, Factory-Hill, &c., all in the county of Cork, Ireland. All settled in Ireland, in 1649, from Edmonton, co. Middlesex, and Changford of Rishford, co. Devon.

This motto, a canting one, is in allusion to the name "*Hoare,*" formerly spelled "*Hore,*" but altered about the 17th century. The word Hore, or Hoare, is of Armoric extraction, and signifies a boundary, from the Greek "*ὁρος,*" whence the Latin "hora," an hour being merely a "boundary of time." The word denotes also the colour white, as hoar-frost, hore-wood, hoary-headed, &c. It is supposed to have been thus designated from the well-known and celebrated boundary-stones, "hoar-stones" and "mein heirs," they being *hoary* or white with age. The armorial bearings are also in accordance with this name, viz. sa. an eagle displayed, with two heads, within a bordure engrailed argent.

"Where only the hoar eagle finds a rest
Safe, and secure in those wild cliffs its nest."
Solitary Moments: Poems.

The family of Hoare also bears the motto "Dum spiro spero," to which refer. For this account of the Hoare motto I am indebted to Capt. Edward Hoare.

Ventis secundis. By favourable winds. HOOD, v. ROWLEY, bt.

Venture and gain. HAY. WILSON, of Fraserburgh.

Venture forward. BRUCE, of Garvet.

Vera trophæa fides. Faith is our true trophy. SWABEY.

Verax atque probus. Trustworthy and honest. RUTTLEDGE.

Verax et fidelis. True and faithful. PEARETH.

Verbum Domini manet in æternum. The word of the Lord endureth for ever. STATIONERS' COMP.

"The word of the Lord endureth for ever."—1 *Pet.* i. 29.

Veritas. Truth. EISTON.

"What pearl is it that rich men cannot buy,
That learning is too proud to gather up;
But which the poor and the despised of all,
Seek and obtain, and often find unsought?
Tell me, and I will tell thee what is truth."—COWPER.

Veritas et virtus vincunt. Truth and virtue prevail. WALSH.

Veritas ingenio. Truth with wit. GORDON.

Veritas liberabit. Truth will liberate. BODENHAM, of Rotherwas.

Veritas liberavit. Truth has freed me. SLINGSBY.

Veritas me dirigit. Truth directs me. BROCKLEHURST.

Veritas magna est. Truth is great. JEPHSON, bt.

Veritas omnia vincit. Truth conquers all things. KEDSLIE.

Veritas prævalebit. Truth shall prevail. PAUL.

Veritas premitur non opprimitur. Truth may be kept down, but not crushed. CALDERWOOD, of Pittedy, and Dalkeith.

Veritas superabit. Truth will conquer. HILL, of Edinburgh.

Veritas temporis filia. Truth is the daughter of Time. QUEEN MARY.

Veritas via vitæ. Truth is the way of life. TYRELL.

Veritas vincet. Truth will conquer. ORPEN, of Glancrough.

Veritas vincit. Truth conquers. FRENCH. KEITH. PARKER, co. Cork. WRIGHT.

Veritate et justitiâ. With truth and justice. XIMENES.

Veritatem. Truth. TATHAM.

Veritatis assertor. The asserter of truth. NIBLETT.

Veritatis et æquitatis tenax. Persevering in truth and justice. RUST.

Vérité sans peur. Truth without fear. BEDFORD. GUNNING. MIDDLETON, b. WILLOUGHBY.

Vérité soyez ma garde. Truth be my protection. BREWSTER.

Vernon *semper viret.* *Vernon always flourishes.* VERNON, b. VERNON, of Hanbury Hall.

> This motto, though appearing at first to assert somewhat arrogantly the unfading fortune of the Vernons, still, when dissected (Ver non semper viret, The spring does not always flourish), warns them that human prosperity, like the fairest season of the year, is liable to changes for the worse.

Vero nihil verius. Nothing truer than truth, or than *Vere.* DE VERE, bt. VERE, of Craigie Hall.

> These words are said to have been pronounced by Queen Elizabeth in commendation of the loyalty of the family of Vere.

Vertitur in diem. It is changed into day. FARQUHAR.

Vertitur in lucem. It is changed into light. BAILLIE.

Vertue vaunceth. Virtue advances (men). VERNEY. WILLOUGHBY DE BROKE, b.

Verum atque decus. The truth and rectitude. BROWN. LEE.

> "Quid verum atque decens curo et rogo."—HOR. *Ep.* i. 1, 11.

Verus. True. PETERS.

Verus amor patriæ. The true love of country. HUGHES, of Wexford.

Verus ad finem. True to the end. DEUCHER LIZARS. PETERS.

Verus et fidelis semper. True and faithful ever. AYLWARD.

Vescitur Christo. He feeds on Christ. ROUS, of Devon.

Vespere et mane. In the evening and the morning. PIERRE. POURIE. PURIE.

Vespertilionis. Of the bat, *i.e. Batson.* BATSON.

Vestigia nulla retrorsum. (Hor. *Ep.* i. 1. 73.) No steps backwards. BAILY. BUCKINGHAMSHIRE, e. CONINGSBY. HAMPDEN. LEVINGE, bt.

Vi aut virtute. By force or virtue. CHISHOLM.

Vi divinâ. By Divine power. PEARSE.

Vi et animo. By strength and courage. HANKINSON. M'CULLOCH.

Vi et armis. By force and arms. ARMSTRONG.

> An ancestor of this family named Fairbairn, having by main force lifted a king of Scotland into his saddle when he had been dismounted in battle, received the name of Armstrong and certain border lands from

his sovereign as a reward, and had assigned him for crest, an armed hand an arm, in the hand a leg in armour, couped at the thigh, all ppr. with the above motto.

Vi et arte. By strength and skill. FERGUSON. STEVENS.

Vi et consiliis. By force and counsels. MEREWETHER.

Vi et industria. By strength and industry. FALCONER.

Vi et virtute. By strength and valour. BAIRD, bt. BAIRD. BOLTON. BARNES. CHISHOLM. FARRIERS' COMP. HURST. M'TAGGART. SMART. SPOIGHT. WHITE.

" To patient valour trained
They guard with spirit what by strength they gained."—GRAY.

Vi nullâ invertitur ordo. Our order is not overthrown by any violence. CORDWAINERS' COMP. EXETER.

Vi si non consilio. By force, if not by reason. SHERBROOKE.

Vi victus non coactus. Overcome by force not compelled. WARTER.

Vi vel suavitate. By force or by mildness. ROCHFORT.

Via crucis via lucis. The way of the cross is the way of life. SINCLAIR.

" Quæ ignorari sine amittendæ salutis æternæ periculo non potest."— GROTIUS, *de Veritate.*

Via trita via tuta. The beaten road is a safe road. AGAR. LAPRIMANDAYE. NORMANTON, e.

Via tuta virtus. Virtue is a safe path. DICK.

Via vi. A way by force. HAYTER.

Via una cor unum. One way one *heart.* HART. M'CORDA.

Vici. I have conquered. COOKE. RAINES.

Vicisti et vivimus. Thou hast conquered and we survive. JOHNSON, of Bath, bt.

This motto alludes to the victory gained over the Irish rebels at New Ross, by which the lives of many Protestants were saved. To commemorate the services of Sir H. Johnson at this place, one of his supporters bears " New Ross" on a flag which he holds. " Nunquam non paratus" is also borne by this family.

Vicit, pepercit. He conquered, he spared. DRAPER.

Victor. Conqueror. JAMES, of Eltham. LINSKILL.

Victor mortalis est. The conqueror is mortal. CLARKE.

Victoria. Victory. CONQUEROR. LA BEAUME. LOCOCK, bt.

Victoria concordiâ crescit. Victory increases by concord. AMHERST, b. AMHERST, of Didlington Hall, co. Norfolk.

Victoria, fortitudo, virtus. Victory, fortitude, and virtue. YOUNG.

Victoria non præda. Victory, not booty. DURHAM, of Largo. SANDILANDS.

Victoriæ signum. The emblem of victory. TAYLOR.

Victoria vel mors. Victory or death. MACDONALD. M'DOWALL.
" Horæ
Momento cita mors venit, aut victoria læta."—HOR. *Sat.* i. 1. 7.
" In a moment's flight
Death, or a joyful conquest, ends the fight."—FRANCIS.

Victoriæ gloria merces. Glory is the reward of victory. T. OF NORTH BERWICK.

Victoriam coronat Christus. Christ crowns the victory. CAMP-
BELL, of Abernchill, bt.
    The motto of this family was formerly "Ex campo victoria."

Victorious. O'ROURKE.

Victrix fortunæ sapientia. Wisdom the conqueror of fortune.
ANDREWS, bt. CALTHROP, of Stanhoe Hall, co. Norfolk.

Victrix patientia. Patience conquers. GORDON.

Victus in arduis. Conquered in difficulties, or, "Their abode
is in steep places," referring to the eagles in the arms.
HARRISON.

Video alta sequorque. I see lofty objects and pursue them.
CARNAGIE.

Video et taceo. I see and say nothing. Fox, of Eppleton.

Vidi, vici. I saw, I conquered. SCURFIELD. TWISELTON.
    These are the two last words of Cæsar's well-known dispatch describing
his success to the Senate.

Vif, courageux, fier. Spirited, courageous, proud. FALCON.

Viget in cinere virtus. Virtue flourishes after death. DAVIDSON.

    " The death of those distinguish'd by their station,
      But by their virtue more, awakes the mind
        To solemn dread, and strikes a saddening awe."—YOUNG.

Viget sub cruce. He flourishes under the cross. COLQUHON.

Vigila et ora. (Matt. xxvi. 41.) Watch and pray. WAKE, bt.
ROGERS. CROXWELL.
    " Take ye heed, watch and pray, for ye know not when the time is."—
    Mark, xiii 33.

Vigila et aude. (Be) vigilant and dare. CAMPBELL, bt.

Vigilance. LAING, of Lothian.

Vigilando. By watching. CAMPBELL, bt. M'LEOD.

Vigilando ascendimus. We rise by being vigilant. O. OF THE
WHITE FALCON.

Vigilando munio. I defend by being vigilant. KIRKALDIE.
ROYAL BURGH, Scotland.

Vigilando quiesco. In watching I rest. TREDCROFT.
    There is a cock in the arms and crest.

Vigilans. Watchful. BURTON. KADWELL. JOHNSON. SMITH.
TAYLOR.

Vigilans et audax. Vigilant and bold. BRADLEY, of co.
Worcester. CORRIE. COCKBURN, bt. CAMPBELL, bt. DUNN.

Vigilans non cadit. The vigilant man falls not CALDER, bt.

Vigilante. Watching. CLARE.
    Crest — A cock, the emblem of vigilance.

Vigilante salus. Safety while he watches. COCHRAN.

Vigilanter. Watchfully. GREGORY. STAWELL. WEGG.

Vigilantia. Vigilance. AIRD. CARFREA.

Vigilantia et virtute. By vigilance and valour. PORTER.

Vigilantia non cadet. Vigilance will not miscarry. CADELL.

Vigilantia, robur, voluptas.　Vigilance, strength, pleasure.
ARUNDELL.　BLAIR, bt.　HUNTER.
Vigilantibus.　While they watch.　ACHESON.　ATCHISON.
GOSFORD, e.
Crest—A cock standing on a trumpet.
Vigilantibus non dormientibus.　For the vigilant not for the
sleeping.　BRISTOWE.
Vigilat et orat.　He watches and prays.　FENNISON.
Vigilate.　Watch.　ALLCOCK.　LEEDS, bt.　LONGSTAFF.　TUCKER.
Vigilate et orate.　(Matt. xxvi. 41, and Mark, xiii. 33.)　Watch
and pray.　CAPRON.　CASTLEMAINE, v.　HANDCOCK.　SHUCK-
BURGH.
Vigilo.　I watch.　DESSE.　GREGSON.　GEIKIE.　M'HADO.
Vigilo et spero.　I watch and hope.　GALBRAITH.　TWITOE.
Vigueur de dessus.　Strength is from above.　O'BRIEN.
O'BRYEN.　BRAIDWOOD.　THOMOND, m.　WILLINGTON.
Vigueur l'amour de croix.　The love of the cross gives strength.
ANDREWS.　DARNOL.
Vill God I sall.　MENZIES, bt.
This motto is sometimes written "Vill God, I zall."
Vim da vi honestæ.　Give strength to honourable force.　DAVY.
Vim vi repellere licet.　It is lawful to repel force by force.
GWYN, of Pant-y-cored.　GWYN-HOLFORD.
The Gwyns of Pant-y-cored, or the Dingle of the Weir, co. Brecon, as well
as those of Glyntawe, always wrote their names with a single *n* and
without the *e* final.　This addition was made, it is said, by Judge Gwyn
of Garth, between whom and the first Gwyn of Pant-y-cored a violent
quarrel arose, whereupon the latter thrust the sword or dagger of
Brychan through the head of Cadwgan, assuming for his crest a sword
in pale, with the point upwards, piercing a boar's head, and adopted
the above motto.
Vimiera.　WALKER, bt.　See "Orthes."
Vincam.　I shall conquer.　GRIFFEN.
Vincam malum bono.　I will overcome evil by good.　ROBINSON.
"Be not overcome of evil, but overcome evil with good."—*Rom.* xii. 21.
Vincam vel moriar.　I will conquer or die.　CATON.　M'DOUGALL.
M'DOWALL.
" Ere even
With parting smile shall gild the west,
This sword shall triumph win, or rest—
Victory on earth, or peace in heaven."
Vince malum bono.　(Rom. xii. 21.)　Overcome evil by good.
JONES, co. Lancaster.
Vince malum patientia.　Overcome evil with patience.　LEE.
TOWNSHEND.
Vincendo victus.　Conquered in conquering.　LEE.
Vincenti *dabitur.*　It shall be given to the conqueror.　VIN-
CENT, bt.
Vincere.　To conquer.　M'COUL.
Vincere est vivere.　To conquer is to live.　SMYTH.

Vincere vel mori. To conquer or die. M'DOWALL. M'GOUGAN.
M'NEIL. M'NELLY. MACNEILL, of Barra. MACLAINE.
NEIL. NEILL.

> " No thought was there of dastard flight ;
> Link'd in the serried phalanx tight,
> Groom fought like noble, squire like knight,
> As fearlessly and well."—SCOTT.

Vincit labor. Exertion will conquer. CAMPBELL, of Blythswood.

Vincit amor patriæ. The love of my country exceeds everything. CHICHESTER, e. COOPER. GUN. HARGREAVES.
JAMES. MOLESWORTH, v. MUNCASTER, b. PENNINGTON.

> "Vincet amor patriæ laudumque immensa cupido."—VIRG. Æn. vi. 823.

Vincit cum legibus arma. He conquers arms by laws. ATKYNS.

> This motto was assumed by Sir Robert Atkyns of Saperton Hall, who
> distinguished himself by his skill in law and by his exertions in the
> cause of liberty previously to the landing of William of Orange. He
> became Lord Chief Baron in 1689.

Vincit omnia veritas. Truth conquers all things. COURCY.
EATON. GOODCHILD. KINGSALE, b. LAFFAN, bt.

Vincit pericula virtus. Virtue overcomes dangers. MAINE.
THORNTON.

Vincit qui curat. He conquers who is cautious. WHITE.

Vincit qui devincit. He conquers who endears. GRIFFEN.

Vincit omnia pertinax virtus. Stubborn virtue conquers all.
STOKES.

Vincit qui patitur. He conquers who endures. ACKWORTH.
AMPHLETT. ADDENBROOKE. ASHURST. COLT, bt. CHESTER,
of Royston. HARRISON. HOMFREY. SHAW, bt. SMERDON.
TURBERVILLE. WIRE. GILDEA. WHITGIFT.

Vincit qui se vincit. He conquers who conquers himself.
ELLIS. WILSON, co. York. HOLLAND.

> " He is the Conqueror, hero true,
> Who his own passions will subdue."

Vincit veritas. Truth conquers. ALISON, bt. BERRY. BURN.
COOTE, bt. DICKIN. EDWARDS. GORT, v. GALWEY. HASTINGS.
NAPIER. M'KENNY, bt. PEACOCKE, bt. O'SHEE. SHEE.
MORRISON. WEBSTER. ORPEN.

Vincit vigilantia. Vigilance conquers. WRIGHT.

Vinctus non subactus. Bound not subdued. BROOKS, Rev.,
St. Stephen's, Paddington.

> In allusion to the crest a bear muzzled.

Vinctus sed non victus. Chained but not conquered. GALWAY.

> The crest is a cat sejant ppr. collared and chained or.

Vincula da linguæ vel tibi lingua dabit. Place restraint on
your tongue, or your tongue will place it on you. HOSKYNS.

> In the reign of James I. Serjeant Hoskyns having ventured to utter in
> the House of Commons certain unpalatable truths, respecting the
> Scotch favourites of the king, was summoned into the royal presence,
> and asked by the indignant James how he had dared to utter such
> things respecting his friends and countrymen. The Serjeant wittily

rejoined to this, "that he had indeed dared to say what all England only dared to think," and for this reply was committed to the Tower, the king jeeringly quoting, as he was led off, the verse which now forms the Hoskyns' motto. The present crest of the family " A lion's head with flames of fire issuing from the mouth," was at the same time assumed by the family, instead of a wheatsheaf the original crest.

Vincula temno. I despise bonds. SINCLAIR.

Vir non semper floret. A man does not always flourish. DAVIDSON.

Virebo. I shall flourish. HAMILTON. *Crest*—An oak-tree.

Vires agminis unus habet. One has the strength of an army. GRYLLS, of Helston. *Crest*—A porcupine.

" In strength each armed hand
A legion "—MILTON.

Vires animat virtus. Virtue animates our powers. CAMPBELL. GARDEN. GAIRDEN.

Vires in arduis. Strength in difficulties. MAC-BAIN.

Vires veritas. Truth gives power. KENNEDY, of Clowburn.

Virescit. He flourishes. MONCRIEF. MONCRIEFF, bt. STEWART.

Virescit in arduis virtus. Virtue flourishes in difficulties, KEIR.

Virescit virtus. Virtue flourishes. JACKSON.

Virescit vulnere. It flourishes from a wound. STEWART.

Crest—A pelican vulning herself, and the motto asserts that by her wounds the pelican's fame for parental affection flourishes.

Virescit vulnere virtus. Her virtue flourishes by her wound. GALLOWAY, e. BROWNRIGG, bt. BURNETT, bt. GREEN. KER. WEBB. FOOT.

The crest of Galloway is a pelican in her piety.

Viresco. I flourish. GREENLESS. MONTEATH. SMELLET. STEWART. TAILEFER.

Viresco et surgo. I flourish and rise. MAXWELL.

Viresco vulnere. I revive by my wounds. OLDFIELD.

Virgini immaculatæ Bavaria immaculata. To the Immaculate Virgin Immaculate Bavaria. O. OF ST. GEORGE OF BAVARIA.

Only the initials V. I. B. I. are inscribed on the cross of the Order.

Virginitas et unitas nostra fraternitas. Chastity and unity form our brotherhood. PIN-MAKERS' COMP.

Viridis et fructifera. Verdant and fruitful. HAMILTON.

Virtue. FERGUSON.

Virtue mine honour. MACLEAN, bt. M'LEAN.

"Virtue . . . . .
Is sense and spirit with humanity;
And if you pant for glory, build your fame
On this foundation."

Virtue is honour. KENRICK.

This motto was first assumed by Edward Kenrick, who married Susanna Cranmer, grandniece of the Archbishop Cranmer, and has since been used by all his descendants.—ELVEN'S *Heraldry of Crests.*

Virtus. Virtue. ERRINGTON.

> " Here Wisdom calls, 'seek Virtue first, be bold ;
> As gold to silver, Virtue is to gold.'"

Virtus acquirit honorem. Virtue gains honour. SPENCE.

Virtus ad æthera tendit. Virtue reaches to heaven. BALFOUR. CAIRNS.

Virtus ad sidera tollit. Virtue raises to the stars. WILSON.

Virtus ardua petit. Valour seeks for difficulties. COOKE.

Virtus ariete fortior. Virtue is stronger than a battering-ram. ABINGDON, e. BERTIE.

> There are three battering-rams in the arms.

Virtus auget honorem. Virtue increases honour. EDMOUN-STONE, bt.

Virtus basis vitæ. Virtue is the basis of life. STAFFORD, b.

> "Virtue
> Stands like the sun, and all which rolls around
> Drinks life, and light, and glory from his aspect."—BYRON.

Virtus castellum meum. Virtue my castle. BENCE, of Thorington. *Crest*—A castle.

Virtus dum patior vincit. Provided I bear patiently, virtue conquers. WEEMS.

Virtus dabit, cura servabit. Valour will give, care will keep. BROWN, of Clonboy.

Virtus dedit, cura servabit. What virtue has given, discretion will preserve. BROWNE.

Virtus depressa resurget. Virtue, though depressed, shall rise again. KENDALL.

Virtus durat avorum. The virtue of my ancestors remains. SETON.

Virtus durissima ferret. Virtue will bear the greatest hardships. M'LEAN.

Virtus est Dei. Virtue is of God. BRIGGS. BROOKE.

Virtus est vitium fugere. It is virtue to flee from vice. REYNARDSON.

> "Virtus est vitium fugere, et sapientia prima
> Stultitiâ caruisse."— HOR. *Ep.* 1. i. 41.

Virtus et honos. Virtue and honour. O. OF ST. HUBERT OF LORAINE AND OF BAR. O. OF MERIT OF THE BAVARIAN CROWN.

Virtus et industria. Virtue and industry. BROWNE, of London.

Virtus fortunæ victrix. Virtue conquers fortune. SANDES.

Virtus in actione consistit. Virtue consists in action. CRAVEN, e. CLAYTON, bt. HALFORD. SIER.

> "Virtutis laus omnis in actione consistit."—CIC. *de Off.*

Virtus in ardua. Courage against difficulties. POTTINGER, bt.

Virtus in arduis. Courage in difficulties. ASHBURTON, b. COCKAIN. CULLEN. COCKANE. GAMON. MACQUEEN.

Virtus incendit vires.   Virtue excites our powers.   STRANG-
FORD, v.

> " He fixes good on good alone, and owes
>   To virtue, every triumph that he knows."

Virtus incumbet honori.   Virtue will rest upon honour.
WILLIAMS, of Eltham.

Virtus insignit audentes.   Virtue renders the bold illustrious.
BEAMISH.

Virtus intaminatis fulget honoribus. (Hor. *Car.* iii. 2. 17.)
Virtue shines with unspotted honours.   TRUSS.

Virtus invicta gloriosa.   Unconquered virtue is glorious.
THOMAS, bt.   BENTHAM, of Lincoln's Inn.

Virtus invicta viget.   Unconquered virtue flourishes.   PENYSTON.

Virtus invidiæ scopus.   Virtue is the mark of envy.   METHUEN, b.

> " Virtutes ipsas invertimus, atque
>   Sincerum cupimus vas incrustare."—HOR. *Sat.* i. 3. 55.

> " Invidere omnes mihi,
> Mordere clanculum : ego flocci pendere :
> Illi invidere miserè."—TER. *Eun.* iii. 1. 20.

Virtus laudanda.   Virtue is praiseworthy.   PATTON.

Virtus, laus, actio.   Virtue, glory, action.   FRAZER.

Virtus maturat.   Virtue ripens.   RIDDEL.   RIDDELL.

Virtus mihi scutum.   Virtue is to me a shield.   WARREN.

> " Let coward guilt, with pallid fear,
>   To sheltering caverns fly,
> And justly dread the vengeful fate
>   That thunders through the sky.
> Protected by that Hand whose law
>   The threatening storms obey,
> Intrepid Virtue smiles secure,
>   As in the blaze of day."—CARTER.

Virtus mille scuta.   Virtue equals a thousand shields.   CLIFFORD,
bt.   DAYRELL.   HOWARD, of Effingham, b.   SADLER.   VYSE.

Virtus nobilitat.   Virtue ennobles.   O. OF THE BELGIC LION
FOR CIVIL MERIT.   GWINNETT.   HENDERSON.

Virtus, non stemma.   Virtue, not pedigree.   EBURY, b.   WEST-
MINSTER, m.   GROSVENOR.

> " Boast not the titles of your ancestors,
>   Brave youths—
> When your own virtues equalled have their names,
> 'T will then be fair to lean upon their fames."

Virtus omnia nobilitat.   Virtue ennobles all things.   HERRICK.
HEYRICK.   EYRICK.

Virtus omnia vincit.   Virtue conquers all things.   WHITE.

Virtus patrimonio nobilior.   Virtue is nobler than inheritance.
TRELAWNEY.

Virtus paret robur.   Virtue begets strength.   BANBURY, bt.
RICHARDSON.

Virtus post facta.   Virtue after exploits.   BORTHWICK.

Virtus post funera vivit. Virtue lives after the tomb. STANS-
FIELD.
> "Still bloom the deeds of those who cannot die!
> Crowned with eternal fame they sit sublime,
> And laugh at all the little strife of time."— CRABBE.

Virtus præ numine. Virtue under the presence of the
Divinity. PRICE.

Virtus præ nummis. Virtue is preferable to money. STUART.

Virtus præstantior auro. Virtue is more excellent than gold.
SEVERNE. WHIELDON.

Virtus pretiosior auro. Virtue is more precious than gold.
ROBINSON.

Virtus probata florebit. Tried virtue will flourish. BANDON, e.
BERNARD.

Virtus probata florescit. Tried virtue flourishes. COLOGAN.

Virtus propter se. Virtue for its own sake. RADCLIFFE, bt.
REPPINGTON, of Arnington.

Virtus pyramis. Virtue is a pyramid. KINCHANT.

Virtus repulsæ nescia sordidæ. Virtue unconscious of base
repulse. DESART, e. LAURIE.
> "Virtus repulsæ nescia sordidæ
> Intaminatis fulget honoribus:
> Nec sumit, aut ponit secures
> Arbitrio popularis auræ."— HOR. *Car.* iii. 2. 17.

Virtus secura sequitur. Virtue follows in safety. SEVERNE.

Virtus semper eadem. Virtue is always the same. TURVILLE.
> "The only amaranthine flower on earth
> Is virtue."— COWPER

Virtus semper valet. Virtue always avails. WOODWARD.

Virtus semper viridis. Virtue is ever *green*. GREEN. BELMORE, e.
CORRY. FRANCE, of Cheshire. LAURIE, bt. LOWRY.
> "The winged day
> Can ne'er be chain'd by man's endeavour;
> The life and time shall fade away,
> While heaven and virtue bloom for ever."— MOORE.

Virtus sibi præmium. Virtue is its own reward. CALDERWOOD.
WILSON, co. Lanark.
> "What nothing earthly gives, or can destroy,
> The soul's calm sunshine, and the heart-felt joy,
> Is virtue's prize."— POPE.

Virtus sibimet merces. Virtue is its own reward. MACKELLAR.

Virtus sine macula. Virtue unspotted. RUSSELL.

Virtus sola invicta. Virtue alone is invincible. EYRE, of
Wilts. FIELD.

Virtus sola nobilitas. Virtue is the only nobility. BLAKE, of
Menlo, bt. THROCKMORTON, bt.
> "Search me the springs,
> And backward trace the principles of things;
> There shall we find that when the world began,
> One common mass composed the mould of man;
> One paste of flesh on all degrees bestowed,
> And kneaded up alike with moist'ning blood:

The same Almighty power inspired the frame
With kindled life, and formed the soul the same.
The faculties of intellect and will,
Dispensed with equal hand, disposed with equal skill,
Like liberty indulged, with choice of good or ill,
Thus born alike, from virtue first began
The difference that distinguished man from man."—DRYDEN.

Virtus sola nobilitat. Virtue alone ennobles. CADDLE. BLAKE, of Furbough. HENRISON. WALLSCOURT, b. WATSON.

" He whose mind
Is virtuous, is alone of noble kind ;
Though poor in fortune, of celestial race ;
And he commits the crime, who calls him base."—DRYDEN.

Virtus sub cruce crescit. Virtue increases under the cross. BURY.

Virtus sub cruce crescit, ad æthera tendens. Virtue grows under the cross, and looks to heaven. CHARLEVILLE, e.

" Virtue blooms
Even on the wreck of life, and mounts the skies."—KIRKE WHITE.

Virtus triumphat. Virtue triumphs. CHURCH.

Virtus tutissima cassis. Virtue is the safest helmet. BARKER. BELLAIRS. FINCH. HATTON. STEPHENSON. WILLIAMS.

Virtus ubique. Virtue everywhere. STEVENSON. VERST.

Virtus vera nobilitas. Virtue is true nobility. ·HENVILLE.

" It's better to be meanly born and good,
Than one unworthy of his noble blood ;
Though all thy walls shine with thy pedigree,
Yet virtue only makes nobility."—ANON.

Virtus verus honos. Virtue is true honour. BURR.

Virtus viget in arduis. Virtue flourishes in difficulties. GURDON.

Virtus vincit invidiam. Virtue overcometh envy. CORNWALLIS, e. CLIBBORN. MANN.

Virtus virtutis præmium. Virtue is its own reward. MAC MORAN.

Virtus vulnere virescit. Virtue gains strength by a wound. LEITH.

Virtute. By virtue. COOPER, bt. CHURCH. DICK. FERGUSON. KEANE.

Virtute acquiritur honos. Honour is acquired by virtue. RICHARDSON, bt. RICHARDSON. RICHIE. RITCHIE. SPENCE.

Virtute ad astra. Through virtue to heaven. HOME, of Staines.

"But only virtue shows the path of peace."

Virtute adepta. Acquired by virtue. PATON.

Virtute avorum. By the virtue of ancestors. WATKINS.

Virtute cresco. I grow by virtue, BURNET. FORBES. LEASK.

Virtute decoratus. Adorned with virtue. GLASSCOTT.

Virtute dignus avorum. Worthy of the virtue of his ancestors. WORTHINTON.

Virtute doloque. By valour and craft. BINNING.

> During the reign of David II. of Scotland, an ancestor of this family
> surprised the English garrison of Linlithgow, by introducing into that
> fortress certain of his comrades in a waggon, apparently laden with
> hay. Hence they carry as an augmentation, on a bend engrailed sa.,
> a waggon ar. with the above motto.

Virtute duce. With virtue for guide. ELDER. SHANNON. SHAND, of the Burn, co. Forfar.

Virtute duce, comite fortunâ. With valour my leader and good fortune my companion. DAVIES. SHAND. VISME.

Virtute et armis. By virtue and arms. MINNITT.

Virtute et constantia. By valour and constancy. AULD or AULDE.

Virtute et fide. By valour and faith. COLLINS. BEAUVALE, b. HARLEY. LAMB. MELBOURNE, v. OXFORD, e. MARRIOTT.

Virtute et fidelitate. By valour and fidelity. BLAIKIE. CROFTS. GOODSIR. LYONS. O. OF THE GOLDEN LION, OF HESSE-CASSEL. REEVES.

Virtute et fortuna. By valour and good fortune. ANDREW.

Virtute et honore. With virtue and honour. WELLS.

Virtute et industria. By virtue and industry. CITY of BRISTOL.

Virtute et ingenio. By virtue and ability. MASTER.

Virtute et labore. By valour and exertion. ALLAN. COCHRAN. DUNDONALD, e. FOSTER, of Norwich, bt. HEADLEY, b. HEDDLE. M'CLINTOCK, of Drumcar. M'KENZIE. RIG. RIGG. WINN.

Virtute et merito. By bravery and merit. O. OF CHARLES III. OF SPAIN.

Virtute et numine. By virtue and providence. CLONCURRY, b. CREAGH. LAWLESS.

Virtute et opera. By virtue and energy. BENNIE. BERNIE. BENZIE. DUFF. FIFE, e. HARRIS. MACDUFF. DEVAS.

Virtute et probitate. By virtue and honesty. MAGAN.

Virtute et prudentiâ. By virtue and prudence. DAMES. HEPBURN.

Virtute et robore. By virtue and strength. BOROUGH, CO. Salop. PILLANS, of East Dereham, co. Norfolk.

Virtute et sapientia. By virtue and wisdom. BROWNRIGG.

Virtute et valore. By virtue and valour. STAMER, bt. BATT. M'KENZIE. PEPPARD. NOBLE. MACKENZIE, of Ganloch, co. Ross, bt. WALDRON.

> "Justitiæ-ne prius mirer, belli-ne laborum?"—VIRG. Æn. xi. 126.

Virtute et veritate. With virtue and truth. BLATHWAYTE.

Virtute et votis. By virtue and vows. NEILSON, of Manwood.

Virtute excerptæ. Plucked by valour. CARY.

> These words refer to the manner in which the roses in his shield were
> won by Sir Henry Cary, temp. Hen. V. from a knight of Arragon, who
> having come to England and challenged all the chivalry of the realm

to single combat, was defeated by Sir Henry in the lists at Smithfield. For this good service the king restored to the victor his paternal lands, which had escheated to the crown in consequence of his father's adherence to the cause of Richard II. ; and, in pursuance of the laws of heraldry, authorised him to assume the arms of his vanquished foe. To this practice Scott alludes in his "Marmion" when he makes the heralds say,

> "We saw the victor win the crest
> He wears with worthy pride."

Virtute fideque. By virtue and faith. ELIBANK, b. MURRAY. M'MURRAY.

Virtute gloria parta. Glory is obtained by valour. NAPIER.

Virtute me involvo. (Hor. Car. iii. 29, 54.) I wrap myself in my virtue. DEREHAM, or DEERHAM.

Virtute non aliter. By virtue not otherwise. MOIR, of Hilton.

Virtute non astutia. By courage not by craft. LIMERICK, e. THOMAS. WHITBREAD.

Virtute non ferociâ. By courage not by cruelty. FORBES.

Virtute non sanguine. By virtue not by blood. SOUTHBY.

Virtute non verbis. By valour not by boasting. BAXTER. COULTHART, of Collyn. FITZ-MORRIS. LANSDOWNE, m. PETTY. ROBINSON. SAWERS.

Virtute non vi. By virtue not by force. BARNEBY. CHIVAS. SHIVEZ. COPPINGER. DERRICK. RUMSEY.

> "Ut errat longè meâ quidem sententiâ,
> Qui imperium credat gravius esse aut stabilius,
> Vi quod fit, quam illud quod amicitiâ adjungitur."—TER. *Adel.* i. 1. 40.

> "O joyless power that stands by lawless force !
> Curses are his dire portion, scorn and hate,
> Internal darkness and unquiet breath ;
> And, if old judgments keep their sacred course,
> Him from that height shall heaven precipitate
> By violent and ignominious death."—WORDSWORTH.

Virtute nulla possessio major. No possession is greater than virtue. CAWARDEN.

Virtute orta occidunt rarius. Things sprung from virtue rarely perish. AITON.

Virtute parata. Acquired by virtue. MELVILLE. WHYTT.

Virtute parta. Acquired by virtue. HALLYDAY. WHITE.

Virtute parta tuemini. Defend what is acquired by valour. BLACKWOOD. PEPPERELL.

Virtute promoveo. I advance by virtue. SIDESERF, of Rochlaw.

Virtute quies. Repose through valour. NORMANBY, m. PHIPPS.

Virtute res parvæ crescunt. Small things increase by virtue. T. OF ANSTRUTHER.

Virtute securus. Safe by virtue. HAWARDEN, v.

Virtute sibi præmium. By virtue he gains reward for himself. FENWICK.

Virtute tutus. By virtue safe. BLAIR. MARSHALL. PHAIRE.

Virtute vici. By valour I conquered. INGRAM. MEYNELL.

Virtute viget. He flourishes by virtue. KEIRIE. PATON.

Virtute vinces. By virtue thou shalt conquer. LEATHAM.

Virtute vincit invidiam. He conquers envy by virtue. MANN.

Virtute viresco. I flourish by virtue. PATERSON.

Virtutem extendere factis. To increase virtue by deeds. FISHER.

" Dubitamus adhuc virtutem extendere factis."—VIRG. *Æn.* vi. 806.

Virtutem sequitur fama. Fame follows virtue. DANCE.

In allusion to the name, Dance after virtue.

Virtuti. To virtue. DICK.

Virtuti beneficentia. Kindness to virtue. O. OF THE LION OF LEMBOURG.

Virtuti comes invidia. Envy is companion to virtue. CUNNING-HAME.

Virtuti damnosa quies. Inactivity is prejudicial to virtue. BRISBANE.

Virtuti et fidelitati. For virtue and fidelity. O. OF THE GOLDEN LION.

Virtuti et fortunæ. To virtue and fortune. GARDINER.

Virtuti et merito. To virtue and merit. O. OF CHARLES THE THIRD.

Virtuti fortuna comes. Fortune is companion to valour. POTTER, of Buile Hill, of Lancashire.

The word " virtus," does not merely refer to valour in war, or to moral excellence, but also to that strenuous energy, which, whether in the pursuits of agriculture or commerce, for the most part ensures success. The above motto was adopted by the Potter family, in allusion to the prosperity which crowned their exertions.

Virtuti fortuna comes. Fortune is companion to valour. FERGUSON. MAYNE, of Powis, &c. ORR. STEWART. WREN.

Virtuti honores soli. Honours to virtue alone. WROWE-WALTON.

Virtuti in bello. To bravery in war. O. OF ST. HENRY OF SAXONY.

Virtuti inimica quies. Inactivity is inimical to virtue. FORBES.

" Næ illi falsi sunt, qui diversissimas res pariter expectant, ignaviæ voluptatem, et præmia virtutis."—SALL. *Bell. Jug.*

" —— For if our virtues
Did not go forth of us, 'twere all alike
As if we had them not."—SHAKSPEARE.

Virtuti mœnia cedant. Let walls yield to valour. WILDER.

Virtuti nihil invium. Nothing is impervious to valour. CHAMBERLAYNE. HILLARY, bt.

Virtuti nihil obstat et armis. Nothing resists valour and arms. ALDBOROUGH, e.

Virtuti non armis fido. I trust to virtue, not to arms. WILTON, e. EGERTON, bt. TWISS, of Kerry.

"Non exercitus, neque thesauri, præsidia regni sunt, verum amici ; quos neque armis cogere, neque auro parare queas, officio et fide pariuntur." —SALL. *Bell. Jug.*

Virtuti pro patria. For valour in behalf of our country. O. OF MAXIMILIAN JOSEPH OF BAVARIA.

Virtutibus præmium honor. Honour the reward of virtues.
FFEILDEN, of Witton.

Virtutis alimentum honos. Honour is the food of valour.
PARKER, of Petteril Green.

Virtutis amore. (Hor. *Ep.* i. 16. 52.) Through love to virtue.
ANNESLEY, e. ANNESLEY, of Bletchingdon. MOUNTMORRIS,
e. STEPHENS, of Tregenna.

Virtutis avorum præmium. The reward of my ancestors'
valour. TEMPLETON, v. UPTON.

Virtutis comes invidia. Envy is the companion of virtue.
DEVEREUX. HEREFORD, v.

Virtutis fortuna comes. Fortune is the companion of valour.
ASHTOWN, b. BROOK. CLANCARTY, e. FERGUSON, of Raith.
HUGHES. HARBERTON, v. TRENCH. WELLINGTON, d.

> This motto is one of the many which, without having any special
> reference to the family coat-of-arms, are assumed by some member of
> a family who has added fresh honours to those already possessed by
> the stock from which he is descended. Thus the motto of the Duke
> of Wellington is peculiarly suited to express the success of the first
> Duke which waited on his valour in the field, and his genius in the
> senate; and, moreover, alludes to the rewards with which a grateful
> nation requited his achievements.

Virtutis gloria merces. Glory is the reward of valour. GYLL.
DEUCHAR. LORIMER. M'DONAGH. M'DONEGH. MAC-
GREGOR. ROBERTSON, of Strowan, Ladykirk and Kindeace,
co. Ross.

> Robert Chief of Clan Donnachie, son of Duncan de Atholia, arrested,
> close to Blair Castle, Graham and the Master of Athol, who were ac-
> complices in the murder of James I. As a reward for such good
> service, he demanded, instead of lands and honours, that he might
> bear with his arms "a man in chains" and the motto "Virtutis
> gloria merces." The king (James II.) granted him this request, and a
> cubit arm erect holding a crown as a crest of augmentation. The old
> motto, "Recte faciendo neminem timeas," is still retained in addition
> by the Robertsons.

Virtutis honor præmium. Honour is the prize of valour.
SPARLING.

Virtutis in bello præmium. The reward of valour in war.
STEUART, of Allanton.

> This motto alludes to the special augmentation of arms granted by
> Robert II. of Scotland to this branch of the Steuart family as a reward
> for their distinguished and repeated services in defence of the liberty
> of their country.

Virtutis laus actio. The praise of virtue is action. CORBET,
bt. RUMBOLD, bt. TANSLEY.

> "Virtutis enim laus omnis in actione consistit."—CIC. *de Off.* i. vi. 6.

Virtutis præmium. The reward of virtue. STEWART, of Overton.

Virtutis præmium felicitas. Happiness the reward of virtue.
JONES.

Virtutis præmium honor. Honour is the reward of virtue.
DENBIGH, e. FIELDEN. FENISCOWLES. MILLINGTON.

> "Honour and shame from no condition rise,
> Act well your part, there all the honour lies."—POPE.

Virtutis præmium honos. Honour is the prize of valour. FIELDEN, bt. FIELDEN.

Virtutis præmium laus. Praise is the prize of virtue. JER- VOISE, bt.

Virtutis regia merces. Royal is the reward of virtue. ALPIN. MACGREGOR. PETER. SKENE, of Skene.

Virtutis robore robur. Strong as an oak in virtue's strength. DACKCOMBE, co. Dorset.

> *Crest* — An oak-tree ppr. fructed or. round the stem a scroll with the above motto.

Vis et fides. Strength and faith. CAMPBELL, of co. Hants and Dunoon, Scotland. WYNDHAM.

Vis et virtus. Strength and bravery. CHISALME.

Vis fortibus arma. Strength is arms to the brave. CRUIKSHANK.

Vis super hostem. Strength over the enemy. O'DONOVAN.

Vis unita fortior. Strength united is the more powerful. BROOK. FLOOD. HALES. HOSKEN. LIDWELL. MOORE. MOUNT- CASHEL, e.

> " But who the limits of that power can trace,
> Which a brave people into light can bring,
> Or hide, at will, for freedom combating,
> By just revenge inflamed."—WORDSWORTH.

Vis viri fragilis. Weak is the strength of man. LILBURNE. RUDDIMAN.

Visa per invisa firma. Things seen are established by things unseen. SPENCE.

> *Crest* — Two hands issuing from a cloud letting down an anchor into the sea.

Vise à la fin. Look to the end. CALDER. HOME, bt.

Vise en espoir. Look forward in hope. HASSARD.

Vita et pectore puro. With pure life and heart (*lit.* breast). BELOE.

Vitâ posse priore frui. To be able to enjoy the recollections of our former life. TOWNSEND.

> This was the motto of Tickell the poet.
> " Hoc est
> Vivere bis, vitâ posse priore frui."—MARTIAL, 10. 23.
> Colley Cibber prefixed this motto to his celebrated " Apology " and it is thus translated by him : —
> " When years no more of active life retain
> 'Tis youth renew'd to laugh them o'er again."

Vita vel morte triumpha. Triumph in life or death. ALLEN.

Vitæ via virtus. Virtue is the way of life. DAWSON. PORT- ARLINGTON, e. RUST. WATKINS. WEEKS.

Vite, courageux, fier. Swift, courageous, proud. HARRISON.

Vittoria. NICHOLSON. See " Waterloo."

Vivat veritas. Let truth endure. DUNCAN.

Vivat rex. Long live the king. M'CORQUODILL. M'CORGUSDELL.

Vive Deo. Live to God. DURHAM.

Vive Deo ut vivas. Live to God that you may live. CRAIG, bt.

> " For none of us liveth to himself."—*Rom.* xiv. 7.

> " To live to God is to requite
> His love as best we may ;
> To make his precepts our delight,
> His promises our stay."—COWPER.

Vive en espoir. Live in hope. STARR.
Vive la plume. Live the pen. SCOTT.
> *Crest*— A hand holding a pen.

Vive la joye. *Joy* for ever. JOY.
Vive le roy. Long live the king. GAIRDEN, of Barrowfield.
Vive revicturus. Live (as if) about to live again. VIVIAN.
Vive ut postea vivas. So live that you may live hereafter.
  FRAZER. JOHNSTON, of Johnston, bt. JOHNSTON.

> " The voice of Nature loudly cries,
> And many a message from the skies,
> That something in us never dies ;
> That on this frail, uncertain state,
> Hang matters of eternal weight ;
> That future life, in worlds unknown,
> Must take its hue from this alone ;
> Whether as heavenly glory bright
> Or dark as misery's woeful night :
> Since then, my honoured first of friends,
> On this poor being all depends
> Let us th' important now employ,
> And live as those that never die."- BURNS.

Vive ut semper vivas. To live that you may live for ever.
  BANCKS. FALKNER. FAULKNER. HOPSON. MANNING.
Vive ut vivas. Live that you may live. ABERCROMBY, b.
  ABERCROMBY, of Birkenbog, bt. BATHGATE. HARTLEY, of
  Bucklebury. HALL. FALCONER, of Halkerton. ILIFF, of
  Newington Butts. M'KENZIE. PRICE, of Spring Grove,
  bt. SLADEN, of Alton Barnes, co. Wilts. VIVIAN, of Pen-
  calenick.

> " Deeply drinking—in the soul of things,
> We shall be wise perforce ; and, while inspired
> By choice, and conscious that the will is free,
> Unswerving shall we move as if impelled
> By strict necessity, along the path
> Of order and of good.   Whate'er we see,
> Whate'er we feel, by agency direct
> Or indirect, shall tend to feed and nurse
> Our faculties, shall fix in calmer seats
> Of moral strength, and raise to loftier heights
> Of love divine, our intellectual soul."—WORDSWORTH.

Vivere sat vincere. To conquer is to live enough. ATTWOOD.
  MOLYNEUX. DE MOLINES. SEFTON, e. VENTRY, b.
Vivis sperandum. Where there is life there is hope. NIVEN.
Vivit Leo de Tribu Juda. The Lion of the Tribe of Judah
  lives. ETHIOPIA or ABYSSINIA.
Vivit post funera virtus. Virtue lives after death. BOYLE.
  CRAIG. SHANNON, e.

> " Only the actions of the just
> Look green and blossom in the dust."

Vivitur ingenio. He lives by skill. DARLEY. COPEN.

Vivunt dum virent. They (the *Forrests*) live as long as they (the trees) are green. FORREST.

In the arms three oak-trees.

Vix ea nostra voco. I scarce call these things our own. ARGYLL, d. BROOKE and WARWICK, e. FOUNTAIN, of Narford and Southacre, co. Norfolk. GRENVILLE. HUSSEY. CAMPBELL, of Weasenham, Cockley Cley, and Fakenham, co. Norfolk. HUSSEY, co. Sussex.

The lines of the poet express his opinion that high ancestry and noble blood avail nothing without personal virtues : —

" Genus et proavos, et quæ non fecimus ipsi
Vix ea nostra voco."—OVID, *Met.* lib. xiii. 140.

" The deeds of long-descended ancestors,
Are but by grace of imputation ours."—DRYDEN.

Vix distat summus ab imo. The loftiest is scarcely removed from the lowest. WHITTAKER.

" Divesne, prisco natus ab Inacho,
Nil interest, an pauper, et infimâ
De gente, sub Dio moreris,
Victima nil miserantis Orci."—HOR. *Car.* ii. 3. 21.

Vixi liber et moriar. I have lived a freeman and will die one. GRAY. IBBETSON, bt.

Volabo ut requiescam. I will fly (away) to be at rest. (Ps. lv. 6.) COLLENS, or COLLINS, of Offwell, co. Dorset.

Crest — A dove.

Volando reptilia sperno. Flying myself I despise creeping things. SERAS. SCARTH.

Crest — On the stump of a tree environed with a serpent, an eagle rising ppr.

Volens et valens. Willing and able. FETHERSTON, bt.

Volenti nil difficile. To the willing nothing is difficult. CRUCH.

Volo non valeo. I am willing but unable. CARLISLE, e. GREYSTOCK. HOWARD.

Volonté de Dieu. The will of God. TYLER.

Volvitur et ridet. He revolves and smiles. FAIRWETHER.

Crest — The sun in splendour.

Voor moed, beleid, trouw. For courage, prudence, and fidelity. O. OF WILHELM, NETHERLANDS.

Vota vita mea. Prayers are my life. BRABAZON, bt. MEATH, e.

Votis et conamine. By vows and exertion. KIRK.

Votis, tunc velis. By wishes, then by sails. MARTIN.

Crest — A ship under sail.

Vows *shall be respected.* VOWE, of Hallaton.

Vraye foy. True faith. BOSWELL, bt.

Vulnerati non victi. Wounded not conquered. COOKS' COMP.

Vulneratur, non vincitur. He is wounded, not conquered. HOMFRAY.

Vulneratus non victus. Wounded not conquered. GUILLAMORE, v. O'GRANDY.

Vulnere sano. I cure by a wound. BALDERSTON.

Crest—A hand holding a lancet.

Vulneror non vincor. I am wounded, not conquered. HOMFRAY. MUSCHAMP, of Brotherlee.

Vultus in hostem. The countenance against the enemy. CODRINGTON.

Horace enumerates this among the sights which Mars loves:—
" —— Acer et Marsi peditis cruentum
Vultus in hostem."—HOR. *Car.* i. 2. 39.

W

Walk *in the way of God.* WALKER-HENEAGE.

Watch. FORBES, of Cragedar. GORDON, of Haddo.

Watch and pray. (Matt. xxvi. 41.) FORBES, of Craigievar Castle, bt.

Watch weel. SCOTT, of Abbotsford, bt.

Watch well. HALYBURTON, of Pitcur, Newmains, &c.

Watch wiel. SCOTT.

Watchful and bold. COATS.

Waterloo. NICHOLSON.

In commemoration of the services of Capt. M'Innes at that battle, who in 1821 assumed the name of Nicholson. He also bears the words "Vittoria" and "Barvach," in memory of the services of Lieut.-Gen. Robert Nicholson.

Wath ein fferwyth yr adnabyddir. We are known according to our actions. ELLIS.

Ways and means. LOWNDES.

William Lowndes, founder of the Buckinghamshire branch of this family, was for many years Chairman of "Ways and Means" in the House of Commons. Hence the motto.

We are one. ARMOURERS' AND BRAZIERS' COMP., London.

We beg you see warily. CORNWALL, of Bonhard.

We have dune. MAC MICKING.

We live in hope. THORBURN.

We rise. MARTINSON, of Newcastle-on-Tyne.

We stoop not. ANDERTON, of Euxton.

Weapon forefendeth evil. MITFORD.

Weave truth with truth. WEAVERS' COMP., London.

Weigh well. URQUHART. URQUHART, of Byth.

Well win, well wear. HORT.

Wer gutes u boses nit kan ertragan wirt kein grose chre erjagen. Who cannot bear good and evil shall not obtain great honours. BRANDER, co. Hants.

West Indies. PREVOST, of Belmont, co. Hants, bt.

Whatsoever thy hand findeth to do, do it with thy might.
BUXTON, bt.
What was may be. OLIPHANT, of Bachiltoun.
Whyll God wyll. TREFFRY.
Whyll lyff lastyth. CORNWALL, Barons of Burford.
𝔚𝔦𝔩 𝔰𝔬𝔫𝔢 𝔴𝔦𝔩. WILSON, of Stowlangtoft Hall, co. Suffolk.

> This motto is expressive of the success that usually attends determined purpose and will, and is explained by the proverb " Where there's a will there's a way," or by " Possunt quia posse videntur."

Will God and I shall. ASHBURNHAM, of Sussex and Suffolk.
Will God, I shall. MENZIES.

> " We may not doubt that who can best subject
> The will to reason's law, can strictliest live
> And act in that obedience, he shall gain
> The clearest apprehension of those truths,
> Which unassisted reason's utmost power
> Is too infirm to reach."— WORDSWORTH.

Will well. URQUHART, of Craigston.
Wisdom, justice, and moderation. GEORGIA, North America.
Wisdom's beginning is God's fear. CAMPBELL.

> "The fear of the Lord is the beginning of wisdom."—*Ps.* cxi. 10.

Wise and harmless. GRANT, of Carron.

> In allusion to the serpent which forms the crest, and to the dove in the arms.

With heart and hand. DUDGEON. RULE.

> The crest of Dudgeon is a hand holding a heart.

With truth and diligence. LUCY, of Charlecote.
Without fear. CAMPBELL, of Gartsford, bt. DUFFUS, b.
SUTHERLAND.
Without God castles are nothing. CASTLEMAN.

> In allusion to the name and to the castles in the arms.

Wrth ein ffrwythan ein hadnabyddir. Let us be seen by our actions. ELLIS, of Merinoth.

Y

Y blaidd nid ofnaf. I fear not the wolf. JENNINGS.
Y cyfiawn sydd hy megis llew. The righteous is bold like a lion. HUGHES, of Alltwyd.
Y ddioddefws orfu. He who has suffering has conquered.
DE AVAN. WILLIAMS.
Y ddioddefws y orfu. He suffered to conquer. MORGAN.
Y cadarn a'r cyfrwys. The mighty and cunning. WYNN-
WILLIAMS.
Yet higher. KINLOCK, of Gourdie.

Yet in my flesh shall I see God. Surman.

"And though after my skin worms destroy this body, yet in my flesh shall I see God."—*Job*, xix. 26.

ורושלם. A vision of peace. Montefiore, bt.

Ysgwyd. A shield. Hughes.

Ystoyeau et ne doubtero. Strangways, of Alne.

Yvery. Perceval. Egmont, e.

The earldom of Yvery, in Normandy, was held by Ascelin Gouel de Perceval, an ancestor of the Perceval family, who accompanied the *Conqueror* to England.

Z

Zealous. Hood, bt.

The name of the vessel commanded by Sir S. Hood at the victory of th Nile, August 1, 1798.

Zeal and honour. Blomfield.